McGraw Hill Education create™

D0139010

Course Taking Sides: Clashing Views in Human Sexuality, 14e

Course Number **Ryan McKee, Jayleen Galarza, & Tracie Gilbert** create™

http://create.mheducation.com

ISBN-10: 1259410463 ISBN-13: 9781259410468

Contents

Credits

Unit 4 181

Detailed Table of Contents

Unit 1: Sexuality Education

Issue: Should Sexuality Education Take an Intersectional Approach?
Yes: Aida Manduley, from " Values-Neutral Education Is a Myth: The Need for Intersectionality and Social Justice in Sex Education," Original Work (2016)
No: Paul Joannides, from "The Luxury of Intersectionality," An original essay written for this volume (2016)

Aida Manduley, sexuality educator, social worker and activist, challenges traditional sex education with the idea that practitioners need to take a more intersectional approach in their work, incorporating lessons that unpack connections between sexuality and other social markers, including race, gender, socioeconomic status, ability, etc. Psychoanalyst and author Paul Joannides argues that the political realities of school-based sex education make taking an intersectional approach difficult outside of academia. He posits that focusing on intersectionality may ultimately limit the reach of more general sex education programs.

Issue: Should Sex Educators Use Trigger Warnings When Discussing Controversial Content?
Yes: Julie A. Winterich, from "Trigger or Not, Warnings Matter," *Inside Higher Ed* (2015)
No: Rani Neutill, from "My Trigger-Warning Disaster: '9 ½ Weeks,' 'The Wire' and how Coddled Young Radicals Got Discomfort All Wrong," *Salon* (2015)

Julie A. Winterich, Associate Professor of Sociology and Director of Women's, Gender, and Sexuality Studies at Guilford College, argues that trigger warnings offer some protections to students who have experienced, or are experiencing, violence and trauma in their lives. Rani Neutill, a former Lecturer and Sexual Assault Prevention Educator at Harvard University, counters that trigger warnings limit free speech by forcing professors to protect students from ideas that may be challenging.

Issue: Should Sex Educators Be Required to Have Formal Training?
Yes: Lexx Brown-James, from "Required Training for Sex Educators is Beneficial for All," An original essay written for this volume (2016)
No: Tyomi Morgan, from "Information Is Power: How Knowledge Trumps Credentials for Any Good Sex Educator," An original essay written for this volume (2016)

Lexx Brown-James, marriage and family therapist, and founder of the Institute for Sexuality and Intimacy, argues that quality sex education depends on facilitators who are highly skilled and trained at their craft, which most often comes through formal training. Tyomi Morgan, a sex coach, columnist, and the founder of SexpertTyomi.com, argues that knowledge and skill gained from independent study and preparation can be just as effective in building a successful sex education career as formal experience.

Issue: Do Reality TV Shows Portray Responsible Messages about Teen Pregnancy?
Yes: Amy Kramer, from "The REAL Real World: How MTV's '16 and Pregnant' and 'Teen Mom' Motivate Young People to Prevent Teen Pregnancy," An original essay written for this volume (2011)
No: Mary Jo Podgurski, from "Till Human Voices Wake Us: The High Personal Cost of Reality Teen Pregnancy Shows," An original essay written for this volume (2011)

Amy Kramer, director of Entertainment Media & Audience Strategy at the National Campaign to Prevent Teen and Unplanned Pregnancy, argues that reality television shows engage teens in considering the consequences of pregnancy before they're ready for it, and motivate them to want to prevent it. Mary Jo Podgurski, founder of the Academy for Adolescent Health, Inc., argues that though such television shows have potential benefits, they inadequately address the issue, and may even have a negative impact on those who participate in them.

Unit 2: Sexual Health, Treatments, and Reproduction

Issue: Is Pre-Exposure Prophylaxis (PrEP) an Effective Method for HIV Prevention?
Yes: Michael Lucas, from "Op-Ed: PrEP Works, So Drop the Backlash," *Out Magazine* (2015)
No: Tom Myers, from "HIV Prevention Pill Will Do More Harm Than Good," *U.S. News & World Report* (2012)

Michael Lucas, founder of all-male erotica studio Lucas Entertainment, argues that the effectiveness of PrEP negates all arguments against its use, and that organizations opposing PrEP are acting in their own self-interest. Tom Myers, Chief Public Affairs and General Counsel for the AIDS Healthcare Foundation, believes incorrect and inconsistent usage of PrEP will lead to more HIV infections.

Issue: Should Sexual Problems Be Treated Pharmaceutically?
Yes: Connie B. Newman, from "Pharmacological Treatment for Sexual Problems: The Benefits Outweigh the Risks," An original essay written for this volume (2011)
No: Anita P. Hoffer, from "The Hidden Costs of the Medicalization of Female Sexuality—How Did We Get Here? An Overview," An original essay written for this volume (2013)

Connie Newman, an endocrinologist and adjunct associate professor of medicine at New York University School of Medicine, explores the definitions and causes of sexual dysfunction and explains how sexual medicines can improve sexual response. Anita P. Hoffer, former associate professor at Harvard Medical School and former director of research in urology at the Brigham and Women's Hospital, argues that the rise of sexual medicine has created a market that benefits the pharmaceutical industry at the expense of the individual.

Issue: Do the Benefits of Male Circumcision Outweigh the Risks?
Yes: Larkin Callaghan, from "Making the Cut: Is It Time to Put the Circumcision Debate to Rest?" *The 2x2 Project* (2012)
No: Elizabeth Reis, from "Circumcision Debate: Cut the Hyperbole," *Nursing CLIO* (2014)

Larkin Callaghan, Managing Director of the Center for AIDS Research, believes the public health benefits, for both men and women, make male circumcision worth the risks. Elizabeth Reis, author and Visiting Professor at the Macaulay Honors College at the City University of New York, argues that circumcision proponents misguide parents by irresponsibly likening its effectiveness to vaccines.

Issue: Is Female Genital Cutting a Violation of Women's Health and Human Rights?
Yes: Olivia Jackson, from "Cutting Out the Devil: Female Genital Mutilation," *Evangelicals for Social Action* (2014)
No: Zelaika Hepworth Clarke, from "Empowered Perspectives of Ethnic Female Genital Modifications (EFGM)," An original essay written for this volume (2016)

Olivia Jackson, a writer and filmmaker who focuses on international social justice issues affecting women and children, argues that female genital mutilation is a violation of women's rights on all fronts, including the political, medical, cultural, and spiritual. Zelaika Hepworth Clarke, an African-centered social worker and cultural and clinical sexologist, argues that "female genital modifications" are an important part of many people's cultural and spiritual practices around the world and should be respected as such.

Issue: Is "Social Transitioning" a Beneficial Treatment for Transgender Children?
Yes: Kristina Olson and Lily Durwood, from "Are Parents Rushing to Turn Their Boys Into Girls?" *Slate* (2016)
No: Alice Dreger, from "The Big Problem with Outlawing Gender Conversion Therapies," *Wired* (2015)

Kristina Olson, Associate Professor of Psychology and founder of the TransYouth Project at the University of Washington, and Lily Durwood, Project Coordinator at the TransYouth Project, argue that researchers have misrepresented findings to suggest that many young people who identify as transgender will ultimately identify as cisgender, and that calls to limit the option of social transitioning can be harmful to transgender youth. Alice Dreger, author and Professor of Clinical Medical Humanities and Bioethics at Northwestern University, argues that controversial "gender conversion therapy" can help prevent unnecessary treatments on gender non-conforming young people.

Unit 3: Sexual Identities and Expressions

Issue: Are Women More "Sexually Fluid" Than Men?
Yes: Ann Friedman, from "Why Should Fluid Sexuality Be Women-Only?" *The Cut* (2013)
No: Joe Kort, from "Going with the Flow: Male and Female Sexual Fluidity," *Huffington Post* (2015)

Ann Friedman, a freelance journalist who writes about gender, media, technology, and culture, notes that while men face more scrutiny for same-sex behaviors, research indicates women experience a greater capacity for same-sex attraction than men. Joe Kort, a psychotherapist, certified sex therapist, and author, draws on his clinical experience as well as recent studies to argue that men's lack of sexual fluidity is a falsehood.

Issue: Is "Kink" a Sexual Orientation?
Yes: Jillian Keenan, from "Is Kink a Sexual Orientation?" *Slate* (2014)
No: William Saletan, from "The Trouble with Bondage: Why S&M Will Never Be Fully Accepted," *Slate* (2013)

Jillian Keenan, freelance journalist and author of the book *Sex With Shakespeare,* presents kink as a sexual orientation more complex and nuanced than attraction to a specific set of behaviors. William Saletan, an author who writes about sexuality, politics, science, and technology, argues against kink as an orientation, noting that BDSM is not about *who* one loves, but *how*.

Issue: Is Sexting a Form of Safer Sex?
Yes: Brent A. Satterly, from "Sexting, Not Infecting: A Sexological Perspective of Sexting as Safer Sex," An original essay written for this volume (2011)
No: Donald A. Dyson, from "Tweet This: Sexting Is NOT Safer Sex," An original essay written for this volume (2011)

Brent A. Satterly, associate professor and bachelor of Social Work Program Director at Widener University's Center for Social Work Education, acknowledges the risks involved in sexting while criticizing fear-based media coverage of the phenomenon. He argues in favor of harm-reduction strategies to reduce the risks associated with sexting rather than continuing the trend of panicked reactions to the expression of youth sexuality. Donald A. Dyson, director of the Center for Human Sexuality Studies and associate dean of the School of Human Services Professions at Widener University, examines sexting through the lens of the World Health Organization's definition of sexual health and determines that the risks inherent in the digital transmission of sext messages is not a form of safer sex.

Issue: Is the Addiction Model Appropriate for Treating Compulsive Sexual Behaviors?
Yes: Isaac Abel, from "Was I Actually 'Addicted' to Internet Pornorgraphy?" *The Atlantic* (2013)
No: Marty Klein, from "Why 'Sexual Addiction' Is Not a Useful Diagnosis—And Why It Matters," *martyklein.com* (2016)

Isaac Abel, a journalist who writes (under a pen name) about sexuality and gender, shares his story of compulsive sexual behaviors while arguing that the sex addiction model, while not perfect, gave support to his struggle. Marty Klein, an author and Certified Sex Therapist, argues that the sex addiction model is harmful to clients, treating normal sexual behaviors as pathologies and gives undue authority to moralizing, sex-negative "experts."

Issue: Should Group Marriage Be Legal?
Yes: Fredrik deBoer, from "It's Time to Legalize Polygamy," *Politico Magazine* (2015)
No: Jonathan Rauch, from "No, Polygamy Isn't the Next Gay Marriage," *Politico Magazine* (2015)

Fredrik deBoer, a writer, researcher, and Continuing Lecturer at Purdue University, believes that despite opposition from both conservatives and progressives, the next logical step in marriage equality is the legalization of polygamy. Jonathan Rauch, an author and Senior Fellow at the Brookings Institution, asserts that there are many reasons, supported by extensive research, to oppose polygamy.

Unit 4: Sex and Society

Issue: Is Having a Sex-Positive Framework Problematic?
Yes: Melissa Fabello, from "3 Reasons Why Sex Positivity Without Critical Analysis Is Harmful," *Everyday Feminism* (2014)
No: Eric Barry, from "I'm Sex-Positive, and Most People in Chicago Have No Idea What That Means," *Huffington Post* (2014)

Melissa Fabello, a body acceptance activist and a Managing Editor of the *Everyday Feminism* media site, argues that without critical analysis, the mainstream sex-positivity movement can ultimately be harmful. Eric Barry, writer, comedian, and creator of the *Full Disclosure* sex-positive podcast, believes that sexpositivity allows people to embrace sex and without feeling shame or applying other inextricable meanings to behaviors.

Issue: Is Pornography Harmful?
Yes: Pamela Paul, from "The Cost of Growing Up on Porn," *The Washington Post* (2010)
No: Megan Andelloux, from "Porn: Ensuring Domestic Tranquility of the American People," An original essay written for this volume (2011)

Pamela Paul, author of *Pornified: How Pornography Is Transforming our Lives, Our Relationships, and Our Families*, argues that studies declaring the harmlessness of pornography on men are faulty, and that consequences of porn consumption can be seen in the relationships men have with women and sex. Megan Andelloux, sexuality educator and founder of the Center for Sexual Pleasure and Health, argues that the benefits of porn on American society outweigh the questionable consequences.

Issue: Should Condoms Be Required in Pornographic Films?
Yes: Sadhbh Walshe, from "Condoms and Porn Don't Mix Is a Stupid and Unhealthy Belief," *The Guardian* (2013)
No: Shay Tiziano, from "Keep Concern Trolling Laws Out of Our Porn: A 'Workplace Safety' Based Argument Against Mandatory Condom in Adult Films," *Stefanos & Shay* (2016)

Sadhbh Walshe, a filmmaker and television writer who also writes about social justice issues for publications around the world, believes arguments against condom use in porn are more about studio profits than performers' rights. Shay Tiziano, an emergency room nurse who is also an educator, host, performer, and advocate within the BDSM community, argues that concerns over workplace safety on pornographic film sets are overblown, and an example of sex-negative moralizing in disguise.

Issue: Should Sex Work Be Decriminalized?
Yes: Matt Hershberger, from "Legalized Prostitution Is a Mess. Here's Why It Has to Happen Anyway," *Matador Network* (2015)
No: Demand Abolition, from "The Evidence Against Legalizing Prostitution," *Demand Abolition* (2016)

Matt Hershberger, writer and blogger, uses the "lesser of evils" argument to suggest that decriminalization may be the best chance society has at present to ensure a safe working environment for today's sex work population. Demand Abolition argues there is insufficient evidence from efforts to legalize and/or decriminalize prostitution in the past to suggest either as a useful option in any sense.

Issue: Do State Laws on Abortion Clinic Safety Make Women Safer?
Yes: Mary Kate Cary, from "Safety First for Abortion Clinics," *U.S. News & World Report* (2013)
No: The American Civil Liberties Union, from "What TRAP Laws Mean for Women," American Civil Liberties Union (ACLU) (2014)

Mary Kate Cary, a former White House speechwriter for President George H.W. Bush and contributing editor for U.S. News and World Report, argues that states have the right to regulate abortion clinics as they see fit, and that increased regulations are in the best interest of patients. The American Civil Liberties Union, a nonprofit organization working to defend and preserve individual rights and liberties, argues that states are increasingly regulating abortion providers in an attempt to restrict and ultimately eliminate women's access to abortion services.

Issue: Has Marriage Equality Set the Gay Rights Movement Back?
Yes: Karma Chávez, from "Intersectional Equality," *Against Equality* (2015)
No: Keegan O'Brien, from "In Defense of Gay Marriage," *Jacobin Magazine* (2015)

Karmen Chávez, an activist, author, and Associate Professor of Rhetoric, Politics, and Culture at the University of Wisconsin-Madison, argues that the singular focus on marriage equality resulted in inaction on a number of other issues important to the LGBT community, and that continued progress and support for LGBT issues and organizations is now at risk. Keegan O' Brien, a queer social activist and writer, argues that marriage equality is but one step on the path toward LGBT liberation, and that it should be celebrated as a major victory.

Preface

In the age of 24-hour news channels and nonstop social media updates, one might think that the only way to think about sexuality is through a lens of outrage and confrontation. It seems as if every day a new (or in some cases *very old*) controversy arises that spurs people of all ages and backgrounds to take completely opposite positions on such issues as abortion, contraception, pornography, gender identity, teenage sexuality, and the like. To some, these topics are highly personal and tied to long held values and beliefs. To others, a lack of knowledge, understanding, and experience may make an issue seem irrelevant or even nonsensical. Deciphering what is at stake, and for whom, in an argument can be difficult; successfully creating and articulating one's own stance can be even more challenging! The purpose of this book, therefore, is to encourage meaningful critical thinking about current issues related to human sexuality. That some of the topics debated (i.e., sex work) have been argued for thousands of years yet still remain relevant should tell you how deeply rooted and controversial sexuality is in our societies. Each issue included in this book, including the essays chosen and their introductory and concluding passages, were designed to assist you in the task of clarifying your own personal values in relation to some common and contentious questions about human sexuality.

Book Organization

This 14th edition of *Taking Sides: Clashing Views in Human Sexuality* presents many lively and thoughtful statements by articulate advocates on opposite sides of a variety of sexuality-related questions. Each issue includes:

- A *question* (e.g., "Should Condoms Be Required in Pornographic Films?");
- *Learning Outcomes* describing the knowledge or skills students should be able to achieve upon reading the selections;
- An *Issue Summary* that presents background information helpful for understanding the context of the debate and information on the authors who will be contributing to the debate;
- Essays by two authors—one who responds *YES*, and one who responds *NO* to the question; and
- *Exploring the Issue* that presents questions for critical thinking and reflection; a summary of the arguments, including discussion about whether common ground exists and additional questions to help you further examine the issues raised (or not raised) by the authors; and print and Internet sources for further reading.

While the arguments made in these essays are strong and well-rounded, they often only represent two perspectives on the issue. The debates do not end there, as most issues have many (far more than 50!) shades of gray. You may find that your own values are not congruent with either author, and that you have a quite different take on an issue presented. Since this book is a tool to encourage critical thinking, you should not feel confined to the views expressed in the articles. You may see important points on both sides of an issue and may construct for yourself a new and creative approach, which may incorporate the best of both sides or provide an entirely new vantage point for understanding.

As you read this collection of issues, try to consider each author's philosophical worldview and beliefs. Furthermore, you should attempt to understand and articulate your own. At the same time, be aware of the authors' potential biases, and how they may affect the positions they articulate. Read each authors' short biography, and even consider researching more about them, in order to better understand their perspectives. What is their background? Where do they work? What other issues do they write about? Consider what impact these things may have on their argument and, ultimately, if that matters to this issue. Be aware, too, of your own biases and privilege. We all have experiences and social capital that may shape the way we look at a controversial issue. Still, try to come to each issue with an open mind. You may find your values challenged or even strengthened, after reading both views. Although you may disagree with one or even both of the arguments offered for an issue, it is important that you read each essay carefully and critically. We also ask that, in this time of intense political and social polarization, you attempt to see the humanity in those with whom you may strongly disagree. It is far too easy to paint someone with whom we disagree as an *other*, or a person whose very existence poses a threat to our well-being or security. Remember that holding different views or values should not be a cause for suspicion or hatred. Some debates may never be won, and some viewpoints may never align.

But to retreat into fear, or lash out at difference, takes us further away from the goal of sharing knowledge and increasing understanding.

A Word to the Instructor

In this issue we pose a question about trigger warnings. Please note that some of the issues presented in this text, as well as almost everything covered in a course on human sexuality, may be potentially traumatic triggers for students in your classes. That said, the decision to offer such warnings before assigning readings is up to you. If you are unsure about whether or not this practice is the right decision for you and your students, we hope that the essays presented in the text, and the suggested resources provided, offer some insight.

Teaching about human sexuality is a difficult task that requires a great deal of patience, practice, and skill; focusing on hot-button and controversial issues is even more challenging. But we believe the risks are worth the ultimate rewards of helping students to clarify their values around sex and sexuality, and to make well-informed, healthier, and more socially conscious decisions. We thank you for choosing *Taking Sides: Clashing Views in Human Sexuality* as a part of your course.

Taking Sides: Clashing Views in Human Sexuality is one of the many titles in the Taking Sides series. If you are interested in seeing the table of contents for any of the other titles, please visit The Taking Sides Collection on McGraw-Hill Create™ at http://create.mheducation.com/, or www.mhhe.com, or by contacting the authors at TakingSidesSexuality@gmail.com—ideas for new issues are *always welcome!*

Ryan W. McKee
Widener University

Jayleen Galarza
Shippensburg University of Pennsylvania

Tracie Q. Gilbert
Widener University

Editors of This Volume

RYAN W. MCKEE, MS, MEd, is a doctoral candidate in the Center for Human Sexuality Studies at Widener University. His research interests include the intersections of masculinities and sexual health, hazing and the health behaviors of fraternity men, and online sexuality education. Along with William J. Taverner, he coedited the 11th,12th, and 13th Editions of *Taking Sides: Clashing Views in Human Sexuality*. An adjunct instructor with over a decade of experience in the classroom, he teaches a variety of health- and sexuality-related courses for Widener University, William Paterson University, and Montclair State University. In addition to teaching, he works as a sexuality education consultant and program evaluator. Recent projects include the development online sexuality education courses for ANSWER and The Religious Institute. He is a certified sexuality educator through the American Association of Sexuality Educators, Counselors, and Therapists, (AASECT) and is a member of the American Men's Studies Association and the Society for the Scientific Study of Sexuality (SSSS).

JAYLEEN GALARZA, PhD, LCSW, is a clinical social worker who specializes in sexuality social justice issues. She is a licensed clinical social worker (LCSW) in Pennsylvania as well as a certified sex therapist through the American Association of Sexuality Educators, Counselors, and Therapists (AASECT). She completed her PhD in Human Sexuality at Widener University with a focus on exploring the intersections of queer, Latina identities, and experiences. Prior to joining Shippensburg University's department of Social Work and Gerontology, Dr. Galarza served as a Frederick Douglass Scholar at West Chester University of Pennsylvania. She also worked extensively as a mental health counselor with adolescents and young adults in the Philadelphia area. Dr Galarza's research and practice interests include: intersectionality, Latina(o) sexuality, sexual/gender identities and experiences, empowerment, sexuality social justice, narrative therapy, and feminist therapy. The focus of her work is on exploring empowering approaches to working with oppressed communities as well as raising awareness around such issues.

TRACIE Q. GILBERT, MSED, MEd, is a doctoral candidate with the Center for Human Sexuality Studies at Widener University, and an adjunct instructor of psychology at Murray State University. She is a writer, educator, and project manager, with nearly 20 years of experience in providing educational opportunities for adolescents and their advocates. Ms. Gilbert completed her Masters of Science in Education degree at the University of Pennsylvania in 2009, shifting her focus specifically to intersections of race and sexuality for African American populations during that time. Ms Gilbert was the inaugural Minority Faculty Fellow for Murray State in 2014, teaching undergraduate courses in both psychology and gender and diversity studies. In addition to serving as a sexual health counselor and educator for several high schools in the Greater Philadelphia area, she is working with the Center for Sex Education on several projects, including the Center's first-ever manual on sexual orientation. She is the 2011 winner of the Women for Social Innovation's Turning Point Prize, which she used to create The Empowered Mom's Think Tank—a 10-month sex education initiative for African American female caregivers. She has also presented at several major events, including the National Conference on Higher Education, the 2011 Annual Meeting for the Society for the Scientific Study of Sexuality (SSSS), the 2013 Widener University Graduate Research Day, the 2014 Careers in Sexuality Conference, and the 2016 Annual Meeting for the American Association of Sexuality Educators, Counselors, and Therapists (AASECT). Ms. Gilbert is a regular lecturer for the History & Ethics in Human Sexuality course, also taught at Widener University. Besides those mentioned above, Ms Gilbert's research interests include adolescent sexuality development, sexuality and faith, and social justice-based sexuality education. She is a passionate scholar of all topics related to the sexuality development of African Americans, including both historical and contemporary elements informing this process.

Acknowledgments

Thanks from the Coeditors

We would like to take the opportunity to collectively thank the many contributors, both new and old, who allowed their work to be included in this volume. Special thanks to Lexx Brown-James, Zelaika Clarke, Paul Joannides, Aida Manduley, and Tyomi Morgan for writing new and original pieces for this 14th Edition. Regardless of the stance each contributor takes, we are thankful that they speak up and contribute to these important conversations by sharing their research, knowledge, and opinions.

We would also like to acknowledge a place that is special to all of us, the Center for Human Sexuality Studies (CHSS) at Widener University. Thank you to all the professors there for teaching us so much, and continuing to support us in our academic and professional endeavors. Thanks and congratulations, as well, to the newest edition to Widener's full-time faculty, Dr. Eli Green. Extra-special thanks to Julissa Coriano for the support and kindness over the years.

Thanks from Ryan W. McKee

The creation of the 14th edition of *Taking Sides* saw a changing of the guard. My long-time collaborator, Bill Taverner, made the tough decision to step away from the book series he worked on for over 15 years. Bill was kind enough to name me as a Coeditor for the 11th edition and, for that, I will be forever grateful. I owe so much of my professional success to the chance he gave me. While I'm sad to see him leave the project, I know that stepping away will give him more time to focus on leading the Center for Sex Education and the National Sex Ed Conference to even greater heights. I have learned so much from Bill over the years and, along with my new coeditors, promise to bring those lessons to the Taking Sides series for many editions to come.

Speaking of new coeditors, I want to thank Jayleen Galarza and Tracie Gilbert for bringing their skill and expertise to the new edition of Taking Sides. I met both Jayleen and Tracie at the Center for Human Sexuality Studies at Widener University, and have leaned on them as trusted colleagues ever since. Jayleen and Tracie are dedicated educators determined to amplify marginalized voices in academia and beyond, and center them in conversations that are too often dominated only by those with great privilege. During the editing process they challenged me (in the true spirit of Taking Sides) to make bold choices and to defend my thought process with logic and rationale. I've learned so much from them as colleagues and friends over the last few years, as well as during the creation of this book. I'm so thankful for the opportunity to work with them during this new phase of *Taking Sides*, and I'm excited to introduce readers to their work.

Thank you to Jill Meloy at McGraw-Hill for the help, support, and patience throughout the development of this edition. Jill was gracious when we needed extra time, and understanding when issues arose that were out of our control. As always, she has been a pleasure to work with. Thanks also to Tanya Bass who served as Research Assistant on the book. Her insights and contributions were invaluable, and her positive attitude was absolutely contagious. I look forward to working with her again soon.

Thanks to my students at Widener University, Montclair State University, and William Paterson University for challenging me and teaching me so much each semester. Thank you to Dr Dyson, my dissertation advisor at Widener for his guidance, understanding, and support. Thanks also to my colleagues at Montclair State and William Paterson, especially Dr Eva Goldfarb, Dr Jean Levitan, and Dr Bill Kernan.

As always, a special thanks to Kelly Wise, Daphne Rankin, Judith Steinhart, and John Schoener.

To my parents, Erma and Paul McKee, my siblings and their partners, nephews and nieces, I owe an unpayable debt of gratitude for the love and support throughout the years. Thanks for always being there for me. Thanks also to Don and Michelle Gee, Bob and Sue Goodwin, and all of my in-laws, for welcoming me into the family.

Finally, thank you to my wife Alison and our son Henry for the love, support, patience, and laughs as I worked on this project. I'm so thankful that I get to share in the joys and challenges of parenthood with such a smart and caring partner. It is my hope that we can raise Henry to be thoughtful, considerate of differing opinions, and steadfast in his values. He will face many tough decisions, during his life, and he won't always make the right ones. But as long as he errs on the side of kindness he will make us proud.

Thanks from Jayleen Galarza

At times, the most marginalized and vulnerable voices are lost in discussions about sexuality. This is why I incorporated Taking Sides into my own teaching. So when Ryan approached me to be a coeditor of the 14th edition, I was honored to have the opportunity to have a voice in this important conversation. Bill Taverner and Ryan had already set a strong foundation acknowledging today's most relevant issues, and I hold their work as educators in high regard. I want to thank Ryan for creating a space for including diverse ways of thinking and knowing about sexuality issues and involving me in this process. I believe an important aspect to teaching sexuality is exploring the various ways that people view these challenging topics. I believe this edition truly reflects an attempt to explore difficult topics while giving voice to the voices that often go unheard.

I want to express appreciation to Jill Meloy at McGraw-Hill for the opportunity to work on this edition and for all her help as we navigated this new and challenging process. We also could not have completed this work without the help from our Research Assistant, Tanya Bass. She was a significant contributor to the development of this project.

There have been several people who have supported me throughout my professional career and development. I want to share my deepest appreciation to my colleagues at Shippensburg University for encouraging me to pursue research, teaching, and practice focused on exploring sexuality content.

Thank you to Dr Crane and Dr Satterly at Widener for your support over the years. I also want to express gratitude to my colleagues committed to social justice-based sexology, Becky, Angie, and Julissa, who are constant sources of knowledge, support, and always keep me grounded.

I want to express thanks to my family. Thank you to my mother, Joan Alomar, for being a model of strength and a guiding light in my life. To my stepfather, brother, sister, grandmother, niece, and nephew, I appreciate their constant and consistent encouragement and belief in my abilities.

Finally, thank you to my wife, Crys, for sharing her life and love with me, celebrating my successes, and supporting me during the challenges encountered in my academic and professional journey. When I was originally approached to coedit Taking Sides, Crys was just as enthusiastic as I was about this opportunity, and I've appreciated her insight and feedback throughout this process.

Thanks from Tracie Q. Gilbert

I stand on the shoulders of many amazing giants, so please forgive me in advance if I miss anyone. To begin, however, I would like to thank Ryan McKee for giving me the opportunity to support him on this next level of Taking Sides. We've worked together as colleagues for some time now; however, for him to think of me first for this was both tremendously humbling and gratifying. I can only hope my first efforts with this volume have set the standard you had in mind. Thank you to Dr Jayleen Galarza also—your reputation as a brilliant, dynamic scholar preceded you, and was further cemented by working with you directly.

Thank you to Jill Meloy and the entire team at McGraw-Hill for your professionalism and patience with the new team and vision. Working with you thus far has been a real joy, and you are sincerely appreciated.

To Tanya Bass, our research assistant (and my fellow sistah-scholar): I don't know how I was so lucky to have our paths cross, but I'm so glad they have.

While I echo collective sentiments of gratitude for our family at Widener, I want to send particular thanks to my advisor and Center Director Dr Donald Dyson, who has been a tremendous light for me during my time there. Thank you for allowing me to be unapologetically me, and for not only recognizing, but also being unafraid to center my voice. You give me wings.

There are several other folks who have supported my professional journey within the past few years, through their feedback, mentorship, and other shows of support. Thank you to my colleagues at Murray State University, and for those who saw fit to allow me to grow roots there as the inaugural Minority Faculty Fellow. Thank you to Ms Micki Davis, Director of Multicultural Student Affairs at Widener University, who has never let me believe I am anything other than amazing at all I do.

Thank you to every friend and scholar alike who took a phone call, social media DM, text thread, or Google Hangout call from me while working through this project. There are too many to name, but you all are appreciated.

Thank you to my partner and best friend, Vince Costello. Your love and faith in me as a scholar and human being is a huge part of what keeps me going each day.

Finally, I want to thank all my family in Milwaukee, WI, especially my mother Linda Jackson, my brother Calvin Woodley, and all my amazing aunts and cousins—again, too countless to name. When my brother shared the rumor that folks thought I was already writing a textbook, I never realized that would become a literal word spoken into my future. Thank you all for your love, encouragement, and nommo!!!

Academic Advisory Board Members

Members of the Academic Advisory Board are instrumental in the final selection of articles for *Taking Sides* books. Their review of the articles for content, level, and appropriateness provides critical direction to the editors and staff. We think that you will find their careful consideration reflected in this book.

Bernardo J. Carducci	*Indiana University Southeast*
Stanley Snegroff	*Adelphi University*
Edward Fernandes	*Barton College*
Harriet Bachner	*Pittsburg State University*
Doug Rice	*California State University, Sacramento*
Bernard Frye	*University of Texas, Arlington*
Kim Kirkpatrick	*Fayetteville State University*
Herb Coleman	*Austin Community College*
Ann Crawford	*Lynn University*
Rachel Dinero	*Cazenovia College*
Dr. Donald Dyson	*Widener University*
James Ferraro	*Southern Illinois University, Carbondale*
Pamela J. Forman	*University of Wisconsin-Eau Claire*
James S. Francis	*San Jacinto College—South Campus*
Jerry Green	*Tarrant County College—Northwest Campus*
Timothy Grogan	*Valencia Community College, Osceola*
Ethel Jones	*South Carolina State University*
Charles Krinsky	*Northeastern University*
Joseph Lopiccolo	*University of Missouri—Columbia*
Amy Marin	*Phoenix College*
Mary McGinnis	*Columbia College Chicago*
Dennis Roderick	*University of Massachusetts-Dartmouth*
Louise Rosenberg	*University of Hartford*
Casey Welch	*Flagler College*

Maria Theresa Wessel	*James Madison University*
David Yarbrough	*University of Louisiana, Lafayette*
Lisa G. Borodovsky	*Pace University*
Andrea Ericksen	*San Juan College*
Natasha Otto	*Morgan State University*
Christopher Ferguson	*Texas A&M International University*
Marissa A. Harrison	*Penn State Harrisburg*
Sandra M. Todaro	*Bossier Parish Community College*
Jane Petrillo	*Kennesaw State University*
Fredanna M'Cormack	*Coastal Carolina University*
Douglas Abbott	*University of Nebraska, Lincoln*
Carol Oyster	*University of Wisconsin, La Crosse*
Carol Apt	*South Carolina State University*
Christine Robinson	*James Madison University*
Joanna Gentsch	*University of Texas at Dallas*
Susan Milstein	*Montgomery College*
Lis Maurer	*Ithaca College*
Linda Synovitz	*Southeastern Louisiana University*
Konstance McCaffree	*Widener University*
Mindy Korol	*Mount Saint Mary College*
Nicole Capezza	*Stonehill College*
Kim Archer Kato	*Stephen F. Austin State University*
Justin Lehmiller	*Harvard University*
Martha Rosenthal	*Florida Gulf Coast University*
Barbara Denison	*Shippensburg University*
Kenyon Knapp	*Mercer University*
Estelle Weinstein	*Hofstra University*
Kevin Gustafson	*University of Texas—Arlington*
Edward Fliss	*St. Louis Community College at Florissant Valley*
Richelle Frabotta	*Miami University, Middletown*
Clint Bruess	*Birmingham Southern College*
Christopher Robinson	*University of Alabama-Birmingham*
Chris Wienke	*Southern Illinois University, Carbondale*
Debra Golden	*Grossmont College*
C. Lee Harrison	*Miami University—Oxford*
Sabra Jacobs	*Big Sandy Community and Technical College*
Laura Widman	*University of Tennessee—Knoxville*
J. Davis Mannino	*Santa Rosa Junior College*

Mark Doherty	*University of Louisiana—Monroe*
Matthew Daude Laurents	*Austin Community College*
Kathy McCleaf	*Mary Baldwin College*
Nicholas Grosskopf	*York College*
Jenny Oliphant	*University of Saint Thomas*
Sandra Reineke	*University of Idaho*
Tracy Cohn	*Radford University*
Tony Talbert	*Baylor University*
Lenore Walker	*Nova Southeastern University*
Alice Holland	*Penn State-Berks*
Catherine Salmon	*University of Redlands*
Margot Hodes	*Teachers College*
David Bogumil	*California State University—Northridge*
Lawrence A. Siegel	*Palm Beach State College*
Steven Hoekstra	*Kansas Wesleyan University*
Steven Reschly	*Truman State University*
Sue Simon Westendorf	*Ohio University—Athens*
Susan Heidenreich	*University of San Francisco*
Alisa Velonis	*University of Colorado Denver*
Linda R. Barley	*York College CUNY*
Aimee Sapp	*William Woods University*
Alexandrina Deschamps	*University of Massachusetts—Amherst*
Bree Kessler	*Hunter College*
Caitlin Killian	*Drew University*
Elizabeth Calamidas	*Richard Stockton College of New Jersey*
Jessica Willis	*Eastern Washington University*
Franklin Foote	*University of Miami—Coral Gables*
Ana Maria Garcia	*Arcadia University*
Kelley Wolfe	*University of North Carolina—Asheville*
Lisa Justine Hernandez	*Saint Edwards University*
Marcia Adler	*University of Nebraska Omaha*
Janice Kelly	*Purdue University*
Adina Nack	*California Luthern University*
Mindy Puopolo	*California Luthern University*
Sara Walsh	*Indiana University Bloomington*
Midge Wilson	*DePaul University*
Adrian Teo	*Whitworth University*
Phyllis Shea	*Worcester State College*

Lou Ann Wieand	*Humboldt State University*
Elham Gheytanchi	*Santa Monica College*
Allan Fenigstein	*Kenyon College*
Jennifer Jossendal	*Kishwaukee College*
Shanti Kulkarni	*University of North Carolina—Charlotte*
Roberta Wiediger	*Lincoln Land Community College*
Timothy Gobek	*Calumet College of St. Joseph*
Clare Chadwick	*Utah Valley University*
Keith King	*University of Cincinnati*
Phillip Bogle	*The Citadel*
Priscilla MacDuff	*Suffolk County Community College*
Jillene Seiver	*Bellevue College*
Daniel Rubin	*Valencia Community College-West Campus*
Deborah Mitchell Robinson	*Valdosta State University*
Jess Kohlert	*King's College*
Janet Griffin	*Howard University*
Michael Coconis	*Ohio Dominican University*
Mercedes Guilliaum	*California State University Long Beach*
Michael Agopian	*Los Angeles Harbor*
Harold Koch	*Penn Valley Community College*
Bertram Garskof	*Quinnipiac University*
B. Jill Smith	*University of Wisconsin—Eau Claire*
Ricia Chansky	*University of Puerto Rico, Mayaguez*
Terry Pettijohn II	*Coastal Carolina University*
John G. Shiber	*Big Sandy Community & Technical College*
Karen Rayne	*AUSTIN Community College*
Janna Edrington	*Luther College*
David Stewart	*Sanford-Brown College*
Norene Herrington	*College of DuPage*
Marina Epstein	*University of Washington*
Adrienne R. Carter-Sowell	*Texas A & M University*

Introduction

Taking Sides: Clashing Views in Human Sexuality is a book that challenges the reader to think deeply and critically about sex and sexuality. As you might imagine, this is not always an easy task. The way that we, in the United States, think about sex is deeply rooted in our society's traditional values. While new technologies proliferate, allowing knowledge and information to travel faster than ever before, our feelings about sex and sexuality are still intertwined with centuries-old sexual taboos. Even those who consider themselves sexually progressive have grown up with, and internalized, a culture that sends many mixed messages about sexuality. Is sex so special it should be shared only with the person you truly love? Or is it "dirty," and potentially hazardous to your health? Is our sexuality to be publicly celebrated without shame? Or is it so personal that it should be hidden and never discussed? And what about our bodies: are they perfect just the way they are? Or do beauty, sexual pleasure, and fulfillment require cosmetic surgery, steroids, or the latest fad diet? Everyone seems to have a different answer, and the resulting anxiety can leave us feeling confused about where we stand on issues related to our own sexual health and behaviors—not to mention those of sex and society as a whole!

One of the goals of this book is to help you clarify your values on a number of current issues related to human sexuality. How you feel about the questions individually, as well as in relation to each other, will largely be influenced by your *worldview*. Simply put, worldviews are "a pattern of beliefs, behavior, and perceptions that is shared by a population based on a similar socialization and life experiences" (Watts, 1994, p. 52). These patterns are usually formed over time without intention or thought, but they influence "how we think, make decisions, behave, and define events" (Sue & Sue, 1990, p. 137). Even if you have never considered or reflected upon your own worldview, it guides your thinking and behaviors in all interactions, including those associated with sexuality. Understanding your worldview, and the worldviews of others, is a critical part of examining one's sexual attitudes and behaviors. As with our knowledge and understanding of human sexuality in general, the way sexologists have conceptualized worldviews have evolved over time. Below we present several models of worldviews that have shaped, and continue to influence, the field of human sexuality studies.

Absolutist and Relativist Worldviews

The late Dr Robert T. Francoeur, a Catholic priest and founding editor of this *Taking Sides* volume, examined social views on sexuality and synthesized them into a model focused on two opposing worldviews: The fixed, or *absolutist*, worldview and the process, or *relativist*, worldview (Francoeur, 1991). These worldviews represent a binary way of thinking that helps explain much of the polarized way our culture views sexuality. While somewhat general, these two perspectives are important in any attempt to understand or debate controversial issues in human sexuality.

The fixed, or absolutist, worldview is founded in an essentialist view of nature (Francoeur, 1991). According to this view behaviors, including sexual ones, are seen as either natural or unnatural. Here, morality is governed by an ideology, most often drawn from a fundamentalist religious perspective. Natural sexual behaviors are those that can lead to procreation, while those that are unnatural cannot. These religious values were based on the views that God created man and woman at the beginning of time, and laid down certain rules and guidelines for sexual behavior and relations. To behave counter to these rules would be to behave "sinfully" or unnaturally. This view has been the dominant cultural perspective upheld by Western imperialism for centuries, and is still very influential in our culture, even for those who are not active in any religious tradition. Recent examples of this perspective, and how it emerges in public discourse, can be seen clearly through political controversies surrounding same-sex marriage, transgender rights and inclusivity, access to abortion, and even sexual assault.

The opposing view, according to Francoeur, is represented by the process, or relativist, worldview. Adherents to this perspective examine issues of morality, including sexual morality, in response to an ever-changing world. While one may feel strongly about an issue, a relativist worldview asserts that there is no fixed sense of right or wrong. Deciding on a moral issue may require contextual consideration; moreover, rules and ethics must constantly be reexamined in light of new information. From a relativist perspective even one's feelings, in their normative evolution, may change over time. Sex is decoupled from procreation, and norms around gender and orientations become more fluid. As a person or culture becomes more sex-positive and less governed by fear or shame, a more pleasure-focused understanding of sex can arise. Behaviors like masturbation, anal sex, or BDSM play, for example, become more acceptable. Having a process, or relativist, worldview does not mean that one is open to participating in, or even understands, these behaviors. It simply means that one does not see them as inherently bad or unnatural in the way someone with a fixed, or absolutist, worldview would.

Sexological Worldview

For most people, worldviews are shaped over time, largely without consideration or thought. But for sexologists, those professionals engaged in the academic study of sexuality, it is crucial to reflect upon and examine their attitudes and beliefs about sex and sexuality. While Francoeur's model helps us understand a general way of thinking about worldviews, those who study sexuality are tasked with having a more nuanced understanding of the subject. Sitron and Dyson (2012) advocated for both students and professionals in the field to cultivate a *sexological worldview* in order to gain and transform their perspective on, and better understand, sensitive topics in sexuality. Through interviews with sexologists, they defined the construct of sexological worldview as follows:

> Sexological worldview is the often unexamined but changeable perspective held by each person about the world around them with regards to sexuality. Sexological worldview emerges throughout life experiences and the socialization process and is influenced by the presence or absence of infinite combinations of the following components and their variations: culture, knowledge, values, beliefs, religion or spirituality, opinions, attitudes and concepts specific to sexuality, relationship style and type, sexual behavior, sexual orientation, and gender identity. Sexological worldview develops across a continuum with worldviews at one end being expressed as "dualistic (right or wrong)" and at the opposing end as "relativist (possible perspectives are endless and no one perspective is right or wrong)" and varied expressions in between. (p. 12)

Like most of us, many sexologists grow up in a culture that, again, is strongly influenced by the acceptance of the fixed or absolutist (or dualistic, as described by Sitron and Dyson) worldview as the norm. But through observation and discussion, academic study and professional (and even personal) experience, sexologists gain a more nuanced perspective that exists somewhere on the continuum between completely absolutist and completely relativist. This perspective is changeable, and adapts over time as new information or experience is integrated into one's sexological practice. To be clear, not having a fixed worldview does not mean that one is completely relativist in thought and action. There is nuance and growth that can only be accomplished through thoughtful reflection on challenging topics. Sitron and Dyson (2012) also found that sexologists may adhere to a more fixed worldview in their personal lives, but take a more relativist approach professionally. What they consider acceptable sexual behavior for others may not appeal to them personally, or even fit their personal definition of moral. However, understanding—if not acceptance—of sexual diversity is crucial for educators, counselors, and therapists, working in the field of human sexuality.

Intersectionality and Sexology

While not explicitly a worldview, the theory of intersectionality also has a significant impact on the way sexologists are beginning to see and understand the subject of human sexuality. Long valued by sociologists, as well as those working in race and gender studies, intersectionality has only recently struck a chord within the fields of sexuality education, research, and clinical practice. The theory, originated by law professor Kimberlé Crenshaw, builds upon Patricia Hill-Collins' theory of "interlocking oppressions" to describe Black women's experiences managing and navigating multiple oppressed identities. This is important to sexologists as it can help us better unpack, for example, differences in how queer-identified women of color experience the world, or see their sexuality, in comparison to queer white women. Additionally, the way a queer, nondisabled woman of color navigates sociosexual environments will differ from that of a queer, disabled woman of color because of the additional, "intersectional" barriers the latter experiences due to ableism. These compounding, interlocking oppressions, as Hill-Collins described, are often minimized by, or even invisible to, those with more social privilege. Moreover, the nature of privilege itself creates unnoticed *multiplied* benefits for those whose overlapping identities most mirror what sociologist Audre Lorde (1984) called the *mythical norm*—"white, thin, male, young, heterosexual, christian [*sic*] and financially secure" (p. 116). Sexologists have, for decades, championed sexual diversity in regard to gender, sexual orientations, and even sexual behaviors. But they have largely ignored how issues of race, disability, or other social identities factor into people's sexual lives. Examining human sexuality through an intersectional lens not only broadens our perspective, allowing us to see the ways in which we are similar, but also deepen our understanding, making space for marginalized voices to express how their various social locations and identities impact their sexuality, and providing opportunities for addressing institutional and systemic sexual health inequity. This perspective challenges educators, researchers, and clinicians to be more thoughtful about the methods they use in their work, and more effective in ensuring long-term wellness outcomes.

Closing

As you examine the 20 controversial issues in human sexuality chosen for this volume, you will find yourself unavoidably encountering the values you have absorbed from your society, your ethnic background, your faith communities, and your personal experiences. These values make up your worldview, and will influence your decisions—often without being consciously recognized. It is important to actively think about the role these underlying themes play in the positions you take on these issues. Notice your initial reactions to the questions and ask yourself what factors from your personal history or worldview influenced your response. As you read the essays arguing either side, take note of the feelings you have and where they may come from. Read the brief author bios, or research them further online, and think about how their social location may influence the way they see the questions raised. Consider if knowing more about the author of an essay changes the way you feel about your own answer. Remember, also, to consider your biases. In our polarized society it is easy to think "I'm a conservative/liberal, so this is how I should feel about this issue. Those who disagree are just ignorant, unintelligent, or worse." We encourage you to set such thoughts aside, challenging yourself to think more critically and dig deeper. While some of the issues presented in this volume could easily be argued along stereotypically conservative/liberal lines, many offer perspectives that are not so easy to categorize. Try to step outside of traditional, politicized, and polarized ways of thinking when deciding your stance. While you may not agree with one (or either!) of the essays for each issue, we hope that by thinking about the questions raised, and the answers presented, you emerge with a more fully developed sexological worldview.

References

Francoeur, R. (1991). *Becoming a sexual person* (2nd ed.). New York: Macmillan.

Lorde, A. (1984). *Sister outsider: Essays and speeches.* Berkeley, CA: Crossing Press.

Sitron, J. and Dyson, D. (2012). Validation of a sexological worldview: A construct for use in the training of sexologists in sexual diversity. *SAGE Open, 2,* DOI: 10.1177/2158244012439072

Sue, D. W., & Sue, D. (1990). *Counseling the culturally different: Theory and practice* (2nd ed.). New York: John Wiley.

Watts. R. J. (1994). Paradigms of diversity. In E. J. Trickett, R. J. Watts, & D. Birman (Eds.), *Human diversity perspectives on people in context* (pp. 49–80). San Francisco, CA: Jossey-Bass.

Editor's Note:

The language used by people in describing their lives and identities is in a constant state of evolution. Some terms may come into, and then fall out of, favor. In other cases individuals may feel terms previously used to describe their identity no longer seem appropriate. Within some communities, there is disagreement over the most appropriate terminology to use. For example, many disability activists prefer *person-first* language ("person with a disability") while others prefer *identity-first* language ("disabled person"). As editors, we strive to use terminology that is most appropriate when describing the wide array of social and sexual identities used today. In deciding on language choices, we consulted *A Progressive's Guide to Style* by Hanna Thomas and Anna Hirsch (http://interactioninstitute.org/wp-content/uploads/2016/06/Sum-Of-Us-Progressive-Style-Guide.pdf), as well as several colleagues from the field of sexuality studies. When there were discrepancies or multiple ways of identifying, we chose terms that were most widely known, or alternated between terminology described as appropriate among members of each community. Attempting to write as inclusively as possible is challenging, and we have undoubtedly erred on occasion. To that end, we appreciate feedback and promise to learn and grow moving forward.

Unit 1

UNIT

Sexuality Education

Despite evidence showing its effectiveness, comprehensive sexuality education remains a hotly contested issue in schools. The stereotypical assumption often made is that debates over content and methods are waged between liberals and conservatives. While this can certainly be true, it is but one aspect of the conversation. Even among supporters of sexuality education, there are debates on when, where, how, and by whom sexuality education should be taught. As the field expands to meet the needs of those who hope to improve their sexual health and better understand their sexuality, debates over best practices continue to arise. In the following unit we ask you to consider four contemporary issues around the teaching and learning of human sexuality.

Selected, Edited, and with Issue Framing Material by:
Ryan W. McKee, *Widener University,* Tracie Q. Gilbert, *Widener University,*
and
Jayleen Galarza, *Shippensburg University of Pennsylvania*

ISSUE

Should Sexuality Education Take an Intersectional Approach?

YES: Aida Manduley, from "Values-Neutral Education Is a Myth: The Need for Intersectionality and Social Justice in Sex Education," An original essay written for this volume (2016)

NO: Paul Joannides, from "The Luxury of Intersectionality," An original essay written for this volume (2016)

Learning Outcomes

After reading this issue, you will be able to:

- Define intersectionality.
- Describe two reasons for the prioritization of intersectionality within sexuality education.
- Describe two challenges to the implementation of an intersectional approach to sexuality education.

ISSUE SUMMARY

YES: Aida Manduley, sexuality educator, social worker and activist, challenges traditional sex education with the idea that practitioners need to take a more intersectional approach in their work, incorporating lessons that unpack connections between sexuality and other social markers, including race, gender, socioeconomic status, ability, etc.

NO: Psychoanalyst and author Paul Joannides argues that the political realities of school-based sex education make taking an intersectional approach difficult outside of academia. He posits that focusing on intersectionality may ultimately limit the reach of more general sex education programs.

While not a new concept, the theory of "intersectionality" has gained larger recognition in academic and other professional settings when discussing the need for understanding the impact of and connections between various social identities and experiences in one's practice. The term intersectionality is rooted in the work of Patricia Hill Collins and Kimberle Crenshaw. The original intentions and application of Hill Collins' "interlocking oppressions" (1990) and Crenshaw's "intersectionality" (1994) were designed to further explore and understand the depth and complexity of Black women's experiences in navigating oppression within diverse spaces and communities. It also emphasized the limited visibility and awareness of the nuances of Black women's lived experiences, which often resulted in their marginalization. As Hill Collins argued, a Black woman's experience, especially in navigating and engaging in the civil rights and women's rights movements, cannot be separated into distinct categories; rather, the dynamic interactions of race, gender, and social class result in unique understandings of, and interactions with, different oppressive forces. In other words, a marginalized person can't, for example, separate their gender identity from their race, or their sexual orientation; these identities are interlocked. Other social markers, such as identifying as transgender, working-class, or able-bodied also intersect and contribute to the ways we approach issues and navigate the world around us.

Recently the field of sex education has been charged with accusations of whitewashed curricula and a limited focus on, or understanding of, the experiences of people of color. Some feel that while inclusion is a stated goal for most sex educators, only sexual identities like gender or sexual orientation are considered, ignoring other intersecting aspects of students' lived experiences. This often leads to the omission of people of color from curriculum materials, classroom examples, and teaching strategies. For example, the content of images used during teaching demonstrations may lack racial or ethnic diversity. Class discussions may fail to make connections to historical or current events that shape racial and cultural injustice in the United States, including systemic violence against people of color such as the recent cases of Trayvon Martin, Freddie Gray, and Sandra Bland.

Professionals who support the idea that sex education needs to address the intersections of sexuality and racial/social justice argue that without critically analyzing how discrimination impacts life experiences, sex educators are unable to fully understand the communities in which they work. As such, the basic information they are trying to relay is limited and prioritizes only the most privileged individuals in the classroom. As the United States becomes increasingly diverse, one can understand why there is a push to address shortcomings in the curricula, materials, and content.

Despite the intentions of many educators to be as inclusive as possible, teaching from an intersectional lens can be challenging. An increased awareness of, and focus on, intersectionality and its applications has led many sexuality educators to reexamine and question their learning goals, as well as their own role in the classroom. Is it appropriate, or even possible, to be truly comprehensive without exploring the ways in which racial justice and social justice are integrated in this work? How will students, parents, or administrators respond to overt discussions of race and ethnicity in a course about sexuality? Many states and school districts do not mandate comprehensive sex education, and many who do rely on limited abstinence-only models of sex education. Because of this, simply attempting to meet the goal of providing medically accurate sexual health education is a challenge in certain parts of the United States. For these teachers, attempting to implement social-justice-informed sexuality education may feel like a fantasy.

Proponents of intersectionality note that despite the challenges, these issues are too critical to ignore, and that they should be a compulsory part of the educational experience—even in human sexuality classrooms. Because of this, they argue, an investment must be made in training sexuality educators to properly address these interlocking components. The conversation about intersectionality in sex education has introduced the controversial topic of race (and other identities) into the always-controversial subject of sexuality education. For many, it is a charged and uncomfortable issue to address. Still, advocates for intersectionality in education argue that the discomfort that comes from recognizing privilege and understanding systemic injustice as it relates to sexuality is part of the learning and growing process.

As you read the YES and NO selections below, think of your own experiences with sex education. In what ways were your lessons or assignments intersectional? In exploring this question, people may have different experiences and understandings depending on where, when, and from whom they received sex education. For some, educators were permitted to provide detailed sexuality content and also provide more context and depth—possibly about topics like the disparate impact of race, disability, and socioeconomic status on our sexual attitudes, values, and behaviors. For others, only foundational content, if any, was provided.

In the YES selection, Aida Manduley argues that it is impossible to provide values-neutral education, and that even attempting is problematic. She emphasizes the need for sex educators to examine the values integrated within their work in order to unearth personal biases, recognize inherent privilege, prevent the perpetuation of systemic oppression, and make space for the varied communities they will encounter. In the NO selection, Paul Joannides discusses the difficulties many sex educators face in attempting to relay the most basic of information, let alone related issues such as consent, interpersonal relationships, or sexual pleasure. While some instructors may have the ability to teach from an intersectional framework, he argues that to expect all educators to have the skill and community support to integrate even more politically charged topics into their work teaching sexuality content is out of step with the realities of school-based sex education.

References

Crenshaw, K. (1994). Mapping the margins: Intersectionality, identity politics, and violence against women of color. In M.A. Fineman & R. Mykitiuk (Eds.), *The public nature of private violence* (pp. 93–118). New York, NY: Routledge.

Hill Collins, P. (1990). *Black feminist thought: Knowledge, consciousness, and the politics of empowerment.* Boston, MA: Unwin Hyman.

YES

Aida Manduley

Values-Neutral Education Is a Myth: The Need for Intersectionality and Social Justice in Sex Education

It is so tempting to believe in values-neutral education. Some may even see this as the holy grail of sexuality education, where there is no controversy or harm being done because everything is so neutralized and harmless that it can cater to everyone. Some may push back against the idea of a "social justice framing" to sexuality education because we cannot be "everything to everyone" and thus we have to make strategic decisions about how, when, and what we educate. And while part of that is true and we do certainly have to make strategic choices of how we convey information, creating a split between being "everything to everyone" and not needing to tend to or at least bend toward a perspective that is intersectional is a false dichotomy. Simply put, values-neutral education is not only a farce, but it is also irresponsible in a culture where there continues to be oppression (defined here as a sustained state of discrimination). To treat all values as equal (whether it's as equally important or equally harmful) and as having no place in our teaching is to do a disservice to society and, furthermore, to allow injustice to flourish through inaction.

Our values are the lenses through which we interpret the world and our role in it. Our value frameworks direct us in our day-to-day life even if we are not able to fully articulate what these values are. Broadly defined, especially through an ethical framework, values are our ideas about preferable courses of action and what we hope the outcomes to be. Thus, ostensibly progressive notions of "empowerment" and allegedly "neutral" ideas of promoting individual choice through "judgment-free" education are not coming out of thin air. They come from individualist lenses, and while they may be very helpful in some cases, they also serve as a tool to perpetuate oppression through ideologies that do not acknowledge systemic forces of marginalization. Educators that promote "values-neutral" education also often aim to stay away from topics they personally deem "politicized," even when tackling things (or ignoring things) that are political for others. This is how we can have cohorts of educators who promote education about safer sex as a human right, and as something basic that everyone should have access to, but fail to discuss issues of race and class in their work.

Because of the diverse nature of our society, and more broadly our human experience, many of us may find the teaching of "prescriptive" sexual worldviews inappropriate. It follows, then, that many of us may believe in a non-directive model of sexuality education that focuses on awareness, knowledge, consideration of options, and choice. Many of us contrast this with models of teaching that are judgmental and strict, value-laden, top-down, and even coercive. We may believe that including values in our educational models is, itself, dangerous and damaging when we serve diverse crowds. In attempts to be accepting and tolerant, we feel we may have to be make space for a variety of views and that all perspectives should be accepted.

However, as stated above, these are not true binaries, and by constructing them as such, we are making it seem like values are in the domain of the dangerous, the domain of the negative, and that the only way to responsibly practice is to remove them from the equation. When, in fact, the very conceptualization of a "values-free" or "values neutral" education has values embedded in it. The arguments for this kind of education eventually self-destruct when followed to their logical conclusion. The very notion of institutionalized sex education has belief systems inherent in it, and it has a particular history as well—one that, when looking specifically at government-based sexuality education, is fairly recent.

Taboo as it may seem for some to explicitly acknowledge this, I believe critical analysis and transparency around these issues is key, and that unexamined worldviews that present ideas like "values-neutral" education can ultimately continue to perpetuate oppression even if they do so in ways that are less noticeable and measurably negative. For those of us who wish to see a world where sex education is commonplace, where sex education is comprehensive and responsive to varied populations, where sex education works to liberate rather than shackle, we "need to be precise about the *kind* of school sexuality education we advocate, rather than uncritically supporting the general concept of mandates that require its inclusion in the curriculum" (Trudell, 1992). Many of us have spent so long fighting abstinence-only education and negative messaging around sexuality that we have, perhaps as a culture of "progressive" educators, come to think of all values in this type of education as inherently negative or dangerous. In fact, in our values lies our strength!

There is also evidence to support the notion of teaching with, through, and about values. The idea of "values education" specifically is one that has been explored in literature and international research on teaching is challenging "earlier beliefs that values were exclusively the preserve of families and/or religious bodies and that, as a result, schools function best in values neutral mode" (Lovat & Hawkes, 2013). Beyond the social justice implications of addressing values, "the content and substance of Values Education . . . has the potential to go to the very heart of the power of quality teaching by focusing teacher and system attention on those features of their professional practice that have the most impact, namely the relationship of due care, mutual respect, fairness, and positive modelling established with the student and, in turn, the network of systemic 'relational trust' that results" (Aspin & Chapman, 2007).

Centering the importance of relationship-building and human interactions in the pedagogical process, Lovat also notes that through forming these kinds of connections, educators can better convey the kind of humanity that is crucial for personal character development and a commitment to the community. Thus, whatever the educational site, quality teaching involves conveying concepts and values as well as modeling them in the space. What this means for sex education is that we cannot simply talk abstractly about social justice, diversity, and equity; we have to embed it in our practice consistently and systematically.

Through this work, I invite us to look more closely at our values, whether it is through formalized tools like a "values inventory" or a more general exploration of our belief systems. I invite us to recognize the importance of an intersectional approach (particularly in the realms of language and values) in institutionalized sex education and the ways in which that language operates to both implicitly and explicitly construct frameworks and narratives that affect/create our understanding of sexuality. I want us to acknowledge the biases and effects of our language, understanding that the discursive production of fear and shame through the language of a sex-ed curriculum undermines self-empowerment and agency (especially under the Foucauldian notion of places like schools as sites of control).

With this knowledge, we can move away from a language that has historically been fraught with fear-mongering and shaming, and instead aim for a validating, liberating, sex-positive, relatable & relevant, comprehensive, and medically accurate language of sex ed—one that recognizes diversity, promotes agency and responsibility, and empowers people to make decisions based on accurate information and their personal values within a larger framework of understanding social marginalization and justice. In doing this, we meet what I feel should be the goal of sexual education: to promote a holistic vision of sexual health and "to create a context for healthy sexual expression and responsible self-fulfillment" (Dailey, 1997). It is both impossible and irresponsible for sexuality educators to truly give comprehensive education that supports sexual health without addressing issues of oppression. As noted by the World Health Organization (WHO), "for sexual health to be attained and maintained, the sexual rights of all persons must be respected, protected and fulfilled." This definition makes sexual health inextricable from activism, inextricable from changing the systematic forces in our societies that uphold discriminatory practices. To solely advance the sexual rights of dominant groups, and particularly at the direct expense of certain communities, is an act of violence.

Sex Education as a Historical Project

In the United States, before the late 1800s, sex education was seen as within the scope of the family rather than the state (Carter, 2001). Then, a rising divorce rate paired with low birth rates of middle-class Anglo, White Americans led critics to blame the "breakdown of society" (symbolized by the breakdown of marriage, seen as a pillar of morality and society) on immigrants and feminism (due to women's advancement and the relation to shifting gender roles and expectations), some going so far as to say that "formal education interfered with women's fertility and femininity, and so made them both biologically and socially unfit for marriage and motherhood" (Carter, 2001).

By 1880, a new socio-sexual problem had arisen in the United States: venereal disease. The spread of gonorrhea and syphilis alarmed doctors, who tied this "epidemic" to "the immorality of life in the city" (which, should be pointed out, is connected to cultural bias and discomfort with the number of immigrants in the cities) and sex work (Moran, Sex Education). This social context, and the ensuing published material on the topic specifically, led many to believe that there was a "direct connection between venereal disease and the breakdown of marriage," and while the old ideas about shifting gender roles and social paradigms still had followers, many people began to argue that the problem with venereal disease "lay in the 'enforced ignorance' about sex that was a prominent component of middle-class culture" (Carter, 2001). Thus, the pressing need for sexual education in a widespread, formalized fashion was born.

Because of the culture in which it flourished—one that made a connection between the individual and society at large—it is unsurprising that mass-produced pamphlets in the early 1900s explicitly reminded every citizen about the importance of protecting both their homes and families in the greater project of serving the nation and its security. This focus on the family and its integral nature to publicly funded sex education meant that a specific *type* of family structure was made highly visible. Through this representation, the mutually monogamous, heterosexual union of marriage was normalized as the "traditional family." Which, in turn, had the effect of "removing" other sexualities, family configurations, and possibilities from the map. During a time when the personal was political, every individual needed to embody a cultural ideal or else they would be read as actively going *against* the fabric of society, which was a dangerous threat. For this reason, coupled with moral panics about sex, the regulation and policing of individuals zeroed in on sexuality.

In the twentieth century, the solution to the problem of education was to institutionalize and standardize information so that it would promote the essential goal of keeping people from having premarital sex, which was tied to the aforementioned anxieties of moral and medical decline. Introducing information to the public was a fineline of "educating not advocating" about sexual desire and practices, with a hard focus on emphasizing dangers in order to deter people from sexual activity. To help in this, society turned to the language of medicine and science (the American Social Hygiene Association—ASHA, playing a huge role), partly because of its clout and "irrefutability" (conveniently, there were no discussions about the constructions of scientific knowledge and how "facts" and "truths" are often later discovered to have been partial), and partly because it was the most relevant discourse for the time (since sex had become an issue of public health). This type of instruction—using the language of contagion, disease, and responsibility—created a climate where there was pressure from all sides to remain "pure" in order to protect oneself and one's future partner, setting up (once again) a heteronormative ideal that naturalized and made logical the notion of chastity.

This continued until the 1920s, when schools began to integrate sex education into their curricula, and develop a different focus due to the social changes in the wake of World War I. The period's socio-cultural shifts, especially in regards to sexual liberation and the changing role of women, refocused the discourse of sexual education; it was no longer acceptable, easy, or useful to broadly condemn sex. During a time when "more Americans came to believe that sexual fulfillment was a crucial part of marriage" (Moran, Sex Education), there arose need to restructure sexual education so that it could continue to promote its core tenets (i.e. sex before or outside of marriage is not only bad, but dangerous) while acknowledging the positive force of sexuality within the sphere of marriage. For this reason, educators put their faith in science—this time social science—to solve the problem. Sexual education then began to focus on development, and "took the position that evolutionary sexual knowledge was identical with sexual conformity," teaching "children to view sex as a natural function, on the one hand, and to conflate sex with marriage and the family, on the other" (Moran, Sex Education).

Throughout the next few decades, the focus would be on the family and married life, bolstered by scientific discoveries that lessened the dangers of diseases like syphilis. Educators shifted away from the notion of "sex education" and instead renamed it "family life education," which was a major semantic move that simultaneously mirrored, reinforced, and constructed the idea of sex as a piece of family life, that had to be discussed within that context (and never outside of it). Furthermore, this new framing expanded the role of sex educators because it brought in lessons about daily-life tasks that one would encounter in a marriage (e.g. child rearing and money). This served as, once again, a tool to pass on norms and expectations that privileged and normalized a white, middle-class existence, and covered more areas of instruction that further enmeshed the concept of sex with marriage.

When the sexual revolution of the 1960s and 1970s hit, the language of sex education changed once again, and "family life education" took more of a backseat to "sexuality education," an approach that hoped to distinguish itself from the "overt moralizing and narrow heterosexual focus of its predecessors" (Moran, Sex Education). The Sexuality Information Education Council of the United States (SIECUS) was one of these leaders in championing for a "sexuality education" that addressed issues of masturbation, gender relations, homosexuality, birth control, and other topics in "a value-neutral manner [that] would allow students to reach their own conclusions about sexual behavior and sexual morality" (Moran, Sex Education) However, though not overly or overtly value-laden, this sexuality education still favored abstinence until heterosexual marriage. Because it was not overt or explicit about its biases (reduced from those in previous educational frameworks, but still prevalent), though, it made it harder to critique on the basis of ideology because its messages—hidden beneath a seemingly "value-free" nature—were harder to detect. In fact, a lot of education in the 20th century was directly impacted by the eugenics movement and had foundational beliefs that dehumanized people with mental illness and disability, not to mention people of "lesser" races.

Even though there were certain shared underlying beliefs (e.g. the delaying of teenage intercourse) in this "sexuality education" and its predecessors, the model and its proposed curricula did not go by without receiving scathing criticism. Sex education was vilified as a project of indoctrinating people into communism, queerness, and other "undesirable" and even "unnatural" positions. By describing their outrage "in socially acceptable terms" (e.g. "protecting children, supporting marriage, preventing disease, honoring women, sympathizing with the problematic 'male sexual psyche'") (Cornblatt, 2010), promoters of fear-based abstinence-centric education have craftily used language to make it hard, if not outright impossible, to publicly disagree with their agenda and not receive a backlash; any criticism has the potential to read as disagreement with the "values" themselves instead of their underlying sex-negativity, homophobia, ethnocentrism, misogyny, and heterosexism. However, a critique of these messages can only take place once they have been made visible in the first place.

The idea of "values neutrality" is enticing because we have been broadly taught that "neutrality" can be a virtue especially in politicized times, framed as the essence of tolerance. To argue against neutrality is seemingly to argue against a blank slate. How can one argue against nothingness? How can one argue against blandness and not be read as someone attempting "indoctrination" (which is seen as inherently negative and moralizing)? How can we, in a nation that focuses so much on alleged individual freedoms, push against even the very notion of individualism? In the United States—where conflicting values about moderation and indulgence are espoused, where people addressing controversial and socially progressive topics have been taught conflicting ideas of both minimizing themselves and their messages for safety's sake as well as the need to fight for visibility and inclusion—we have gotten mixed messages about how to create a sexually healthy culture. And we have been misled into believing that a neutral approach will save us.

It will not. It will be our collective downfall. Unless we do something to stop it.

We Need Intersectional Sexuality Education and We Need It Now

As we have seen through the targeted historical context above, sex education that is not intersectional works as a tool of control and oppression. In present-day, many of the underlying values and issues that created the world of institutionalized sexuality education remain at play. Our sociopolitical contexts have shifted, but many of the same issues remain. By looking at our approaches from a less insular perspective, by exploring modalities that center decolonization, and by inviting new voices into the mix, we can better shape the kind of sexuality education that will transform our world for the better.

At its core, we need to address our definition of what sex education is, what it tackles, and who it is for. Comprehensive sex education is a much broader topic than just mechanics. For those of us already on the progressive sexuality education bandwagon, we know that sex education involves discussing healthy relationships, safer sex, reproductive rights, anti-bullying, emotions, vulnerability, sexual desire or lack thereof, coercion, gender, and so forth. But how can we curb unwanted pregnancies when we only speak to the experiences of heterosexual, cisgender students having sex with their first boyfriend or girlfriend at, say, prom? How can we stop sexual violence when, overwhelmingly, narratives of prevention focus on "stranger danger," ordering women to cover themselves up, and oppressive ideas about who is targeted, what trauma looks like, and how consent should look? How can we eliminate domestic violence when only recently as a nation did we acknowledge the need for specific protections and approaches for LGBTQ people, immigrants, and Native American individuals in tribal lands through a contentiously reauthorized Violence Against Women Act? How can we preach a politic of love and autonomy when we live in a capitalist society with a school-to-prison pipeline that prioritizes incarceration over restorative justice and rehabilitation?

Just as we adopt racist, sexist, ableist beliefs in other areas of our lives, we adopt them in our sexual life and sexuality too. It's our responsibility to interrogate what we want and how that intersects with the world around us. Unless we actively work to deconstruct and understand our conditioning, we cannot do this work to the fullest extent possible. For those of us who are educators, it is imperative that we do this work within ourselves and also give those we work with the tools to do it as well. We must not only teach with values that center justice and anti-oppression, but we must also teach with tools for critical thinking and analysis.

When we do not have intersectional sex education and spaces to discuss sexuality issues, we may be making great strides in some arenas for promoting sexual health while undermining justice in others. When we are given sex toys and assistive devices that avoid misogynist traps, they are often not affordable and their marketing can even be racist. When we discuss reproductive rights education and ostensibly progressive activists lobby for women's rights to comprehensive reproductive medical care, we often see transgender people left behind as their identities and bodies do not neatly fit into mainstream discourse of reproduction. When we have event organizers putting on events for "alternative sexuality communities" and especially those who are interested in BDSM and kink practices, we see rampant racism and cultural appropriation in the form of "Asian-style" fonts, butchered cultural traditions cannibalized for sexual pleasure, fetishizing and non consensual dehumanizing of specific peoples, and outright exclusion of certain identities and communities from sites of pleasure. When we have radical sex-positive spaces for community education, teach-ins, and consciousness-raising discussions but hold them in spaces that are not accessible by people in wheelchairs, not accessible by people who need emotional support animals or service dogs, not accessible by people who have chemical sensitivities and fragrance allergies . . . we need to reevaluate our methodologies and values.

When we have non intersectional education and approaches, we get people like Margaret Sanger, the founder of the organization that would become Planned Parenthood—someone who pioneered birth control and reproductive rights . . . for some. She and many others in this era could, on one hand, advocate for free access to birth control and family planning services for the "able-minded" while also advocating for restrictive immigration policies, forced sterilizations of those considered "unfit" (to use one of the least inflammatory and offensive terms), and compulsory social segregation.

This is, of course, not to say that sexuality education is the root of all these problems. Discrimination and structural violence were here long before institutionalized sex education! However, when we approach sexuality from a values-neutral angle or one that does not acknowledge and explicitly address these forces, we end up in situations like those described above. We end up with inequitable distributions of resources and seemingly "radical" politics that still somehow manage to uphold certain systems of power.

Moving Forward

There are strong and inclusive educators out there today, and an emerging body of literature around incorporating social justice in educational settings (not just in discussions of sexuality). And though we have institutionalized many ways of learning about sexuality, the schoolhouse and the government are only two of the myriad spaces where people learn about sexuality and its meanings. In this discussion, though very systemically focused, we must remember that there are always alternate sites for knowledge production and narrative.

While it is beyond the scope of this article to conclusively and comprehensively outline what a social justice curriculum might look like, especially because social justice first would have to be defined concretely, a key place to start would be to list the social forces impacting society and strategize around how to address or incorporate each of them (e.g. ageism, ableism, classism, sexism, racism, etc.). Another key part of such a project is to clarify our own personal values and deconstruct at a very core level what assumptions we are making about sexuality. Instead of keeping them under the surface as if they were invisible, we must openly tackle them and see how they inform our worldviews. Oppression itself thrives off making itself seem normal or unintentional, like "the way things are." By airing out the unspoken or invisible, we can better work to dismantle these systems and point out how they have been built throughout history to specifically keep power in certain people's hands, even if some people in the current day do not realize it.

This work around social justice, anti-oppression, and diversity broadly defined is not just a project for those marginalized by it. In this case, this is not even about if marginalized groups "can do it alone" or not; it is that none should have to. The work of dismantling oppressive systems should never be just the task of the oppressed. How convenient and completely irresponsible, to tell someone being marginalized that not only do they have to deal with their marginalization, but they also have to educate their oppressors about it and bear the complete burden of changing the system! We all have to work on this, and the people in power need to uplift and amplify (not replace) the voices of those at the margins. This is not a simple task because we all have varying degrees of power and social capital, not just in different contexts, but also just because we have overlapping identities and thus are not all-powerful or all-oppressed. It is also important to note that certain kinds of discrimination leveled at specific communities have been pursued more aggressively and consistently across history (e.g. slavery, genocide, etc.), so we must balance not falling into an "Oppression Olympics" while also not trying to promote the idea that all peoples have been "equally oppressed" somehow.

In this work, we must also acknowledge the disconnect and difference among the written materials intended to regulate what goes on inside a teaching space, how the dynamics inside a space actually play out, and what people understand of the material. What's written in a curriculum or a set of government standards may not be what's taught in a classroom, due to the distance between the educator and the curriculum (and, to a degree, the distances between class and life, theory and practice). While a progressive teacher may subvert a restrictive, standardized curriculum, the opposite can happen as well. As Trudell (1992) points out: "No matter how restrictive or progressive, the planned curriculum or teaching materials may acquire alternate cultural meanings as they work their way through teacher and students in a particular context." Furthermore, the way in which things are taught and the way students receive them can vary considerably. In Trudell's experience teaching ninth-graders, students constructed their own versions of the information relayed to them and didn't just accept the definitions for appropriate sexual behavior from the classroom experience, even though they seemed to acquiesce "to classroom information and procedures to get a good grade in the required course and avoid embarrassment"(1992). Harkening back to an earlier point: we are all woven into a social fabric where multiple sites of knowledge production exist and affect us, and whatever information we receive is filtered through human relationships and sociopolitical contexts.

Most of us are neither huge oppressive monsters [n]or magical selfless creatures of social justice light; we are somewhere in the gray middle along the continuum of action and our positions may change depending on our environment. The key is to keep moving ourselves and our organizations toward liberation, toward becoming groups of dismantling oppression. We will all inevitably take harmful actions. We will all fail to take action at some point where we should have made a move, especially in this imperfect world rife with pain and power imbalances. The goal is to continuously do better and work toward a world of equity and joy. We are not excused from addressing our harmful actions "because nobody's perfect" and thus we are all absolved. To paraphrase a passage from the Perkei Avot, a compilation of teachings from the Jewish faith: the task of repairing the world does not fall solely on our individual shoulders and we are not going to complete the work ourselves, but that does not mean we get to opt out or desist from the endeavor.

References

Carter, J. B. (2001). Birds, Bees, and Venereal Disease: Toward an Intellectual History of Sex Education. Journal of the History of Sexuality, 10(2), 213–249. http://doi.org/10.1353/sex.2001.0022

Crenshaw, K. (1989). Demarginalizing the intersection of race and sex: A black feminist critique of antidiscrimination doctrine, feminist theory and antiracist politics. *U. Chi. Legal F.*, 139.

Dailey, D. "The Failure of Sexuality Education," *Journal of Psychology & Human Sexuality* 9(3) (1997): 96.

Lovat, T., & Hawkes, N. (2013). Values Education: A Pedagogical Imperative for Student Wellbeing. *Educational Research International*, *2*(2), 1–6.

Moran, J.P., "Sex Education," in *Encyclopedia of Children and Childhood in History and Society*, accessed November 28, 2010, http://www.faqs.org/childhood/Re-So/Sex-Education.html.

Trudell, B. "Inside a Ninth-Grade Sexuality Classroom," in *Sexuality and the Curriculum: The Politics and Practices of Sexuality Education*, ed. James T. Sears (New York: Teachers College Press, 1992) 223.

Aida Manduley is a trained sexuality educator, social worker, and nonprofit management professional. She obtained a Bachelor of Arts in Gender and Sexuality Studies from Brown University and is currently a MSW student at Boston University. Beyond her academic studies, she leads a vibrant career and is intricately connected to several sexuality social justice initiatives, including serving as a member of the Executive Committee of the Women of Color Sexual Health Network.

Paul Joannides

NO

The Luxury of Intersectionality

I wish we lived in a world where we as sex educators could make Intersectionality a priority instead of having to battle for basic reproductive rights, and freedom to teach basic and accurate information about healthy sexuality. And I wish we lived in a world where trained sex educators, rather than the producers of porn, were providing the sex education for our young. But that world does not exist either.

In the world I live in, we don't have the luxury of asking how women of different cultural backgrounds perceive abortion, which would be an important way of learning about the intersections of ethnicity and sexuality. In my world, the search terms "how to give myself an abortion" have soared recently because our United States Congress, which has been dominated by conservative male members who millions of women voted for, are doing everything under the sun to make abortion illegal and to limit women's rights.

In my world, a Title IX administrator at a large university recently cancelled my talk on sex and consent after she discovered my book is "more on how to have a meaningful sexual relationship." So in my world, administrators do not consider consent to be a central part of meaningful sexual relationships. Consent is apparently a dictum that college administrators believe they can enforce while avoiding the subject of sexual relationships altogether.

Being able to discuss how culture influences the ways that different women perceive abortion would be like discussing whether you want to be vegan or vegetarian in a world where people are starving.

I am the author of a book on sex that now has more than 90 chapters. Only one of those chapters is on penis-in-vagina intercourse, and with good reason. I, like many sex educators, have wanted to help people see that there is more to sex than sticking a penis into a vagina. Yet if you asked the vast majority of the population to define sex, penis-in-vagina intercourse would be the answer. We've hardly made a dent in expanding how people define what sex is, yet now we're supposed to board the Intersectionality train?

I think it would be wonderful for us to be able to consider issues like how an able-bodied lesbian-identified Latina perceives gay marriage in comparison to a genderqueer person with a disability who was raised in a black or white neighborhood. But at the time I am writing this, the political party who is in power has a litmus test that requires the next Supreme Court Justice be opposed to same-sex marriage and LGBT rights. Even if conservatives were to lose their majority in Congress, does anyone believe that the pervasive anti-LGBT sentiment is going to magically go away? Look at what happened when we elected a black president. In spite of our best hopes, it merely served as a catalyst for eight years of relentless racist attacks. And what about the impossible situation school educators are in when parents who are opposed to sex education storm the local school boards? (Contrary to what you might think, it's not just the evangelical parents who are opposed to sex education in the schools.)

At times, it seems like the proponents of Intersectionality feel they invented cultural sensitivity and empathy. Yet I've often found sensitivity and empathy to be the hallmarks of people who choose to be sex educators.

So I am not saying that our work as sex educators is inconsistent or incompatible with the goals of Intersectionality. Most of us share these goals (even if we don't always know the academic terminology) and would love to incorporate the ideas into our lessons. But I am concerned that the recent focus on Intersectionality takes us even further away from the basic health and relationship information that students need, and battles over basic women's and LGBT rights. It also blurs how much we are failing to reach the vast majority of young adults with credible sex education.

As for helping to inform the PE and health instructors at public schools who are assigned to teach the units on sex—these are individuals who are often cut from the abstinence-only cloth. It will be a huge victory if we as sex educators can help these teachers talk to their students about consent, and to stop shaming girls about their bodies and for wanting to have sex. These battles are so basic they don't even get us to the front door of Intersectionality.

Does Sex Education Even Exist?

University Gender Studies and Sociology departments are the birthplace of Intersectionality. I find it interesting that people in these departments believe that sex education still exists. Perhaps it does for the few students who are lucky enough to receive competent sex education. But we live in a time the United States has spent $2 billion on abstinence sex education to spread lies and shame—a time when porn has become the de facto sex educator for just about every young adult.

Teenage girls today are more interested in how to shave their pubic hair than how to masturbate or explore their sexuality. Yet if a sex-ed teacher at a public middle or high school were to have a class discussion about women's orgasms or women's masturbation, they would immediately be fired. If they tell their middle school or high school students that anal sex can often be very painful for women, or that ejaculating in a woman's face is not going to fill her with delight, the instructor would likely be fired. As a result, there is no effective voice to counter the lessons of the world's most prevalent sex educator—porn.

I have some amazing colleagues who teach college sex-ed courses. I wish I could have taken their courses when I was young. But at most colleges, fewer than 5% of the students will ever take a sex-ed course. And what about the millions of young adults who don't go to college? Where do they get their sex education? As sex educators, we haven't even begun to reach these young adults with the most basic information about the importance of consent and talking to a partner about the things they do and don't like when having sex. Instead, the sex education they are getting on their laptops and phones tells them that women want sex every minute of every day, that "real men" are always ready for it, and that conversation, foreplay, and fun are a waste of time.

On my sex survey, which more than a thousand people take each year, the average time couples say they spend on foreplay is 5 to 10 minutes before they start to have "real sex"—and 5 minutes is mentioned far more often than 10 minutes. I haven't seen where Intersectionality even deals with issues like this, yet these are the things that impact the lives of millions of people.

Sex Education Today—Males Need Not Apply

If 95% of sex educators were men, there would be a crisis in the world of sex education. At the nation's premiere sex educators' conference, there would have been speaker after speaker imploring us to do whatever is necessary to encourage more women to become sex educators. Students in gender studies, sociology and psychology would be picketing outside of the sex educator conferences to protest their 95% male membership, and I would be outside picketing as well.

Today, approximately 95% of sex educators are women. Yet, at the nation's premiere conference for sex educators, there were no protests, no keynote speakers addressing the need to encourage men to become sex educators, and there have been no workshops dedicated on how we can enlist more men to become sex educators.

I'm not seeing where the advocates of Intersectional sex ed are addressing the tremendous gender imbalance in sex education. However, when more than 90% of women who are sexually active are having sex with men, we should be very concerned about the lack of male sex education instructors and our failure to reach young men with accurate and competent sex education.

"The Male Problem" and the Marginalization of Gay and Straight Males in Sex Education

One of mantras of the Intersectionality movement is its support of those who identify as having a sexual orientation other than heterosexual. Yet I'm not seeing where sex education today is concerned about effectively engaging gay or bisexual males. Instead, sex education seems to be quietly lumping all males, regardless of orientation or behaviors, into a generic metrosexual mold. One way we are doing this is by making sex education inclusive, which means the same lesson must speak to all people of all orientations and identities, be they straight, gay, bisexual, genderqueer, or anything else. We don't realize that inclusivity, along with the easy availability of free porn, have been the death knell of effective sex education.

More than twenty years ago, when I was working on the first edition of my book on sex, I met with a group of gay men who worked in bookstores. I told them I wanted my book to be one of the most inclusive books on sex ever written. I wanted it to speak to gays and lesbians as much as to straight men and women.

I assumed these gay men would embrace and welcome my approach, and would provide words of wisdom on how to best accomplish it. Not for a moment did I think they would totally reject inclusivity, and change my mind entirely about the wisdom of it.

The first thing one of them did was point to a shelf in the corner of the gay and lesbian bookstore where we met. (This was back in the day when we had vibrant gay and lesbian bookstores.) He said it was the one shelf in the bookstore that they had to dust the most often. I asked why, and he said it was the shelf where they put the inclusive books on sex.

The men then thumbed through my manuscript and said, "What gay man do you think will want to look at a book with all of these illustrations of women's genitals, or at the one of a guy's face between a woman's legs?" And "What lesbian do you think would want a book with this illustration of a woman with a guy's penis in her mouth, or this one of a woman putting a partner's penis into her vagina?"

And then they said "What straight guy wants to see to gay men blowing each other or having anal sex? But that's what these illustrations in this chapter are showing."

Their conclusion was, "If you write it for everyone, it will speak to no one."

The[y] also asked "Do you wake up most mornings wanting to suck cock?" When I answered no, they said "Why would you think you can write about our experience when it isn't your experience?" They encouraged me to write what I know. Otherwise, they said I would be pandering.

So instead of writing an inclusive book on sex, I wrote a book for straight people that had a sense of humor about being straight; a book that has made respect for sexual differences one of its cornerstones. It introduced being LGBT as being every bit as normal as being straight. My book is now in its 8th edition and it is used in a number of college courses—often being assigned by instructors who are gay or lesbian.

In the years since I met with the group of gay men, the world of sex education now requires that every aspect of every lesson be inclusive. What those gay men warned me about has come true. Sex education today is made for everyone, but speaks to no one—at least not to straight or gay males.

One thing that sex educators can't see through the forest of political correctness is that we are trying to force heterosexual images on gay men—the kind of heterosexual images that represent the shadow of oppression they had to grow up with. And there can be no presentations about sex for straight males on college campuses. If a presentation doesn't include illustrations of gay couples and people who are transgendered, it will be criticized as being heteronormative or homophobic—of not being inclusive enough.

The Future of Sex Education

I am convinced that sex education in the schools will never be able to deal with the questions about sex that today's porn watching young adults might have. Even if we take porn out of the equation, sex ed in public middle schools and high schools will never be able to discuss women's masturbation and orgasms, using vibrators or dildos, and the importance of sexual pleasure, much less take an intersectional approach to these topics.

This doesn't mean I feel sex education is not important. Quite to the contrary—I think it's more important than ever. But only if it can transform itself in two different directions.

The first direction is for sex education in middle school and high school. It needs to be about relationships and human relatedness more than being about sex.

I keep hearing from people who work with teens how much of a spike there has been in social anxiety among teenagers. Kids still love to communicate, but with their thumbs. As a result, face to face interactions for emotional issues have become increasingly difficult. Problems we used to associate with Asperger's are now appearing in kids who aren't on the autism spectrum.

There are many students today who desperately need help in learning about emotional relatedness. They need help in knowing how to talk to a partner about what they are feeling, and the different kinds of emotions that people have when they are in relationships. And students need help in learning about breaking up when they are in a relationship, because too many people stay in relationships they don't want to be in, but are afraid of hurting their partner if they should be the one to break it off. All too often, the unhappy partner will end up cheating, which compromises his or her integrity as well as hurting their partner even more than breaking up would. Students also need help with the emotions they might feel when a partner wants to break up with them. While we can't prevent heartache, we could prepare them with healthy coping strategies.

This is a context where sex educators could take intersectional approach and, depending on the local political climate, safely lead discussions about how different kinds of relationships are viewed in different cultures and how women are perceived in different religions—although that's a discussion that could quickly go wrong for all sorts of reasons.

Sex educators can also help students become more aware of how sex and bodies are represented in the media. While I don't think it's safe for sex educators in public middle schools and high schools to include how bodies and genitals are represented in porn, many students will be able to make the connection on their own.

What I'm saying is that sex educators in public middle schools and high schools should consider giving up on the idea that they can teach about sex in depth. They should focus instead on the huge impact they can have on students' lives by helping them learn more about relationships, whether casual or traditional. And if students can be helped to be better at relationships, the benefits will cross over into their sex lives.

The other direction sex education needs to take is the highway—or to use a dated term—the information superhighway. It needs to be made for YouTube, and it needs to be way more explicit, upbeat, and dynamic than the schools will ever allow. That's because it will be competing with viral comedy and music videos, web series, and the thousands of other videos that are uploaded every hour on YouTube. It will have to be something young adults seek out and want to see, because no one will be assigning it to them as required viewing.

Fifteen years ago, I wrote a weekly column on sex for alternative weekly newspapers that needed to be 750 to 1,200 words long, and they would be annoyed if I included any images. Today, if I write more than 300 words for my blog, nobody will read it, and I often spend more time in Photoshop trying to create the perfect image than I spend writing the actual post.

College level courses can take time to discuss readings that examine sexuality through an intersectional lens, but your average high school student wants bite-sized content tailored to their experiences, and good luck getting them to read more than 200 or 300 words. Where there are opportunities, however, are in blogs and online communities. There are Tumblers, Pins, Snaps, Vines, and Instagrams where issues can be presented using images and brief videos instead of just words. I know the proponents of Intersectionality are developing more media-savvy ways of spreading their important messages that will extend beyond academic and liberal audiences.

Finding a way to teach sex education by using new mediums and in new ways are the challenges we as sex educators face today. Intersectionality is certainly a new and important theory, but in practice it isn't likely to find space in public middle or high schools. Sex educators who teach in the real world, and not on a college campus, live and work in a world that is so very different from the one where the nuances of Intersectionality can be at the forefront of our lessons.

Paul Joannides is a research psychoanalyst and the author of the *Guide to Getting It On*, an award-winning book on sex that is used in dozens of college sex-education courses. Paul has been on the editorial boards of the *Journal of Sexual Medicine* and the *American Journal of Sexuality Education*. He was awarded the 2014 Professional Standard of Excellence Award by the American Association of Sex Educators, Counselors and Therapists.

EXPLORING THE ISSUE

Should Sexuality Education Take an Intersectional Approach?

Critical Thinking and Reflection

1. What is the theory of intersectionality?
2. What, if any, is the sex educator's role in addressing intersectionality in their lessons?
3. What, in your opinion, are the overarching goals and objectives of sexuality education? How might intersectionality and racial/social justice align with these goals?
4 Are all sex educators equipped, skilled, or ready to address issues related to the intersections of sex education and racial/social justice? Why or why not?

Is There Common Ground?

What are the ultimate goals of sexuality education? Are they simply to help students make decisions that keep them free of infections or unwanted pregnancies? Should they help students navigate issues of consent? To understand their sexual identities? How can educators achieve these goals while balancing the need to affirm the experiences of people of color or other marginalized groups and integrate racial/social justice into sex education? Should an overarching goal of the field be to address more structural social issues, like helping students to understand the ways issues of race and disability intersect with sexuality? In their own ways, both authors see a need for intersectionality can be an asset to sex education. However, issues surrounding the politically charged nature of sex education and the responsibilities of educators bring about some key differences.

Aida Manduley highlights the value of intersectionality within sex education, and argues that sex education cannot truly be deemed comprehensive unless it examines the impact of oppressive forces in society. Can a young woman of color, for example, truly reflect on and understand the complexities of her sexuality and body without understanding the implications of historical and current race relations in the United States? Can sex education be truly holistic without talking about racism, sexism, classism, xenophobia, transphobia, ableism, and heterosexism?

While affirming the potential benefits of adopting intersectional approaches for discussing sexuality, Paul Joannides critiques sexuality education in the United States as being woefully unable to meet students' most basic needs. While intersectionality may be the ideal approach to university-level sex education, attitudes around basic sex education in many local communities create an unwelcoming environment for more complex discussions to occur. How, he argues, can we talk about the intersections of sex, race, gender, disability, or other common points of marginalization when many sex educators are still fighting to discuss foundational sexuality content in their classrooms? Can educators facilitate discussions about race and give this topic the attention it deserves when some school districts are hesitant to even include accurate presentations about condom usage or birth control?

In what ways do you believe sexuality education can move forward? Both Manduley and Joannides emphasize the importance of interpersonal relationships and relationship building as central aspects of comprehensive sex education, as well as subject areas that can integrate an intersectional lens. How can we build off of and capitalize these areas to develop more meaningful and in-depth conversations about sex and sexuality, while also addressing interlocking identities and oppression? In what ways can school administrators support sex educators? Should intersectional approaches to education be used in additional classes or activities? In what ways can technology and online spaces supplement school-based sexuality education? Is an intersectional approach a luxury, as Joannides claims? Or, as Manduley argues, is it a necessity?

Additional Resources

Carastathis, A. (2008). The invisibility of privilege: A critique of intersectional models of identity. *Les Ateliers De L'ethique, 3*(2).

Crenshaw, K. (September 2015). Why intersectionality can't wait. *The Washington Post.* Retrieved from *https://www.washingtonpost.com/news/in-theory/wp/2015/09/24/why-intersectionality-cant-wait/*

Kyra. (December 2014). How to uphold white supremacy by focusing on diversity and inclusion, *Model View Culture.* Retrieved from https://modelviewculture.com/pieces/how-to-uphold-white-supremacy-by-focusing-on-diversity-and-inclusion

Lewis, H. (February 2014). The uses and abuses of intersectionality, *The New Statesman.* Retrieved from http://www.newstatesman.com/helen-lewis/2014/02/uses-and-abuses-intersectionality

Masucci, V. (2016). How Sex Education Fails People of Color in the United States, *Black Girl Dangerous.* Retrieved from http://www.blackgirldangerous.org/2016/04/how-sex-education-fails-people-of-color-in-the-united-states/

Internet References . . .

Sexuality Information and Education Council of the United States (SIECUS)

www.siecus.org

Teaching Sex Ed

teachingsexed.com

Women of Color Sexual Health Network

http://www.wocshn.org

Selected, Edited, and with Issue Framing Material by:
Ryan W. McKee, *Widener University,* Tracie Q. Gilbert, *Widener University,*
and
Jayleen Galarza, *Shippensburg University of Pennsylvania*

ISSUE

Should Sex Educators Use Trigger Warnings When Discussing Controversial Content?

YES: Julie A. Winterich, from "Trigger or Not, Warnings Matter," *Inside Higher Ed* (2015)

NO: Rani Neutill, from "My Trigger-Warning Disaster: '9 ½ Weeks,' 'The Wire,' and how Coddled Young Radicals Got Discomfort All Wrong," *Salon* (2015)

Learning Outcomes

After reading this issue, you will be able to:

- Define the concept of trigger warnings.
- Explain two reasons instructors use trigger warnings in sexuality education courses.
- Explain two reasons some may feel trigger warnings are problematic.
- Clarify your own values around the use of trigger warnings.

ISSUE SUMMARY

YES: Julie A. Winterich, Associate Professor of Sociology and Director of Women's, Gender, and Sexuality Studies at Guilford College, argues that trigger warnings offer some protections to students who have experienced, or are experiencing, violence and trauma in their lives.

NO: Rani Neutill, a former Lecturer and Sexual Assault Prevention Educator at Harvard University, counters that trigger warnings limit free speech by forcing professors to protect students from ideas that may be challenging.

Have any subjects covered in your human sexuality courses made you uncomfortable? What was the feeling like? Was it simply discomfort, or something more? At what point in the lesson did you notice the feelings? How did you manage them? Did your instructor say anything to the class about the potential for discomfort before the lesson? If not, would you have preferred a warning about the content in advance?

Such advanced notice is known as a "trigger warning" and, over the last few years, a debate over their use in classrooms has emerged. Originating among therapists who treat clients with Post Traumatic Stress Disorder, the term "trigger" refers to any content such as a comment, image, or other piece of media that may cause someone to recall, and be negatively affected by, a trauma from their personal history. Trigger warnings (TW), sometimes called content warnings (CW), are typically given in advance of a conversation or activity that may result in harm for the triggered individual. Many writers, especially bloggers, have normalized the practice of including the acronyms TW or CW, along with a short description of the triggering content, before their articles (for example, "TW—sexual violence, victim blaming"). Many social media users include the warnings before sharing links to potentially alarming sites or videos.

Calls for the use of trigger warnings have become increasingly common in academic settings, leading to conversations, debates, and even protests, from those who disagree over their inclusion in lessons. For many students, trigger warnings provide advance notice of classroom topics like sexual assault or domestic violence that, given past experiences, may be re-traumatizing. For many educators, the calls feel like an unnecessary encroachment on academic freedom. While most conversations about trigger warnings have focused on higher education, some advocate for their inclusion in middle and high school settings as well.

While triggering sexual content may be covered in many classes (English Literature, Art History, Sociology, etc.) the debate over trigger warnings are of particular relevance to sexuality educators. Regardless of the setting, those who teach about sexuality occupy a unique space in comparison to those who teach less politicized courses. Because of sex-negative socialization and shame almost any lesson, regardless of content, could be triggering for some students.

Take, for example, a typical college course on human sexuality. An Intro to Human Sexuality Course may include lessons and discussions on topics that some, but not others, may consider sensitive. These topics include sexual orientations, gender identities, sex and disability, sexuality throughout the lifespan (including childhood sexuality), pornography (including violent images, or pornography depicting children), sexual behaviors (ranging from masturbation to anal sex to BDSM), sexual fantasy (including rape fantasies), sexually transmitted infections, infertility, and sexual assault. Because of the politicized nature of sex education, and sexuality in general, many instructors teaching courses on sexuality included disclaimers in their syllabi long before the term trigger warning was coined. Many go so far as to encourage students who think they may be uncomfortable with the content to withdraw from the course early on. However, not all feel the need to issue such stern declarations. Some believe that those students who need sexuality education the most may be the ones who are initially the most uncomfortable, and that such warnings may frighten students away from the opportunity to gradually become more comfortable with the material.

Recently Oberlin College made headlines by recommending trigger warnings as part of their policy on sexual offenses. Additionally, the policy guidelines noted that "[t]riggers are not only relevant to sexual misconduct, but also anything that might cause trauma. Be aware of racism, classism, sexism, heterosexism, cissexism, ableism, and other issues of privilege and oppression," and that "anything could be a trigger" (Flaherty, 2014). Some members of the faculty felt that the trigger requirements could take pedagogical decisions out of their hands and prevent them from teaching certain controversial or sensitive subjects. The policy, and others like it, was criticized by several media outlets from across the political spectrum. The American Association of University Professors (AAUP, 2014) came out in opposition to mandated trigger warnings, stating "[t]he presumption that students need to be protected rather than challenged in a classroom is at once infantilizing and anti-intellectual" (aaup.org). As more student groups on other campuses advocated for the inclusion of trigger warnings, they drew further media attention from writers, talk show hosts, and comedians accusing them of being oversensitive.

Oberlin eventually withdrew the policy, citing the desire for further faculty input. However, many educators and students across the country were eager to defend trigger warnings against what they felt were politicized attacks. Few, if any, campuses have actually mandated the use of trigger warnings, they argued. Many simply encouraged instructors to consider using them. Supporters argued that to label students as coddled, rather than empowered and able to advocate for their own health and well-being, was reductive and insulting. Critics, they believe, misunderstood the difference between trauma and discomfort. Discomfort, according to some university guidelines, "has a positive place in the learning process" (University of St. Thomas, 2015), whereas trauma is an issue that deserves special care. Instead of learning about the benefits and proper use of trigger warnings, they reacted as if a grave injustice had been committed against their lesson plans. They failed to realize, advocates say, that rather than limiting pedagogical choice, teaching from a trauma-informed approach can open new avenues for getting through to students—even on challenging material.

In the following YES and NO selections, Julie A. Winterich argues that trigger warnings simply provide advanced notice to those who, based on past experiences, may experience real trauma from the discussion of certain subjects in the classroom. Rani Neutill counters by arguing that trigger warnings, while originally well intentioned, have become tools to limit speech on topics that some students may disagree with or feel uncomfortable discussing.

References

American Association of University Professors (2014). On trigger warnings. Retrieved from http://www.aaup.org/report/trigger-warnings

Flaherty, C. (2014). Trigger unhappy. *Inside Higher Ed*. Retrieved from https://www.insidehighered.com/news/2014/04/14/oberlin-backs-down-trigger-warnings-professors-who-teach-sensitive-material

Remarks by the President at Town Hall on College Access and Affordability (September 14, 2015). Retrieved from https://www.whitehouse.gov/the-press-office/2015/09/15/remarks-president-town-hall-college-access-and-affordability

University of St. Thomas. Trigger warnings in the classroom—Resources for UST faculty (Fall 2015). Retrieved from https://www.stthomas.edu/media/lyris/facultydevelopment/TriggerWarningHandout.pdf

YES

Julie A. Winterich

Trigger or Not, Warnings Matter

Recently, a nonacademic friend asked, "If you were teaching William Butler Yeats's 'Leda and the Swan,' would you use a trigger warning?"

"Leda and the Swan" is a vivid account of Zeus, in the form of a swan, raping a young woman named Leda. I hadn't read that poem since high school, and after rereading it, I can't say for certain what I would do as an English professor. I probably would take an approach similar to the one I use as a professor in sociology as well as women's, gender and sexuality studies.

The concept of a trigger warning has become quite controversial in recent years, with some people on campuses encouraging or demanding its use, and others discouraging it—such as the Faculty Senate at American University, which recently passed a resolution citing the potential negative impact on academic freedom. As a faculty member who regularly teaches course content on trauma, I take more of a middle ground.

The term "trigger warning" has come to refer to introductory statements on web postings of graphic descriptions of rape, eating disorders, and self-harm. They are used to alert readers who may be struggling with post traumatic stress disorder (PTSD) related to those topics so that they can choose whether to continue reading. The purpose of using a trigger warning in the classroom is to let students know that the material that their professors have assigned may cause physiological or psychological reactions as a result of past traumas.

I started teaching in 2000, before the term was regularly used in academe or had received any news media attention. I now teach many of the same topics I taught then, about rape, violence, trauma and eating issues.

My approach on the first day of class, when I discuss the purpose of the course and learning goals, is to review the syllabus, pointing out topics that may be emotionally difficult, such as trauma and eating issues. I explain the content in the texts and any films that I plan to show in class.

In the past two years, I've also said something like, "I can't predict what material may trigger someone suffering from post traumatic stress disorder or what will upset people for other reasons. If you are concerned or uncertain about this course, please closely review the course materials and decide whether you want to continue taking it."

I tell students that I'm available to meet with them to discuss any questions they may have about any aspect of the course. Typically, the week before we engage content that explicitly depicts violence or trauma, I remind students about the upcoming material.

If a student cannot view a film or discuss raw readings in the class setting, they are still responsible for that material, just as is a student who cannot attend class because they have a fever or other illness. I do not change my expectations or assessments concerning quizzes, exams, papers, and so on—regardless of the reason a student misses class. In the handful of cases when a student (typically a rape victim) has met with me to tell me that she cannot attend an upcoming class because the material is too emotionally charged, I tell her that she can use one of the two allotted absences that I give all students for any reason, such as if they are sick or need to attend a family event. I also tell her about the mental-health resources available to her to encourage her to seek help if she has not yet done that. I've never had students tell me they cannot read the course material because they are dealing with PTSD. (The reality is that some students don't read all course material for a variety of reasons.)

The intent of a trigger warning is to acknowledge that some students may need to prepare themselves before engaging with explicit texts or films that might otherwise catch them off guard. But what preparing oneself looks like differs based on where each specific student is in the healing process. As noted by Mental Health America, people can have very different reactions. One student may need to seek counseling, while another may need to focus on mindfulness techniques and other strategies before coming to class. And yet another may need to skip class altogether.

How professors should use the phrase "trigger warning" is a source of contention. Students often do not have an accurate understanding of what it means, so they need an explanation of PTSD to appreciate the warning's purpose. They may not realize there is a difference between course content that they will find emotionally disturbing for reasons other than trauma, and course content that is triggering due to PTSD. Some types of course content are upsetting for most students, such as films that depict genocide or natural disasters. Not all students who become visibly emotional are reliving memories of trauma (unless, of course, they have direct, traumatic experiences with genocide or natural disasters).

Then there's the issue of whether to use trigger warnings at all. Discerning whether material is potentially triggering due to PTSD is arguably a slippery slope. And no professor can warn students about all possible triggers that might occur in their classroom.

I certainly don't have all the answers when it comes to the debates about trigger warnings, but I never only use the term "trigger warning," if I use it at all. If we as professors incorporate the phrase "trigger warning," we should include more information than those two words, whether in a syllabus or before showing a film. I'm not trained about all possible PTSD triggers, so I risk misleading students by labeling some material as triggering and overlooking other content altogether. Instead, I continue to prefer course content overviews and reminders about upcoming content on violence and trauma.

All that said, things can get especially complicated in an academic setting. Outside of academe, a person with PTSD who is learning how to manage triggers may successfully avoid news, films, or other potentially difficult stimuli. What is distinct about college is that students may be enrolled in courses that *require* them to read, watch, or discuss content that graphically depicts violence or trauma.

Sexual assault, in particular, is associated with a greater risk of developing PTSD symptoms, and a new survey among 27 universities finds that ciswomen, transgender, and gender nonconforming students experience the highest rates of sexual assault and misconduct during their college years.

So, whether using the term "trigger warning" or not, I strongly believe that professors should say something about that content before requiring students to engage it. Here's an example of a time when I regret that I didn't do that.

In a senior sociology seminar, I showed a clip from *The Invisible War*, a documentary about sexual assault in the military. I described the film's content, but I did not specify that the clip we were about to view included distraught, first-person interviews. One segment showed a young woman shaking as she described a rape's impact on her life. The film then cut to her father weeping about his failed attempts to reassure her that she is still a virgin.

A student became agitated. She shifted in her chair, wiped away tears, and left the room for a few minutes while we wrapped up the clip.

After class, I sent an email to check in with her. She wrote back first thanking me for covering these issues in class rather than avoiding them. Then she said that she wished that I had better prepared the class for the content of this particular film. Watching first-person accounts of rape is much more difficult to absorb in a class setting than academic readings on the same topic. Not acknowledging that difficulty risks leaving sexual assault victims in the classroom feeling more isolated than they already do.

She's right.

I had unexpectedly received a copy of the film, and I could have sent an email giving a more detailed description of the film before we met in class that day. And I wish I had.

Higher education cannot identify all possible topics or classroom moments that might trigger students suffering from PTSD. Professors may decide to abandon the language "trigger warning" altogether to avoid the impression that they have drawn a bright line between material that is and is not triggering. But let's not forgo giving students advanced descriptions of course content on violence or trauma. Whether it's a content alert or a preparatory overview, professors have a responsibility to let students know about such content.

Not giving students a heads-up risks a return to the status quo of intellectualizing violence and trauma as something that happens only outside the classroom. And those in the classroom who have suffered such trauma may needlessly suffer even more.

Julie A. Winterich is an Associate Professor of Sociology Anthropology and the Director of Women's, Gender and Sexuality Studies at Guilford College.

Rani Neutill

NO

My Trigger-Warning Disaster: "9½ Weeks," "The Wire," and how Coddled Young Radicals Got Discomfort All Wrong

About a year ago I was asked to teach a class about the evolution of the representation of sex throughout American Cinema. I started with the silent film (*The Cheat*) and ended with Spike Jonze's disembodied sex in *Her*. Along the way, I showed a number of sexually graphic films that caused a great deal of controversy.

At the time I was teaching the course, I was also figuring out a life outside of academia. I had been a wandering postdoc for a long time and was tired. A friend of mine had recently been violently sexually assaulted. I was a witness. The trauma she suffered, from the assault and the long, drawn-out trial of her assailants, led me to volunteer at my local rape crisis center. Working directly with folks who have experienced trauma, I entered the course believing in trigger warnings and gave them throughout the class, even though it seemed as though the title of the course was a trigger warning in and of itself. Regardless, I gave them for almost every film I showed. I even gave them for films that really shouldn't have needed them (i.e., *Psycho*).

Midway through the semester, because of my work in sexual assault prevention, I was asked to fill in for the Director of the Office of Sexual Assault Prevention Services at the university. The Director had to take a short leave so I was there to fill in temporarily. In accepting the position, I took on a dual role. First, I was an activist against sexual violence, supporting survivors on campus, but I was also an educator who believed that learning is about shaking up one's world and worldview. I didn't realize that occupying both roles at once would be impossible; failure was inevitable.

The first "uh-oh" moment came when I taught *Pillow Talk* with Rock Hudson and Doris Day. Rock Hudson plays the role of a womanizer (the irony of all this, of course, is that he was closeted). When he gets women into his home there are a series of "booby traps" meant for getting it on (who says that anymore? me). One seemed like a literal trap—the door locks itself shut. I suggested that this might be a predatory act. The class was suddenly divided—there were the ones who vehemently believed that Hudson's character was a rapist, and those who vehemently argued that he was not. This divide would get deeper and uglier throughout the semester, with me caught irrevocably in the middle.

Next, I assigned a reading by Linda Williams, a chapter from her book, *Screening Sex*. It looked in intimate detail at the first blaxploitation film ever made—Melvin Van Peebles', *Sweet Sweetback's Badasssss Song* (SSBAS). The chapter outlined (with pictures), the plot of the movie and all the sexual acts that were in the film. Williams' argument is that Blaxploitation and SSBAS arose from a reclamation of masculinity by black men who were historically emasculated and castrated (think of the killing of Emmett Till).

I assumed everyone had done the reading. I showed one of the scenes that Williams writes about in detail. Before I screened it, I gave a warning, indicating that it was one of the disturbing scenes to which Williams refers. The scene shows a young Sweetback (played by the director's son Melvin Van Peebles) having sex with a 30-year-old woman. She finds him irresistible and thus starts the hyper-sexual evolution of Sweetback—every woman on earth wants to fuck him, including a whole bunch of white women. This, of course, is statutory rape. When the lights went on and the scene was over, two students left the room in tears. I was perplexed. I started to ask questions about Williams' reading, how it felt to read about and then watch the scene, what questions of race and masculinity it provoked. Crickets man, crickets. Clearly no one had done the reading.

Later that day, I had a white female student come to my office hours crying. Between picking up tissues and blowing her nose she said, "I'm doing a minor in African

American Studies. How could your first images of black people be that horrible?" I told her that I understood her concerns. I went on to explain how the class was a historical look at sex on screen and as the reading for the class articulated, it was one of the first film's to show black people having sex and was important to film history. She still didn't get it. She said I had to show some positive images, otherwise it was unfair, that the other students weren't African American Studies minors so they didn't understand race politics as she did. I told her that I would bring a positive image to the next class to address her concerns. Finally, she smiled.

That night I went home and thought about it, hard. Isn't confronting difficult issues what learning is about? My classes were about race, gender, and sexuality. These are inherently uncomfortable topics that force students to think critically about their privilege and their place in the hierarchy of this world.

It's not fun to talk about inequality. It's not fun to talk about slavery. It's not fun to talk about the complexity of sexual desire. It's terribly, terribly, uncomfortable. But it was my job as their teacher to navigate through this discomfort. I felt like I handled the class poorly. I had kowtowed too much, so I went to class the next day prepared to break this shit down.

I also thought about a positive image of black sexuality and sex. I decided to show a clip from *The Wire* that shows Omar in bed with his boyfriend just after having sex, a tender moment where they kiss. Omar's character, a black, gay dude who steals from drug dealers, is a revolutionary representation of black masculinity that stands in stark contrast to SSBAS. I was excited to show it. I mean, it's *The Wire*: who doesn't want to talk about *The Wire*?

I began class by talking briefly about learning through discomfort. The students were silent. I turned to them for questions about moments of feeling uncomfortable and how we could read these as productive. The student who came to my office raised her hand and asked, "Are we gonna talk about SSBAS."

"Yes," I said, "but I want us to talk about any of the films that made people uncomfortable. Let's discuss the discomfort." Her face fell. She started crying and ran out of the room. Her friend followed her. Right after she left I showed the scene with Omar. Later that day, she came to my office again, sobbing.

For the rest of the semester, I gave trigger warnings before every scene I screened. Every. Single. One. This wasn't enough. A student came to me and asked that I start sending emails before class outlining exactly which disturbing scenes I would be showing so that I wouldn't "out" survivors if they had to walk out of class when hearing what I was about to show. This took all the free form and off the cuff ability to teach. It stifled the teaching process. There would never be a moment for me to educate them by confronting them with the unknown, by helping them become aware of their own biases by making them feel uncomfortable.

Nevertheless, I did it. Each night I sent a meticulous email detailing which scene I was showing, where in the film the scene was, and what the content of the scene included. My role as a sexual assault prevention services specialist and survivor advocate eclipsed my role as a professor as I tried to accommodate students over and over again.

The next film to piss them all off was *9 1/2 Weeks*. The film is about a[n] S&M relationship between a character played by Micky Rourke and one played by Kim Basinger. At first Basinger's character is drawn to Rourke and they begin an S&M style consensual relationship. As the film goes on, Rourke becomes abusive and the sex becomes non consensual, but the beauty of the film is that Basinger is eventually able to let go and take something from the relationship—a heightened sense of her sexuality and desires. There's an infamous scene with Rourke feeding Basinger a number of food items while she's blindfolded. It's basically a series of soft core money shots. It *is* a consensual scene. When conversation began in class, a white male student started talking about the scene as one of consent. Four hands shot up. One said, "no—it is clearly not consensual." Other students concurred. They argued that if someone is in an abusive relationship, they can never consent to sex because they are being manipulated.

This *triggered me*. I was furious.

Sexual assault survivor support is about empowerment. The model says, "Hey! It's not for you to tell the survivor what happened to them; that's their story, they know, don't fucking label it." What these students were essentially doing was stripping every person in an abusive relationship of all their agency. They were telling every survivor that they were raped, even when the survivor may have wanted to have sex with their abuser. They were claiming god like knowledge of every sexual encounter. And they were only 20. If that. Their frontal lobes haven't even fully developed.

I was done with it. I was drained. I was anxious. I was tired. I was fed up. But I didn't want to be. I had been teaching for ten years with passion.

I went to get advice from a colleague in the department. He listened and said that during that time of the semester, students tended to get testy. He thought it was seasonal. I asked him if he ever had such a hard time with his students and he said, "No, I am an old white dude, I really think that as a young woman of color they probably just aren't afraid of you, they see you as a peer." For the record, I'm not that young but he may have been right. And here's the irony, all of the students who were upset were the feminists, the activists, and there they were, treating a woman of color professor like she wasn't an authority while treating old white dudes like they are.

There has been a lot written about triggering and trigger warnings, discussions about how triggers are often not explicit references to one's traumatic experiences. Smells, tastes, different objects, they can all be triggering. Think of Proust's madeleine and the surge of memories about his mother. Memory, emotional trauma, grief and healing are complicated and unique to an individual's experience. Blanket trigger warnings treat them as impersonal predictable entities. The current movement of calling for trigger warnings prioritizes the shielding of students from the traumatic, whereas, ironically, so many other therapeutic models focus on talking through and confronting trauma as a mode of healing.

Recent work by Greg Lukainoff and Jonathan Haidt looks in depth at this phenomenon, the call for safe spaces and trigger warnings. Their tone could be read as condescending to people who are survivors of trauma, but I do think they raise a number of important points. Similarly, the work of Laura Kipnis on trigger warnings is crucial and illuminating, but in an unfortunate and sometimes typical academic fashion, it can be snobbish and dismissive (Jack Halberstam is also in this camp). Here lies the problem. Taking a tone like that just pisses students off even more. I'm not saying that if we said these things nicely, students would suddenly get it; they won't. I am living proof of that. I'm just pointing out the fact that putting on an academic face of elite speak isn't helping either. Maybe pointing out the horrifying political stance these students are making would be more effective.

When a Duke Student refuses to read a book because it has lesbian sex in it and students who are liberal, who are activists, also refuse to read and watch things because they see it as triggering, we see the collusion of the right and left wing. When I get an evaluation from this course that says, "as a white male heterosexual I felt unsafe in this course," and another that reads, "as a survivor this course was traumatizing," we are at a moment that needs some radical re thinking. Do students of a radical nature think that if they are seeing eye to eye with the most extreme conservative element of the population that they are doing something right? Fighting for something positive? Participating in something different?

I don't have the answers. Hell, I gave up on the whole thing. This was the last straw for me. I didn't know the answers but I knew this was a crisis. Colleges are the new helicopter parents, places where the quest for emotional safety and psychic healing leads not to learning, but regression.

I don't know about trigger warnings outside classes that deal with race, gender and sexuality, but I do know that if you promote trigger warnings in subjects that are supposed to make people feel uncomfortable, you're basically promoting a culture of extreme privilege, [be]cause I'm pretty sure that the trans women who are being murdered weekly, the black men who are victims of police brutality daily, and the neighborhoods in America that are plagued by everyday violence, aren't given any trigger warnings. Let's be honest: life is a trigger.

Rani Neutill is a former Lecturer and Sexual Assault Prevention Educator at Harvard University. She is currently a Marketing Manager at CoachUp.

EXPLORING THE ISSUE

Should Sex Educators Use Trigger Warnings When Discussing Controversial Content?

Critical Thinking and Reflection

1. What are the concerns regarding trigger warnings expressed by Neutill? How effective might Winterich's approach resolve Neutill's issues?
2. How can teachers and students discern the difference between discomfort and trauma?
3. Is there sexuality-related content that you may find triggering? If so, do you believe instructors should include trigger warnings?
4. Do sexuality educators have the responsibility to create a totally "safe space" for learning to occur? If so, what might this look like? If not, how can educators reduce the potential for harm in their classrooms?

Is There Common Ground?

Criticism of Oberlin's trigger warning policy came swiftly and sharply from conservative and liberal media alike. Many on the right see trigger warnings as an attack on free speech, and an example of the effects of liberal education policies on a generation of oversensitive millennials. Many on the left see the warnings as an attack on academic freedom and the right of instructors to determine which teaching methods best suit the content. Even President Obama chimed in on the subject from a Town Hall meeting on educational issues. He noted:

> I've heard of some college campuses where they don't want to have a guest speaker who is too conservative. Or they don't want to read a book if it has language that is offensive to African Americans, or somehow sends a demeaning signal towards women. And I've got to tell you, I don't agree with that either. I don't agree that you, when you become students at colleges, have to be coddled and protected from different points of views.
>
> (whitehouse.gov, 2015)

In a report by the National Coalition Against Censorship, 23 percent of faculty surveyed reported providing warnings about course content. However, 62 percent believed trigger warnings will negatively impact academic freedom, and only 17 percent view them favorably. Academic freedom is a hallmark of higher education. Having one's values challenged, and ultimately clarified, through the discussion of challenging issues has been a rite of passage for generations of college students. But what responsibilities come with such freedom? Do sexuality educators, or other instructors teaching content related to sexuality, have a special responsibility to ensure their students' well-being? Should assigned books like a sexually explicit novel in an English Literature course, or even *Taking Sides: Controversial Issues in Human Sexuality* come with trigger warnings on their covers (or from the instructors who assign them)?

An often overlooked part of this discussion deals with changing demographics on college campuses. While students are becoming increasingly diverse, college professors remain largely white and male. What part might these changes play in the debate over trigger warnings? Should care be taken to understand if each student is mentally and emotionally ready for challenging material? Or, as President Obama mentioned, do some students simply want to be coddled and protected? Is there a way to protect both academic freedom and the students who may be re-traumatized by certain classroom content?

Additional Resources

Flaherty, C. (December 2, 2015). Trigger warning skepticism. *Inside Higher Ed*. Retrieved from https://www.insidehighered.com/news/2015/12/02/survey-sheds-new-light-faculty-attitudes-and-experiences-toward-trigger-warnings

Hanlon, A.R. (August 14, 2015). The trigger warning myth. *New Republic*. Retrieved from https://newrepublic.com/article/122543/trigger-warning-myth

JESSINCAMBODIA (2015). My trigger warning dilemma. *Feministing*. Retrieved from http://feministing.com/2015/12/02/my-trigger-warning-dilemma/

Lukianoff, G., & Haidt, J. (2015). The coddling of the American mind. *The Atlantic*. Retrieved from http://www.theatlantic.com/magazine/archive/2015/09/the-coddling-of-the-american-mind/399356/

McQuade, M. (Sept. 19, 2015). Why I use trigger warnings. *New York Times*. Retrieved from http://www.nytimes.com/2015/09/20/opinion/sunday/why-i-use-trigger-warnings.html?_r=0

National Coalition Against Censorship (2015). What's all this about trigger warnings? Retrieved from http://ncac.org/wp-content/uploads/2015/11/NCAC-TriggerWarningReport.pdf

Internet References . . .

American Association of University Professors

www.aaup.org

University of St. Thomas: Trigger Warnings in the Classroom— Resources for UST Faculty (Fall 2015)

www.stthomas.edu/media/lyris/facultydevelopment/TriggerWarningHandout.pdf

National Coalition Against Censorship

http://ncac.org

Selected, Edited, and with Issue Framing Material by:
Ryan W. McKee, *Widener University,* Tracie Q. Gilbert, *Widener University,*
and
Jayleen Galarza, *Shippensburg University of Pennsylvania*

ISSUE

Should Sex Educators Be Required to Have Formal Training?

YES: Lexx Brown-James, from "Required Training for Sex Educators Is Beneficial for All," An original essay written for this volume (2016)

NO: Tyomi Morgan, from "Information Is Power: How Knowledge Trumps Credentials for Any Good Sex Educator," An original essay written for this volume (2016)

Learning Outcomes

After reading this issue, you will be able to:

- Identify three types of formal training opportunities available for aspiring sex educators.
- Discuss the potential benefits and challenges of leveraging professional networks to increase sexuality knowledge.
- Discuss the potential benefits and challenges of using one's personal experience as pedagogy.

ISSUE SUMMARY

YES: Lexx Brown-James, marriage and family therapist, and founder of the Institute for Sexuality and Intimacy, argues that quality sex education depends on facilitators who are highly skilled and trained at their craft, which most often comes through formal training.

NO: Tyomi Morgan, a sex coach, columnist, and the founder of SexpertTyomi.com, argues that knowledge and skill gained from independent study and preparation can be just as effective in building a successful sex education career as formal experience.

If you are reading these pages, you have likely been exposed to at least one formal sex education experience. Through it, you've probably explored a reasonable range of concepts—most of which (if not all) helped increase your intellectual understanding of sexuality as a whole. In thinking about the facilitator of that experience, what would you say were the qualities that made them most suitable for their job? Was it important to you that, for example, they have personal experience with the topics they discussed? Or was it enough for them to have only studied them beforehand? If you found them to be charismatic, or the course itself entertaining or personally helpful, would it matter to you to find out later that their knowledge base was not acquired through traditional means? While you might find significant concern with a biology or mathematics instructor with no formal training in the subject matter they taught, would you feel the same way about a teacher or professor in human sexuality?

Debate on the necessary qualifications for sexuality educators is not new, and has wavered between several different perspectives since emergence of the profession in the early 1900s. Influencing factors on such debates have also varied, though they have almost always been informed by the collective social expectations of the time. At present, the list of professional standards for sex educators is long, and covers such areas as content proficiency, sexual attitude awareness, and learner sensitivity, among others. At minimum, it is mostly expected that good sex educators be knowledgeable about the topic of instruction, and be willing to create a safe space for others to become knowledgeable as well. Unfortunately, not all sexuality educators have the training or experience to meet this expectation. Educators from organizations including the Sexuality Information and Education Council of the United States (SIECUS), Advocates for Youth, and ANSWER, have worked diligently to create the National Sexuality Education Standards, a document that attempts to clearly guide educators in the essential minimum core content for sexuality education across grades K–12. Interestingly, the standards encourage professional development and training, but set no minimum formal education requirement for sex educators.

An important point to consider in the debate on formal educator training is how it makes assumptions about sex education's usefulness in preventing unwanted sexual outcomes among young people—specifically, sexually transmitted infections and unintended pregnancy. In order to engage with either of these topics effectively, teachers must have accurate, up-to-date knowledge, all of which is key in clarifying facts and dispelling untruths. For this reason, most people might argue in favor of formal training, as it would be perceived to be the ideal way to ensure timely and cost-effective access to needed information. That said, a focus on adolescent sex education in this debate makes many assumptions about the ways that sex education is enacted in nontraditional settings, and among other audiences. Adolescents, after all, aren't the only people in need of quality sex education. For example, an alternative perspective might focus on sexual skill building or technique. While formal training may exist for learning how to teach better coital techniques, or best strategies for beginning a polyamorous relationship, some may have concerns over its effectiveness. How much more beneficial would such training be to an instructor versus teaching from one's own personal experience? In this case, some might argue that formal training is not only unnecessary, but an impossible goal for acquiring that particular kind of knowledge base.

Where the biggest challenge to requiring formalized training may lie is in the vast diversity of content areas from which sexuality research and, by extension, sexual knowledge emerges. Indeed, sexuality is a large enough body of conceptual knowledge that many disciplines (e.g., public health, sociology, anthropology, biology, gender/women studies, psychology) have influenced. While current practitioner credentials relative to sexuality (e.g., MPH, MSW, MFT, LPC) might be easy enough to acquire on their own, necessitating that all sex educators garner formal content training might leave many unable to curate a thorough enough list of credentials to qualify as a legitimate "expert." Additionally, while one might argue that required credentialing in teacher education is ideal, or even intuitive in charting a formal sex-ed training path, those for whom it is not their primary job might find adding this extra step an unwieldy extra burden. Furthermore, completing the work of even one formalized program of study often comes at great personal and financial cost to the learner; requiring it to be the standard runs the risk of pricing out those from marginalized communities, many of whom have been historically excluded from the field.

While much of the debate centers on knowledge versus experience, some may see formal education programs as experience themselves. While independent study may contain as much content acquisition, and a self-taught educator may possess natural charisma and open-mindedness, most formal training programs prepare learners with both content and methodology simultaneously—which is key in addressing one the biggest challenges in effective sex education, those around teacher and learner affect development. In this way, a formal learner might not only acquire basic sexual content knowledge, but also the tangible skills needed to successfully address unexpected challenges in one's learning space, like inappropriately personal questions, learner derailing, revelations of trauma, or any other threat to the learning experience as a whole. Moreover, formal learning through traditional degree programs often affords practitioners community they might not be able to find otherwise, from which insight and opportunities for collaboration may abound. Others, however, may argue that such community can be found anywhere, thanks to the proliferation of content and the myriad of ways to connect, both professionally and personally, online.

As collective social interest and support grows for comprehensive sex education, the time may quickly approach to standardize the credentialing expectations for sex educators. In the meantime, however, the debate continues in new and unexpected spaces.

YES

Lexx Brown-James

Required Training for Sex Educators is Beneficial to All

Sexuality educators work in many settings and across multiple disciplines, including formal and informal educational institutions, sexuality-based coaching and counseling, sociology and public health. These professionals might not all identify as sexuality educators, but they work within the broad realm of sexuality and are therefore in need of formal training. Within each of these spaces sexuality educators are responsible for the education students, administrators, clients, and other service providers receive. Sexuality education is uniquely able to impact multiple institutions and has the power to cause systemic change. The people doing this work, whether intentionally or not, need to be formally trained in human sexuality, because with knowledge comes great power.

What is formal sexuality education training?

The Sexuality Education and Information Council of the United States (SEICUS) believes sexuality education should "address the biological, sociocultural, psychological, and spiritual dimensions of sexuality within the cognitive learning domain (information), the affective learning domain (feelings, values, and attitudes), and the behavioral learning domain (communication, decision-making, and other skills)." Sexuality education should be appropriate for the age and developmental levels of the students, take into consideration their cultural backgrounds, and provide medically accurate information, while recognizing the expansive and diverse values and beliefs that exist in the classrooms. A sexuality educator needs to be able to teach students with these issues at the forefront of their learning goals.

Untrained sexuality educators, as well as those who do not teach from a comprehensive perspective, cause harm. Research from the 2015 National Survey of Family Growth found that when educated using a comprehensive sexuality education curriculum teenagers were 50% less likely to get pregnant than those teens who only received abstinence only education. In the United States only 22 states and the District of Columbia require sexuality education to be taught in school, and only 19 of those require that information to be medically, factually, or technically accurate (National Conference of State Legislatures, 2016). This means that over half of the children in the US are not receiving regulated sexuality education, and that even those who do receive it are subject to varying interpretations of what is actually beneficial to their sexual development. Formally trained sexuality professionals, however, work to prevent misinformation and reduce its long-term effect.

Wait, I know people who have been working in the field for years, who aren't 'formally trained' and are better educators than those with PhDs. Are you discrediting them because of an expensive piece of paper?

No. Formalized training comes from many different places, not only sexuality education programs at institutions of higher learning. Fortunately, there are a myriad of ways to gain comprehensive, fact-based sexuality education training. Currently, a number of organizations offer trainings which allow a person to earn certification without having to have a specific degree. The World Association of Sex Coaches offers its own certification training program. Additionally, if you already have experience as a sexuality educator, you can apply for the credentials based on your experience without having to have a higher education degree specific to sexology. The National Coalition of Sexual Freedom (NCSF) also offers certification and will designate professionals as Kink Aware Professional (KAP) on their listserv and directory (Martin, 2016). Membership in the NCSF does not require an academic degree and members stem from various employment backgrounds (Martin, 2016). Additionally, the Association of Somatic & Integrative Sexologist (ASIS) offer a certification without educational background restrictions (Martin, 2016). Sexuality is a vast field, with many different avenues of formal training available. Each of these sexuality-based organizations provides pertinent information for the advancement of sexuality education and there are additional groups that offer training as well.

Organizations like health agencies, public school systems, and governmental organizations may also offer certifications and continuing education for formalized sexuality education. For example, the United States Army provides training in the Sexual Harassment/Assault and Prevention (SHARP) training to professionals to help prevent or assist with traumatic events experienced by service members (n.d.).

That there are so many different types of institutions creates the opportunity for any professional who educates about sexuality to receive formalized training. Taking advantage of them can help to reduce harm, while helping lead students and consumers to sexually positive, healthy, and affirming lives.

Outside of traditional academic institutions, ways to gain formal sexuality education include taking workshops from non profit establishments like Planned Parenthood, and ANSWER, as well as other sexual heath or advocacy groups. These programs can have trainings on a variety of topics including disease prevention, healthy relationships, or LGBTQ issues, ranging anywhere from 10 to 40+ hours. Such workshops create sound sexuality educators ready to support and educate others about specific sexuality topics.

Okay, I don't want to teach adolescents or work in a school. I talk about sex and I'm a professional, but I'm not a typical sexuality educator. I don't need formal training, do I?

Yes. You do. Sexuality is a sensitive and complex topic that is imbued with personal morals and values. If you are going to teach anyone about topics within sexuality you need to be aware of the most medically accurate and up-to-date information. Consider the following example:

> A person who works for a sex toy distributor finds themselves hosting an event at a home. This party is unique and exciting because it is for couples. After the general demonstration, one of the participants asks how a man can enjoy other sexual stimulation outside of penile touch. This specific sex toy distributor took the mandated online formal training class the company offers and is able to educate the man about safe prostate play, types of toys to use, lubricants that are safe and durable, and even remove some of the stigma and bias that might come along with a question like this.

It is through formal training that despite the variety of fields sexuality education occurs within (and) educators are able to teach about the subject comprehensively.

What about somatic sexuality education? I find touch to be a super important part of sexuality education and all of these formal institutions have rules against it. They aren't accepting of non-academic or therapeutic professionals.

Sexual touching from professional to client can be difficult to navigate and negotiate, but many find it to be a healing and therapeutic process. It is important to understand that formal education doesn't necessarily mean acquiring licensure or certification. Dr. Betty Dodson is a sex coach in New York City who has been working with individuals in somatic pleasure-based touch for nearly 40 years. She now hosts regular "bodysex" workshops where individuals can earn a certification to become bodysex coaches (again, another form of formalized education). During these all-nude seminars, women work together to overcome anxieties and fear around sexual pleasure. As a somatic and tactile sexuality practitioner, Dodson eventually earned a PhD through the Institute for the Advanced Study of Human Sexuality. She decided not to become licensed or go into psychology because of the restrictions it would put on her work. Formal training allows her to specialize in a specific realm of sexuality education not addressed by many organizations, while successfully helping many women and sexuality educators.

Are there any other benefits to having formal training as a sexuality educator?

Formal education connects students to a vast network of sexuality educators in one overarching field, and allows future practitioners to become a part of that community. Along these lines, one can also gain formal training and support, as well as a sense of belonging, by joining professional organizations. For example, The Women of Color Sexual Health Network (WOCSHN) provides a safe space for women of color to collaborate on projects, post job opportunities, share educational materials, and discuss relevant news and challenges met in the field of sexuality. The group is comprised of women from various ethnic, religious, socioeconomic, sexual identity, and educational backgrounds. And quite importantly, the organization is free to join. Each woman there has created her own path in the field of human sexuality and accrued various types of formalized training to hone her skills as a professional sexuality educator. She also has the support of hundreds of women who can provide constructive feedback or just moral support. Without formalized training, whether initial or continued, there is a chance an educator would miss out on building community with other skilled practitioners.

Outside of community, formally trained sexuality educators are also more likely to have support from another sexuality professional as their supervisor. The field of sexuality professionals has supervisors in education, therapy, bodywork, sex magic, and counseling. Although they might not be called supervisors in every area of the field, one will typically have access to more seasoned sexuality professionals who are able and willing to provide educational, emotional and professional support. Having guidance from established educators in the field potentially increases access to future opportunity, knowledge, and skill. Additionally, having a larger collective of sexuality professionals who can both share and challenge one's perspective on topics helps one to decipher and/or solidify one's own positionality and attitudes about challenging subjects. Ways to meet sexuality professionals include attending seminars, conferences, specialization classes, volunteer education, academic institutions, and sexual health organization training—all formal education avenues.

In closing, all sexuality educators need to have formal training. There are many options to gain this training, but it needs (to) be medically accurate, comprehensive and fact based. To become a professional sexuality educator or to educate about sexuality without formal training is risky and can cause harm to those who are in that person's care. Formal training has to extend beyond scholastic institutions in order to meet the varied and vast needs of sexuality practitioners. I believe that formal training is necessary for all sexuality educators and is just as important as medical training is for doctors and law school is for lawyers. It is how sexuality professionals get their fundamentals. To build anything that will last, the foundation has to be strong.

References

Dodson, Betty. (2012). About me. Retrieved April 2, 2016 from www.bettydodson.com.

Martin, Sarah. (2016). *6 Sexology Credentials You Need to Know About.* Retrieved April 2, 2016 from https://www.linkedin.com/pulse/6-sexology-credentials-you-need-know-sarah-martin

National Conference of State Legislators. (2016). Retrieved April 2, 2016 from http://www.ncsl.org/research/health/state-policies-on-sex-education-in-schools.aspx

Sexual Harassment/Assault Response & Prevention. (n.d.) Retrieved April 4, 2016 from http://www.sexualassault.army.mil/

Sexuality Education and Information Council of the United States. (n.d.) Retrieved April 3, 2016 from http://www.siecus.org/index.cfm?fuseaction=Page.viewPage&pageId=490&parentID=472

World Health Organization. (2016). *Defining Sexual Health.* Retrieved March 11, 2016 from http://www.who.int/reproductivehealth/topics/sexual_health/sh_definitions/en/.

Lexx Brown-James is a marriage and family therapist, and the founder of the Institute for Sexuality and Intimacy.

Tyomi Morgan

NO

Information Is Power: How Knowledge Trumps Credentials for Any Good Sex Educator

On September 8th, 2011 I entered into the field of sexuality education, without any formal training or institutionalized education, with the click of a button. On this day, my sex education blog Glamerotica101.com launched after two solid years of planning and contemplation. My associates, colleagues, and social media following were floored. I was a successful model and music writer before becoming a "sexpert," and the arrival of my blog was not only intriguing but a bit perplexing for those who only saw me as a sexy vixen who curated compelling music reviews.

What inspired me to drop my successful modeling career and take on an industry many are afraid to enter? It is a question that continues to be asked of me on every radio interview, blog feature, and TV appearance I encounter.

I made the decision to enter the field of sexuality because I recognized the lack of people of color within its mainstream representation. I wasn't seeing people who looked like me, that I felt I could relate to when it came to sexuality and relationships. I felt my presence was the remedy for that issue. The field of sexuality was missing someone of color who was young and had fresh, innovative ideas, who spoke from the perspective of the Millennial generation while keeping conversations about sexuality relatable, classy, solidly educational, and entertaining. I began my blog at the encouragement of my father, who required that I use my natural gift for writing to make a difference and achieve the goal of healing and reaching the masses. All of that said, my prior schooling only boasted a few college credits from an art and design school and a high school diploma.

I didn't wait to go through formal training in order to begin speaking to the world about things that I already had knowledge of. I weighed my options, got over my fears of being judged and scrutinized by the world, and decided to use what I had gathered from self-study. For me, time was of the essence, and every minute spent behind a desk in formal study was a minute lost in being able to broadcast vital information to the world. My finances at the time also didn't support my desires to gain a formal education. I had to make a decision to go forward in faith, knowing that my ability to gather knowledge on my own was sufficient enough to supply my blog with information the masses needed. Eventually I plan to receive formal training in sexuality coaching to [e]nsure I am competent and confident in the work I'm doing, but the need for formal training isn't necessary to do great work within the field of sexuality now.

Without formal training I have gained the trust and respect of millions of people around the globe, secured a residency as the official sexpert at EBONY.com, become a member of the National Coalition for Sexual Health, written hundreds of articles on the topic of sexuality scattered throughout the World Wide Web, and am currently coaching singles and couples to success. The millions across the globe who view my sex education videos via YouTube have accepted me as a reputable source for sexual knowledge, and dozens contact me daily for advice or help with the most intimate parts of their lives. Formal education is an amazing way to amass knowledge, know-how and confidence in presenting information, but ambition, passion, tenacity and vision trump formality when one is aware that the work can be done without it. There are several factors, presented below, that contribute to the success of anyone who has a desire and the passion to go into the field of sexuality as a practitioner without the backing of formal education or training.

Knowing Your Niche

The field of sexuality is extremely vast, ranging from education to entertainment, but within the education or therapy spectrum there are important concerns that must be addressed. Before jumping into the field, one must have a solid awareness of what he or she would like to focus on as a primary niche. Each educator or therapist will be equipped with the basic knowledge of sexual health, but the success of any brand or practice is rooted in knowing exactly where his or her knowledge is best served. Before I entered into the field, I took the time to brainstorm the concerns I wanted to meet and the audience I wanted to serve. I made the decision to focus on sexual pleasure, technique and awareness for women and couples in need, and as I did, my career, audience and reach began to blossom. Eventually, I wasn't only talking to women as when I first began. The demand from men who also wanted advice on how to become better lovers grew so great that my niche began to expand. Formal training will give any student the tools to help remedy issues within relationships with self and others, but what it doesn't teach is how to go within and find one's true purpose in the field of sexuality. Knowing your niche is a personal decision that requires intimate reflection beyond the classroom setting.

Using Your Gifts to Create a Platform

One consistent complaint I have heard from young people currently in sexuality education programs is about the lack of guidance or support in knowing how to build a platform to reach the public and gain a clientele. This is another aspect of working in the real world that formal training doesn't teach. Some receive suggestions on how to go about reaching the masses, but the science behind sexuality education business-building in the new millennium is far more intricate than in previous generations. Knowing one's gifts and how he or she comfortably presents information is vital for establishing a rapport with the public.

In my personal practice I decided to go the route of the writer and broadcaster, via blogging, YouTube, and radio. My natural gift of gab and writing talent helped me spread my message confidently and grow my following exponentially, while maintaining integrity in my messaging gained from consistent self-study. The success of any practitioner's work is heavily dependent on how information is received by potential clients. Knowing how you will deliver that information sets you apart from the next educator.

Using Social Media to Reach the People

The invention of the Internet has forever changed the way we communicate with the world, and has also altered how consumers shop and search for services to utilize. Social media adds to this, as a direct connection to real people in real time. Using various platforms can help one establish a brand voice, while spreading educational messages and counseling directly to mobile devices and computer screens. No longer does one have to schedule an appointment with a counselor for simple questions to be answered. With the click of a button, a sex educator can publish a status update, refer a link to a blog post, or send a consumer straight to his or her website. Through social media, practitioners have the opportunity to see exactly what concerns are troubling the public, and meet those needs by speaking directly to those who have issues. Social media has been the driving force behind my success in sexuality, and has given me access to media influencers who helped promote my sex positive message. From celebrities, to major publishers and television networks, I have received support and affirmation that further established my authority within the field.

Networking with Industry Leaders

A strong network is what every practitioner needs—not only to refer out when cases are beyond his or her expertise, but (also) to learn from and receive encouragement when working within the ever evolving field of sexuality. Mentors help mold efficient teachers. Making associations with established educators, researchers, doctors and organizations within the field is also helpful in establishing one's authority. Having these individuals on your side to authenticate your knowledge and refer you to their client base reaffirms trust in those who may have questions about your credentialing. I have received support and mentorship from Dr. Logan Levkoff, Trojan Condoms, The Alexander Institute, SIECUS, Sherri Winston, Dr. Patti Britton, Dr. Tamara Griffin and many others who have been well established for a decade or more. It is the support and backing of these individuals and organizations that continues to propel my success within sexuality. Through the work I have put in over the course of my career, I have landed on the radar of prominent figures who respect the great work that I am doing, and who are impressed with my passion and tenacity, despite my lack of formal education.

Referencing Reputable Sources for Information

Although formal education isn't necessary, it is imperative to stay abreast of updates in the field, and to study on one's own to remain reputable and knowledgeable for your clientele. There are several sources online that publish information about the broad spectrum of sexuality; however, all sources aren't created equal. For the person taking the path of self-study over formal education, seeking out literature and journals from higher learning institutions is the best way to remain current. Attending workshops, learning from other educators, and purchasing self-help books published by leaders in the field are also valid ways for continuing education. Formal education makes it easier for the learner to retain information by preparing the lessons in a format that is easy to digest, but those same lessons can be learned independently.

Life Experiences Are Necessary Educators

Possessing academic knowledge in sexuality is necessary to do the work; however, life experiences make one more authentic to the public and to potential clients. The most consistent question I receive from viewers and members of my social media after giving a live broadcast or having a discussion on Twitter or Facebook is "have you experienced this?" The average viewer wants to know that the educator isn't just speaking from a book, but from life experience. Knowing that the person who gives you advice is relatable creates closeness and establishes a level of trust that many have complained is missing from the client-counselor dynamic. People want to be able to see themselves in you, and want to know that the techniques you recommend have been proven to work. I will never forget one of my most successful coaching sessions with a client who was feeling insecure about re-entering the dating space because he had lived with a micropenis all his life. He was a successful middle-aged man who had been married twice and had children to show for it, but his success with women in the past wasn't enough to reassure him. He came to me with his concerns about how women would react to his revelation, and was worried about being rejected. I, however, was able to encourage him to move forward. I had previously dated a man who also had a micropenis and from that experience I was able to give him advice on how to approach the situation when sex was discussed. I placed an emphasis on his personality versus his physicality and encouraged him to place his focus on being confident no matter what the outcome of the dating experience. A year after our brief coaching sessions together, he sent an email revealing just how influential my advice was on how he currently viewed himself and how he now approached dating. My words resonated so deeply within him that he remembered the exact day I spoke them and changed his life. He celebrates this day as the anniversary of his awakening. The power of personal experiences not only made me more relatable to this man, but (also) enabled me to empathize with what he was going through more than someone who had only read about the *biology* of a micropenis.

My stance will always be that formal education isn't necessary to do the work required of competent sexuality educators and practitioners, because it isn't credential that makes people feel secure in trusting a coach or counselor with their most intimate concerns and desires. It is the connection they feel towards the person who possesses the knowledge, along with his or her ability to suggest solutions that have been proven first by the teacher themselves. What I believe is more important than credentials is mastery of self, a process that can only take place by living in real time and using one's self as a testing ground for sexual techniques and expressions. To be a great educator means to first be a great student, and to be a student of sexuality through personal life experiences helps establish an understanding of sexuality that books and formal institutions could never teach. Becoming a master over your own sexuality requires fearlessness—the same fearlessness that any educator will ask their clients to adopt in moving toward improvement. And through that same fearlessness, the ambitious student who is eager to change the world through sexuality will venture forward in establishing his or her place within the field, with or without the backing of formalized training. Effective teaching doesn't require certificates or diplomas. It simply requires innovation, compassion, self-awareness, and the ability to always remain a student of life.

Tyomi Morgan is a sex coach, columnist, and founder of SexpertTyomi.com. She is the official Sexpert for ebony.com.

EXPLORING THE ISSUE

Should Sex Educators Be Required to Have Formal Training?

Critical Thinking and Reflection

1. Should sex educators be allowed to teach about sex and/or sexuality if they have not been formally trained? Why or why not?
2. Are there certain spaces or educational settings where formally trained educators would be preferable? What about those who have been informally trained?
3. What role should professional organizations play in shaping expectations for sex educator training?

Is There Common Ground?

After reading the two divergent perspectives presented in this issue, one thing is clear—many people are in need of sexuality education, and they are searching for it through many means. To this point, both YES and NO selections assert the flexibility of being able to find formal training through alternative, nontraditional means, including conferences, organizations, informal professional networks, and other nonacademic institutions. Beyond this, however, is where the similarities appear to end, with each professional raising significantly different yet powerful arguments on the most important aspects of being a sexuality education professional

Brown-James argues that potential harm may be caused by sex educators who receive no formal training, suggesting that they are more likely to teach from an abstinence-only perspective that, at best, emits important information and, at worst, utilizes scare tactics to get its message across. That said, does a comprehensive perspective automatically ensure a sex-positive attitude in the classroom? An important point to consider related to this is the diversity of educators of who teach from a comprehensive perspective, including those who may still employ a wholly preventative or sex-shaming lens when thinking about sexual expression. Formal training might not prevent the infliction of harm as well as one intends, if it does not also address the perspective one takes in their teaching methodology.

Morgan raises several strong points about the *business* of sex education—a topic not often discussed within formal training circles. She also focuses on the use of the Internet and social media on sex education. Again, a skill not traditionally taught in formal training programs. How effective can a sex educator in the twenty-first century be without comprehensive knowledge of social media, and the ways in which social media interacts with the sex lives of the public? Morgan also speaks strongly about the salience of personal experience as effective reference for advising others sexually. What are the benefits and challenges (including ethical) that could come from using one's personal sexual experience as methodology for teaching sexuality to others? And what precedence might it set for those who are not as sexually experienced or adventurous as others?

Given the similarities in their positions on training and networking, there may be a chance to build connectors between both perspectives. Return to the original question with this in mind and ask yourself: "Would it matter to me if my sexuality educator had no formal training?"

Additional Resources

Fields, J. (2012). Sexuality education: Shared cultural ideas across a political divide. *Sociology Compass, 6*(1), 1–14. doi: 10.1111/j.1751-9020.2011.00436.x

Goldfarb, E. S. (2009). A crisis of identity in sexuality education in America: How did we get here and where are we going? In Schroeder, E., & Kuriansky, J. (Eds.) *Sexuality education: Past, present, and future* (Chapter 2). Westport, CT: Praeger.

Kantor, L. M., Rolleri, L., & Kolios, K. (2014). Doug Kirby's contribution to the field of sex education. *Sex Education 14*(5), 473–480. doi: 10.1080/14681811.2014.881336

Kelly, G. F. (2009). Will the good sexuality educators please stand up? In Schroeder, E., & Kuriansky, J. (Eds.) *Sexuality education: Past, present, and future* (Chapter 11). Westport, CT: Praeger.

Internet References . . .

American Association of Sexuality Educators, Counselors, and Therapists (AASECT)

http://www.aasect.org

Future of Sex Education: National Sexuality Education Standards

http://www.advocatesforyouth.org/publications/publications-a-z/1947-future-of-sex-education-national-sexuality-education-standards

Sexuality Information and Education Council of the United States (SIECUS)—Comprehensive Sex Education

http://www.siecus.org/index.cfm?fuseaction=Page.viewPage&pageId=514&parentID=477

So You Want to Be a Sex Educator?

http://www.sexualityeducation.com/sexeducator.php

Selected, Edited, and with Issue Framing Material by:
Ryan W. McKee, *Widener University,* Tracie Q. Gilbert, *Widener University,*
and
Jayleen Galarza, *Shippensburg University of Pennsylvania*

ISSUE

Do Reality TV Shows Portray Responsible Messages about Teen Pregnancy?

YES: Amy Kramer, from "The REAL Real World: How MTV's '16 and Pregnant' and 'Teen Mom' Motivate Young People to Prevent Teen Pregnancy," An original essay written for this volume (2011)

NO: Mary Jo Podgurski, from "Till Human Voices Wake Us: The High Personal Cost of Reality Teen Pregnancy Shows," An original essay written for this volume (2011)

Learning Outcomes

After reading this issue, you will be able to:

- Describe the current rates of teen pregnancy in the United States.
- Compare the rates of teen pregnancy in the United States to other developed nations.
- Describe how shows like "16 and Pregnant" might affect and impact American attitudes and behaviors.
- Explain some of the possible negative effects of reality TV shows about teen pregnancy.

ISSUE SUMMARY

YES: Amy Kramer, director of Entertainment Media & Audience Strategy at the National Campaign to Prevent Teen and Unplanned Pregnancy, argues that reality television shows engage teens in considering the consequences of pregnancy before they're ready for it, and motivate them to want to prevent it.

NO: Mary Jo Podgurski, founder of the Academy for Adolescent Health, Inc., argues that though such television shows have potential benefits, they inadequately address the issue, and may even have a negative impact on those who participate in them.

Television has evolved during the past five decades. Just 50 years ago, families could gather around one immovable set with a limited number of channels, and observe Desi Arnaz and Lucille Ball occupy different beds in the wildly popular sitcom "I Love Lucy." Considered prudent for television standards at the time, it would strike many today as an odd family life arrangement for the famous couple—who were married both off-the-air and in-character! Fast forward two decades, and we see Mike and Carol Brady sharing the same bed on "The Brady Bunch," with not a hint of sexual interest or attraction between them.

Today's television has a much more substantial representation of sexual relationships and themes. Leaps and bounds from then-landmark events such as William Shatner and Nichelle Nichol's "first interracial kiss" on television's "Star Trek," Ellen DeGeneres coming out on-the-air in the mid-1990s, and Kerr Smith's and Adam Kaufman's "first gay male kiss" on prime-time television in 2000, many of today's television programs include overtly sexual messages, and a greater range of sexual identities and orientations. Indeed, many shows rely and bank on sexual innuendo, humor, and steamy scenes. While the representation is greater, the *accuracy* of the portrayals is questionable. Is the infrequent gay character actually a *caricature* manifesting common stereotypes? Is sex so closely and frequently tied to crime as portrayed in various crime dramas? Does the constant use of sexual humor mirror and reinforce society's discomfort with sex?

Do sexual scenes in prime-time dramas make sex appear seamless—and only for the young and beautiful? (Note the hilarious response to 90-year-old Betty White discussing her "Dusty Muffin" on "Saturday Night Live.")

Another way in which television has changed is with the emergence of the so-called "reality TV show" genre. Popularized with the success of MTV's "The Real World" and CBS's "Survivor," many reality TV shows and formats have followed. Perhaps it was inevitable that the worlds of reality TV and sexuality would collide, and new shows addressing specific sexual themes emerged in the last few years. Some shows address issues of pregnancy and family life. In 2007, we were introduced to the family life of parents of octuplets on Discovery Health's "Jon and Kate Plus 8." Later, MTV introduced the real-life teen-focused pregnancy dramas "16 and Pregnant" and "Teen Mom," which follow the lives of real young people dealing with teen pregnancy, parenting, and in some episodes, abortion. VH-1 also airs "Dad Camp," a show in which young men go through "boot camp-style group therapy" in preparing them to take responsibility for fatherhood.

Some sexuality educators, looking for ways to connect with students in authentic, meaningful ways, have embraced the popularity of these shows for their potential as teachable moments. Educators can show a clip to build discussion questions themed around the premise, "What would you do if . . .?"

Other sexuality educators express concern over the reality and impact of the shows. Do the networks do an adequate job of portraying all the hardships of teen pregnancy, or will students perceive the characters as TV stars to be admired and emulated?

In the following selections, Amy Kramer, the director of Entertainment Media & Audience Strategy at The National Campaign to Prevent Teen and Unplanned Pregnancy, describes the positive potential these shows can have as allies in sexuality education. Kramer explains how the shows help motivate young people to want to prevent pregnancy before they are ready to be parents. Mary Jo Podgurski, founder of the Academy for Adolescent Health, Inc., who routinely works with pregnant and parenting teens, explains her reasons for declining the opportunity to work with "16 and Pregnant" when producers approached her. While noting the potential benefits of such shows, Dr. Podgurski expresses reservations about the impact the shows might have on the teens who appear on a national stage.

YES

Amy Kramer

The REAL Real World: How MTV's "16 and Pregnant" and "Teen Mom" Motivate Young People to Prevent Teen Pregnancy

Like it or not, media is a huge influence in the lives of young people. Teens spend more hours each week in front of a screen than they do in a classroom.[1] Many teens know a lot more about their favorite shows than they do about any academic subject, and characters on television are often more familiar than neighbors. What young people learn in sex ed, if they have sex ed at all, is a fraction of what pop culture serves up on a daily basis. Which is why parents and educators alike should be thankful that MTV has emerged as a sort of accidental hero in the campaign against teen pregnancy.

Thanks to the reality shows "16 and Pregnant" and "Teen Mom," millions of young people are now thinking and talking about teen pregnancy. These shows were developed as nothing more than good entertainment but they have succeeded in ways public health initiatives have not—that is getting young people to stop, pay attention, consider, and discuss what happens when someone becomes a parent before they're ready.

Although we know how to avoid teen pregnancy—get teens to avoid having sex at all or to use contraception carefully and consistently when they do have sex—prevention isn't always as easy as it looks. Getting young people to commit to waiting or protecting themselves is tough. After all, they're kids. The consequences of their actions might not seem as likely as the benefit of the risks. Nearly half of teens admit they've never thought about how a pregnancy would change their lives[2] and most girls who get pregnant say they never thought it would happen to them. It's no wonder young people don't always take precautions to prevent pregnancy—if you never consider that something might happen to you, or what life would be like if it did, why would you consider taking steps to prevent it?

But "16 and Pregnant" and "Teen Mom" seem to be changing that. These shows are bringing the reality of too-early pregnancy and parenthood smack into the middle of the lives and minds of young people in powerful and important ways. Teens come to these shows on their own and they say they come away with a new appreciation for some of the consequences of unprotected sex. In fact, in a nationally representative poll conducted by The National Campaign to Prevent Teen and Unplanned Pregnancy in 2010, 82% of teens who had seen "16 and Pregnant" said that watching the show "helps teens better understand the challenges of pregnancy and parenthood." Only 17% said the show makes teen pregnancy look glamorous.[3] Already, the fact that young people are tuning in week after week makes what MTV is doing more successful than many PSA campaigns could ever hope to be.

* * *

Rates of teen pregnancy and birth are higher in the United States than in any other industrialized nation. The teen birth rate in the US is more than three times higher than the rate in Canada, and nearly twice that of the United Kingdom (which has the highest rate in Europe). One out of every ten babies born in the US is born to a teen mother. Three out of every ten girls in the US get pregnant before their 20th birthdays—750,000 girls each year. That's 2,000 girls getting pregnant *every day*. These numbers—as shocking as they are—actually represent dramatic improvements. In the past two decades, rates of teen pregnancy and childbearing in the US have dropped by more than one-third.[4]

According to the National Center for Health Statistics, in early-1990s America, 117 out of every 1,000 girls ages 15–19 got pregnant, and 62 out of every 1,000 girls ages 15–19 gave birth. Not even twenty years later those rates are down to 72 per 1,000 teens getting pregnant and 39 per 1,000 teens giving birth. Put another way, teen pregnancy has declined by 38% and teen births are down by one-third. Still too high, but a remarkable improvement on an issue once thought to be intractable.

To what do we owe this astonishing decline in teen pregnancy and teen births? Quite simply and perhaps not surprisingly, it's a combination of less sex and more contraception. According to the National Survey of Family Growth (NSFG), a household-based nationally representative survey conducted periodically by the Centers for Disease Control and Prevention to study families, fertility, and health in the U.S., in 1988, 51% of girls and 60% of boys ages 15–19 had ever had sex. In 2006–2008 those numbers had declined to 42% of girls and 43% of boys. Condom use increased during that time as well: In 1988, 31% of girls and 55% of boys who had sex in the past 90 days said they used a condom the last time they had sex. In 2006–2008, those numbers had grown to 53% for girls and 79% for boys. So, for a complicated array of reasons, teens have been doing the only two things you can do to prevent pregnancy: delaying sex and being better about contraception when they do have sex.

It's also important to note that abortions to teens declined as well over that same time period. In 1988, 39% of pregnancies to teens ended in abortion, in 2006, it was 27%, meaning that the decline in teen births was not due to an increase in terminations.[5]

* * *

Consider the following: While rates of sexual activity, pregnancy, birth, and abortion among teens were declining enormously, the media was growing exponentially and becoming coarser and more sexualized. There are hundreds of channels now and an infinite number of websites. Finding sexually suggestive content on television and explicit content online—or it finding you—is a fact of life for many young people. If media influence on teens' decisions about sex is so direct and so negative, why might it be that teen sexual behavior has gotten more responsible at exactly the same time the media and popular culture has become more sexualized? Simply put, the media can't be solely to blame for teens having sex, or having babies. However, the media can help write the social script and contribute to viewers' sense of what's normal and acceptable—and can make sex seem casual, inconsequential, or serious. In fact, polling for The National Campaign to Prevent Teen and Unplanned Pregnancy shows that year after year 8 in 10 teens say they wish the media showed more consequences of sex (not less sex).[6]

So television alone doesn't cause teen pregnancy, but could it actually help prevent it? Teens themselves suggest that it can. Most teens (79% of girls, 67% of boys) say that "when a TV show or character I like deals with teen pregnancy, it makes me think more about my own risk of becoming pregnant/causing a pregnancy, and how to avoid it," according to the National Campaign to Prevent Teen and Unplanned Pregnancy.[7] "Thinking about my own risk" is an important piece of the prevention puzzle.

In that same study from The National Campaign, three-quarters of teens (76%) and adults (75%) say that what they see in the media about sex, love, and relationships can be a good way to start conversations about these topics. Communication between parents and teens about their own views and values regarding these issues is critical. Children whose parents are clear about the value of delaying sex are less likely to have intercourse at an early age. Parents who discuss contraception are also more likely to have children who use contraception when they become sexually active.[8] These conversations can be awkward and intimidating (on both sides), but they are important. So anything that encourages such talk, or makes it easier to start the conversation, is valuable.

MTV's "16 and Pregnant" is a conversation starter. Certainly among teens, but also within families. In a 2010 study of more than 150 teenagers involved with Boys & Girls Clubs after-school programs in a southern state, 40% of teens who watched "16 and Pregnant" with their group at the Club, and then talked about it in a facilitator-led discussion, also talked about it again afterward with a parent. One-third discussed it with a boyfriend/girlfriend. More than half discussed it with a friend.[9] That 40% went home and talked about with mom or dad is particularly exciting—because the more opportunities parents have to discuss their own ideas and expectations about pregnancy and parenting, the better. Teens talking about these shows—articulating their own thoughts about a teen parent on MTV or a situation depicted in an episode—brings them one step closer to personalizing it, which is an important step along the behavior change continuum, and the path to prevention.

Educators and leaders in youth-serving organizations are using the MTV shows as teaching tools. A social worker in the Midwest who frequently speaks at schools in both urban and rural areas, has used episodes of "16 and Pregnant" in her work: "With the boys, we had great discussion about what makes a man a 'father'." Boys were a little defensive about the portrayal of the teen dads, but after talking it through, began to empathize more with the young women." A teacher in the South incorporated the series into high school lesson plans: "I use it as part of a unit on teen parenting and parenting readiness to discourage teen pregnancies and to encourage students to wait until they are older and 'ready' before having children. . . . Students enjoy watching the 'real-life' stories of teens and are able to really identify with them." A private special education teacher who works with a teen population especially vulnerable to abusive relationships and pregnancy has also watched the series with students: "The kids were very much engaged because it was something they would watch at home. Some of them had seen the episodes already but looked at them differently once viewed in a group, clinical setting. The conversations were often very serious and enlightening for the students. They were able to put themselves into the girls' shoes and talk about how they would feel, react, respond in each of the situations that came up." Staff at a county juvenile detention center in the Southwest includes the show in teen pregnancy prevention programs and calls it "heavy-hitting and impactful": "They cater to the very media-driven nature of teens today—they aren't dry book material, but rather a great combination of reality and entertainment in a condensed format. . . . A whole year in the life of these teen parents in just an hour of viewing."[10]

* * *

Television shows like MTV's "16 and Pregnant" and "Teen Mom" are created for entertainment purposes with the hope of attracting viewers and keeping them engaged. By that measure, these shows are indisputably successful. Millions of people tune in to each new episode—and the ratings are among the highest on the cable network. Recent episodes have drawn more viewers than even the major broadcast network competition. Public attention to the storylines extends beyond the episodes themselves and into Internet discussion forums, where theories and speculation about the lives depicted on the shows are rampant.

Thanks to these very real reality programs, teen pregnancy is no longer a mysterious topic to millions of young people. Viewers have seen in the most vivid way possible what happens when contraception fails, when babies arrive, when boyfriends leave, when money is tight, when parents are disappointed, and when graduating from high school is impossible. Conversations are happening around dinner tables and in carpools, allowing parents and teens to explore their own opinions and behavior. Parents now have an opportunity to discuss their own values and expectations as they pertain to family formation and romantic responsibility. Friends, siblings, and partners are talking to each other about what happens when young people become parents before they're ready. Maybe they're even talking about how to prevent it from happening in the first place.

Every episode of "16 and Pregnant" includes a scene in which the expectant teenager talks about how she got pregnant. Many weren't using any protection at all, others had problems remembering to take their pills every day, some found out that prescribed antibiotics can interfere with the effectiveness of birth control pills, a few missed their Depo shot appointments, others stopped using a method after a break-up and then never returned to its use after reconciliation, etc. This information is presented honestly and in peer-to-peer terms, inviting viewers to listen and learn, and perhaps explore a type of contraception they hadn't previously known about. On "Teen Mom" viewers see the young parents taking steps to prevent subsequent pregnancies: cameras have captured the girls' discussions with their doctors about the vaginal ring, IUDs, and other long-acting methods of contraception. Even the "reunion" episodes devote time to discussion about birth control between updates on the babies and the relationship drama.

Watching what happens to girls who "never thought it would happen to them" encourages viewers to assess their own risk. When teenage fans of the shows see time and again that having a baby as an adolescent often means educational goals are abandoned, family relationships erode, financial challenges become insurmountable, and romantic fantasies are dashed, the prospect of early parenthood in their own lives becomes far less attractive. Rosier depictions of teen pregnancy and its consequences from movies, scripted television shows, and daydreams start to look silly in comparison. Seeing that teen pregnancy happens in the lives of girls from every sort of background (even a familiar one) reminds viewers that it could happen to them and it pushes them to figure out how to avoid a similar fate.

Separate from the shows themselves is the tabloid coverage they receive, though it is so pervasive right now it deserves mention here. That the tabloid media have decided to treat these struggling young mothers like celebrities is certainly unfortunate. That the real-life people around the teen mothers have obviously decided to cooperate with the tabloids (in the form of photos, tips, and other information) is sadder still. However, the bulk of even that coverage focuses on the turmoil in their lives. These are young mothers agonizing over money, men, family drama, health issues, the law, and the unending responsibility of parenthood. Followers of this often repugnant news stream may know even more about the chaos that swirls around young parents than do mere viewers of the show. Coverage does not necessarily equal glamorization. Bottom line: if you sit through a full episode, any episode, of "16 and Pregnant" or "Teen Mom," glamour is totally absent.

* * *

MTV's "16 and Pregnant" and "Teen Mom" are not evidence-based teen pregnancy prevention programs. They aren't a substitute for talented teachers or comprehensive sex ed curricula. These shows aren't more meaningful than traditions of faith. They aren't more important than access to quality healthcare or relevant health information. They aren't more powerful than engaged parents willing to talk openly about tough topics. But teen pregnancy prevention needs to happen everywhere, including in the popular media teenagers love to consume. Everyone who cares about teens, babies, and the next generation of Americans needs to do their part to keep rates of teen pregnancy on a downward trajectory. Families, schools, health care professionals, businesses big and small, religious communities, and yes, the media, all have a role to play. Teen pregnancy prevention requires sustained effort over time by all sectors. This isn't an issue where a vaccine or a cure will lead to a drop in incidence. Even new and better methods of contraception won't do the trick if young people aren't motivated to use them. Making headway on this complex topic requires young people to make better choices over and over again. Any way they can get the message that the teen years are not the appropriate time for parenthood matters.

MTV is doing more than most—even if inadvertently—with "16 and Pregnant" and "Teen Mom." Millions of young people tune in each week and four out of five viewers say that doing so "helps teens better understand the challenges of pregnancy and parenthood." Anyone who cares about reducing rates of teen pregnancy and teen birth should listen to what teens themselves are saying and tune out the rest.

Footnotes/Sources

1. Kaiser Family Foundation, (2010). *Generation M2: Media in the Lives of 8- to 18-Year-Olds.* http://www.kff.org/entmedia/upload/8010.pdf
2. National Campaign to Prevent Teen and Unplanned Pregnancy, (2007). *With One Voice 2007: America's Adults and Teens Sound Off about Teen Pregnancy.* http://www.thenationalcampaign.org/resources/pdf/pubs/WOV2007_fulltext.pdf
3. National Campaign to Prevent Teen and Unplanned Pregnancy, (2010). *With One Voice 2010: America's Adults and Teens Sound Off about Teen Pregnancy.* http://www.thenationalcampaign.org/resources/pdf/pubs/WOV_2010.pdf
4. National Campaign to Prevent Teen and Unplanned Pregnancy, various fact sheets. http://www.thenationalcampaign.org/resources/fact-sheets.aspx
5. Guttmacher Institute, (2010) *U.S. Teenage Pregnancies, Births and Abortions: National and State Trends and Trends by Race and Ethnicity.* http://www.guttmacher.org/pubs/USTPtrends.pdf
6. National Campaign to Prevent Teen and Unplanned Pregnancy, (2007, 2004, 2002). *With One Voice 2007/2004/2002: America's Adults and Teens Sound Off about Teen Pregnancy.* http://www.thenationalcampaign.org/resources/pdf/pubs/WOV2007_fulltext.pdf http://www.thenationalcampaign.org/resources/pdf/pubs/WOV_2004.pdf http://www.thenationalcampaign.org/resources/pdf/pubs/WOV_2002.pdf
7. National Campaign to Prevent Teen and Unplanned Pregnancy, (2010). *With One Voice 2010: America's Adults and Teens Sound Off about Teen Pregnancy.* http://www.thenationalcampaign.org/resources/pdf/pubs/WOV_2010.pdf
8. Blum, R.W. & Rinehard, P.M., (1998). *Reducing the Risk: Connections that Make a Difference in the Lives of Youth.* Center for Adolescent Health and Development, University of Minnesota. Minneapolis, MN.
9. Suellentrop, K., Brown, J., Ortiz, R., (2010) *Evaluating the Impact of MTV's '16 and Pregnant' on Teen Viewers' Attitudes about Teen Pregnancy,* The National Campaign to Prevent Teen and Unplanned Pregnancy, Washington DC. http://www.thenationalcampaign.org/resources/pdf/SS/SS45_16andPregnant.pdf
10. Telephone interviews and email inquiries by the author.

Amy Kramer is the director of Entertainment Media & Audience Strategy at The National Campaign to Prevent Teen and Unplanned Pregnancy.

Mary Jo Podgurski NO

Till Human Voices Wake Us: The High Personal Cost of Reality Teen Pregnancy Shows

Having a baby young took away my childhood and there's no way I'll ever get it back.

—16-year-old mother

I wouldn't be alive today if I hadn't had her. She's the reason I'm still alive.

—15-year-old mother

The "voices" above are direct quotes from the video I produced in 1998 entitled *Voices: The Reality of Early Childbearing—Transcending the Myths*. The video was marketed nationally by Injoy Productions until 2009 and is still used in the Lamaze teen program Creativity, Connection and Commitment: Supporting Teens During the Childbearing Year (Lamaze International, 2010). Over the course of a year my team interviewed and videotaped young parents with the intent of using their voices and wisdom as a catalyst for teen pregnancy prevention. I share these voices to underscore an acute need to protect teens. When editing the film I discovered that the teen mothers consistently wanted to reveal very intimate aspects of their lives. Data including early drinking, number of sexual partners, an incestuous relationship, nonconsensual sex, and sexual experimentation were all freely revealed. I cautioned them to think of the future. Would their children relish such revelations a decade later? Were these details pertinent to their messages? I persisted, and only information that was truly educational and not sensationalized remained in the film. I believed then that 16-year-old parents could provide a priceless service to other teens as peer educators; I continue to believe such teaching is effective and significant. I simply refused to expose the truly personal details of their lives to scrutiny. I was interested in education, not drama.

My staff and I remain in contact with many of the teen parents in *Voices*. More than ten years after its production they are in 100% agreement: our careful screening spared their children (now young teens) embarrassment. The young parents I've served have taught me to put a face on the statistics surrounding teen pregnancy; while I will always strive to educate all young people about the risks associated with bearing children young, I am deeply cognizant of the price a teen parent pays when offering his or her life as a lesson plan.

The last 30 years of my life have been dedicated to providing comprehensive sexuality education to young people; our programs reach over 18,000 youth a year in all 14 Washington County school districts. Concurrently I've mentored young parents. I served as a doula (providing labor support) for my first adolescent in the '70s; that young mother became one of many. My staff and I provide educational services and support for nearly 100 pregnant and parenting teens annually. When the MTV program "16 and Pregnant" was in its planning stages I was approached by the producers and asked to provide teens for the show. I declined after much soul searching. This article explores my rationale for that decision.

Why Rethink Reality TV Using Teen Parents?

As an educator I seek teachable moments in everyday life. I am thrilled to have the opportunity to teach; I consider the field of sexuality education a vocation and am blessed to be in a role where life-affirming information is at my disposal and I am free to convey it to teens. I don't deny the impact reality shows like "16 and Pregnant" and "Teen Mom" (now "Teen Mom 2") can have on teens. The April 10, 2011, edition of *The New York Times* reports anecdotes of teachers using the shows as a part of curriculum in life skills and parenting classes (Hoffman, 2011, April 10). The National Campaign to Prevent Teen and Unplanned Pregnancy has distributed DVDs and teacher guides on "16 and Pregnant" and these materials seem to be well received by educators. I also am not deterred by fears that these reality shows glamorize teen pregnancy. The Campaign conducted a national telephone poll of young people ages 12 to 19; 82% said that the shows aided their understanding of the reality of teen pregnancy. Only 17% stated that the shows gave pregnancy a glamorous spin (Albert, 2010). In the hands of a skilled educator the shows' influence can be directed away from glamour to empathic awareness. There is no doubt that there are lessons to be learned from these shows, but at what price?

My primary concern with reality TV shows like "16 and Pregnant" and "Teen Mom" deals with the human cost of these lessons. Young parents, like most young people, are not immune to the appeal of fame. I question a teen's ability to give full permission to a life-changing activity that will reframe his or her identity on a national stage. I am concerned that these young people cannot developmentally grasp the far-reaching implications of their decision to participate. Exploitation is a strong word and I use it with a caveat; I do not believe the shows aim to exploit. I believe that their intentions are good; it is society that removes all boundaries and exposes tender lives to the scrutiny of tabloids and the manipulation of the media. When I filmed *Voices* I stressed the need for discretion; in ten or twenty years, I said, would your baby want to be known for the things you now reveal? In a decade and more, how will the babies in "16 and Pregnant" view their lives? How will they react to their parents, their families, and their infancy and toddler years exposed for posterity?

I am also troubled by a nagging sense that these shows hope to provide a simple solution to the problems associated with adolescent sexuality in America. There are no Band-aids that can be applied to the multi-faceted, complicated situations that arise when teens are sexually involved, yet our culture consistently seeks an easy fix. I was afforded the privilege of attending an Advocates for Youth European Study Tour in 2001. As part of that experience I was exposed to European approaches to sexuality education. In contrast to American culture, European culture does not deny the fact that teens need education that helps them achieve sexual health; comprehensive sexuality education is the norm. Are reality TV shows that focus on the lives of young parents yet another simplistic answer that distracts from the need to mandate comprehensive sexuality education to all of our children?

No Band-Aids

Research points to antecedents to early pregnancy and risky behavior; I question whether the teen parents in reality TV shows reflect those antecedents or are selected for their "camera" quality and the appeal of their families' dramas. I also ponder the use of dollars to develop these TV shows instead of creating programs that would target youth that evidence-based data show are at risk.

Dr. Doug Kirby's work (2002, 2007) alone and with colleagues (Kirby, Lepore, & Ryan, 2006) is considered seminal in the areas of comprehensive sexuality education and teen pregnancy antecedents. Research into the role of siblings in early childbearing from East and associates (1996 through 2007) is pivotal to understanding generational teen pregnancy (East, Reyes, & Horn, 2007; Raneri & Constance, 2007). Kristen Luker (1999, 2006) is considered a founding theorist of the sociological and political theories surrounding early childbearing and linked poverty to teen pregnancy as an antecedent, not a consequence of the pregnancy. Young people who are survivors of sexual and physical abuse (Boyer & Fine, 1992) are at risk for early childbearing, as are children in placement or foster care (Kirby, Lepore, & Ryan, 2006) and children living with domestic violence, drug/alcohol abuse, or incarcerated parents (Coyle, 2005; Goode & Smith, 2005; East & Khoo, 2005; Jekielek, Moore, Hair, & Scarupa, 2002). Do the teens in reality TV reflect these antecedents?

Research at the University of Arkansas showed that girls are more likely to experience teen pregnancy if they live with internal poverty (measured as a low locus of control and future expectations) as well as external poverty (Young, Turner, Denny, Young, 2004). Internal poverty "describes a person's lack of internal resources, such as attitudes and beliefs that attribute outcomes to individual effort, high future expectations, and few perceived limitations for life options" (Coles, 2005, 10). Certainly internal and external poverty are antecedents in the pregnancies of some reality TV participants; at any time are those teens given guidance that will help them develop the skills and self-efficacy they need to succeed?

Antecedents to teen pregnancy in the United States lead dedicated sexuality educators to explore the need for education that affects behavioral change. Dr. Michael A. Carrera's Children's Aid Society is a well-respected and researched youth development approach that targets the whole child through early intervention (Children's Aid Society, 2010). On a much smaller scale, my team and I have tried to emulate his efforts. Although we remain committed to comprehensive sexuality education, we first approached teen pregnancy prevention through proactive education in 1999 with the initiation of an early intervention educational mentoring program entitled Educate Children for Healthy Outcomes (ECHO). ECHO provides one-on-one mentoring to young people who have been identified as at risk for engaging in high-risk behavior. Specifically, we target girls in grades 2–12 who have experienced sexual abuse, abandonment issues, placement problems, truancy, early sexual acting out, and/or familial teen pregnancy and provide them with a supportive, consistent, empowering educator and role model. Our advisors educate participants on youth development topics that guide them in making healthy life choices. Our program topics include: decision making, refusal, communication, and problem solving skills, assertiveness training, anger management, conflict resolution, puberty education, socialization skills, life skills, and prevention education. We strive to empower families to communicate well with each other, help children avoid risky behavior during their adolescent years, and strengthen the family unit as a whole. Only three of the 511 high-risk girls we've mentored since 1999 experienced a pregnancy, and all three of those young women were older than 18 when they gave birth.

Reality shows target all teens without the capacity to address the real and complicated issues that may lead to actual teen pregnancy. Focusing on sexual health for all young people is vital; providing personalized instruction to teens at highest risk, while costly, could maximize positive outcomes.

Voices to Break the Cycle: A Phenomenological Inquiry into Generational Teen Pregnancy

I completed my doctoral work late in life; my dissertation was not only informative but also humbling. I looked at the lived experiences of women who gave birth as adolescents to investigate how these adults might help their pubertal aged children avoid teenage pregnancy. Research participants gave birth as teens (defined as under 19 years of age) and were parenting their biologic children ages 10–15. A key criteria for selection in the study was generational teen pregnancy; participants in the study came from families with a history of teen pregnancy through at least one generation prior to the former teen mother's birth. The study reinforced the antecedents of poverty, foster placement, sexual abuse, and familial patterns of early childbearing (Podgurski, 2009).

Stigmatizing women who conceive and bear children during adolescence is common in American culture and can lead to social inequalities (McDermott & Graham, 2005). Data reinforces young mothers' continuing need for support while teens (Pai-Espinosa, 2010) and as their lives move forward beyond adolescence (Jutte et al., 2010). The voices of former teen mothers in my study also revealed lives deeply affected by their adolescent pregnancies. Many women expressed a desire to move away from the community in which they gave birth; 30% of the former teen mothers in the study did relocate. One participant in the study stated: "When I got married I left the area. I found it easier to reinvent myself than deal with people who had labeled me as that pregnant girl. My life here is better than it would have been if I'd stayed where I was." Where can a teen parent whose life has been exposed on a national reality TV show relocate?

Adult empathic understanding and compassion for the lives of teen parents was not common among the participants in my study; over 80% described self-reported disrespectful treatment during their births, upon their return to school, or while seeking employment. If, as the National Campaign for Teen and Unplanned Pregnancy reports, 41% of adults report the show "16 and Pregnant" glorifies teen pregnancy (Albert, 2010), will that compassion diminish?

Till Human Voices Wake Us

What is the effect of fame on the young parents made into instant celebrities by reality TV? What do they and their children sacrifice to the altar of TV ratings?

To examine the possible long-term effects of fame and celebrity status on young parents, it is illustrative to look at fame as it is perceived in youth culture. Halpern (2007) surveyed 5th to 8th grade students in Rochester, New York, and found 29% of males and 37% of females selected fame over intelligence as a desired trait. The study participants viewed at least five hours of TV daily; that figure is consistent with other studies of youth screen time (defined as TV and computer time). For example, Burnett and her research team (2008) found that 60% of teens spent an average of 20 hours in screen time, a full third spent closer to 40 hours per week and 7 percent were exposed to greater than 50 hours of viewing time weekly. Perhaps most significantly, Halbern's work showed that 17% of the students felt that celebrities owed their fame to luck, and believed that TV shows had the power to make people famous. If fame is valued over intelligence and luck is perceived as a better indicator of future well-being than industry among average children, would pregnant and parenting teens buy into that delusion as well?

An intense desire for fame can lead reality TV participants to believe that "every reality show is an audition tape for future work" (Wolk, 2010, p. 32). If adults are affected by fame hunger that directs their actions and choices, how can adolescents avoid influence from reality TV fame? The sad drama of Amber, violence, and child custody revealed on the show "Teen Mom" was popular among tabloids, magazines, and advertisers. As an educator I am troubled. Did Amber receive guidance or were her actions considered fodder for higher ratings? One need go no further than the cover story of a current *OK! Magazine* to read that "More Teen Mom Babies!" are planned, including one baby that is being conceived to save a relationship (2011, April 18). The same issue proclaims that Amber and Gary will reunite. What type, if any, relationship skill education do these young "reality celebrities" receive as their lives are broadcast nationally?

Putting a Face on the Numbers

The names of the young parents in the following anecdotes are fiction but their stories are not. Any of these young people would produce high ratings on a reality TV show. Protecting their anonymity is a fundamental educational task. Ethical treatment of pregnant and parenting youth demands that respect is rendered at all times.

Picture Tracy: This lively young woman was a National Honor Society student when she found she was pregnant at the age of 16. Articulate, empathetic, and soft-spoken, she is now a caring social worker completing her master's degree in counseling. Tracy did not disclose her history of sexual assault until the baby she birthed as a teen was four years old; she now uses her life experiences to help her connect with young women at risk for early childbearing.

Nina is a bright, intelligent 27 year old. Her hair color and body piercings change often but her striking hazel eyes and determined expressions remain constant. She is perceptive, a hard worker, and one of the most resilient young people I've ever known. Nina is also the parent of a 12 year old. She lived in a series of foster homes while pregnant and parenting; her mother gave birth to her as a 15 year old and her grandmother had her first pregnancy as a 16 year old. Nina was born into poverty and continues to struggle to make ends meet. She left school at 17 and hasn't completed the GED (General Equivalency Diploma) she frequently talks about. She often bemoans the fact that her daughter "does without" things she too was denied as a teen. She is proud that she has been her child's only parent and that her daughter has never been in foster care. Like her own parents, Nina fights addiction to alcohol and drugs and has been in and out of rehab several times.

Meet Samantha: Sammy planned her baby to prove that she was heterosexual. Her first kiss at 11 was with a girl; she reacted violently to the fear that she was lesbian in a homophobic family and made a conscious decision to conceive a baby to a man ten years her senior. She was only 12 when her pregnancy was discovered; she didn't tell anyone until she was in her third trimester. She came out when her son was two years old and is currently in a five-year relationship with her female partner.

Jodi gave birth as a tenth grader but only disclosed her stepfather as her baby's daddy when he starting hitting on her younger sister. Her baby was two years old at the time. Disclosure led to her stepfather's arrest and incarceration for over four years of sexual abuse. Her five siblings were divided and sent to three different foster homes. While Jodi is intermittently proud of her disclosure, she blames herself for the dissolution of her family. She is in a new school district where few know her family's history and is starting to shine academically.

Trevor's father reacted to his girlfriend **Amy's** pregnancy by denying his parentage; within an hour he was homeless at 18. Too old for children and youth services, he wandered from one friend's sofa to another until the single mother of his girlfriend allowed him to move in with her family. The baby is due this spring. Trevor is determined to remain with his partner and states firmly that he will not "be a statistic." His girlfriend's mother, while kind and supportive, is skeptical. She sees Amy's father in Trevor. Although she hopes for the best, she expects him to leave before the baby is two.

It's Not about the United States

Those in the United States who have committed our lives to supporting, empowering, and educating young people approach this charge in unique ways. I humbly acknowledge that there are many paths to reaching youth. I have learned more from listening to the young people I serve than from any other resource. When I train new staff I reinforce a common theme: our work is not about us, it's about the young people. I am reminded of the old admonition: First, Do No Harm. As adults we are responsible for the needs of all youth, regardless of sexual orientation, gender and gender identity, race, ethnicity, socio-economic status, religion, or level of sexual involvement. I challenge all who serve pregnant and parenting teens to examine the effects adult interventions have upon the lives of these young people and their children, bearing in mind that we do not yet have full knowledge of the long-term implications of national exposure at a time of great vulnerability. When in doubt, protect.

References

Albert, B. (2010). *With one voice 2010: Teens and adults sound off about teen pregnancy.* National Campaign to Prevent Teen and Unplanned Pregnancy. *Retrieved from* http://www.thenationalcampaign.org/resources/pdf/pubs/WOV_2010.pdf

Barnett, T., O'Loughlin, J., Sabiston, C., Karp, I., Belanger, M., Van Hulst, A., & Lambert., M. (2008). Teens and screens: The influence of screen time on adiposity in adolescents. *American Journal of Epidemiology, 172*(3), 255–262.

Boyer, D. & Fine, D. (1992). Sexual abuse as a factor in adolescent pregnancy and child maltreatment. *Family Planning Perspectives, 24*(1), 4–11.

Children's Aid Society. (2010). Dr. Michael A. Carrera, Retrieved from http://www.childrensaidsociety.org/carrera-pregnancy-prevention/dr-michael-carrera

Coles, C. (2005). Teen pregnancy and "internal poverty." *Futurist, 38*(7), 10.

Coyle, J. (2005, September). Preventing and reducing violence by at-risk adolescents common elements of empirically researched programs. *Journal of Evidence-Based Social Work, 2*(3/4), 125.

Goode, W. W. & Smith, T. J. (2005). *Building from the ground up: Creating effective programs to mentor children of prisoners.* Philadelphia, PA: Public/Private Ventures.

East, P. L., & Khoo, S. (2005, December). Longitudinal pathways linking family factors and sibling relationship qualities to adolescent substance use and sexual risk behaviors. *Journal of Family Psychology, 19*(4), 571–580.

East, P. L., Reyes, B. T. & Horn, E. J. (2007, June). Association between adolescent pregnancy and a family history of teenage births. *Perspectives on sexual and reproductive health, 39*(2), 108–115.

Halpern, J. (2007). *Fame junkies: The hidden truth behind America's favorite addiction.* New York: Houghton Mifflin Company.

Hoffman, J. (2011, April 10). Fighting teen pregnancy with MTV stars as Exhibit A. *The New York Times*, p. ST 1, 11.

Jekielek, S. M., Moore, K. A., Hair, E. C., & Scarupa, H. J. (2002, February). Mentoring: A promising strategy for youth development. *Child Trends Research Brief.* Retrieved from www.mentoring.ca.gov/pdf/MentoringBrief2002.pdf

Jutte, D., Roos, N., Brownell, M., Briggs, G., MacWilliam, L., & Roos, L. (2010). The ripples of adolescent motherhood: social, educational, and medical outcomes for children of teen and prior teen mothers. *Academic Pediatrics, 10*(5), 293–301.

Karcher, M. (2005). The effects of developmental mentoring and high school mentors' attendance on their younger mentees' self-esteem, social skills and connectedness. *Psychology in the Schools, 42*(1), 65–77. Retrieved from www.adolescentconnectedness.com/media/KarcherPITS_mentoring&conn.pdf

Kirby, D. (2002). Antecedents of adolescent initiation of sex, contraceptive use, and pregnancy. *American Journal of Health Behavior, 26*(6), 473.

Kirby, D. (2007). *Emerging answers: Research findings on programs to reduce teen pregnancy and sexually transmitted diseases.* Washington, DC: National Campaign to Prevent Teen Pregnancy.

Kirby, D., Lepore, G., & Ryan, J. (2006). *Sexual risk and protective factors—Factors affecting teen sexual behavior, pregnancy, childbearing and sexually transmitted disease: Which are important? Which can you change?* Scotts Valley, CA: ETR Associates.

Lamaze International. (2010). *Creativity, connection and commitment: Supporting teens during the childbearing year.* Retrieved from http://www.lamaze.org/ChildbirthEducators/WorkshopsConference/SpecialtyWorkshops/SupportingTeensDuringtheChildbearingYear/tabid/494/Default.aspx

Luker, K. (1997). *Dubious conceptions: The politics of teen pregnancy.* Boston: Harvard University Press.

Luker, K. (2006). When sex goes to school: Warring views on sex—and sex education since the sixties. New York: W. W. Norton & Company.

McDermott, E. & Graham, H. (2005). Resilient young mothering: social inequalities, late modernity and the 'problem' of 'teenage' motherhood. *Journal of Youth Studies, 8*, 59–79.

(2011, April 18) More teen mom babies. *OK! Magazine, 16*, 32–35.

Pai-Espinosa, J. (2010). Young mothers at the margin: why pregnant teens need support. *Children's Voice, 19*(3), 14–16.

Podgurski, MJ. (2009). *Voices to break the cycle: A phenomenological inquiry into generational teen pregnancy.* (Doctoral dissertation). University of Phoenix, Phoenix, AZ.

Raneri, L., & Constance, M. (2007, March). Social ecological predictors of repeat adolescent pregnancy. *Perspectives on Sexual & Reproductive Health, 39*(1), 39–47.

Young, T., Turner, J., Denny, G., Young, M. (2004, July). Examining external and internal poverty as antecedents of teen pregnancy. *American Journal of Health Behavior, 28*(4), 361–373.

Wolk, J. (2002). Fame factor. *Entertainment Weekly,* (665), 32.

Mary Jo Podgurski is the founder of the Academy for Adolescent Health, Inc., in Washington, Pennsylvania. She is an adjunct professor in the Department of Education at Washington and Jefferson College.

EXPLORING THE ISSUE

Do Reality TV Shows Portray Responsible Messages about Teen Pregnancy?

Critical Thinking and Reflection

1. In what ways could reality TV programs educate the public and impact the prevention of teen pregnancy?
2. How might reality TV programs about teen pregnancy have a negative impact on the teens involved?
3. What strategies, other than television, might be effective in addressing high rates of teen pregnancy?
4. European nations have much lower teen pregnancy rates than the United States. Why might this be?

Is There Common Ground?

Amy Kramer notes that the shows depict realistic consequences of sexual activity and teen pregnancy without glamorizing these outcomes. She says, "Families, schools, health care professionals, businesses big and small, religious communities, and yes, the media, all have a role to play." Do you agree with her assessment of the role of various institutions, including the media in addressing teen pregnancy prevention?

Mary Jo Podgurski does not dispute the potential benefit that reality TV shows about teen pregnancy can have. She notes their merits and their good intentions. However, she is concerned about the potential for teens who appear on the show to be exploited. She says that, developmentally, teens can't fully "grasp the far-reaching implications of their decision to participate." What might be some examples of far-reaching implications? Think back to when you were 15 or 16. How prepared do you think you would be to share your life story on national television, if you experienced early pregnancy or became a teen parent?

Noting that young people may be blinded by fame, Podgurski also commented on how participants on the show may be selected for their "camera quality." What do you think she meant, and how do you think this might be problematic? Podgurski also expressed concern about society applying a "Band-aid" solution to a complex, multi-faceted issue, and that perhaps money would be better invested in programs that actually address the variety of antecedents to early pregnancy and risky behavior. Kramer likewise acknowledges that these TV programs do not make a singular solution. Is there room for *both* evidence-based teen pregnancy prevention programs *and* media-driven shows that open the door for discussion between parents and children? Is one approach better than the other? If you were in a position to award a million dollar teen pregnancy prevention project, would you invest in both approaches, or would you support one more than the other?

Additional Resources

Alford, S. & Hauser, D. (March, 2011). *Adolescent Sexual Health in Europe and the United States: The Case for a Rights, Respect, Responsibility Approach.* Washington, DC: Advocates for Youth.

Chang, J. & Hopper, J. "Pregnancy Pressure: Is MTV's 'Teen Mom' Encouraging Pregnancy for Fame?" *ABC News*, February 11, 2011.

Sharp, S. "16 and Pregnant and Almost True," *Mother Jones*, April 21, 2010.

Stanley, A. "Motherhood's Rough Edges Fray in Reality TV . . . And Baby Makes Reality TV," *The New York Times*, January 21, 2011.

Internet References . . .

16 and Pregnant: Important Things to Know about Teen Pregnancy

Developed by the National Campaign to Prevent Teen and Unplanned Pregnancy, this page presents a summary of key facts about teen pregnancy.

www.thenationalcampaign.org/resources/pdf/16-and-preg-fact-sheet.pdf

Evaluating the Impact of MTV's *16 and Pregnant* on Teen Viewers' Attitudes about Teen Pregnancy

This page, also by the National Campaign to Prevent Teen and Unplanned Pregnancy, has links to fact sheets about the media and teen pregnancy.

www.cnn.com/2011/SHOWBIZ/TV/05/04/teen.mom.dolgen/index.html

Sexuality and Reality TV

This article critically examines the portrayal of gender identity, sexual orientation, and other aspects of sexuality on reality television.

http://mkopas.net/courses/soc287/2012/08/06/sexuality-and-reality-tv/

Why I Created MTV's "16 and Pregnant"

Laura Dolgen, senior vice president for MTV series development, explains her rationale for creating "16 and Pregnant" and "Teen Mom."

www.cnn.com/2011/SHOWBIZ/TV/05/04/teen.mom.dolgen/index.html

Unit 2

UNIT

Sexual Health, Treatments, and Reproduction

Some of the most contentious modern debates about sexuality center on health and reproduction. Issues like contraception and abortion, gender and body autonomy still have the ability to raise eyebrows and voices. These issues force us to consider our values amid a rapidly changing world. The ethical questions we must consider go far beyond our own families because the decisions we make and stances we take can have a strong influence on society. In the upcoming unit you will examine five issues related to sexual health and reproduction.

Selected, Edited, and with Issue Framing Material by:
Ryan W. McKee, *Widener University,* Tracie Q. Gilbert, *Widener University,*
and
Jayleen Galarza, *Shippensburg University of Pennsylvania*

ISSUE

Is Pre-Exposure Prophylaxis (PrEP) an Effective Method for HIV Prevention?

YES: Michael Lucas, from "Op-Ed: PrEP Works, So Drop the Backlash," *Out Magazine* (2015)

NO: Tom Myers, from "HIV Prevention Pill Will Do More Harm Than Good," *U.S. News and World Report* (2012)

Learning Outcomes

After reading this issue, you will be able to:

- Describe the effect of pre-exposure prophylaxis (PrEP) medication in regard to HIV transmission.
- List two benefits of PrEP.
- List two reasons why some are concerned about reliance on PrEP as an HIV prevention method.

ISSUE SUMMARY

YES: Michael Lucas, founder of all-male erotica studio Lucas Entertainment, argues that the effectiveness of PrEP negates all arguments against its use, and that organizations opposing PrEP are acting in their own self-interest.

NO: Tom Myers, Chief Public Affairs and General Counsel for the AIDS Healthcare Foundation, believes incorrect and inconsistent usage of PrEP will lead to more HIV infections.

Since the emergence of HIV as a global public health crisis, people have longed for a cure or preventative medical treatment, such as a vaccine, that is easy to use and widely available. While many drugs have shown promise, most have fallen short during clinical trials. There are, however, some medical treatments that provide protection against the accidental transmission of HIV. Two kinds of medications, an emergency treatment called post-exposure prophylaxis (PEP) and a preventative medication called pre-exposure prophylaxis (PrEP), are highly effective, but not widely-known outside the medical community.

PEP has been available for years and is used in a variety of instances. Babies born to HIV-positive mothers, for example, are protected from transmission while in utero but may be exposed to HIV when they come into contact with blood and other body fluids occurs during birth. Health care providers and first responders run the risk of accidental exposure to HIV when caring for those in medical or emergency situations. Despite precautions like latex gloves or other protective barriers, contact with blood or needles may occur. In situations like these, PEP can dramatically reduce (but not eliminate) the risk of contracting HIV. Medication treatment should begin as soon after potential exposure as possible (within 72 hours) and be adhered to over a 28-day regimen to maximize effectiveness. PEP may also be offered to victims of sexual assault. The Centers for Disease Control and Prevention (CDC) also recommends PEP for those exposed to HIV through the sharing of needles or unprotected sex. While these last recommendations caused some controversy when originally released, PEP treatments have become largely accepted in a wide-variety of instances.

In 2012, the U.S. Food and Drug Administration (FDA) approved a drug called Truvada, as the first pre-exposure prophylaxis (PrEP) for HIV. Originally a medication used to treat those who had already contracted HIV, a new, more groundbreaking use made headlines. Simply put, Truvada, used for PrEP, is a pill that is taken once daily by a person who is HIV-negative that greatly reduces the risk of contracting HIV. Findings from several studies have shown that the drug is highly effective in reducing the risk of infection among gay and bisexual men, heterosexual men and women, transgender women, and even IV drug users. Truvada has relatively few side effects, and has been shown to be 99 percent effective among users who take the pill daily, without fail. The effectiveness rate falls to 96 percent among those who only take four pills per week, and 76 percent for those who take the pill twice per week. It has been hailed by some as a miracle drug.

Despite the high effectiveness rates, not everyone sees PrEP as a panacea, and it has been somewhat slow to catch on. The cost of the medication may be one reason; some insurance companies have been reluctant to cover the drug, and individuals without insurance can expect to pay up to $2,000 per month to fill a prescription (though subsidies are available for some low-income users). The price, many advocates argue, means that only the affluent can actually afford the drug, putting it out of reach to those most at-risk for contracting HIV. The controversial AIDS Healthcare Foundation, a Los Angeles-based community medical care provider, has been strongly critical of the FDA for approving PrEP and launched a media campaign designed to discourage use of the drug. The group believes that inconsistent use of PrEP will lead to more HIV infections—not less. While studies have shown high rates of effectiveness, additional research, they argue, is needed to confirm the results. Furthermore, media outlets have incorrectly reported that Truvada is *100% effective*, without additional clarification on how often, or for how long, the medication should be used. This reporting, along with the tag of "FDA Approved" may lead some to rely on PrEP, rather than condoms, as their primary HIV prevention method. Distrust of the pharmaceutical industry, government systems like the FDA, as well as what they perceived as a too-good-to-be-true pill also resonated with older gay men who had witnessed the impact of HIV/AIDS during eighties and nineties. They warned that replacing condoms with PrEP could lead to skyrocketing rates of infection. Shortly after its release some Truvada users who began using PrEP and stopped using condoms reported being harassed and stigmatized as "Truvada whores" who were putting others at risk.

The majority of HIV prevention advocates have taken a much more favorable stance on PrEP. While not 100 percent effective, the drug offers an incredibly high degree of protection against HIV. Condoms, they note, are not 100 percent effective either. Additionally, not everyone uses condoms for every sexual act. Truvada may, for some people, be a more viable option. PrEP should be seen simply as another (highly effective) tool in the fight against HIV—not a miracle drug.

In the YES selection, Michael Lucas argues that the effectiveness of PrEP negates all arguments against its use, and that organizations opposing PrEP, who may lose financial support if HIV infections are reduced, are acting in their own self-interest. In the NO selection, Tom Myers counters, arguing that incorrect and inconsistent usage of PrEP will lead to more HIV infections rather than fewer.

Reference

San Francisco AIDS Foundation (2015). The Basics. Retrieved from http://men.prepfacts.org/the-basics/

YES

Michael Lucas

Op-Ed: PrEP Works, So Drop the Backlash

It's never polite to say, "I told you so." But I think I'm justified in using the somewhat less offensive, "Now do you believe me?" in this case.

I'm referring to the game-changing results of a new study on the antiviral drug treatment "pre-exposure prophylaxis," known as PrEP, or by its brand name, Truvada. Researchers at Kaiser Permanente San Francisco tracked 647 men, 99% of whom have sex with men, over the course of 32 months. Not a single participant taking PrEP contracted HIV.

I have been speaking out in support of PrEP for several years, so let me repeat the stunning conclusion of this study: Taking PrEP in the real world had an HIV prevention rate of 100%. Previous smaller clinical trials had indicated about 90% protection from the virus. Nothing is perfect, but this is clear: PrEP works.

One would think that all who deal with HIV and AIDS would embrace a nearly miraculous medication like this with open arms. Not the case, despite the fact that approximately 50,000 Americans are newly infected with HIV every year.

So allow me to respond to some of the misconceptions about and objections to PrEP that have been heard for years, and are still being pushed by opponents of the treatment:

1. **"It's too expensive."** Not true. PrEP is FDA-approved, and may be largely covered by health insurance (depending on your policy and provider). It's available free from the maker, Gilead, for those without health insurance and on low or moderate incomes, or who don't qualify for Medicaid. And that includes every immigrant living in the U.S., regardless of his or her legal status.
2. **"It doesn't protect from STDs."** True. But this is irrelevant. Those supporting PrEP have never claimed it would prevent STDs. PrEP also doesn't prevent diabetes, but why should that diminish its value in protecting people from HIV?
3. **"It encourages men to have more sex without condoms."** PrEP is the most highly-effective tool we now have to help sexually active people avoid contracting HIV. The corollary of the bareback argument is "Only gay men with high risk behavior need to take PrEP." That is a shameful contention that creates an unnecessary stigma. All you need is to have had one instance in your entire life of not using a condom, with a partner you don't know and trust 100%, to find value in taking PrEP. Each individual now can decide if PrEP fits his or her life, and if their risk for HIV is high enough to merit taking a pill every day.
4. **"It doesn't guarantee 100% protection, and hasn't been studied enough."** These arguments hold no weight after the publication of the Kaiser Permanente results in *Clinical Infectious Diseases,* a top publication in the field. Condoms should theoretically work 100%, but sometimes they break. The chance of condoms not working doesn't mean you shouldn't use them. PrEP will work 100% of the time, even in the real world outside of a clinical study, if taken as prescribed.
5. **"Taking PrEP has side effects."** Actually, so many people have no side effects that they reportedly question whether the drug is actually working. About one in ten people studied do report short-term effects such as headaches, weight loss, and stomach problems; most of those problems lessened after the first few weeks. But what drug doesn't have side effects? Where would we be if people never took antibiotics, due to the drastic side effects often associated with those powerful drugs?

I interview models for Lucas Entertainment in person or by Skype, and if they live in New York I will recommend that they visit the Mount Sinai Comprehensive Health Care Clinic in Manhattan. Since it's just a couple of blocks from my office, I often take them myself. I've brought at least 60 young men there in the last year.

If their blood test shows they are negative, they start taking PrEP; if it's positive for HIV, they begin medication.

The medication has serious side effects, and there's no choice other than to take it daily until a cure is found. I begged a close friend to go on PrEP for the last two years. He hesitated for all the reasons cited above. When he finally decided to discuss it with a doctor, he was found to be HIV positive. He's now on HIV medication, which he takes along with a daily dose of regret. And there's no option to stop.

I should also point out that those who take PrEP automatically will be seeing their doctors on a regular basis, with the increased health awareness that brings. Often, taking PrEP means these people are getting appropriate sexual and other healthcare for the first time. This in itself may prevent HIV and STDs.

I often wonder why there has been such a backlash against PrEP. I have come to the conclusion that many of the opponents lived through the horrific time when sex equaled death, and they cannot imagine people having sex without fear. They cannot conceive of gay men enjoying sex without being paranoid about contracting HIV.

Then there is the most strident voice against the use of PrEP: the AIDS Healthcare Foundation. That's the Los-Angeles organization accused in April of bilking Medicare and Medicaid in a $20 million scam spanning twelve states. Three former managers of AHF, the country's largest supplier of HIV and AIDS medical care, alleged a system of kickbacks for referrals that would increase funding from federal health programs. Let me be very blunt here: PrEP prevents HIV. Without HIV and AIDS, this foundation would be out of business.

Despite all the attempted distractions, the focus must remain on the simple message in the new study: If you take PrEP, you will not get HIV. Period. It is time to wake up, stop the endless debating, and take action.

The war against HIV rages on, and when scientists actually win a battle, we must avail ourselves of the powerful weapon they have developed.

Michael Lucas is the founder of all-male erotica studio Lucas Entertainment.

Tom Myers **NO**

HIV Prevention Pill Will Do More Harm Than Good

When pre-exposure prophylaxis (PrEP)—the idea of using an existing AIDS drug treatment as an HIV prevention pill—was first introduced, it heralded the promise of allowing people to protect themselves from becoming infected with HIV. Unfortunately for all, this simply will not work the way that scientists and supporters had hoped.

Truvada PrEP will not work on a widespread scale because in order for it to be effective at preventing HIV infection, pills must be taken every single day. No missed doses. However, study after study has shown that people generally cannot meet this ideal.

Even people who are sick, and have the most incentive to take medicine to get better, don't take it as directed. For example, people taking statins for heart disease generally take them properly only 61 percent of the time. When was the last time you finished even a two-week course of antibiotics instead of stopping once you started feeling better?

If we know that people don't take their medicines regularly when they are sick, how can we expect them to take pills when they are not sick? We can't, of course.

In the primary study of PrEP, participants were regularly counseled on taking their pills daily. They had monthly doctor visits, where they again were counseled on taking their medications. Further, they were paid to participate in the study. And yet, even with all this support, only 18 percent of the study participants were taking the pills with any regularity. In the real world, where people don't get paid to take medicine, and where people don't have medication counseling, the results will be even lower. And that's where the danger lies. Not taking Truvada for PrEP properly is more serious than just not having protection from HIV infection.

First, if a person taking Truvada becomes infected, there is a greater chance that their HIV will be resistant to Truvada. Currently, Truvada is the backbone of successful AIDS treatment. The creation of Truvada-resistant strains of HIV is incredibly worrying.

Second, Truvada has serious side effects, including kidney damage and bone loss. These risks may be acceptable when a person has HIV or AIDS, but people taking PrEP are healthy. There will be healthy people who will not get the preventive benefits of PrEP, but who will suffer kidney damage and other harms.

Third, many people, thinking they are protected by taking PrEP, will abandon or reduce the use of other proven preventive measures such as condoms. "Risk compensation," the phenomenon of engaging in more risky behavior when you believe you are protected from harm, has been documented in virtually all areas of life, including the sexual arena. Because many people will not take Truvada properly, but think they are protected, it is entirely likely that widespread use of PrEP will actually increase HIV infections.

The cost of Truvada is over $13,000 per year. For that kind of money, the government, which is the primary payer of AIDS care through Medicaid, Medicare, and the Ryan White CARE Act, could provide treatment for a similar number of people with HIV/AIDS (currently, about 450,000 Americans living with HIV/AIDS lack access to care). Treatment not only makes people healthier and able to take care of their families; treatment itself is up to 96 percent effective in preventing HIV transmission, according to studies.

While I very much wish it would work, I fear that PrEP is one tool in the prevention kit that will do more harm than good.

Tom Myers is the Chief of Public Affairs and General Counsel for the AIDS Healthcare Foundation.

EXPLORING THE ISSUE

Is Pre-Exposure Prophylaxis (PrEP) an Effective Method for HIV Prevention?

Critical Thinking and Reflection

1. How confident would you be using PrEP as your only protection against HIV? What would contribute to your confidence or reluctance?
2. In what ways are arguments for and against PrEP similar to those used when discussing hormonal contraceptives?
3. Lucas repeats accusations of misconduct against the AIDS Healthcare Foundation, for whom Myers works, in an attempt to discredit the organization. Do these statements make you less likely to trust Myers' arguments? Why or why not?

Is There Common Ground?

In February 2016, it was reported that the first person on a daily regimen of Truvada had tested positive for a rare, drug-resistant strain of HIV. Those skeptical of PrEP's utility in the fight against HIV now had a concrete example of the drug's shortcomings. However, the Truvada user who was infected, along with most in the medical community, still argue that the drug is highly effective and should be seen as an important HIV prevention option. Focusing on the one infection, caused by a very rare strain of HIV, ignores the countless other users who are protected by the drug every day.

To longtime sexuality educators, criticism of PrEP and its users sounds similar to that of early hormonal contraceptive pills and the women who took them. Concern for contraceptive users over side effects, consistent adherence, increased risky sexual activity, and reduced condom usage have all been expressed at various points in time to argue against contraception. Even the stigmatization and shaming leveled against Truvada users is similar to that of women who sought access to birth control.

What are your thoughts on PrEP as an HIV prevention tool? Would you trust its effectiveness, or are you skeptical? Does the revelation of an HIV-infected Truvada user make you less likely to trust PrEP? If you are HIV-negative, how do you protect yourself against HIV? If you are HIV positive, would you encourage your partners to take PrEP? What is your tolerance for risk in sexual situations, and how do you determine what preventative measures are best for you? Do you use condoms with every partner, every time you have sex? Why or why not? If you had access to Truvada, how likely would you be to take it consistently, every day? What, if anything, would impact your ability to do so?

Additional Resources

Centers for Disease Control and Prevention. (2016). Pre-exposure prophylaxis (PrEP). Retrieved from http://www.cdc.gov/hiv/risk/prep/

Murphy, T. (September 9, 2013). Is this the new condom? *Out Magazine. Retrieved from http://www.out.com/news-opinion/2013/09/09/hiv-prevention-new-condom-truvada-pill-prep*

McCollom, R. (April 16, 2016). What's so controversial about AIDS Healthcare Foundation? *thebody.com*. Retrieved from http://www.thebody.com/content/75720/whats-so-controversial-about-aids-healthcare-found.html

Straube, T. (March 3, 2016). Meet the man who got HIV while on daily PrEP. *Poz*. Retrieved from https://www.poz.com/article/meet-man-got-hiv-daily-prep

Internet References . . .

AIDS Healthcare Foundation

aidshealth.org

Keep It Real with PrEP

men.prepfacts.org/

Truvada for PrEP

https://start.truvada.com/

Selected, Edited, and with Issue Framing Material by:
Ryan W. McKee, *Widener University,* Tracie Q. Gilbert, *Widener University,*
and
Jayleen Galarza, *Shippensburg University of Pennsylvania*

ISSUE

Should Sexual Problems Be Treated Pharmaceutically?

YES: Connie B. Newman, from "Pharmacological Treatment for Sexual Problems: The Benefits Outweigh the Risks," An original essay written for this volume (2011)

NO: Anita P. Hoffer, from "The Hidden Costs of the Medicalization of Female Sexuality—How Did We Get Here? An Overview," An original essay written for this volume (2013)

Learning Outcomes

After reading this issue, you will be able to:

- Describe some of the sexual problems experienced by women and men.
- Explain some of the factors that may contribute to sexual problems.
- Describe some of the treatments available for sexual problems.
- Differentiate between treatments available to men and those available to women.

ISSUE SUMMARY

YES: Connie B. Newman, an endocrinologist and adjunct associate professor of medicine at New York University School of Medicine, explores the definitions and causes of sexual dysfunction and explains how sexual medicines can improve sexual response.

NO: Anita P. Hoffer, former associate professor at Harvard Medical School and former director of research in urology at the Brigham and Women's Hospital, argues that the rise of sexual medicine has created a market that benefits the pharmaceutical industry at the expense of the individual.

If you watch much television, chances are you have seen ads for Viagra, a drug that treats erectile dysfunction in men. In fact, 2013 marked the 15-year anniversary of the "little blue pill." Since its release, several additional erectile dysfunction drugs, including Levitra and Cialis, have made the process of getting erections much easier for millions of men around the world. The products have been so successful that pharmaceutical companies have, for years, been attempting to replicate their success with medications for a variety of sexual dysfunctions in women (including hypoactive sexual disorder, otherwise known as low libido). Authors of a controversial study from 1999 found that 43 percent of women between the ages of 18 and 59 had some type of sexual dysfunction (1). Pharmaceutical companies invested billions of dollars into research for elusive remedies. It was thought that the profits from women's treatments would rival, if not surpass, those of male treatments.

Clinical trials of a women's version of Viagra, as well as several other potential medications, ended with mixed results. Intrinsa, a testosterone patch designed to increase women's libido, showed promise, but did not get approval from the Food and Drug Administration (FDA) (the patch was approved in several European countries, however). The desire for the product was there; the desired results, on the other hand, were not.

Why has the search for a women's prescription treatment proven so challenging? If men can have some of their sexual issues taken care of with a prescription medication, critics argue, why have women's sexual problems proven so difficult to treat? Some women's health advocates take issue over the disparity between FDA-approved drugs available for men and women. Some saw sexism and a fear of women's sexuality at play in the FDA's decisions. Others theorized there were subtle differences between the ways men and women experienced arousal. A pill may have a difficult time differentiating between such body–mind nuances.

Another camp holds that pharmaceutical treatments for such complex issues (for both men and women) may be off-base to begin with. Many therapists and sexologists warn against what they see as the "medicalization" of sexual problems. An over-reliance on prescription drugs is seen as a one-size-fits-all approach that ignores larger issues. Some point to the far more common psychogenic causes of sexual dysfunction that cannot be treated by medication. They contend that nonmedical treatments (improving partner communication, for example) would be far more effective. They charge that pharmaceutical companies are making a hefty profit through the "medicalization" of sexuality. Still others argue that the estimated number of sexual dysfunction cases is inflated, and that the vast majority of real cases of both female and male sexual dysfunction are caused by psychological or interpersonal factors that are better treated with nonmedicinal interventions like counseling or therapy.

In the YES selection, Dr. Connie B. Newman describes the common problem of sexual dysfunction in both men and women, and explores the ways that sexual medicines may alleviate these problems. In the NO selection, Dr. Anita P. Hoffer argues that pharmaceutical companies, not their patients, are the primary beneficiaries of sexual medicine.

YES

Connie B. Newman

Pharmacological Treatment for Sexual Problems: The Benefits Outweigh the Risks

Introduction

In the past decade considerable controversy has emerged over whether medicines that improve sexual function are truly needed. In fact, some experts have accused the pharmaceutical industry of creating sexual diseases in order to profit from new medicines specifically designed for these "invented" diseases (1, 2). In November 2010, while at a sex education conference sponsored by The Center for Family Life Education (The CFLE), I had the opportunity to preview the movie *Orgasm Inc.*, a documentary about the development of therapies to improve women's sex lives. The movie questioned whether female sexual dysfunction was a real disorder or a pseudo-disease created by the pharmaceutical industry in order to develop and market sex-enhancing medicines for women. In doing this, the movie made light of the real sexual problems that some women have. It did not explain the nature of the highly regulated drug development process, which requires pharmaceutical companies to adhere to strict standards in developing safe and effective medicines. It also put forth a distorted image of practicing doctors, showing them to be too eager to fix their patients' problems by prescribing medications.

To my surprise many people in the audience seemed to believe every word in the film and did not understand that there might be another side to this story. I am writing this article to explain the other point of view, or at least a more balanced point of view. Sexual dysfunction is a real disorder that occurs in women, especially as they age, as well as in men. Women's sex problems can have a physiological as well as a psychological basis, and are not solely due to lack of sex education, poor relationships, or working long hours. Sexual medicines that enhance sexual performance can benefit individuals and society. Pharmaceutical companies are interested in making a profit (after all they would not be in business if they did not), but in addition many scientists who work in pharmaceutical companies want to help people have healthier and more satisfied lives. Doctors prescribe medicines for patients only after a diagnosis is reached by evaluation of the patient's history, symptoms, physical findings, and laboratory tests, and after consideration of the benefits and risks of available therapies.

This article assesses the benefits and risks of using pharmacological treatments (sexual medicines) for individuals with sexual dysfunction. The following topics will be considered: the definitions and causes of sexual dysfunction in men and women, the prevalence of sexual dysfunction, therapeutic options for individuals with sexual problems, and an analysis of currently available medicines for sexual dysfunction.

Changing Definitions of Sexual Dysfunction: A Shift from Psychological Factors to Combined Organic and Psychological Causes

Sexual dysfunction is a broad general term that includes abnormalities in libido (sex drive), erections, orgasms, and ejaculation in men, and in sexual desire, arousal, orgasm in women, as well as painful intercourse and vaginal spasm. The sexual response cycle differs in men and women (3). In men, sexual desire often occurs before sexual stimuli and subsequent arousal. In contrast, women, especially those in established relationships, often engage in sex with their partners for reasons other than desire (3). Data suggest that sexual desire, as expressed by fantasizing, anticipating sexual experiences, and spontaneously thinking about sex in a positive way, varies in frequency among women and may be infrequent in many women who have normal sexual function (3, 4). In women, desire can be triggered during the sexual encounter (5), and desire then follows sexual arousal.

In both men and women many hormones, peptides, and neurotransmitters have a role in sexual desire and arousal. One of these hormones, testosterone, and its potential therapeutic uses, will be discussed later. Various medical conditions can adversely affect sexual responsiveness, as can depression, other psychiatric diseases, and psychological and social factors. In addition, medications including antidepressant agents can cause sexual problems as a side effect.

Defining sexual dysfunction has been difficult because of incomplete understanding of sexual disorders, especially in women. Classification of sexual disorders has been based on the *Diagnostic and Statistical Manual of Mental Disorders, 4th Ed.* (*DSM-IV*), a manual published by the American Psychiatric Association, reflecting the long-held belief that most sexual problems are psychologically based (6). This in itself might explain some of the resistance to pharmacological therapies that is still present today. *DSM-IV* recognized five disorders in female sexual function: hypoactive sexual desire disorder (reduced desire for sexual activity), female sexual arousal disorder, female orgasmic disorder, dyspareunia (genital pain associated with sexual intercourse), and vaginismus (spasm of the muscles of the outer third of the vagina that interferes with sexual intercourse). *DSM-IV* classified sexual disorders in men into the following main categories: erectile disorder, orgasmic disorder, premature ejaculation, hypoactive sexual desire disorder, and dyspareunia due to general medical condition. A new, revised manual of sexual disorders, with more precise definitions, is targeted for publication in 2012 [DSM-5 published May 27, 2013].

Prevalence of Sexual Disorders: What Do We Really Know?

It is difficult to know the true prevalence of sexual disorders in different age groups because most of the information comes from large surveys, rather than from detailed assessment by interviews. Although both the Food and Drug Administration (FDA) and the American Psychiatric Association require personal distress as part of the definition of sexual dysfunction, some of the older studies did not specifically evaluate this parameter. In the following section, data from the following surveys are presented: Massachusetts Male Aging Study (MMAS) in 1,709 men ages 40–70 years (7) and in 847 men ages 40–69 years (8); National Health and Social Life Survey (NHSLS) in 1,749 women and 1,410 men ages 18–59 years (9); National Social Life, Health and Aging Project (NSHAP) in 1,550 women and 1,455 men ages 57–85 years (10); Prevalence of Female Sexual Problems Associated with Distress and Determinants of Treatment (PRESIDE) in 31,581 women ages 18–102 years (11).

Estimates of Prevalence of Sexual Disorders in Men

Premature ejaculation is the most prevalent sexual disorder in young adult men and is defined by *DSM-IV* as "persistent or recurrent ejaculation with minimal sexual stimulation, before, upon, or shortly after penetration and before the person wishes it." In addition, the disturbance must cause marked distress or interpersonal difficulty. This definition of premature ejaculation has been criticized because it is not precise and is dependent upon the judgment of the clinician as well as the patient (12). The exact prevalence is unknown because of the lack of a universally accepted definition and the fact that, like most data on sexual function, the available data are self-reported. In NHSLS, early climax was reported by 30% of men between the ages of 18 [and] 29 years, and by 28–32% of men in the older age groups: 30–39, 40–49, 50–59 (9). Performance anxiety was less common than premature ejaculation, and was reported by 19% of men in the youngest age group, and 14% of men in the oldest age group.

Erectile dysfunction also occurs in younger men, although less frequently than in older men. How much of this is related to performance anxiety in younger men is not known. In NHSLS (9), difficulty in maintaining an erection was reported in less than 10% of the youngest men (18–29 years), and in 18% of men between the ages of 50 [and] 59 years. As men are more likely to overstate than understate their sexual capacity, these percentages are probably underestimates. Among older men the most prevalent sexual problem is erectile dysfunction (7, 8, 10), which increases with age and disease. In MMAS (7, 8), 52% of men between the ages of 40 [and] 70 years reported some degree of erectile dysfunction. With more advanced age, the prevalence of erectile dysfunction increases, affecting as many as 75% of men over the age of 80.

Lack of interest in sex is a less frequent complaint for men than either premature ejaculation or erectile dysfunction. In NHSLS, about 15% of men reported lack of interest in sex (9). In NSHAP, in older men between the ages of 57 and 85 years, lack of interest in sex was reported by 28% of respondents (10).

Estimates of Prevalence of Sexual Disorders in Women

There is uncertainty about the overall prevalence of sexual problems in women. NHSLS concluded that in women aged 18–59 years the prevalence of sexual dysfunction was 43%. More recently, PRESIDE, a survey of about

31,000 women (age 18–102 years, mean age 49), found that while 43% had at least one sexual problem, only 22% reported sexually related personal distress (11). The most common sexual problems reported by women are low desire, low sexual arousal, and inability to achieve an orgasm (9–11). In PRESIDE, 27% of women in the youngest age group reported any of these sexual problems, compared with about 45% of middle-aged women, and 80% of women 65 years of age or older (11). In NHSLS, in the youngest women studied (ages 18–29), 32% reported lack of interest in sex, 26% reported inability to achieve orgasm, 21% reported pain during sex, and 16% reported performance anxiety (9). In PRESIDE low desire was the most common sexual problem reported by 39% of the entire group; less common were low arousal (26%) and orgasm difficulties (21%) (11). Distressing sexual problems were more common in middle-aged than in younger or older women. Women with depression had more than twice the chance of having distressing sexual problems. This may be due in part to the adverse sexual side effects of antidepressant drugs, which can interfere with the ability to have an orgasm.

Taking all these data into consideration, it appears that at least one-third of men and women of all ages report sexual problems. In younger men, premature ejaculation is the most commonly reported problem, and in younger women, the most commonly reported problems are low desire, low arousal, and difficulty achieving an orgasm. Problems due to low libido and orgasm difficulties in women and to erectile dysfunction in men increase with age.

Therapeutic Options for Sexual Dysfunction

The "VIAGRA Revolution"

As noted by Segraves (6), after the publication of *Human Sexual Inadequacy* by William Masters and Virginia E. Johnson (13) the majority of sexual problems were considered to be treatable by psychologically based methods. Psychosexual counseling to reduce performance anxiety, develop sexual skills, change sexual attitudes, and improve relationships became first-line therapy for sexual dysfunction, regardless of cause (3). The introduction of sildenafil (VIAGRA) in 1998, dramatically changed the therapeutic approach to men with erectile problems. VIAGRA quickly became accepted as first-line therapy for male patients with erectile dysfunction. Now doctors had available an oral medication that was effective in about 70% of men with this problem, effective both in those with organic (vascular and neurologic disease) and psychological causes. The use of VIAGRA and similar medications changed the emphasis of treatment for erectile dysfunction from psychological and behavioral therapies to medicinal interventions. Improved sexual performance increases self-confidence and improves interpersonal relationships. Thus, in individuals with a psychological basis for erectile dysfunction, pharmacological treatment may be used together with psychological therapies.

Medicines for Men

Table 1 lists approved medicines that are used to treat disorders of sexual function in men along with the approved indications. Information about potential side effects may

Table 1

Medical Therapies for Sexual Dysfunction in Men

Drug (Brand Name)	Therapeutic Use	Approved Indications in United States
Sildenafil (VIAGRA) Vardenafil (LEVITRA) Tadalafil (CIALIS)	Erectile dysfunction, Selective Serotonin Uptake Inhibitor (SSRI)—induced sexual dysfunction*	Erectile dysfunction
Alprostadil [intraurethral (MUSE), intracavernosal]	Erectile dysfunction	Erectile dysfunction due to neurogenic, vasculogenic, psychogenic, or mixed etiology
Fluoxetine (PROZAC, SARAFEM) Sertraline (ZOLOFT) Paroxetine (PAXIL) Escitalopram (LEXAPRO) Citalopram (CELEXA)	Premature ejaculation*	Depression, obsessive compulsive disorder, panic attacks, post traumatic stress disorder, social anxiety disorder, premenstrual dysphoric disorder, generalized anxiety disorder
Bupropion (WELLBUTRIN, ZYBAN)	SSRI-induced sexual dysfunction*	Depression, seasonal affective disorder, smoking cessation
Testosterone†	Hypoactive sexual desire disorder when low testosterone is present	Replacement therapy in men with deficiency or absence of endogenous testosterone

Information is from the United States Product Circulars for the medications listed. Approved indications may not apply to all drugs in that class. Information about possible side effects can be found in the "Patient Information" for each drug, and the "Important Safety Information" which are available on each product's website.

*Off-label use in the United States SSRIs include fluoxetine, sertraline, paroxetine, escitalopram, citalopram.

†Preparations include injectable testosterone, transdermal gels, transdermal patches, buccal tablets, implantable pellets.

be found in the Patient Information and Important Safety Information brochures (available on the medication's website). Although all of these medicines are approved by the FDA, not all are approved for use in sexual dysfunction. Premature ejaculation is the most prevalent sexual dysfunction in men aged 18–59 years, but there is no FDA-approved medication for premature ejaculation. Ejaculation is regulated by serotonin, and similar chemicals produced by the brain that are responsible for good feelings (14, 15). This has led to the off-label use of some medications that block serotonin, known as "selective serotonin reuptake inhibitors" (SSRIs), including fluoxetine (PROZAC), sertraline (ZOLOFT), and escitalopram (LEXAPRO) for the treatment of premature ejaculation.

Conversely, the use of SSRIs for depression and other psychiatric diseases has led to sexual side effects such as difficulty in reaching orgasm and difficulty maintaining an erection. SSRI-induced sexual dysfunction is often treated with VIAGRA and similar medications, although VIAGRA is approved for use in erectile dysfunction but not for orgasmic difficulties.

Although libido is not completely understood in either men or women, the hormone testosterone is necessary for sexual desire in men and is also believed to contribute to sexual desire and function in women. The average testosterone level in premenopausal women is about 10% of the average male level. Hypoactive sexual desire disorder in men, commonly known as decreased libido or lack of sexual interest, can have many causes including depression, medications, and chronic illness, but may also be due to deficiency of testosterone (16, 17), especially in older men. A variety of testosterone preparations are available for treating men with low levels of testosterone, and this treatment usually restores libido. Testosterone is not recommended for use in men with normal levels of testosterone or in men who simply want to increase their sexual desire, as levels above normal increase the risk of prostate cancer.

Table 2

Medical Therapies for Women with Sexual Dysfunction

Drug (Brand Name)	Therapeutic Use	Approved Indications in United States
Estradiol vaginal tablets (VAGIFEM); Conjugated estrogens vaginal cream (PREMARIN vaginal cream); Estradiol vaginal ring (ESTRING)	Vaginal atrophy in menopausal women (vaginal dryness, pain during sexual intercourse, vaginal itching)	Vagifem: atrophic vaginitis in menopausal women. Estring: moderate to severe symptoms due to postmenopausal vaginal atrophy (dryness, burning, itching, and pain during intercourse) and for urinary urgency/pain with urination
Bupropion (WELLBUTRIN, ZYBAN)	Selective serotonin uptake inhibitor (SSRI)—induced sexual dysfunction*	Depression, seasonal affective disorder, smoking cessation
Testosterone†	Hypoactive sexual desire disorder (low libido) usually when low testosterone is present*	Not approved for use in women in the United States INTRINSA (transdermal testosterone patch) is approved in the European Union for treatment of hypoactive sexual desire disorder in women with surgically induced menopause receiving estrogen therapy

Information in this table is from the United States Product Circulars for the medications listed and from the EU Summary of Product Characteristics for INTRINSA. Information about possible side effects can be found in the "Patient Information" for each drug, and the "Important Safety Information" which are available on each product's website.

*Off label use in the United States SSRIs include fluoxetine, sertraline, paroxetine, escitalopram, citalopram.

†Preparations approved in the United States for men include injectable testosterone, gels, patches, buccal tablets (absorbed through the gums), implantable pellets.

Medicines for Women Are Lacking

Unfortunately, there are few medications available for the sexual disorders that affect women (Table 2). This is particularly true for younger women who most commonly suffer from low desire, low arousal, or difficulty with orgasm. More research is needed. Presently, the only FDA-approved medications for treating sexual dysfunction in women are estrogen preparations for dyspareunia related to vulvovaginal atrophy (a post-menopausal condition that is associated with vaginal dryness, irritation, soreness, urinary frequency and urgency, and pain during intercourse).

The clinical success of VIAGRA in men increased interest in finding pharmacological treatments for women with sexual dysfunction. However, trials of VIAGRA in women failed to show significant benefit and the drug development program for this indication has been discontinued. Unfortunately, the quest for medications to help women with sexual problems has led to criticisms of both the pharmaceutical industry and physician-experts who consult for the industry. Despite the epidemiological data, which shows that a significant proportion of women have sexual dysfunction, these critics insist that female sexual dysfunction is an illness created by doctors under the influence of their pharmaceutical industry allies.

Many factors—biological, psychological, and social—contribute to sexual response in women, and it is challenging to find an abnormality that can be corrected with medication. Thus, behavioral, cognitive, and sexual therapies continue to be the main therapies for sexual dysfunction in women (3). While some studies have found varying degrees of improvement with non-pharmacological therapies [with response rates varying from 37% to 82% in 9 studies reviewed by Basson (3)], outcome data evaluating these non-pharmacological approaches are severely limited by the different durations of treatment and follow-up, different methods for assessing the benefits of treatment, and the fact that not all studies are controlled (3, 18).

Clearly there is still a need for safe and effective sexual medicines that can be used in younger as well as older women. Fortunately research efforts continue. Investigational drugs which act upon neurotransmitters, increasing dopaminergic and decreasing serotoninergic activity, are postulated to have a favorable effect on sexual responsiveness (19), and several compounds are under evaluation in younger women (20).

Should Testosterone Be Used to Treat Low Sexual Desire or Low Arousal in Women?

It should be pointed out that testosterone is a promising treatment for older, postmenopausal women with decreased libido and low levels of testosterone. Testosterone, long considered the "male hormone" because of its role in the development of secondary sex characteristics in men (deeper voice, facial hair, etc.), is also produced in women and is thought to have an important role in female sexual function. Some but not all studies in women have found a direct correlation between testosterone levels, sexual desire, and frequency of sexual intercourse (21).

To date efforts to gain regulatory approval for testosterone use in postmenopausal women have been unsuccessful in the United States, but more successful in Europe. A testosterone patch, INTRINSA, for surgically menopausal women (women who had had their ovaries and uterus surgically removed) with hypoactive sexual disorder (low libido) was rejected by the FDA in 2005, and subsequently approved by regulatory authorities in the European Union in 2006 for specific use in surgically menopausal women with hypoactive sexual desire disorder who were also taking estrogen therapy. In the United States, some experts had concerns over the cardiovascular safety of this medication, because heart attacks in men occur at a much younger age than in women. However, it should be pointed out that in women who use the testosterone patch, blood levels of testosterone increase only to levels seen in pre-menopausal women (22), which are far lower than testosterone levels in men (22). In a recent review of potential safety issues in women taking testosterone because of symptoms of testosterone deficiency, Mathur and Braunstein found no good evidence for adverse cardiovascular effects, nor for increased risk of breast cancer (21).

The testosterone patch was subsequently studied in naturally menopausal women with hypoactive sexual desire disorder, showing benefit both in women taking estrogen and in women not taking estrogen (23). Use of the testosterone patch in naturally menopausal women has not as yet been approved by regulatory authorities in the United States or Europe. Nevertheless, despite the fact that in the United States, testosterone is not approved for use in women, about 2 million prescriptions of testosterone annually are written for women (24). Unfortunately, some of these preparations are prepared by pharmacies that mix testosterone with other ingredients to create topical creams, lozenges, oral gels, and drops. The standardization of such therapies is in question and therefore experts in the field do not encourage their general use (21).

However, some physicians with expertise in reproductive endocrinology (the study of hormones as it relates to fertility and the menopause) prescribe low doses of testosterone (by gel applied to the skin) on a case by case basis to individual patients with decreased libido who are postmenopausal, have low testosterone levels, and have not responded satisfactorily to treatment with estrogens. For many of these patients, especially those who are in healthy relationships and have suffered from loss of libido and markedly diminished sexual satisfaction with aging, the benefits of testosterone supplementation are worth the potential risks. As with many medications there are as yet no long-term safety data for this treatment. The main adverse effects include acne, oily skin, and increased hair growth at the site of application of testosterone. Virilization (the development of unwanted male sex characteristics such as facial hair, baldness, deepened voice) is rare.

Women who take testosterone should be made aware of the potential benefits and potential risks of therapy, and should be told that the treatment is not approved by the FDA at this time. Also, serum levels of total and free testosterone should be monitored to keep these levels in the normal range for young women.

One might ask whether testosterone would benefit younger premenopausal women with decreased sexual desire if such women had low levels of testosterone. There are few clinical trials evaluating this. However, one placebo-controlled study in 51 women of reproductive age with low testosterone levels due to pituitary gland disease found a positive effect of the testosterone patch on some but not all parameters of sexual function, including a positive effect on arousal (25).

Summary and Conclusions

Sexual dysfunction is a common problem of men and women and may have both organic and psychological components. Abnormalities such as vascular or neurologic disease in men with erectile dysfunction, low levels of testosterone in men and some women with decreased sexual desire (hypoactive sexual desire disorder), and possibly alterations in neurotransmitters in women with low desire and low arousal may be the initial cause of the problem. The evaluation of patients with sexual problems should take into account organic and psychological factors, and treatment should combine medical and psychosocial therapies, as appropriate for the individual patient. The introduction of VIAGRA for men with erectile dysfunction, which is often due to vascular or neurogenic causes, has dramatically improved the prognosis of men with erectile dysfunction. Nevertheless psychological factors may still need to be addressed in patients who respond to VIAGRA and similar treatments. When choosing a medicine for an individual patient, as with any treatment, the benefit/risk balance must be taken into account and the patient should be fully informed about potential benefits as well as potential side effects. When there are no medications approved for use for a sexual disorder, such as premature or early ejaculation, the doctor and patient may sometimes cautiously use medications that are approved for other uses, but have been found effective in that particular sexual disorder.

There are very few medicines for sexual dysfunction in women. For women with low libido (hypoactive sexual disorder) and low levels of testosterone, the testosterone preparations that are available for men are not approved for use in women in the United States. Yet, physicians may prescribe testosterone in some women because the clinical trial data support the effectiveness of testosterone replacement, and both physician and patient perceive that the benefit/risk balance is acceptable. The lack of approved medications for women with sexual problems is of concern and argues for more research to understand the appropriate drug targets for women with sexual problems such as low desire, low arousal, and difficulties with orgasm.

References

1. Goldbeck-Wood, S. (2010). Commentary: Female sexual dysfunction is a real but complex problem. *BMJ, 341*, p. c5336.
2. Moynihan, R. (2010). Merging of marketing and medical science: female sexual dysfunction. *BMJ, 341*, p. c5050.
3. Bhasin, S. and Basson, R. (2008). Sexual dysfunction in men and women. In: Kronenberg H, Melmed, S, Polonsky, K, Larsen, PR ed. *Williams Textbook of Endocrinology*, 11th ed. Philadelphia: Saunders Elsevier; pp. 701–737.
4. Basson, R. (2006). Clinical practice. Sexual desire and arousal disorders in women. *N. Engl J. Med, 354*, pp. 1497–1506.
5. McCall, K. and Meston, C. (2007). Differences between pre- and postmenopausal women in cues for sexual desire. *J Sex Med, 4*, pp. 364–371.
6. Segraves, R.T. (2010). Considerations for diagnostic criteria for erectile dysfunction in DSM V. *J Sex Med, 7*, pp. 654–660.
7. Feldman, H.A., Goldstein, I., Hatzichristou, D.G., Krane, R.J., McKinlay, J.B. (1994). Impotence and its medical and psychosocial correlates: results of the Massachusetts Male Aging Study. *J Urol, 151*, pp. 54–61.
8. Johannes, C.B., Araujo, A.B., Feldman, H.A., Derby, C.A., Kleinman, K.P., McKinlay, J.B. (2000). Incidence of erectile dysfunction in men 40 to 69 years old: longitudinal results from the Massachusetts male aging study. *J Urol, 163*, pp. 460–463.
9. Laumann, E.O., Paik, A., Rosen, R.C. (1999). Sexual dysfunction in the United States: prevalence and predictors. *JAMA, 281*, pp. 537–544.
10. Lindau, S.T., Schumm, L.P., Laumann, E.O., Levinson, W., O'Muircheartaigh C.A., Waite, L.J. (2007). A study of sexuality and health among older adults in the United States. *N Engl J Med, 357*, pp. 762–774.
11. Shifren, J.L., Monz, B.U., Russo, P.A., Segreti, A., Johannes, C.B. (2008). Sexual problems and distress in United States women: prevalence and correlates. *Obstet Gynecol, 112*, 970–978.

12. Segraves, R.T. (2010). Considerations for an evidence-based definition of premature ejaculation in the DSM-V. *J Sex Med, 7,* pp. 672–679.
13. Masters, W., Johnson, V. (1970). *Human Sexual Inadequacy.* Boston: Little, Brown, and Company.
14. Waldinger, M.D., Olivier, B. (2004). Utility of selective serotonin reuptake inhibitors in premature ejaculation. *Curr Opin Investig Drugs, 5,* pp. 743–747.
15. Waldinger, M.D., Zwinderman, A.H., Olivier, B. (2003). Antidepressants and ejaculation: a double-blind, randomized, fixed-dose study with mirtazapine and paroxetine. *J Clin Psychopharmacol, 23,* pp. 467–470.
16. Diaz, V.A. Jr., Close, J.D. (2010). Male sexual dysfunction. *Prim Care, 37,* pp. 473–489, vii–viii.
17. Bhasin, S., Cunningham, G.R., Hayes, F.J., Matsumoto, A.M., Snyder, P.J., Swerdloff, R.S., Montori, V.M. (2010). Testosterone therapy in men with androgen deficiency syndromes: an Endocrine Society clinical practice guideline. *J Clin Endocrinol Metab, 95,* pp. 2536–2559.
18. Heiman, J.R. (2002). Psychologic treatments for female sexual dysfunction: are they effective and do we need them? *Arch Sex Behav, 31,* pp. 445–450.
19. Pfaus, J.G. (2009). Pathways of sexual desire. *J Sex Med, 6,* pp.1506–1533.
20. Nappi, R.E., Martini, E., Terreno, E., Albani, F, Santamaria, V., Tonani, S., Chiovato, L., Polatti, F. (2010). Management of hypoactive sexual desire disorder in women: current and emerging therapies. *Int J Womens Health, 2,* pp. 167–175.
21. Mathur, R., Braunstein, G.D. (2010). Androgen deficiency and therapy in women. *Curr Opin Endocrinol Diabetes Obes, 17,* pp. 342–349.
22. FDA. (2004). Transcript, FDA Advisory Committee for Reproductive Health Drugs, December 2, 2004.
23. Davis, S.R., Moreau, M., Kroll, R., Bouchard, C., Panay, N., Gass, M., Braunstein, G.D., Hirschberg, A.L., Rodenberg, C., Pack, S., Koch, H., Moufarege, A., Studd, J. (2008).Testosterone for low libido in postmenopausal women not taking estrogen. *N Engl J Med, 359,* pp. 2005–2017.
24. Snabes, M.C., Simes, S.M. (2009). Approved hormonal treatments for HSDD: an unmet medical need. *J Sex Med, 6,* pp.1846–1849.
25. Miller, K.K., Biller, B.M., Beauregard, C., Lipman, J.G., Jones, J., Schoenfeld, D., Sherman, J.C., Swearingen, B., Loeffler, J., Klibanski, A. (2006). Effects of testosterone replacement in androgen-deficient women with hypopituitarism: a randomized, double-blind, placebo-controlled study. *J Clin Endocrinol Metab, 91,* pp. 1683–1690.

Connie B. Newman is an endocrinologist and adjunct associate professor of medicine at New York University School of Medicine, New York.

Anita P. Hoffer

NO

The Hidden Costs of the Medicalization of Female Sexuality—How Did We Get Here? An Overview

Medicalization in our society wields enormous socioeconomic influence and this influence is underestimated, particularly as it pertains to female sexuality. Medicalization has traditionally referred to a "process whereby non-medical problems become defined and treated as medical problems, usually in terms of illnesses or disorders" (Conrad, 1992; Farrell and Cacchioni, 2012) or a process wherein "more and more areas of everyday life have come under medical dominion, influence and supervision" (Zola, 1983). Especially in the arena of women's health, Tiefer (2012) and Starr (1982) have pointed out that the expanding cultural and institutional authority of medicine in the 20th century has been responsible for medicalization becoming a defining social process that places sexual problems and their treatments in an authoritarian framework of diagnoses and therapies that is overseen by healthcare providers (medical and non-medical) with expertise in the field of sexuality. The result is a system which favors a traditional medical approach and offers women as well as the doctors who care for them biomedical interventions in preference to other possible sexuality therapies. In addition, all too often, unfortunately, a system so deeply embedded in the fabric of our society leads to an ideal of sexual normalcy which in turn fosters market demand for "solutions"—products, pills, procedures and potions which will cure the illness and enable a captive population of consumers to experience improved, aka "normal," sex that conforms to social norms. The quest for female sexual "normalcy" results in a very large market which benefits the biomedical and biopharmaceutical industries that sell these remedies. But it also has costs that include personal and psychological harm, theoretical distortions in the way we conceptualize health and well-being, and political as well as socioeconomic impact.

An excellent example of this phenomenon is the disease entity known as "female sexual dysfunction," or FSD, which is listed in the *Diagnostic and Statistical Manual of Mental Disorders-IV* (hereafter, "the DSM"). For those unfamiliar with this publication, the DSM is published by the American Psychiatric Association and is used in the United States and to various degrees around the world. It provides a common language and standard criteria for the classification of mental disorders. Because it is relied upon by clinicians, researchers, psychiatric drug regulation agencies, health insurance companies, pharmaceutical companies, and policy makers, its sphere of influence is very wide and it has played a significant role in how the healthcare industry deals with female sexuality as well as other medical issues.

In the middle of the 20th century, medical experts commonly used the term "frigid" to describe women who were unable to experience "normal sex," as the word "normal" was being defined by the medical, mostly male, establishment. Kroger and Freed (1950) wrote an article in a leading medical journal stating that frigidity was a common gynecological problem that affected 75% of American women. Heading into the 21st century, the label of frigidity has morphed into female sexual dysfunction or "FSD." This is a new illness which may be used to describe any woman who has experienced ordinary, run-of-the-mill sexual problems and is bothered by them. The notion of a sexual "dysfunction" is relatively recent, appearing for the first time in the DSM in the 1980s. Since then, the definition of FSD has changed many times. In simplest terms, the condition is currently described as consisting of four sub-disorders: desire, arousal, orgasm, and pain (*Diagnostic and Statistical Manual of Mental Disorders-IV-TR,* 2000). Arousal disorder, also known as FSAD (female sexual arousal disorder) is defined as inadequate genital lubrication and swelling in response to sexual excitement. Female orgasmic disorder describes a condition in which a woman is unable to reach orgasm or is delayed in having one. A disinterest in sexual activity or lack of fantasies is called low desire or hypoactive sexual desire disorder (HSDD). Pain disorder is also known as dyspareunia or vaginismus, the experience of pain during sexual intercourse.

One problem with the aforementioned definition of FSD is that it is focused so narrowly on "function," such that experiences or difficulties once considered to be a common part of women's day-to-day experience have come to be labeled as the symptoms of a dysfunction (Leiblum, in Goldstein et al. 2006). Given that definition, it is not surprising that research protocols, surveys and psychometric questionnaires (often written by the drug companies or the medical experts whom they hire as consultants) that explore and document these common experiences and sub-disorders have "revealed" that nearly one in two women in the USA suffers from this "new" medical disease. Findings of this sort, which are increasingly common (Laumann et al. 1999; Laumann et al. 2005), are being widely publicized and incorporated into corporate-sponsored marketing campaigns for new drugs. But wait . . . red flags should be going up here. If roughly half of a study population has a condition and the other half does not, who's to say which half is "abnormal"? Indeed the distinction between a "difficulty" and a "disorder" has become seriously blurred. If left unchecked, the long-term impact of this trend on women (as well as their partners), and how they experience their sexuality, is potentially disastrous—not only as it applies to FSD but also as it applies to how they feel about themselves.

In order to understand some of the factors that have contributed to such a sweeping definition of FSD, it is necessary to explain how the academic and corporate worlds interact around the subject of research and development. The nature of this complex and co-dependent relationship is clearly laid out in the excellent book, *Sex, Lies and Pharmaceuticals* (Moynihan and Mintzes, 2010). Basic research is traditionally the province of academia whereas development is typically left to biomedical and pharmaceutical companies ("Big Pharma") which have the vast resources needed to conduct huge lengthy clinical trials navigate and comply with endless Food and Drug Administration (FDA) requirements and, once regulatory approval by the FDA is gained, market and sell the product. Historically, there has been a close collaboration between the drug companies and the thought leaders in academic medicine and psychology. Many of the academics that have played a fundamental role in helping Big Pharma ferret out "symptom patterns" end up shaping companies' assumptions about women's sexual problems. Often they have been paid by companies with a vested interest in seeing the scope of a new disease entity broadened as much as possible. At the heart of the matter is the question of whether common sexual ailments should be interpreted and treated as aspects or fluctuations of normal female sexuality, or as the symptoms of widespread medical conditions that are treatable with some sort of biomedical intervention. The potential for financially driven conflict-of-interest is significant and rarely acknowledged. On the one hand, it is understandable, and indeed part of their fiduciary responsibility to their shareholders, for drug companies to grow their markets and develop medications that can be marketed to the broadest range of people possible. On the other hand, some healthy skepticism may be warranted when we are exposed to messages that FSD is so highly prevalent, affecting anywhere from 20–50% of women (Moynihan and Mintzes, 2010).

Once armed with a functional definition of a "new disease," a biomedical company can then move ahead to gather together large groups of women and conduct surveys that are designed to evaluate the scope of the problem they have identified and defined. By designing and scoring these surveys so that an affirmative answer to any one of several questions places the respondent in the category of the condition under examination, women who don't necessarily feel sick may end up being told that they are. This is what is called "selling sickness to the wealthy healthy" (Moynihan and Mintzes, 2010). The data collected from these surveys is used to substantiate the claim that there is a huge unmet need for new treatments, including the drugs or procedures made by the company that conducted the survey in the first place. To facilitate these studies further, corporate employees move ahead with development of new devices and tools to measure and diagnose the symptoms their company identified. The availability of these tools tends to influence the problems that get investigated in the sense that if you have a ruler, you are probably going to be engaged in measuring length. By using these tools, countless numbers of women (the ones who did not feel sick in the first place) come to be labeled as suffering from the "condition" and thus become eligible to receive the sponsor's drug.

The USA is one of the very few countries in the world where direct-to-consumer (DTC) advertising in healthcare is legal. This allows the American consumer, male *or* female, to be directly targeted with information on TV and other media that allegedly is essential to their well-being. Even though DTC is regulated by the FDA if a pharmaceutical company is promoting their own drug, destructive or unhealthy stereotypes still often manage to find their way into these advertisements. The drug companies are eager to help potential patients recognize that they have a treatable illness so that they will consult their doctors for a remedy. Patients naturally take the information they hear from the media, and questions engendered by it, to their doctors. The local medical doctors (LMD's) are genuinely eager to provide the latest and best possible care for their patients. They may be eager to attend free, industry-sponsored educational programs, held during professional meetings or at corporate conferences and industrial centers. There the doctors are exposed to "cutting-edge" thinking about new clinical problems/conditions and the solutions that the company has developed for them. Prestigious thought leaders often serve as faculty at these educational programs, and it probably won't come as a big surprise that the speakers who are given the honor of lecturing to their peers very often are the same experts who were the consultants who have worked all along with the company to study, identify and define the clinical problem (Angell, 2004). While there is increasing scrutiny and legislation recently that addresses the tight relationship between biomedical marketing and the medical community, it is neither uniform nor universal and much of this activity is still permitted in most states. (Exceptions which restrict or prohibit some activities, as of this writing, include Massachusetts, Vermont, California, Minnesota, New Hampshire, West Virginia and Washington, DC.) It is worth noting that the above-described system operates to showcase the work of the thought leaders whose perspectives coincide with those of Big Pharma. These individuals are thus the ones who gain visibility among their peers. By contrast, dissenting voices, or alternative treatment approaches to these ailments are less likely to get comparable high-profile publicity. A potential result over time may be a trend toward a pro-drug bias which thus becomes the status quo in the medical community as well as in the wider public arena of debate about sex (Caplan and Cosgrove, 2004).

So far we have examined the forces that have allowed "more and more areas of everyday life in general to fall under medical dominion, influence and supervision" (Zola, 1983) and we have seen one example of this process of medicalization at work—namely the creation of FSD, an entirely new woman's sexual disease and its carefully defined sub-disorders (Moynihan and Mintzes, 2009).

What are the opportunity costs of the medicalization of female sexuality? In the business world, an opportunity cost is defined as the value of the next best choice that one gives up when making a decision—in other words, "what you would have done if you didn't make the choice that you did." What then are these costs, or what is the harm, if any, that results from a system which, according to some, favors a traditional medical approach and offers women as well as the doctors who care for them biomedical interventions in preference to other possible sexuality therapies?

Leonore Tiefer, the founder of the global grassroots campaign known as the New View (www.newviewcampaign.org), is a leading researcher, New York University psychology professor, sex therapist and renowned global activist who advocates for women's health and sexual rights. While she acknowledges that the conventional medical perspective does take non-biomedical interventions into account, she argues that the DSM definition of FSD and its four sub-types is much too focused on functional problems and too often leaves the whole patient out of the equation. Rather than the four *sub-disorders* of sexual illness, Dr. Tiefer proposes four *causes* of women's sexual difficulties: (i) psychological factors such as depression or abuse, (ii) relationship challenges including discrepant desire problems, (iii) broad societal factors that impact sexuality (e.g., religious taboos that leave us feeling ashamed of our bodies, economic factors that leave us exhausted from struggling to meet work and family responsibilities, and sex-negative cultures that help create our inhibitions), and finally, (iv) medical causes like surgical damage to nerves or adverse side effects (ASE's) from drugs (including but not necessarily limited to antidepressants) which can interfere with sexual desire or the ability to climax (Kaschak and Tiefer, 2001).

In the author's opinion, Dr. Tiefer's approach embodies a wiser and more thoughtful, holistic perspective. It leaves room for the whole person and doesn't force an individual into a mold constructed by external "experts." Sadly, constraining definitions in the field of sexuality are not new and they are not limited to FSD. In fact, they creep into other models of women's sexual behavior as well. For example, in Masters and Johnson's classic model of the sexual response cycle published nearly 50 years ago, four stages of response were defined: excitement, plateau, orgasm, and resolution (Masters and Johnson, 1966). But this linear model is desire-driven and postulates the arousal pattern is the same for men and women. As sexuality educators, we now know that many women do not move through all these phases sequentially and many do not even experience all of these phases. The Masters and Johnson biologic model ignores context, pleasure, satisfaction, and relationship. It sets up expectations that leave many women who don't experience it feeling like they have failed or may be doing something wrong. A few years ago, a Canadian researcher published a less biologically focused model of female sexual response; she named it the circular or "non-linear model of female sexual response" which runs on triggered or responsive sexual desire (Basson, 2001). Like Dr. Tiefer's consideration of female sexual problems, Dr. Basson also leaves room for the individual . . . ALL of her . . . and much less room for self-criticism, shame and depression.

There are additional downsides, or opportunity costs, to classifying the normal fluctuations of everyday sexual life as a medical dysfunction and using pills, potions or procedures to treat them. Not only is it expensive (and potentially dangerous) to take medicines that are not really needed, or that are ineffective, but also it places an additional financial burden on a healthcare system that is already struggling to keep its head above water. Equally important is the ever-present potential for the new "wonder drug" to cause direct ASEs or cross-reactivity with other medicines that a patient may already be taking. For example, a man who is taking nitroglycerin for angina or amyl nitrates ("poppers") for recreational use should *not* be taking Viagra because it can cause a precipitous drop in blood pressure and even a heart attack. In addition, treating a symptom without knowing its cause may gloss over a deeper medical problem which does indeed require a medical intervention. Here again, Viagra is a useful case in point because it is well-documented that erectile difficulties can be a predictor of cardiovascular problems or predisposition to stroke (Banks et al. 2013; Hall et al. 2010). If the Viagra appears to solve the problem temporarily by enabling an erection, the underlying circulatory issues may go undetected until they become dangerously severe. Alternatively, the erectile difficulty may have nothing at all to do with a physiological problem and rather be an expression of relationship problems or other psychosocial pressures (Rosen, 2007). This is not an anti-Viagra admonition . . . it is merely a recommendation that pills be used when the etiology of the problem is clearly understood. And finally, there are no pills or procedures that can be prescribed to deal with psychosocial or cultural components of sexual difficulties. The quest to find them can siphon off energy from doing a different kind of research, namely taking psychological and emotional inventory and uncovering non-biological contributors to the problem.

In addition to the above-described opportunity costs, there are also examples of potentially harmful procedures that have emerged recently and are available to women who have concluded, or been convinced, that their dissatisfaction with their vulvas can best be addressed by creation of designer-vaginas through surgical intervention. Female cosmetic genital surgery (FCGS) includes the practices of labiaplasty, re-virginization (tightening and/or hymen restoration), and other vaginal rejuvenation protocols.

Notwithstanding warnings from the American College of Obstetricians and Gynecologists about severe complications that may arise from these procedures (ACOG, 2007), FCGS is one of the fastest growing fields of surgery in the country and is "increasingly affordable, available, and normative" (Tiefer, 2010). FCGS has moved from insurance-reimbursed procedures to "cash-only" with private financing plans offered by the individual surgeon in his (or her) office. This obsession with genital beauty is now embraced by doctors who are members of the International Society of Cosmetogynecology (ISCG; information available at www.iscg.com). The ISCG is exploiting the body insecurity issues of their patients and promoting the impression that so-called aberrations are abnormal by failing to inform them that genitals are as diverse as faces or fingerprints. It has even gone so far as to be on record as promoting, marketing and even national franchising of cosmetic genital procedures . . . all this despite documented potential consequences of this surgery such as infection, altered sensation, pain, adhesions, severe hemorrhaging, scarring and even obstetric risks! Surely there must be a "next best choice" for resolving sexual dissatisfaction that is better than opting for a procedure as extreme and potentially harmful as this one.

Perhaps the most subtle and insidious of all of the opportunity costs arising from this troubling trend toward creating diseases is how the focus on the quick fix can distract us from recognizing that conscious reframing of the meaning of sexual satisfaction throughout the life cycle is a gradual but rich, ongoing opportunity for personal growth. This growth process is disrupted by the crippling sexual stereotypes that abound in our society. It starts early with the sexualization of our children. Then, preconceived notions of how we should feel about sex, how much of it we should want and have in order to be "real women," whether we should shave, wax, color (www.mynewpinkbutton.com), pierce, be-jewel (www.themodernsavage.com/2010/03/06/theart-of-vajazzling) or surgically alter our genitals in order to be considered young and attractive, and how (or if) we should continue to perform sexually as we age (Marshall, 2012) are all expectations that women (and men) are saddled with in American society. It is most assuredly unfair to blame Big Pharma and the biomedical establishment in general for these cultural issues. But to the extent that they capitalize on these trends and exploit these messages to persuade women they have newly defined "diseases" for which they need products, medications, and services, the phenomenon of medicalization of sexuality is contributing to collective sexual angst and depriving women of becoming their own unique sexual selves.

In closing, balance is important. It is crucial to emphasize that many of the medical advances that have come about as the result of collaboration between corporate and academic medical researchers are vitally important; our health would be sorely compromised without the fruits of their efforts. The author, who was trained in academic medicine, was privileged to work for several years in the field of women's health in one of the world's leading pharmaceutical companies. It would be difficult to find a more sincere, dedicated, intelligent group of professionals. Not all are as cynical as sometimes portrayed in discussions of this topic. There are professionals of unimpeachable integrity in both worlds.

Being skeptical about medical approaches and pharmaceutical solutions does not mean losing all trust in the value of these contributions. Critical analysis of the phenomenon of medicalization is not a rejection of medicine; rather it highlights the potential for unnecessary pathologization, biological reductionism, the downplaying of social factors and the prioritizing of profit and career expansion over health and well-being (Farrell and Cacchioni, 2012). As Moynihan and Mintzes (2009) point out, we all need to take a little more time to sort out the fake hype from the genuine hope. The milder a problem is, the smaller the benefit that can come from a medical label and a pill, and the bigger the risk of doing more harm than good. But there are medical and physiological components to all behavior, including sexual behavior. There are many women and their partners whose sexual difficulties cause real suffering and in whom real medical problems are affecting their ability to experience sexual pleasure. Psychosocial approaches may not work for, or may not be available to, all of these people. Therefore, innovative companies that may be able to offer drugs, devices, or procedures for these women have the potential to make a needed contribution, *provided* that their remedies are proven to be necessary, safe, and effective (Hoffer, 2011).

References

1. ACOG (American College of Obstetricians and Gynecologists), Committee on Gynecologic Practice. (2007). ACOG Committee Opinion No. 378: Vaginal 'rejuvenation' and cosmetic vaginal procedures. *Obstet Gynecol.,110*(3), 737–738.
2. Angell, M. (2004). *The Truth About the Drug Companies: How They Deceive Us and What to Do About It.* New York and Canada: Random House.
3. Banks, E., Joshy, G., Abhayaratna, W. P., Kritharides, L., Macdonald, P. S., Korda, R. J., et al. (2013). Erectile Dysfunction Severity as a Risk Marker for Cardiovascular Disease Hospitalization and All-Cause Mortality: A Prospective Cohort Study. *PLoS Med 10*(1).
4. Basson, R. (2001). Human Sex-Response Cycles. *Journal of Sex & Marital Therapy 27,* 33–43.
5. Caplan, P. J., & Cosgrove, L. (Eds.). (2004). *Bias in Psychiatric Diagnosis* [Hardcover]. Oxford, UK: Rowman and Littlefield Publishers.
6. Conrad, P. (1992). Medicalization and Social Control. *Annual Review of Sociology, 18,* 209–232.
7. *Diagnostic and Statistical Manual of Mental Disorders-IV-TR* (2000). American Psychiatric Association, Arlington, VA, http://psych.org/MainMenu/Research/DSMIV.aspx
8. Farrell, J., & Cacchioni, T. (2012). The Medicalization of Women's Sexual Pain. *Journal of Sex Research, 49*(4), 328–336.
9. Goldstein, I., Meston, C., Davis, S., & Traish, A. (Eds.). (2006). *Women's Sexual Function and Dysfunction: Study, Diagnosis and Treatment.* Boca Raton: Taylor and Francis. P. 263
10. Hall, S. A., Shackelton, R., Rosen, R. C., & Araujo, A. B. (2010). Sexual Activity, Erectile Dysfunction, and Incident Cardiovascular Events. *American Journal of Cardiology, 105*(2), 192–197.
11. Hoffer, A. P. (2011). A Review of ORGASM INC.: The Strange Science of Female Pleasure. *American Journal of Sexuality Education, 6,* 317–322.
12. Kaschak, E., & Tiefer, L. (Eds.). (2001). *A New View of Women's Sexual Problems. Part I, 1–8.* New York: The Haworth Press, Inc.
13. Kroger, W., & Freed, C. (1950). Psychosomatic Aspects of Frigidity. *Journal of the American Medical Association (JAMA), 143,* 526–532.
14. Laumann, E., Paik, A., & Rosen, R. (1999). Sexual dysfunction in the United States: prevalence and predictors. *JAMA, 281,* 537–544.
15. Laumann, E. O., Nicolosi, A., Glasser, D. B., Paik, A., Gingell, C., Moreira, E., et al. (2005). Sexual problems among Women and Men Aged 40–80 Years: Prevalence and Correlates Identified in the Global Study of Sexual Attitudes and Behaviors. *International Journal of Impotence Research, 17*(1), 39–57.
16. Marshall, B. (2012). Medicalization and the Refashioning of Age-Related Limits on Sexuality. *Journal of Sex Research, 49*(4), 337–343.
17. Masters, W. H., & Johnson, V. E. (1966). *Human Sexual Response.* New York: Bantam Books.
18. Moynihan, R., & Mintzes, B. (2010). *Sex, Lies and Pharmaceuticals: How Drug Companies Plan to Profit from Female Sexual Dysfunction.* Vancouver, BC: Greystone Books.
19. Rosen, R. C. (2007). Erectile Dysfunction: Integration of Medical and Psychological Approaches. In S. R.

Leiblum (Ed.), *Principles and Practices of Sex Therapy - 4th edition*. New York: The Guilford Press.
20. Tiefer, L. (2010). Female Genital Cosmetic Surgery. Paper presented at Framing the Vulva: Genital Cosmetic Surgery and Genital Diversity, Las Vegas.
21. Tiefer, L. (2012). Medicalization and Demedicalization of Sexuality Therapies. *Journal of Sex Research, 49*(4), 311–318.

ANITA P. HOFFER, a clinical sexologist and sexuality educator, originally worked at Harvard Medical School in the field of male reproductive biology and chemical male contraceptives before moving into the pharmaceutical industry to work in women's health. She now lectures at universities, medical schools, and nonprofit organizations, and presents at national and regional conferences on sexuality and aging.

EXPLORING THE ISSUE

Should Sexual Problems Be Treated Pharmaceutically?

Critical Thinking and Reflection

1. What are the main causes of sexual problems?
2. Do you think most Americans would prefer a pharmaceutical treatment for sexual problems or psychological treatment? Why?
3. Is there potential for an integrated approach for addressing sexual problems? Explain.
4. Why do you think there are so many more medicinal treatments available to men?

Is There Common Ground?

Advocates both for and against sexual medicine express concern for patients suffering from sexual difficulties. The disagreements between them center around understanding—and treating—the root causes of sexual problems. Are sexual difficulties biologically, psychologically, or socially constructed? Or, are they the result of a combination of these factors?

Connie Newman explains that "sexual dysfunction is a common problem of men and women and may have both organic and psychological components." Since it is not only a psychological problem, it shouldn't be treated only with psychosexual therapy. Treatment needs to combine medical and psychosexual therapies "as appropriate for the individual patient." She also notes that men have a variety of medications available to treat sexual dysfunctions, but that there are few such medical options for women. More research is needed to develop safe and effective sexual medicines for women. Why do you think there are fewer medical treatments available for women?

In citing activist and psychology professor Leonore Tiefer, Hoffer outlines four root causes of sexual difficulties: psychological factors, such as depression and abuse; relationship problems, including problems with desire; societal factors, such as sexual shame imparted by religious messages; and medical causes. What overlap do you observe between these two authors with respect to the causes of sexual problems?

One of the most interesting, yet least discussed, aspects of the controversy over the medicalization of sexuality is the future of sex therapy. If people are able to have their sexual issues treated chemically by their general practitioners, OB-GYNs, and urologists, what role will the therapist fill? Newman suggests that pharmacological and psychological treatments can co-exist, and even used together. Hoffer similarly says that skepticism of sexual medicine does not mean an outright rejection of it. It may, indeed, have its right uses for the right people. How comfortable would you be taking medications for sexual problems? Would you rather deal with these issues through counseling first? Or would you be more comfortable raising the issue in doctor's office than on a therapist's couch?

In their new book, *Older, Wiser, Sexually Smarter,* sexuality educator Peggy Brick and her colleagues argue that many of the physical changes that people experience related to their sexuality as they grow older are not inherently problematic and may not necessarily require medication or therapy. Rather, they necessitate a new understanding of one's sexuality and, perhaps, new sexual behaviors that may not be quite the same as when they were age 18. What do you think of this viewpoint? Can sexuality be experienced differently as one grows older? What adjustments might a person need to their sexual expectations and behaviors as they grow older?

Reference

(1) Laumann, E., Paik, A., & Rosen, R. (1999). Sexual dysfunctions in the United States. *Journal of the American Medical Association, 281*: 537–544.

Additional Resources

Brick, P., Lunquist, J. Sandak, A., & Taverner (2009). *Older, Wiser, Sexually Smarter: 30 Sex Ed Lessons for Adults Only.* Morristown, NJ: The Center for Family Life Education.

Frank, J.E., Mistretta, P., & Will, J. (2008). Diagnosis and treatment of female sexual dysfunction. *American Family Physician, 77*(5): 635–642.

Green, B. The quick fix: *Orgasm Inc.* examines the treatment of female sexuality. *Honolulu Weekly,* May 4, 2011.

Katz, S. Return of desire: Fighting myths about female sexuality. *AlterNet,* July 23, 2008.

Tiefer, L. (2008). *Sex Is Not a Natural Act & Other Essays.* New York, NY: Westview Press.

Internet References . . .

International Society for Sexual Medicine (ISSM)

Established in 1982 to promote erectile dysfunction research, the ISSM today encourages research and education across a broad spectrum of human sexual functioning. The ISSM publishes the *Journal of Sexual Medicine.*

www.issm.info

New View Campaign

The New View Campaign is an educational campaign that challenges myths promoted by the pharmaceutical industry and calls for research on the causes of women's sexual problems. Visitors will find developing information on Intrinsa at this website.

www.NewViewCampaign.org

World Association for Sexual Health

The World Association for Sexual Health (WAS) promotes sexual health throughout the lifespan and through the world by developing, promoting, and supporting sexology and sexual rights for all. WAS accomplishes this by advocacy actions, networking, facilitating the exchange of information, ideas, and experiences, and advancing scientifically based sexuality research, sexuality education, and clinical sexology, with a transdisciplinary approach.

www.WorldSexology.org

Selected, Edited, and with Issue Framing Material by:
Ryan W. McKee, *Widener University,* Tracie Q. Gilbert, *Widener University,*
and
Jayleen Galarza, *Shippensburg University of Pennsylvania*

ISSUE

Do the Benefits of Male Circumcision Outweigh the Risks?

YES: Larkin Callaghan, from "Making the Cut: Is It Time to Put the Circumcision Debate to Rest?" *The 2x2 Project* (2012)

NO: Elizabeth Reis, from "Circumcision Debate: Cut the Hyperbole," *Nursing CLIO* (2014)

Learning Outcomes

After reading this issue, you will be able to:

- List at least two reasons why male circumcision is practiced.
- List two critiques of routine male circumcision.
- List two reasons for the decline in male circumcision rates in the United States.

ISSUE SUMMARY

YES: Larkin Callaghan, Managing Director of the Center for AIDS Research, believes the public health benefits, for both men and women, make male circumcision worth the risks.

NO: Elizabeth Reis, author and Visiting Professor at the Macaulay Honors College at the City University of New York, argues that circumcision proponents misguide parents by irresponsibly likening its effectiveness to vaccines.

Circumcision, a practice in which the foreskin of the penis is cut and removed to expose the glans, is one of the most common surgical procedures in the United States. It is typically performed when a child is an infant, and it is carried out for a variety of reasons. Many Jewish parents, as well as those who practice a number of other religious traditions, perform the procedure as a religious rite. Others have their child circumcised because there are presumed health benefits which make the practice worthwhile. For example, several studies have shown that circumcision reduces the risk of urinary tract infections, as well as sexually transmitted infections—including HIV. Other parents simply do it because the child's father was circumcised. "*Like father, like son*" is all the rationale they need.

Despite these reasons, the number of newborn males being circumcised in the United States has declined dramatically since the 1960s. Many American parents who choose not to circumcise their sons question the perceived health benefits, pointing out that studies showing the most dramatic results were conducted in sub-Saharan Africa. They question if the practice is really necessary given higher rates of condom usage and greater access to sexuality education in the United States. These questions, combined with the pain felt by infants during the surgery and recovery period, have caused some to not only question the necessity, but to argue that the practice is a violation of a child's human rights. Anti-circumcision activists (known in activist circles as "intactivists") compare the practice to female genital cutting (FGC), sometimes called female genital mutilation (FGM) or female circumcision, which is condemned by organizations like the World Health Organization. While FGC can vary in severity from culture to culture, the practice typically involves cutting and removing the exposed clitoral tissue from infant or adolescent girls as a religious or cultural ritual. Both FGC and male circumcision, critics argue, are based on tradition and religious belief rather than science or necessity. However, comparisons of male circumcision to FGC often draw stern reprimands from anti-FGC activists, as female cutting is seen as far more invasive and physiologically damaging.

Though male circumcision is still commonly practiced in the United States, opponents have made great strides in raising awareness about their stance. In 2012, anti-circumcision activists in San Francisco, California, succeeded in placing a measure on the ballot for the November elections. Passage of the ballot would have banned male circumcision within the city, and imposed fines or even jail sentences on doctors who performed the procedure on anyone under the age of 18. The measure was widely criticized by the medical and religious communities. To ban the procedure outright, medical groups argued, could pose risks to public health and infringe upon a family's right to make medical decisions for their children. Members of the Jewish community, along with other religious groups and the American Civil Liberties Union, argued that a ban would infringe on religious freedom. Many considered the measure an outright expression of anti-Semitism, pointing to Internet comics featuring an anti-circumcision superhero named "Foreskin Man." In one comic the character, with blonde hair and blue eyes, "rescued" Jewish infants from rabbis depicted as "sinister-looking" villains (Watson, 2011). Several groups, including the Anti-Defamation League, sued the government to have the measure stricken from the ballot.

In July of 2012 a Superior Court Judge removed the measure, noting that the regulation of medical services falls to the state, rather than individual cities. Despite the setback, anti-circumcision advocates promised to continue their efforts. While they have had little success in stopping the practice through legal means, changing circumcision rates indicate that there is, indeed, an evolving view of the practice.

Guidelines from health organizations have also had an impact on circumcision rates in the United States. In 2012 the American Academy of Pediatrics (AAP), which had previously suggested that there were only *potential* benefits to male circumcision, changed their policy statement to read that "there are clear medical benefits that outweigh the risks" and encouraged insurance companies to cover the procedure (American Academy of Pediatrics, 2012). They did not, however, suggest infant male circumcision become routine. After the AAP's change, circumcision rates in the United States began to rise slightly. In late 2014, the Centers for Disease Control and Prevention echoed the AAP's stance in a preliminary set of guidelines, stopping short of encouraging routine circumcision, but suggesting that for male infants, and even uncircumcised adult men, it is worth the risk. Still, the debate continues.

In the following YES selection, Larkin Callahan describes research pointing to the public health and interpersonal benefits of male circumcision. She argues that the procedure, along with behavioral interventions like condom use and testing, is an important tool in reducing the spread of sexually transmitted infections. Furthermore, in order to increase circumcision rates, parents of male infants, as well as uncircumcised adults, need to be "sold" on the practice to advance public health. In the NO selection, Elizabeth Reis provides a historical perspective on male circumcision and explains why exaggerated claims on both sides of the debate prevent parents from making the best and most informed decision for their child. Parents should be provided with not only information about the perceived public health benefits of the procedure, Reis argues, but also with basic information about infant and adult male sexual anatomy and physiology.

References

American Academy of Pediatrics (2012). Circumcision policy statement. Retrieved from http://pediatrics.aappublications.org/content/130/3/585

Watson, J. (June 18, 2011). Ánti-circumcision comic hero called anti-semitic, *Huffington Post.* Retrieved from www.huffingtonpost.com/2011/06/18/anticircumcision-comic-he_n_879739.html

YES

Larkin Callaghan

Making the Cut: Is It Time to Put the Circumcision Debate to Rest?

Circumcision is not a new practice by any means. It is well known as a religious practice in many communities. But its implementation for public health purposes has been controversial. Raising ethical concerns and questions of tractable population health impact, the procedure has gained increasing attention in the past couple of years as it treads on unprecedented ground—surgery for the prevention of infectious disease.

Research in support of circumcision as a protective measure against the spread of HIV and other sexually transmitted diseases is mounting, countering concerns of its potential risks. Most recently, the American Academy of Pediatrics officially articulated that the health benefits outweigh the risks.

The circumcision debate turns largely on biological, behavioral, and relational factors.

Biologically speaking, the foreskin is the ideal environment for bacterial and viral infections to flourish. Heat and lack of oxygen facilitate the growth of pathogens. When the inner foreskin is retracted during heterosexual intercourse, for example, it is exposed to the vaginal secretions of a female partner, which if carrying HIV and other sexually transmitted infections easily fosters transmission. A 2009 study indicated that the greater the size—and therefore surface of—the foreskin, the higher the incidence of HIV in an infected male, underscoring how it can be a breeding ground for the virus.

A recent study conducted by Dr. Ronald Gray of Johns Hopkins University, in which researchers followed Ugandan adult study participants after a circumcision intervention, showed that the subsequent risk of acquiring HIV was reduced for the 40-month follow-up period. In addition, circumcision decreased the viral load of high-risk human papillomavirus—the strains that can cause penile, cervical, and anal cancers—in men.

Other studies have shown significant reductions in bacteria after circumcision, which also benefits the female partners of the men. Adverse events or complications appear to be rare in both HIV-positive and HIV-negative men who undergo the procedure, with one study documenting moderate-to-severe complications occurring between [3 and 4] percent of men regardless of HIV-status.

Behavior change also features prominently in the circumcision debate. Opponents of circumcision express concerns that the procedure may contribute to a perception of immunity against HIV and result in the reduction of condom use. Additionally, there is a question of whether or not it may increase the number of sex partners one has, for the same reason of rationalizing post-surgery invincibility.

Many circumcision intervention studies are not so cut and dry, so to speak. A number contain significant education components, which makes the procedure's contribution to HIV risk reduction less clear.

One study examined the length of time men who had undergone circumcision waited before engaging in sexual activity. If a man is HIV-positive, the risk of infecting a partner is notably higher if he engages in sexual activity before the wound heals, highlighting the importance of the quality of the surgery to minimize healing complications and the importance of concurrent education to delay sexual activity. Since a 2008 study showed that after 30 days, 73% of HIV-positive men had healed wounds, compared to 83% of HIV-negative men (the discrepancy owing to greater time HIV-positive individuals may take for any kind of wound healing), this is of particular importance.

It seems that being married, not single, might diminish concerns about the length of time it takes wounds to heal. There was no statistically significant difference in time waited to engage in sex post-surgery between HIV-positive and HIV-negative men who were married; nearly 28 percent and 29 percent, respectively, engaged before the wound healed, which is the single greatest cause of post-procedure complications. However, among single men, roughly 13 percent of HIV-positive men resumed sex before their wound was fully healed, compared to about 6 percent of HIV-negative men.

The significant difference between the single HIV-positive men and the single HIV-negative men underscores the potential for altered beliefs about post-circumcision HIV transmission. However, HIV-positive men reported more sexual partners and less consistent condom use than the HIV-negative men throughout the study—itself underscoring the difficulty of risky behavior change. Encouragingly, condom use among HIV-positive men increased over the course of the study.

The relational impacts of circumcision have also been examined. Researchers have assessed the perceptions and opinions of the women in relationships with those who have undergone the surgery. A 2009 study indicated that women whose male partners were circumcised were either more sexually satisfied than they had been previously, or felt no difference. Thirty-nine percent of women indicated more satisfaction, 57 percent noted no change, and less than 3 percent said they were less satisfied than they had been when their partners were uncircumcised. The greater satisfaction, according to the women, was primarily attributed to better hygiene.

These results are important, as one of biggest issues around circumcision is "the sell." The best way to make that sell, researchers argue, is to have the female partners articulate their preference for and encouragement of circumcision to their male partners. It appears that there may also be a generational difference in the acceptance and uptake of the procedure. Dr. Gray and his colleagues have found that adolescent males disproportionately access circumcision procedures. Even some fathers who encouraged circumcision in their sons refused the procedure themselves.

Precautions are of course essential. Research has shown that it takes practitioners approximately 100 circumcision procedures before they can be considered adept at performing the surgery.

And not all the research being done has produced promising results, specifically for women. While some studies suggest that HIV-discordant couples—HIV-negative woman and HIV-positive man—benefit from circumcision and the procedure prevents infection of the woman, other studies have produced conflicting results.

Biologically, the circumcision seems to benefit primarily men in preventing the contraction of HIV from an HIV-positive female partner. The same is not necessarily true for HIV-negative women whose male partners are HIV-positive. This biologically higher risk of infection for women is well known among public health researchers. Of course, decreasing the prevalence of HIV-positive men will ultimately, in the long run, help to lower the HIV incidence in women.

Indeed, population health benefits are already emerging. Dr. Gray and colleagues showed earlier this year that in Uganda, 37 percent of the reduction in HIV incidence could be attributed to circumcision, since there was no change in risk behaviors. The impact was not observed in women.

Circumcision seems to make economic sense. The male circumcision procedure costs \$30-\$60 in adults, and \$5–\$10 in infants. For each HIV infection avoided due to five to 15 male circumcisions performed, the savings reach well into the billions of dollars with the assumptions of a \$150–\$900 cost per infection (depending on HIV incidence in a specific region) over the next ten years.

Critics of course remain, and most vocally claim that other strategies, like education and behavior change, are viable solutions that should be championed. Regarding the sustained HIV epidemic and the hopeful strategies of condom use, testing, and treatment, Dr. Gray himself remarked, "I don't know how to change behavior, I wish I did."

So while behavior change strategies are perhaps the most important intervention to counter the HIV epidemic, they are not the only effective HIV interventions. The evidence seems to indicate that voluntary circumcision also makes the cut as a contender in the global fight against HIV.

Larkin Callaghan is the Managing Director of the Center for AIDS Research.

Elizabeth Reis

NO

Circumcision Debate: Cut the Hyperbole

What frustrates me about the circumcision debate is that both sides exaggerate their claims. Maybe this happens with most controversies, but I am particularly attuned to this one because I have been researching the history of circumcision in the United States. A recent article by Brian J. Morris and others in the *Mayo Clinic Proceedings* overstates the health benefits of circumcision and downplays the risks [1]. They argue that the public health benefits (i.e. reducing sexually transmitted diseases) are so great that circumcision should be mandatory. Mandatory?

Inflammatory statements such as this have been around for a while. In the nineteenth century, proponents alleged that circumcision prevented masturbation and syphilis.

Yes, you read that right. Physicians as well as parents believed that an uncircumcised boy would fuss unnecessarily with his penis, tugging on the annoying foreskin, ultimately leading to masturbation. In fact, some doctors looked to Jewish boys as exemplars of good morality; since Jews mandated infant circumcision, these boys, the theory went, never masturbated to excess. One doctor went so far as to say that Jewish boys only masturbated when they associated with uncircumcised boys, those "whose covered glans have naturally impelled them to the habit [2]." Such a habit among Jews, he claimed, though not unheard of, was exceedingly rare. Ya, right.

With syphilis too, Jewish men stood out. Many circumcision advocates, Jews and non-Jews alike, held that Jewish men had a remarkable immunity to the sexually transmitted disease. Not all agreed, however, as some physicians had actually treated circumcised Jewish patients for syphilis. Yet Jews continued to be praised for what was seen as their hygienic practices. One nineteenth-century doctor who performed scores of circumcisions on adult men as a way to cure genital herpes suggested that this problem could be alleviated if we would "follow in the footsteps of Moses and circumcise all male children [3]."

Despite competing claims about circumcision's purported benefits, the health assertions persisted, shifting from a focus on masturbation and syphilis to urinary tract infections, phimosis (a restricted foreskin), cancer, and AIDS. Today it's easy to dismiss the threat of masturbation as a reason to remove an infant's healthy foreskin, and even penile cancer is quite rare, but it's harder to argue against stemming the spread of HIV/AIDS. Everyone wants to put an end to this disease, but I have to wonder if permanently altering a baby's genitals is a likely way, or even a sensible way, to do that.

Morris is a well-known circumcision advocate, and in this article he suggests that circumcision is so beneficial that parents should consider it akin to vaccination. From his perspective, circumcision keeps the individual boy from getting urinary tract infections and phimosis as a child, and then later when he becomes sexually active his circumcision keeps him from becoming a public health risk. Hence, Morris argues, it's like a vaccine in that it prevents future illness.

Treating circumcision as a vaccine sets us on a dangerous path. If men think that their circumcisions alone will protect them from sexually transmitted diseases, they are sorely mistaken. Circumcision may decrease the risk of some diseases (though even that is contested), but having had the procedure does not work like a vaccine—it does not confer resistance or immunity—and men still need to use condoms to protect against STIs and HIV/AIDS.

Morris says that those parents who refuse circumcision are analogous to parents who refuse vaccination for their children. While it might be true that both groups of parents subscribe to a less interventionist medical model, the two decisions are very different, and it's inflammatory to link them. There are other ways to avoid sexually transmitted diseases—condoms, for example. Vaccines, by contrast, are our only way to prevent the spread of devastating childhood diseases like measles, mumps, rubella, and polio.

Yet how, then, can parents make an informed decision when both sides overstate their claims? Those who advocate circumcision inflate the benefits and dismiss the risks; and those who oppose circumcision amplify the risks and minimize the benefits. For example, "intactivists" raise the issue of pain, physically at the time of the surgery and emotionally for years beyond. Certainly babies feel pain, but are they permanently, psychically scarred for life, as some intactivists suggest? That would be difficult to prove. Similarly, sensitive nerve endings are destroyed with circumcision, and so it's likely that sexual sensitivity would be diminished, but how much that weakens sexual pleasure is hard to ascertain, since circumcised infants grow up to be men with no pre-circumcision sexual experience with which to compare their current sensation. And I'm sure many of us know circumcised men who think the sex they are having is just fine. Better than fine, even.

To me, arguments that are less prone to hyperbole are the most compelling. And in this debate I stick to what is undisputed: opting for circumcision is a decision to permanently change someone else's body. That is a big responsibility. If we are committed to allowing parents this choice, then I would like to see them presented with the most basic and clearly stated information: what exactly happens during a circumcision? What is the foreskin for? What is being cut away? How is it done? How long does it typically take? How long does it take to heal? What does a circumcised and uncircumcised penis look like at infancy and in adulthood? Many new parents do not know even these fundamental facts. I know I didn't.

The circumcision decision should not be made lightly, and parents should not feel pressured by exaggerated claims of benefits or risks. We owe our baby boys that much.

References

[1] Brian J. Morris, Stefan A. Bailis, Thomas E. Wiswell. "Circumcision Rates in the United States: Rising or Falling? What Effect Might the New Affirmative Pediatric Policy Statement Have?" *Mayo Clinic Proceedings*, 2014. DOI:10.1016/j.mayocp.2014.01.001

[2] M. J. Moses, "The Value of Circumcision as a Hygienic and Therapeutic Measure," *New York Medical Journal* 14:4 (November 1871), 368–374

[3] A.U. Williams, "Circumcision," *Medical Standard* 6 (1889), 138–39

Elizabeth Reis is an author and Visiting Professor at the Macaulay Honors College at the City University of New York.

EXPLORING THE ISSUE

Do the Benefits of Male Circumcision Outweigh the Risks?

Critical Thinking and Reflection

1. What are the perceived health benefits of male circumcision?
2. In what ways do religion and cultural norms influence the practice and popularity of male circumcision?
3. How does public health research and policy influence the popularity of male circumcision?
4. Do you feel that comparisons between male circumcision and female genital cutting are valid?
5. If, in the future, you have a son, would you have him circumcised? Why or why not? For those who already have sons, what influenced your decision to, or not to, circumcise?

Is There Common Ground?

Callighan summarizes recent research on circumcision, which points to significant public health benefits associated with the procedure. She also makes note of one study that examined female partners' circumcision preference and sexual satisfaction rates. Should data like this be taken into account when deciding whether or not to circumcise?

Reiss takes a historical perspective when examining the cultural practice of circumcision. Can you think of other common medical procedures that have fallen out of favor over the years? What caused their decline in popularity? Ultimately Reiss decries the use of hyperbole, or exaggeration, from both sides of the debate. What are some examples of these exaggerations, according to Reiss? What information does she suggest parents need to know before deciding on whether or not to circumcise their infant?

Hyperbole aside, it is clear that infants cannot consent to a procedure such as circumcision and that, ultimately, parents must make the best decision possible with the information they have. Opponents liken the procedure to FGC or nonconsensual genital surgeries performed on intersex infants. Many supporters, however, look at routine male circumcision in the same way they view preventative vaccines. After comparing these two selections, are you more or less likely to support the circumcision of male infants?

Additional Resources

Idov, M. (October 26, 2009). Would you circumcise this baby? *New York Magazine*. Retrieved from http://nymag.com/health/features/60135/

Morris, B., Bailis, S., & Wiswell, T. (2014). Circumcision rates in the United States: Rising or falling? What effect might the new affirmative pediatric policy statement have? *Mayo Clinic Proceedings*. Retrieved from http://www.mayoclinicproceedings.org/article/S0025-6196(14)00036-6/fulltext

Rosin, H. (October 26, 2009). The case against the case against circumcision: Why one mother heard all of the opposing arguments, then circumcised her sons anyway. *New York Magazine*. Retrieved from http://nymag.com/health/features/60146/

Silva, C. (March 1, 2016). To circumcise or not to circumcise: A new father's question. *New York Times*. Retrieved from http://www.nytimes.com/2016/03/04/fashion/mens-style/circumcision-fatherhood-dilemma.html

Internet References . . .

American Academy of Pediatrics, "Where We Stand: Circumcision"

https://healthychildren.org/English/ages-stages/prenatal/decisions-to-make/Pages/Where-We-Stand-Circumcision.aspx

Centers for Disease Control and Prevention, "Male Circumcision"

http://www.cdc.gov/hiv/pdf/prevention_research_malecircumcision.pdf

Intact America

http://www.intactamerica.org/

Selected, Edited, and with Issue Framing Material by:
Ryan W. McKee, *Widener University,* Tracie Q. Gilbert, *Widener University,*
and
Jayleen Galarza, *Shippensburg University of Pennsylvania*

ISSUE

Is Female Genital Cutting a Violation of Women's Health and Human Rights?

YES: Olivia Jackson, from "Cutting Out the Devil: Female Genital Mutilation," *Evangelicals for Social Action* (2014)

NO: Zelaika Hepworth Clarke, from "Empowering Perspectives of Ethnic Female Genital Modifications (EFGM)," An original essay written for this volume (2016)

Learning Outcomes

After reading this issue, you will be able to:

- Define female genital cutting, and distinguish between four main types of FGC processes.
- Describe the debate between uses of the terms cutting, circumcision, and mutilation.
- Compare and contrast ideas about the physical harm of genital cutting with our current understanding of sexual physiology.
- Discuss the connection between FGC and socioeconomic disempowerment.

ISSUE SUMMARY

YES: Olivia Jackson, a writer and filmmaker who focuses on international social justice issues affecting women and children, argues that female genital mutilation is a violation of women's rights on all fronts, including the political, medical, cultural, and spiritual.

NO: Zelaika Hepworth Clarke, an African-centered social worker and cultural and clinical sexologist, argues that "female genital modifications" are an important part of many people's cultural and spiritual practices around the world and should be respected as such.

Around the world, an estimated 140 million women and girls have had parts of their genitals surgically removed in ceremonies intended to honor and welcome them into womanhood within their communities. Most often, part of the clitoris is cut away, but in some cases even more of the external anatomy is removed. The ritual, nearly four millennia old, is said by many of its supporters to promote chastity, religion, group identity, cleanliness, health, family values, and marriage goals. The practice, known to many as female genital cutting (FGC), is deeply embedded into the sub-cultures of many African and Asian countries, including Ethiopia, Sudan, Somalia, Sierra Leone, Kenya, Tanzania, Chad, Gambia, Liberia, Mali, Senegal, Eritrea, Ivory Coast, Nigeria, Egypt, and Indonesia. While most often practiced in developing countries within in the Southern hemisphere, FGC is no stranger to the West, having been routinely recommended by psychiatrists during the early 1900s, as a means to stave off masturbation and perceived hypersexual desire. Though the procedure has been deemed illegal in the United States, over half-a-million women and girls there are considered either at-risk for undergoing FGC, or have already undergone the procedure through covert means.

Female genital cutting is known by several different names. In this issue we utilize the term "cutting" in an attempt to reduce bias. Other terms used include female circumcision, female genital modification, and female genital mutilation. Each of these terms, however, female genital cutting included, carries with it some bias depending on one's perspective. Supporters of the practice, or those who take a relativist approach, often refer to the practice as female genital modification to simply imply a change from one physical state to another. Opponents typically prefer to use female genital mutilation as it brings to mind a brutal or destructive process. Both the United Nations and World Health Organization use the term mutilation, highlighting the procedure's connection to a host of sexual health problems, including hemorrhaging, urinary and pelvic infection, painful intercourse, infertility/natal delivery complications, and, in some cases, death.

From a human rights perspective, many argue that FGC amounts to systemic violence against women and girls, many of whom undergo the process in infancy long before they can consent or have an awareness of what is happening. Besides denying women sexual pleasure and orgasm through the removal of clitoral tissue, opponents argue, the consequences of FGC also strain the overburdened health care systems in the developing nations where it is practiced.

Proponents of female genital cutting deny claims about sexual dissatisfaction and social disempowerment, citing its connection to intracultural ideas about beauty, hygiene, non-clitoral sexual pleasure, elevated social status, and feminine matriarchal empowerment. While the assumption many hold is that women are cut by men in the community, many women report having had the procedure conducted by elder women, with entire female clans designated to make sure the tradition is continued. One challenge to understanding the arguments in support of the practice (or even the full nature of the practice itself) rests in its esoteric nature. Many women who experience genital cutting often do so through secret societies, in which traditions are orally transmitted and the members are sworn to life-long confidentiality. Failure to submit to the ritual of FGC and the expectation of confidentiality may result in permanent ostracism from the group or, in extreme cases, forced cutting at a later point in time.

Cultural clashes can occur when families migrate from countries where FGC is customary to parts of the world where it is not practiced. In their new countries, some parents may ask traditional practitioners or local health professionals to perform the circumcision on their daughters which could, depending on the law, lead to child endangerment charges. Women who have already undergone the procedure may run the risk of being stigmatized by healthcare professionals who hold negative views of, or are unfamiliar with the practice. In other cases, women who fear forced FGC in their home countries may apply for political asylum in the United States and other countries where it is outlawed.

In 1999, Western researcher Carla Obermeyer caused great controversy when she published a review of empirical data on FGC. Her findings indicated that, while there were some related health issues reported, there was no statistically significant correlation between the practice and a number of health conditions thought to be directly linked. Since that time, several other authorities have come out in favor of more medicalized and/or harm-reductive approaches to the practice, including the use of standard, more hygienic tools, and consistent antiseptic access. At each turn, however, this perspective has been challenged by feminist activists and FGC survivors who assert that no real alternative interpretation of FGC can be made outside of seeing it as a violent, repressive re-imagining of women's bodies and female sexuality.

Ultimately, the question at hand is whether or not the traditional practice of female genital cutting should be seen as a violation of women's health and human rights or as a powerful symbol of cultural identity. Accepting FGC would allow those who have cherish the practice to maintain the essence of their traditional rites of passage for young girls. Advocating against FGC could ultimately save many girls from the risk of adverse short- and long-term outcomes, and even save lives. In the following YES and NO selections, writer and filmmaker Olivia Jackson, speaks out against female genital mutilation as a ritual whose time has passed and a violation of human rights. Zelaika Hepworth-Clarke argues that, while extreme cases may still occur, the value of the practice can be seen in its connections to a group's cultural heritage and spiritual traditions.

YES

Olivia Jackson

Cutting Out the Devil: Female Genital Mutilation

"I saw dried blood on the jagged edge of the blade. She spat on it and wiped it against her dress . . . The next thing I felt was my flesh, my genitals, being cut away. I heard the sound of the dull blade sawing back and forth through my skin."

"They see it as an act of love, they see it as preparing their child for adulthood."

Controversy surrounds the custom of female genital mutilation. Even the name itself has been the subject of dispute: Circumcision? Cutting? Mutilation? Western physicians attending to circumcised women in the 1970s quickly decided that "circumcision" did not nearly describe the practice. Activists argue that "cutting" also implies a simpler procedure and result than the procedure often entails, yet for those whose traditions require it, "mutilation" indicates Western judgment of a misunderstood custom. For the purposes of this article I shall refer to it as female genital mutilation (FGM), in line with international legal norms and the increasing number of women from practicing cultures who have become advocates against it.

The World Health Organization (WHO) definition states: "Female genital mutilation comprises all surgical procedures involving partial or total removal of the external genitalia or other injuries to the female genital organs for cultural or non-therapeutic reasons."

They classify four types of FGM:

Type 1—Clitoridectomy: partial or total removal of the clitoris and sometimes the prepuce (clitoral hood).

Type 2—Excision: partial or total removal of the clitoris and the labia minora, with or without excision of the labia majora (the labia are "the lips" that surround the vagina).

Type 3—Infibulation: narrowing of the vaginal opening through the creation of a covering seal, formed by cutting and sewing together the remainder of the outer labia, with or without removal of the clitoris.

Type 4—Other: all other harmful procedures to the female genitalia for non-medical purposes, e.g. pricking, piercing, incising, scraping, and cauterizing the genital area.

The age at which FGM is performed also varies. In Ethiopia, it is soon after birth. Elsewhere it is shortly before marriage. Generally, however, girls are operated on between the ages of 4 and 14.

FGM is practiced in 28 African nations, some Middle Eastern nations such as Yemen, and in other parts of the world, such as Indonesia. While it is not a requirement of any major religion, it is performed on girls from Muslim, Christian, and Jewish communities.

The practice affects 100–135 million women and girls who have already been operated on, and a further 2–3 million more each year. That's 6,000 to 8,000 per day, or up to six girls per minute.

Immigrants in Western nations sometimes bring the practice with them: The African Women's Health Center at the Brigham and Women's Hospital in Boston used the 2000 Census to estimate that 228,000 women in the United States either have had FGM or are at risk, and the number has risen 35 percent since 1990. Canada, Europe, and Australia have similar statistics, and report girls being taken back to their nation of origin to have FGM performed during school vacations.

Records of FGM being practiced date back at least 3,000 years. Its origins lie in ensuring female fidelity and thus paternity confidence (infibulation, Type 3, creates a "chastity belt" of scar tissue across the vaginal opening). It slowly became a matter of family honor, ensuring virginity and therefore marriageability.

Many of these beliefs still stand, alongside others. Meanings are added as time goes by—something which is a symbol of purity and honor can quickly become seen as aesthetic too. Myths about FGM include that it makes a woman smell more attractive to her husband, that it is necessary for hygiene and health, and, more recently, that it prevents HIV transmission. In a culture where every woman has a particular type of FGM performed on her, there is no way to know what healthy, intact female genitals are actually like: "Excision is our tradition. The clitoris grows long if we don't remove it, like the male part. In order to be clean and to wash yourself it must be removed. I'm told that in Congo, women hang weights on that female part until it grows as long as an elephant's trunk!" an elderly woman in Mali, West Africa, told the *Independent*.

Somali-born former Dutch politician Ayaan Hirsi Ali recalls learning from her grandmother that "this hideous *kintir*, my clitoris, would one day grow so long that it would swing sideways between my legs."

Without honor and the assurance of virginity/fidelity, and with the clitoris intact, it is assumed that a girl's libido will become uncontrollable and she will be promiscuous, "dirty," her genitals even possessed by the devil, who must be cut out. No one will marry her and she will bring shame on her family, become an outcast in her community. Both Hirsi Ali and Somali supermodel and UN spokeswoman Waris Dirie remember being labeled "disgusting" and "impure" at only 5 years old because they were not yet circumcised.

Other beliefs include the enhancement of fertility and the husband's sexual pleasure. In some cultures the clitoris is seen as causing disease, even death, if the baby's head or husband's penis should touch it.

When religion and tradition become the same thing, some mistakenly see it as a religious requirement, and it is even promoted by some religious leaders. In Bandung, Indonesia, where 100 percent of women undergo FGM, "mass circumcision" events are free of charge, sponsored by the Assalaam Foundation, a Muslim educational and social-services organization, believing that if a girl prays with unclean genitals, her prayers will not be heard.

These beliefs would not have sounded too far-fetched in the US or UK a century ago, however. Medicalized male and female circumcisions became seen as a "cure" for epilepsy, masturbation, and hysteria in the 1900s (thus the origins of the continued practice of male circumcision in the US today). L. E. Holt's standard pediatric textbook *Diseases of Infancy and Childhood*, in publication 1897–1940, advised cauterizing the clitoris and blistering the vulva. In *Sexuality and the Psychology of Love*, Freud claimed, "The elimination of clitoral sexuality is a necessary precondition for the development of femininity."

Long- and short-term medical consequences have been widely documented. Ironically, most highlight the fact that the purposes of FGM actually achieve quite the opposite:

- 10 percent of girls die as a direct result of the surgery (hemorrhage, shock, infection, and septicemia), and up to 25 percent die of later complications. Generally, no anesthetic or antiseptic are used. Dr. Comfort Momoh, a Nigerian-Ghanaian midwife, recounts: "Anybody with scissors and a blade can perform it. It could be a barber. In some markets in Nigeria quite openly there is a queue, and this is performed by a man removing the clitoris, and at the same time, using the same blade, performing some tribal marks on the chest. More than 90 percent of the circumcisers don't have any anatomical knowledge and no medical training. They go in with the aim of removing it and sealing the area and they do more damage to the vulva area."
- High ongoing infection rates and the formation of abscesses do nothing to improve hygiene, fertility, or the "attractive smell" of a wife.
- The use of shared instruments to perform the surgery can only further, rather than prevent, HIV transmission.
- Infibulated women, due to the vulva being sewn up, find urination can take around 15 minutes. The urethra has been covered, causing bladder stones and sometimes incontinence. When a hole the width of a matchstick has been left, menstrual flow can also back up, causing pelvic inflammation and infertility.
- Long-term pain from nerve damage, and pain during sex (for infibulated women, the husband must force his way through the scar tissue seal in order to penetrate her). This has been documented as reducing the husband's sexual pleasure, rather than increasing it.
- Scar tissue cannot dilate during childbirth, so prolonged labor, excessive bleeding, tearing, and obstetric fistula are prevalent: The WHO estimates that maternal mortality doubles and infant mortality quadruples as a result of infibulation.
- Trauma occurs when girls are held down, often by their mother or grandmother, while the procedure is carried out. Most will not have known beforehand what is about to happen, and to be held down by a trusted adult deeply damages the mother/child bond. Dirie recounts that, as she lay in pain for weeks with high fever and infection, "All I knew was that I had been butchered with my mother's permission, and I couldn't understand why." Post-traumatic stress, anxiety, and

depression have all been observed as a result of the above complications which follow women throughout their lives.

With so many dangers inherent in the practice, why does FGM not stop? The reasons are as deep-seated as the original objectives. Gerry Mackie, professor of political science at the University of California at San Diego, points out that it can be equated to straightening children's teeth: If an outsider were to tell us that it was bad for children, we would not believe them. If they proved that it caused long-term problems, we would still not want to be the only parents whose children had crooked teeth. If all the girls in a society undergo FGM, there is no basis for comparison with those who have not, and when it is a taboo subject there is no forum for discussion. Mackie also mentions "belief traps" and "self-enforcing beliefs: a belief that cannot be revised because the believed costs of testing the belief are too high."

Where medical knowledge is extremely limited, the connection between FGM and complications may not be made: Are these problems not simply part of every woman's life? Even when understanding is present, the benefits are seen to far outweigh the risks. If this is necessary for becoming an adult and being accepted in society, why would anyone risk ostracism (which, when resources are scarce, could also affect survival)? Coupled with the belief that female genitals are evil or shameful, and the bullying associated with not having undergone FGM, this leads some girls to actually request the surgery. The exact nature of this "informed consent" thus becomes a moot point.

Most of those who continue the tradition are women: mothers and grandmothers. This is because these women know very well how difficult a daughter's life will be if she is unable to marry. As Dr. Momoh explains, it's a question of providing as much security for your daughter as you can. "[FGM] is like insurance to them: Whereas in the Western community we want to educate our children, we want them to go to university, in some of the villages they are not educated, they don't have means of education and so to secure a future for your daughter would be to FGM her. As a mother you want to do the best for your daughter, so they continue with FGM."

In a culture where girls/women are dependent on their parents, then their husband, they have no choice over their own bodies (or, later, those of their daughters). Unmarried girls risk becoming a burden to their parents. For parents, ensuring a daughter's virginity and therefore marriage ensures that she will no longer be an expense. Frances Althaus, executive editor of *Inter-national Family Planning Perspectives*, quotes Rogaia Abusharaf, "To get married and have children, which on the surface fulfills gender expectations and the reproductive potential of females, is, in reality, a survival strategy in a society plagued with poverty, disease, and illiteracy. . . . The socioeconomic dependency of women on men affects their response to female circumcision."

She also quotes Nahid Toubia: "This one violation of women's rights cannot [be abolished] without placing it firmly within the context of efforts to address the social and economic injustice women face the world over."

The socioeconomic factor is also why circumcisers themselves will not easily give up the practice: It is their livelihood, and in a close-knit community they have every reason to know who has not yet been operated on and to make sure she soon is.

In recent decades, the practice has continued, or even increased, as a reaction against external intervention and perceived cultural imperialism. It is seen to preserve cultural identity and has been associated with nationalist and anti-modernization movements, which is perhaps why FGM is on the rise amongst immigrants to the US.

This perceived attack on culture is at the heart of some of the international controversies. Opponents of FGM have been accused of seeing African women purely as oppressed victims of culture, not as social agents in their own right. Practicing cultures point out Western double standards, observing our high abortion rates—even more harmful to children—and unnecessary cosmetic surgery. Increasingly popular "vaginal reconstruction," "labia trimming," and "hymen recreation" surgeries certainly involve "partial or total removal of the external genitalia or other injuries to the female genital organs for cultural or non-therapeutic reasons."

Arguing the right to cultural expression is entirely valid, but feminists have pointed out that "culture" is not a monolith but constantly in flux, and while women do benefit from cultural rights, they suffer simply because they are women. Cultural rights and relativism do not address intra-group suffering and perhaps protect the perpetrators of FGM more than those at risk. Writers such as Nanci Hogan have suggested focusing on an ethic of human thriving rather than trying to universalize human rights or cultural rights.

Numerous pieces of legislation have been enacted that prohibit the practice (as I write, the Ugandan Parliament has unanimously voted in favor of illegalization). For those to whom FGM is an essential part of life, this is an encroachment by Westernism. For many years the UN hesitated to prohibit FGM outright, yet recent international, regional, and national laws that support the right to cultural expression are outlawing the defense of custom or tradition to perpetrate violence against women. FGM is condemned as a violation of human rights: the right to freedom from torture or cruel treatment; the right to life when FGM results in death; the right to the highest attainable health, bodily integrity, gender equality, and child rights.

Western nations have taken strong action against FGM: The US passed the Federal Prohibition of Female Genital Mutilation Act in 1995, and the case of Togolese teenager Fauziya Kassindja set a precedent in US law in 1996, allowing women to seek asylum on the basis of the risk of FGM if they went home.

Legislation can only do so much to change attitudes, however, and it is increasingly being backed up by initiatives in many nations: In November 2009 Burkinabe First Lady Chantal Compaore called for a "zero tolerance" ban on FGM in Africa and asked all Africa's first ladies to join her.

At a community level, education programs led by organizations like Tostan have been highly successful, challenging attitudes, raising awareness, and encouraging religious leaders to speak out against the practice. They provide practitioners with alternative means of income, persuade governments to include this taboo subject in school curricula, and teach men what really happens to their daughters due to FGM. Some communities have adopted alternative initiation ceremonies: In Kenya and Senegal, "circumcision by word of mouth" is gaining popularity, replacing traditional rites with a program of holistic education and coming-of-age ceremonies that celebrate the girls.

Among medical practitioners fighting FGM is Dr. Comfort Momoh, who advises women both at risk of and living with FGM and performs two to three infibulation reversal surgeries per week in London, UK. She advises healthcare workers worldwide, speaking on behalf of the World Health Organization and as an expert witness to the UK Parliament.

She stresses the importance of engaging with communities, rather than simply labeling traditions as "wrong." In 2008 Queen Elizabeth II presented her with an MBE (Member of the British Empire) award for outstanding service to the Commonwealth. In Western nations, social workers, teachers, and police are slowly learning the warning signs when a girl is at risk of FGM. The French surgeon Pierre Foldès has perfected an operation that reverses FGM, which he performs free of charge to any woman who requests it. Despite death threats from Muslim extremists, he continues to operate, explaining, "Excision is worse than rape because the family are involved."

In the arts, outspoken Senegalese rap artist Sister Fa held a tour last year titled Education sans Mutilation (Education without Mutilation), and speaks openly against what she underwent as a child. Former Somali supermodel Waris Dirie now serves as UN special ambassador for the elimination of FGM, using her status to speak on behalf of women world- wide. The movie of her autobiography, *Desert Flower*, was released at the 2009 Venice Film Festival.

FGM is a practice which often elicits moral outrage. But in reality we are all affected by harmful traditions in our own cultures: The pressures for girls (and boys) to look, dress, and act in certain ways are doubtless detrimental and are horrifying to most African cultures. We consent, or simply turn a blind eye, to many "normal" practices: What do we do to please the opposite sex, to be accepted, to get ahead? It is important to question our own reliance on cultural explanations of social practices: What core beliefs do we have which are less than God's standard?

FGM is not in line with a gospel of health, healing, wholeness, and liberty. But in exposing abuses within a culture, we must not discard or denigrate the culture altogether. FGM can be stopped, but success is only possible through holistic engagement with our fellow human beings.

Olivia Jackson is a writer and filmmaker who focuses on international social justice issues affecting women and children.

Zelaika Hepworth Clarke

NO

Empowering Perspectives of Ethnic Female Genital Modifications (EFGM)

Genital modifications of African women evoke strong emotive reactions in the West. There are many types of genital modifications that have been performed around the world and in different complex ritual contexts. Members of the Uganda-based initiative Reproductive, Education, and Community Health Programme (REACH) have proposed the term "female genital cutting" (FGC) as a more precise, less value-laden term (Eliah, 1996). Ahmadu (2007) uses the terms "female circumcision" (FC), "female genital cutting" (FGC), and "female genital surgeries or operations" as generic descriptions for the various types of traditional female genital operations. The terms "female genital alteration" (FGA) and "female genital modification" (FGMo) can also be used instead of "female genital mutilation" (FGM), which is judgmental. The term "ethnic female genital modification" (EFGM) (Puccioni, 1904; Erlich, 1986; Fusaschi, 2003) can be used as a substitute, as "modification" is an acceptable term to both Western women and African immigrants and "ethnic" underlines the plurality of populations with altered genitalia (Gallo, Tita, & Viviani, 2006).

The hegemonic perspectives of FGM—emphasis "mutilation"—dictates that it is "backward," "barbaric" and "primitive," in order to establish the practice as unacceptable. "Westerners, perceiving the practices from outside the culture, can only regard them as barbaric anachronisms" (Lightfoot-Klein, 2000, p. 449). However, "the people of the countries where FGM is practiced resent references to 'barbaric practices imposed on women by male-dominated primitive societies', especially when they look at the Western world and see women undergoing their own feminization rites intended to increase sexual desirability: medically dangerous forms of cosmetic plastic surgery, for instance, or high heels" (Toubia,1995, p. 232). I do not seek to romanticize practices of any genital modifications but rather to highlight the cultural nuances and offer a counter hegemonic narrative often missing in clitocentric discourse.

Most women who have ethnic genital modifications do not interpret their vulvas as being mutilated and are offended by the term FGM (Anuforo, Oyedele, & Pacquao, 2004). Ahmadu, a first-generation Sierra Leonean/American academic, professional anthropologist who is circumcised comments: "I often wonder whether if I had not been sexually active prior to my own initiation I would not also doubt my sexual capacity and ability to experience pleasure and orgasm, especially after being told over and over again by the Western media, 'FGM experts,' as well as the general society, that I am sexually 'mutilated'. I would certainly be confused by all these negative messages and misinformation" (Ahmadu, 2007, p. 285). The word "mutilation" has been criticized because it is "thought to imply excessive judgment by outsiders and insensitivity toward individuals who have undergone the procedure" (Eliah, 1996, p. 13). Critics have argued that the discussion of EFGM by Westerners has been excessive, essentializing, and paternalistic (Shell-Duncan & Herlund, 2000). A number of African scholars (Abusharaf, 2000; Ahmadu, 2000; Amadiume, 1987; and Oyěwùmí 2003) have critiqued the dominant discussion on female circumcision as "the 'maternalistic' approach of Western women out to 'save' their African 'sisters'" (Herlun & Shell-Duncan, 2007, p. 28). Anti-FGM campaigns have also "been dubbed the 'white woman's burden' to liberate affected African women and future generations from sexual oppression and human indignity" (Ahmad, 2007, p. 283). In general, adult African women are seen as in need of protection, while adult Western women are considered capable of making their own decisions (Kjoller, 2005).

Imagining Third World women as powerless victims incapable of self-determination, self-expression, or reasoned decision-making is problematic, demeaning, and inaccurate. These colonial constructions are in contrast to the image of the emancipated Western woman, who is in control of her income, her body, and her sexuality (Kapur, 2002). These arrogant assumptions are associated with the legacy of imperialism, where the freedom, autonomy, and right to self-determination of non-Western people are crushed by the belief in the superiority and power of one culture over another (Coomaraswamy, 2004). Many writings on FGC fail to recognize the diversity of African women, based on nationality, class, ethnicity, education, and age, and instead imagine homogenized, essentialized African women who are "powerless, constrained by tradition, defined by men, unable to think clearly, and having only problems and needs, not choices" (Kratz, 1999, p. 108). Instead, they are classified and defined by the shared victimization of FGC (Krats, 1999; Obiora, 1997). Although women can share a sense of unity after having experienced ethnic genital modifications, their experiences, opinions, and feelings vary significantly. Yet, despite the obvious diversity of African cultures, ethnicities, rituals, spiritualities, and concerns, genital modifications have been casually lumped together under the label FGM/FGC/FC.

The Diversity of Genital Modifications

There are many different types of genital modifications found throughout the world, and they are performed for many reasons. There are reductive forms, such as clitoridectomy and labial excision; vaginal restriction, including infibulations or the cutting-off of the vulva and sewing up of the vagina (considered one of the most extreme forms of FGM); castration, defined as the removal of clitoris or ovaries; sterilization surgeries that modify the genitals; and nymphotomies or surgical procedures that cut away the inner labia, which can cause the shrinking scar tissue to restrict the size of the vaginal opening, making sex more pleasurable for some men (Love, 1992). Expansive forms of genital modifications include: labia stretching, and dilation of the vaginal canal and of the vagina. There are also women who choose to enlarge their clitorises through anabolic steroids, testosterone, or clitoral pumps. Other classifications of genital modification that do not fall under reductive or expansive forms include ritual defloration, or altering the hymen; hymenorrhaphy, which includes thickening the hymen; elimination of the natural lubrication through the insertion of herbs, grass, ground stones, etc.; introcision; abortion practices; clitoral piercings; genital tattoos; gender reassignment surgeries like metoidioplasty (clitoral release) or phalloplasty (the creation of a penis), as well as genital cosmetic surgeries (GCS) including labiaplasty (alters the labia minora and/or majora); elective genitoplasty (alterations of the vulva); vaginoplasty (tightening the inside of the vagina) hymenoplasty (reconstructing the hymen); Labia majora augmentation (plumping up the outer lips); vulvar lipoplasty (using liposuction to remove fat deposits in the mons pubis); G-spot augmentation (enhancing the size of g-spot); and clitoral hood reduction, aka hoodectomy (used to reduce the hood of skin surrounding the clitoris).

Counterproductive Medical Discourses

The United Nations (UN) Special Working Group assigned to study legal claims applied to female genital modifications concluded that no international treaty could directly address female genital cutting, finding that the issue raises a number of challenging questions (UN, 1986). Although I recognize extreme cases of infibulation can cause great harm, the generalizations made about health risks associated with all forms of FGC are highly problematic. Complications should be differentiated by type of female genital modification. Much of the medical discourse on FGC has been found to be exaggerated and counterproductive. A number of researchers, discussed below, have found credibility gaps that often appear between well-meaning propaganda and the real-life experiences of affected women. Statistics on a type of genital modification from a specific region are not necessarily applicable to other modifications carried out in other regions: e.g. data about infibulation gathered from Sudan may not be comparable to procedures performed in Sierra Leone.

When data collected about FGC becomes closely examined and scrutinized, the association between health problems and FGC is difficult to establish through medical "facts" (Shell-Duncan & Hernlund 2000). Each source of data (e.g. case reports, clinical and hospital records, hospital-based case control comparisons, self-reported retrospective survey data, etc.) bears serious limitations. Obermeyer (1999) completed the first systematic review of the biomedical literature on female genital modifications and concluded that complications from genital surgeries are very scarce and "severe complications are relatively infrequent" (p. 97). Not all ethnic female genital modifications are dangerous, and the procedures can be performed safely to minimize alleged health risks.

Shell-Duncan published a comprehensive review of the literature about reporting on the frequency of complications differentiated by type of female circumcision and found, after considering the limitations of clinical and cross-sectional survey data, that long-term and obstetrical consequences was quite rare for all types of FGC. There are many factors to consider when determining the causal role of FGC, with health risks including the training of the circumciser, geographical location of the operation, and availability of medical support. Health effects of FGC have failed to find an association between these practices, especially clitoridectomy and excision, with several purported long-term health outcomes, including fistulas, tumors, infertility, painful intercourse, prolapse of the uterus, and reproductive tract infections (Morison et al., 2001). This large-scale community-based study conducted in The Gambia, which included physical examination of most of the respondents, confirmed that there does not seem to be a measurable connection between noninfibulating genital cutting and obstructed labor and other often reported long-term medical consequences.

The Right to Self-Determination

The legacy of colonial imperialism echoes in international human rights. The global eradication campaign itself appears to violate several human rights, including "the right of people and nations to autonomy and self-determination, rights of parents to raise children as they see fit, the right of members of a family to be free of government intrusion into decisions that are private, the right of members of a group to favor their own traditions in the education and socialization of their children, their right to freedom of religion" (Shweder, 2002).

The human rights regime should respect the doctrine of "margin of appreciation." This doctrine recognizes that national governments can be better placed than the European Court of Human Rights to appreciate local circumstances and local needs and, thus, human rights claims (Dembour, 2001). In addition to "individual rights," there also exists a demand for group rights, especially from indigenous populations, minority ethnic or religious groups, and formerly colonized populations (Okin, 1999). Societal cultures play a fundamental role in the lives of their member; however, cultures that are threatened with extinction/minority cultures should also be protected by special group rights. Persons should have the ability to develop the capacity to make choices about how to lead their lives. The institution of sovereign autonomy (i.e. local rule without outside interference) should be valued and respected, especially in postcolonial Africa. Local circumstances should be taken into account.

The UN Declaration on the Rights of the Child (UNDRC) asserts that every child has the right to "develop . . . in a normal manner." This can include cultural contexts where being circumcised is to develop in a normal manner. It is also tricky to determine when the parent's right to exercise their culture outweighs the child's right to protection from the culture (Renteln, 2002). Shweder et al. (2002) asks an important question "Does the state's assessment of a child's best interest include the child's membership in a given culture or does it abstract the child from that membership, as if the child had no such connection and was really a 'citizen of the world'? (p. 13).

Although various campaigns may have good intentions, it is important to listen to the diverse voices and perspectives of the women who have experienced genital modifications. Empowered perspectives of those who have ethnic genital modifications include thinking that their genitals are enhanced, "clean," erotic, and have aesthetically pleasing ethnic markings. It is difficult to receive judgmental and condescending suggestions to stop ancient ritual practices from people whose cultures participate in similar body-altering practices. Research has shown that EFGM is "viewed from a Western ethnocentric perspective that often is counter to the actual experiences of the women" (Khaja, Lay, & Boys, 2010, p. 693). In many circumcised communities, there is a conspiracy of silence, due to the distrust of global female circumcision eradication agendas, because general discourse on women's health issues stemming from the practice has been viewed as sensationalized, ethnocentric, racist, culturally insensitive, and simplistic (Khaja, 2004).

People have the right to understand, experience, and interpret sexuality outside of western concepts. Ahmadu (2005) describes how the disembodiment of the "external phallus" (peripheral clitoris) symbolizes a true separation from masculinity and thus defines, paradoxically, the quintessence of matriarchal power. Western feminist should not deny African women a critical aspect of becoming a woman in accordance with their unique and powerful cultural heritage (Ahmadu, 2007). It is imperative not to cause "psychological mutilation" to circumcised women by dictating how they should feel and think about themselves as sexual beings (Ahmadu, 2007). Possibilities of pleasure regardless of the presence of a clitoris

There is an assumption that almost all women who have undergone FGC have sexual problems or are unable to achieve pleasure from sex. Many opponents justify their views on the basis of core assumptions and beliefs about the female anatomy and the role of the clitoris in achieving sexual pleasure. However, many women who have undergone FGC generally report achieving orgasm and sexual satisfaction (Dopico, 2007). "That the external clitoris is key to women's sexual experience and liberation is as much as symbolic construction as the idea that its removal suppresses women's sexuality" (Ahmadu, 2007, p. 306).

The origin of and rationale for genital surgeries remains obscure but, according to Nzegwu (2011), they "do not seem to have been for curbing women's sexuality—the much-hyped explanation that many feminists propound. Such an explanation is unpersuasive given the efforts made in African cultures to reinforce female sexuality and sexual agency and to make a women's lack of sexual fulfillment legitimate grounds for divorce" (p. 262). Inhibiting sexual desire and antisocial sexual behavior are not intended as the main goals of female genital surgeries in many practicing societies (Ahmadu, 2007). Not only is pleasure still possible for circumcised women, it is also said that women who are circumcised are believed by men to be better sexual partners because they enhance the sexual pleasure of man (James and Robertson, 2002). A considerable amount of pleasure is attainable for both candidates in this situation.

Many women who have undergone EFGM have reported achieving orgasm and sexual satisfaction, "an unpredictable response from women who cannot, at least according to western medical discourses, enjoy the act" (Kirby, 1987, p. 44). However, the effects of genital surgeries are diverse and drastically different effects for different women. Toubia and Izette (1998) document a broad range of findings: in some cases up to 90 percent of infibulated women reported pleasurable sex with frequent orgasm (Lightfoot-Klein, 1989); in other cases, 50 percent claimed diminished sexual pleasure (El Dareer, 1982). Megafu (1983) found that 58.8 percent of circumcised Nigerian participants experienced orgasm in contrast to 68.7 percent of uncircumcised women. "[Some] women reveal lack of sexual satisfaction and others report healthy and satisfying sexual experiences" (Dopico, 2007, p. 225). The partial removal of the clitoris does not guarantee inhibition of arousal or orgasm (Dopico, 2007). Toubia (1995) argues that some of the sensitive tissue of the body and the crura of the clitoris are embedded deeply and are not removed when excision takes place. Additionally, some women feel they have a healthy and satisfactory sexual life without experiencing orgasm (Obermeyer, 1999; Vance, 1989). Having an enjoyable and satisfying sex life is highly subjective and personal.

No two people, not even identical twins, have the same pattern and distribution of nerves (Krantz, 1958). The clitoral system has tremendous potential for arousal and sensitivity and women's preferences for sexual stimulation vary (Dopico, 2007). Healthy sexuality and sexual enjoyment are not dependent on an intact clitoris (Obermeyer, 1999). Weijmar-Schultz and colleagues (1989) found that women who had radical vulvectomy, due to tumors, could still experience orgasm with elaborate foreplay, without their clitorises. It should be noted that many women with clitorises still have complaints about sexual dysfunction and loss of desire, and have never experienced orgasm (Ahmadu, 2007). "African girls and women who happen to be circumcised today are entitled to see themselves as okay the way they are, as 'normal' and healthy and not as 'mutilated' objects who are in some pathetic 'search for missing clitorises'" (Ahmadu, 2007, p. 308). People are capable of orgasm and sexual pleasure with or without a clitoris.

The Right to Culture: Empowering Stamps of Legitimacy

One type of EFGM that has been stigmatized by the World Health Organization (WHO) is the practice of manually elongating the inner folds of the labia minora to create a culturally approved organ modification. The practice is widely common in East and Southern Africa (Uganda, Rwanda, Malawi, Lesotho, Zimbabwe, Tanzania, Namibia, Botswana, Mozambique and South Africa) and is "deemed sensuous and critical for enhanced sexual pleasure" (Nzegwu, 2011, p. 262). This acculturating genitalia serves as a "stamp of legitimacy" (Tamale, 2005, p. 40) and is considered the ultimate sexual toy (Nzegwu, 2011). Labia stretching introduces young girls to their genitalia and encourages them to explore, massage, and become familiar with their bodies. In addition to acculturating genitalia, it introduces them to the act of self-stimulation or masturbation, which can also lead to the discovery of other erogenous zones (Nzegwu, 2011). This can happen alone or with groups of girls, where the regular manipulation of labia minora allows them to get familiar with their vulva. Labia elongation is said to enhance the erotic experience of both the male and the female when touched during foreplay or mutual masturbation. It is sometimes described as a "door" (Bagnol & Mariano, 2008, 2009). "Prior to the sexual act the partners should 'open the door,' because 'the man can't come in just like that'" (Bagnol & Mariano, 2011, p. 276). Therefore, foreplay is encouraged before penetration.

Arnfred (2003) reported that elongation of the labia was highly praised by both women and men as a contributing factor to a pleasurable life. During coitus, the elongated labia increases the sexual pleasure of the man, and later when the woman is older, the lips are used to strengthen the diameter of the vagina (OMM, 1983). "Within Africa's broad sexual universe and its many cultural schemes, there is an awareness of the complex nature of sexuality and understanding that female pleasure is not exclusively located in the clitoris, so the former is not compromised by the removal of some parts of the latter (Nzegwu, 2010, p. 262).

Nzegwu (2011) presents narratives of EFGM as "sculpting the erotic body" which gives voice to women who alter their genitalia to become a part of the community's sexual scheme. "On the aesthetic grid of African cultures, natural bodies require some modification to bring them within communities' sexual schema" (Nzegwu, 2011, p. 261). Most theories of African sexualities treated the natural body, both female and male, as not ready for sexual experience until after the completion of certain modifications (Nzegwu, 2011). Body or genitalia sculpting is essential to create a sensual body (Nzegwu, 2011). Practices are diverse and can range from nicks of the clitoris to the excision of the clitoris and infibulation. Sculpting the erotic body can be important for girls' rites of passage to enhance the erotic by creating the ethnically desired aesthetic markings (Nzegwu, 2011).

Excision, a form of EFGM, has been connected to "knowledge" (Johnson, 2000). Dellenborg (2006) explains a localized status given as a result of the genital modification: "An excised girl knows something that a non-excised girl does not, no matter her age. The circumcision ritual is a socialisation process and an important education for girls. This knowledge—a practical, theoretical and corporeally 'magical' knowledge—can only be transferred from older women to girls through the excision ceremony and the subsequent initiation ritual" (p. 85).

Circumcision among the Efik—a practice known as mbobi—was important for a girl's rite of passage, or nkugho; its objective was to beautify the genitalia by making it cultured and enhancing the erotic (Ikpe, 2006). In the African context, there are two types of women: those with cultural legitimacy, who belonged, and those who lacked legitimacy, who did not belong (Nzegwu, 2010). Like "scarifications that many African communities perform, the sculpting of the genitalia as well marked ethnic identity, social hierarchy and perhaps the boundaries of legitimacy in intimacy matters" (Nzegwu, 2011, p. 262).

Conclusion

If the real issue is health then alternative, minimal, and safe genital alterations should be tolerated. EFGM, such as the nonwounding pricking of the clitoris, "nicking" or "pinching" of the prepuce skin, and verbal declarations of altered status can be done in a safe clean environment and medical consequences can be eliminated or drastically reduced. In 2010, the American Academy of Pediatrics suggested that "It might be more effective if federal and state laws enabled pediatricians to reach out to families by offering a ritual nick as a possible compromise to avoid greater harm." But the policy was met with such intense backlash that AAP changed its position to oppose all forms of female genital cutting. Those who wish to eradicate female genital modification practices tend to have "zero tolerance," even if genital surgeries already are—or could be made—medically safe. "They think it is wrong for Africans to modify female genitals (although not male genitals), and it is wrong, many advocates will argue, even if the body modification can be done hygienically, with anesthesia and with no effect on sexual functioning. In other words, the human rights advocacy groups are not really interested in making the world safe for these types of medical procedures. Their goal is to eradicate the practice, whether it is medically harmful or not" (Shweder, 2005). In February 2016, physicians published an article in the Journal of Medical Ethics, that argue female genital "nicks" and other such cuts that respect cultural and religious traditions but cause minimal harm should be legally permitted. This strategy can protect females from the long-term negative health consequences associated with more severe forms of genital cutting.

The narratives of EFGM are as diverse as the experiences women have. There are many perspectives and voices that deserve to be heard. Anti-FGM advocates only make room for the traumatized stories of mutilation and human rights violations. However, there are women who choose to alter their genitals and feel empowered by their decision. Telling women from other cultures what they should not do with their genitals is a form of body policing. I think the hegemonic discourse of FGM is a form of body shaming. I believe people have the right to choose for themselves what to do with their genitals. I believe people have the right to explore their bodies, including experimenting with pleasure and/or pain. I believe people should be able to express themselves sexually, in the privacy of their homes, without the interference of government or international human rights organizations. I respect people's right to pursue consensual sexual pleasure while respecting the diversity of subjective interpretation. "Denying young Wesern(ized) African girls and women the freedom to choose is tantamount to refusing them fundamental, universal human rights- rights to their own bodies and to sexual autonomy, as well as to uphold their cultural identities, however they may define this" (Ahmadu, 2007, p. 308). I believe people have the right to express their culture without fear of deliberate and systematic destruction of that culture from the dominance of non-comprehending Others. Consenting females who choose to alter their genitals for reasons outsiders may not be able to understand, appreciate or value should not be accused of human rights violations. I believe people have the right to choose to do what they want with their bodies.

References

Abusharaf, T. M. (2000). Revisiting feminist discourses on infibulation: Responses from Sudanese feminists. In B. Shell-Duncan & Y. Hernlund (Eds.) *Female "circumcision" in Africa: Culture, controversy, and change* (pp. 151–166). Boulder, CO: Lynne Rienner.

Ahmadu, F. (2000). Rites and wrongs: An insider/outsider reflection on power and excision. In B. Shell-Duncan & Y. Herlund (Eds.), *Female "circumcision in Africa: Culture, controversy, and change* (pp. 283–312). Boulder, CO: Lynne Rienner.

Ahmadu, F. (2007). Ain't I a woman too? Challenging myths of sexual dysfunction in circumcised women. In Y. Hernlun & B. Shell-Duncan, *Transcultural bodies: Female genital cutting in global context* (pp. 278–310). New Brunswick, NJ: Rutgers University Press.

Anuforo, P., Oyedele, L., & Pacquiao, D. (2004). Comparative study of meanings, beliefs, and practices of female circumcision among three Nigerian tribes in the United States and Nigeria, Journal of Transcultural Nursing, 15(2), 103–113.

Amadiume, I. (1987). *African matriarchal foundations: The case of Igbo societies*. London, UK: Karnak House.

Arnfred, S. (2003, June). Contested construction of female sexualities: Meanings and interpretations of initiation rituals. Paper presented at the Conference on Sex and Secrecy, Johannesburg, South Africa.

Bagnol, B., & Mariano, E. (2008). Vaginal practices: Eroticism and implications for women's health and condom use in Mozambique. *Culture, Health and Sexuality*, 10(6), 573–585. doi: 10.1080/13691050801999071

Bagnol, B., & Mariano, E. (2009). Cuidados consigo mesmo,sexualidadeeerotismo.Physis,19(2),387–404. http://dx.doi.org/10.1590/S0103-73312009000200008

Bagnol, B., & Mariano, E. (2011). Politics of naming sexual practices. In S. Tamale (Ed.), *African sexualities: A reader* (pp. 271–287). Capetown, South Africa: Pambazuka Press.

Coomaraswamy, R. (2004). Fighting violence against women as and international right. Paper presented at the University of Washington Speaker Series: Human Rights from the Bottom Up, Seattle, March 8.

Dellenborg, L. (2006). A reflection on the cultural meanings of female circumcision: Experiences for fieldwork in Casamance, Southern Senegal. In S. Arnfred (Ed.*). Rethinking Sexualities in Africa*. (pp. 79–94) Stockholm: Alfa Print AB.

Dembour, M.B. (2001). Following the movement of a pendulum: Between universalism and relativism. In Culture and rights: Anthropological perspectives, ed J.K. Cowan, M.B. Dembour, and R.A. Wilson. Cambridge: Cambridge University Press.

Dopico, M. (2007). Infibulation and the orgasm puzzle: Sexual experiences of infibulated Eritrean women in rural Eritrea and Melbourne, Australia. In Y. Hernlun & B. Shell-Duncan (Eds.), *Transcultural bodies: Female genital cutting in global context* (pp. 224–247). New Brunswick, NJ: Rutgers University Press.

El Dareer, A. (1982). *Woman, why do you weep? Circumcision and its consequences*. London, UK: Zed Press.

Eliah, E. (1996). Reaching for a healthier future. *Populi* (May): 12–16.

Erlich, M. (1986). La femme blessée: essai sur les mutilation sexuelles feminines, Paris: L'Harmattan.

Fucaschi, M. (2003). I segni sul corpo. Per un'antropologia delle modificazioni dei genital femminili. Torino: Bollati Boringhieri.

Gallo, P.G., Tita, E., & Viviani, F. (2006). At the roots of ethnic female genital modification: Preliminary report. In G.C. Denniston, P.G. Gallo, F.M. Hodges, M. F. Milos, & F. Viviani (Eds.), *Bodily integrity and the politics of circumcision: Culture, controversy, and change*. New York, NY: Springer.

Herlund,Y & Shell-Duncan, B. (2007). Transcultural bodies: Female genital cutting in global context. New Brunswick, NJ: Rutgers University Press.

Ikpe, E. B. (2006). Culture and pleasurable sexuality in South Eastern Nigeria. *Sexuality in Africa Magazine*, 3 (1), 4–8. Retrieved from http://www.arsrc.org/publications/sia/sep06/feature.htm

James, S., and C. Robertson. Eds (2002). Genital cutting and transnational sisterhood: Disputing U.S. polemics. Urbana: Univeristy of Illinois Press.

Johnson, M. (2000). Becoming a Muslim, becoming a person: Female "circumcision", religious identity, and personhood in Guinea-Bissau.

In B. Shell-Duncan. & Y. Hernlund (Ed.), *Female "circumcision" in Africa, culture, controversy, and change* (pp. 215–234). London: Lynne Rienner.

Kapur, R. (2002). The tragedy of victimization rhetoric: Resurrecting the 'native' subject in international/post-colonial feminist legal politics. Harvard Human Rights Journal, 15, 1–37.

Khaja K. (2004). Female circumcision: Life histories of Somali women. Salt Lake City, Utah, USA: University of Utah (Ph.D. dissertation)

Khaja K., Lay K., Boys S. (2010). Female circumcision: Toward an inclusive practice of care. Health Care for Women International. 31:686–699

Kirby, V. (1989). On the cutting edge: Feminism and clitoridectomy. *Australian Feminist Studies*, 2(5), 35–55.doi:10.1080/08164649.1987.9961564

Kjöller, H. (2002). Oskydigt misstänkt måste också höras[A suspect, although innocent, must also be interrogated] Dagens Nyheter, October 11

Kratz, C. (1999). Contexts, controversies and dilemmas: Teaching circumcision. In M. Bastian (ed), *Great ideas for teaching abut Africa*. Boulder, CO: Lynne Tienner.

Lightfoot-Klein, H. (1989). *Prisoners of ritual: An odyssey into female genital circumcision in Africa*. New York, NY: Harington Park Press.

Lightfoot-Klein, H. Chase,C. Hammond, T. Goldman, R (2000). Genital surgery on children below the age of consent. In L.T. Szuchman & F. Muscarela(Eds.) Psychological Perspectives on Human Sexuality, New York:John Wiley & Sons Inc.

Love, B. (1992). *Encyclopedia of unusual sex practices*. Fort Lee, NJ: Barricade Books Inc.

Megafu, U. (1983). Female ritual circumcision in Africa: An investigation of the presumed benefits among the Ibos of Nigeria. *East African Medical Journal*, 40,793–800. Retrieved from http://www.ajol.info/index.php/eamj

Morison, L., A. Dirir, S. Elmi, J. Warsame, and S. Dirir. (2004). How experiences and attitudes related to female circumcision vary according to age on arrival in Britain: A study among young Somalis in London. Ethnicity and Health, 9, 75–100.

Nzegwu, N. (2010). "Osunality," or African sensuality-sexuality: Going beyond eroticism. *Jenda: A Journal of Culture and African Women Studies*, (16), 1–24.

Nzegwu, N. (2011). 'Osunality' or African eroticism. In S. Tamale (Ed.), *African sexualities: A reader* (pp. 253–270). Cape Town, SA: Pambazuka.

Obermeyer, C. M. (1999). Female genital surgeries: The known, the unknown, and the unknowable. *Medical Anthropology Quarterly*, 13, 79–106. doi: 10.1525/maq.1999.13.1.79

Obiora, L.A. (1997). Bridges and barricades: Rethinking polemics and intransigence in the campaign against female circumcision. Case Western Law Review, 47, 275–378.

Okin, S. (1999). Is multiculturalism bad for women? In Is multiculturalism bad for women? Ed. J. Cohen, M. Howard, M. Nussbaum. Princeton, NJ: Princeton University Press.

Organização da Mulher Moçambicana (OMM) (1983). Preparação da conferencia extraordinária da mulher: Relatório da provincial de Tete. Tete: OMM.

Oyěwùmí, O. (2003). *African women and feminism: Reflecting on the politics of sisterhood*. Trenton, NJ: Africa World Press.

Puccioni, N. (1904). Delle deformazioni e mutilazioni artificiali etniche piu in uso, *Archivio per l' Antropologia e el'Etnologia*, 34, 391–401.

Renteln, A. D. (1988). Relativism and the search for human rights. American Anthropologist, 90, 56–68.

Shell-Duncan, B. & Hernlund, Y. (2000). Female circumcision in Africa: Dimensions of the practice and debate. In B. Shell-Duncan and Y. Herlund (Eds.), *Female Circumcision in Africa Culture, Controversy and Change* (pp. 1–40). Boulder, CO: Lynne Reinner.

Shweder, R. (2002). What about female genital mutilation? And why understanding culture matters in the first place. In Engaging cultural differences, Ed R. Shweder, M. Minow and H.R. Markus. New York: Russell Sage Foundation.

Shweder, R. (2005). When cultures collide: Which rights? Whose tradition of values? A critique of the global anti-FGM campaign. In Global justice and the bulwarks of localism: Human rights in context, ed. C. Eisgruber and A. Sajo. Leiden and Boston: Martinus Nijhoff.

Shweder, R. M. Minow, and H.R. Markus eds. (2002). Engaging cultural differences: The multicultural challenge in liberal democracies. New York: Russell Sage Foundation.

Tamale, S. (2005). Eroticism, sensuality and "women's secrets" among the Baganda: a critical analysis. *Feminist Africa*, 5, 9–36.

Toubia, N. (1995). *Female genital mutilation: A call for global action* (2nd ed.). New York, NY: Rainbo/ Women Ink.

Toubia, N., & Izette, S. (1998). Female genital mutilation: An overview. Geneva CH: World Health Organization. Retieved from http://www.who.int /reproductivehealth/topics/fgm/en/

United Nations. (1986). Report of the working group on traditional practices affecting the health of women and children. United Nations Sub Commission for the Prevention of Discrimination and the Protection of Minorities Special Working Group on Traditional Practices Item 19.

Weijmar-Schultz, W., van de Wiel, J., Klatter, J., Sturm, B., & Nauta, J. (1989). Vaginal sensitivity to electric stimuli- Theoretical and practical implications. *Archives of Sexual Behavior*, 18(2), 87–95. doi: 10.1007/BF01543115

Zelaika Hepworth Clarke is an African-centered social worker, sexual epistemologist, decolonizing autoethnographer, and cultural and clinical sexologist.

EXPLORING THE ISSUE

Is Female Genital Cutting a Violation of Women's Health and Human Rights?

Critical Thinking and Reflection

1. How is female genital cutting a women's health issue? Is it a Human Rights Issue?
2. How is FGC similar or different to Western vulvar cosmetic surgical practices (e.g., labiaplasty)?
3. How might female economic empowerment influence how FGC is practiced around the world?
4. Is there a way to balance cultural traditions with human rights when it comes to FGC?

Is There Common Ground?

Jackson provides a comprehensive review of female genital cutting (described in her essay as female genital mutilation) and its history, as it has evolved across the globe. She highlights connections between FGC and gender norms she believes to be harmful to both women and their communities. What does a debate on FGC look like when placed within the context of gender-based injustice as a whole? In most, if not all of the countries in which FGC is practiced, poverty is a significant issue for women and men alike. How might changing cultural norms regarding FGC impact the issue of poverty? How might devoting resources to combat poverty help to reduce FGM?

Conversations about the ethics of female genital cutting often result in a debate on cultural imperialism. Hepworth Clarke cautions against viewing what she describes as Ethnic Female Genital Modification (EFGM) through a Western lens. Doing so, she argues, ignores the values of the cultures in which it is practiced and replicates the damaging tradition of colonialism. Furthermore, she offers several studies that attempt to debunk the notion that the physical and sexual effects of EFGM are as pervasive as has been reported; still, one might question, is one adverse outcome (or, in this case, a reported several thousand) one too many? Is the severity of this phenomenon enough to encourage a ban altogether?

Both authors make comparisons between the practice of FGC and procedures more common in the West, including labiaplasty, vaginal tightening, and other genital cosmetic enhancements. A common critique is the connection of these practices to the goal of increasing one's sexual attractiveness to men—a position considered antithetical to self-empowerment. If what Jackson suggests about the potential universality of gender-based cultural pressures follows, do Westerners have a right to criticize FGC in other cultures?

On one hand there is a compelling argument for allowing a valued cultural practice to stand on its own. On the other, what is the cost of said practice when (a) it is often conducted through unsanitary means that can lead to infection, or worse, and (b) members of the community in which it is practiced are unable to break tradition and forge their own path with any sense of safety or security? What do you think about the practice of FGC? How does it compare to Western body modification practices like breast augmentation or labiaplasty? How does it compare to the traditional practice of male circumcision? Is there a middle ground that can protect body autonomy and human rights while also preserving traditional cultural practices?

Additional Resources

Davis, A. N. (January 2012). Female genital cutting: The pressures of culture, international attention, and domestic law on the role of African women. *Gender and Sexuality Law Online*. Retrieved from http://blogs.law.columbia.edu/gslonline/files/2012/01/Davis-Female-Genital-Cutting.pdf

Khazan, O. (April 8, 2015). Why some women will choose to get circumcised. *The Atlantic*. Retrieved from http://www.theatlantic.com/international/archive/2015/04/female-genital-mutilation-cutting-anthropologist/389640/

Obermeyer, C. (1999). Female genital surgeries: The known, the unknown, and the unknowable. *Medical Anthropology Quarterly, 13*(1), 79–106.

Walker, A. (1992). *Possessing the secret of joy*. San Diego, CA: Harcourt.

Internet References . . .

Cut: Slicing Through the Myths of Circumcision

http://www.cutthefilm.com/

International Day of Zero Tolerance for Female Genital Mutilation

http://www.un.org/en/events/femalegenitalmutilationday/

The Cut: A Documentary by Beryl Magoko

https://thecutdocumentary.wordpress.com/

The Female Genital Cutting Education and Networking Project

http://www.fgmnetwork.org/index.php

Selected, Edited, and with Issue Framing Material by:
Ryan W. McKee, *Widener University,* Tracie Q. Gilbert, *Widener University,*
and
Jayleen Galarza, *Shippensburg University of Pennsylvania*

ISSUE

Is "Social Transitioning" a Beneficial Treatment for Transgender Children?

YES: Kristina Olson and Lily Durwood, from "Are Parents Rushing to Turn Their Boys into Girls?," *Slate* (2016)

NO: Alice Dreger, from "The Big Problem with Outlawing Gender Conversion Therapies," *Wired* (2015)

Learning Outcomes

After reading this issue, you will be able to:

- Define the terms transgender, cisgender, and gender dysphoria.
- Describe the process of social transitioning for transgender and gender non-conforming youth.
- Distinguish between social transitioning and medical/surgical transitioning.
- Describe the benefits and challenges of social transitioning for transgender and gender nonconforming youth.

ISSUE SUMMARY

YES: Kristina Olson, Associate Professor of Psychology and founder of the TransYouth Project at the University of Washington, and Lily Durwood, Project Coordinator at the TransYouth Project, argue that researchers have misrepresented findings to suggest that many young people who identify as transgender will ultimately identify as cisgender, and that calls to limit the option of social transitioning can be harmful to transgender youth.

NO: Alice Dreger, author and Professor of Clinical Medical Humanities and Bioethics at Northwestern University, argues that controversial "gender conversion therapy" can help prevent unnecessary treatments on gender non-conforming young people.

For many people, the terms "sex" and "gender" are synonymous. The two terms, however, describe distinct concepts. Biological sex is determined by a combination of a person's sex chromosomes and their gonadal and genital anatomy. At birth, we are assigned a sex based on this anatomy. Depending on our assigned sex, there are certain societal expectations of how society tells us we should feel or behave. Men in the United States, for example, are expected to be less emotional than women. Women are expected to be less aggressive than men. These expectations are called gender roles. Gender identity, to go a step further, is how one feels about and identifies with their assigned sex and the role expectations that come along with it. Most people would say that their gender identity is congruent with their anatomical sex. While some men may feel more (or less) masculine than others, the majority would strongly identify as men. The same could be said for most women; regardless of how feminine they feel (or don't feel), the majority identify as women. These men and women, whose gender identities are in-line with social expectations of their biological sex would be considered "cisgender" ("cis" is a prefix with Latin origins, meaning "on the same side"). Most cisgender individuals have the privilege of never needing to give much thought to their gender, or how they present it to the world.

But what about those having gender identities that differ from what is usually expected of people with their assigned sex? For those whose feeling and expression of gender doesn't fall in line with the social expectations of their assigned sex, gender identity can be hard to ignore. Their gender identities may not fit the binary gender system, historically seen as standard in the United States. Many (but not all) people who feel this way may identify as transgender or transsexual and, according to the fifth edition of the American Psychiatric Association's (APA) *Diagnostic and Statistical Manual of Mental Disorders* (DSM), may be diagnosed with Gender Dysphoria. While the language describing this has changed over time (it was called Gender Identity Disorder in the previous DSM), its inclusion in the book remains controversial, as does the focus on medicalized (hormonal or surgical) treatments. However, access to most medical care related to transitioning, should one choose to do so, requires an official psychological diagnosis. This has provided sufficient rationale for psychiatrists and psychologists to maintain a place for gender dysphoria in the diagnostic manual.

Some, but not all, adults with gender dysphoria may elect to take hormones and/or undergo sex reassignment surgeries in order to facilitate their gender transition. This is not an overnight process and, in order to adhere to accepted standards of care, requires the guidance of a person's mental health care provider and medical doctors. Before any medical or surgical transition takes place, a series of events (known as social transitioning) including, but not limited to, additional counseling, family and peer disclosure, and the fulfillment of certain legal requirements must occur.

When a child is diagnosed with gender dysphoria, the support of parents or legal guardians is crucial in securing appropriate treatment. Even with a support team that includes therapists and doctors, decisions about treatment can be stressful. Even supportive parents may wonder, at times, if their children's dysphoria is "just a phase." Indeed, findings from an often-quoted study claim that childhood gender dysphoria persists into adulthood in somewhere between 12 and 27 percent of cases (Drummond et al., 2008). Still, very few studies have examined this issue, and a childhood diagnosis must not simply be ignored. Early treatment options, according to The World Professional Association for Transgender Health (WPATH), include counseling and therapy for the child, as well as counseling and support for family members. Some children may desire a social transition, during which they begin to express their gender by dressing in different clothing or going by a different name or pronouns. When discussing social transition during early childhood, WPATH acknowledge the debates among healthcare and mental healthcare professionals. While challenging, many young people and their families navigate social transitions with success. However, there is little research on the topic, and social transitioning for children may bring certain risks not associated with adults. Within their Standards of Care, WPATH states,

> Families vary in the extent to which they allow their young children to make a social transition to another gender role. Social transitions in early childhood do occur within some families with early success. This is a controversial issue, and divergent views are held by health professionals. The current evidence base is insufficient to predict the long-term outcomes of completing a gender role transition during early childhood.

How is the controversy over social transitioning in childhood evolving? There has been much debate over whether initiating social transition in childhood is appropriate or necessary given the "low persistent rates of childhood gender dysphoria" (WPATH, 2012). However, the intensity of each side of this debate is highlighted in the recent firing of Dr. Kenneth Zucker, the director of the Child Youth and Family Gender Identity Clinic in Toronto, Canada. In December 2015, Dr. Zucker, who assisted in co-authoring the recommendations for treatment outlined in WPATH's Standards for Care, was dismissed following an internal review of his practice and accusations of practicing harmful reparative therapies on transgender children. Those calling for Dr. Zucker's dismissal from the clinic argue that he consistently pressured children to suppress any desires to socially transition, and urged them to conform to the gender expectations associated with their assigned sex. The negative consequences of such reparative therapy, including the internalization of systemic oppression and increased struggles with depression and anxiety, have been well established by sexuality researchers.

Supporters of Dr. Zucker's work contend that he was only acting in accordance to WPATH's Standards of Care for treatment of transgender children. These protocols suggest that mental health and other healthcare professionals proceed with caution in making choices about social transitioning to avoid premature decisions that may lead to regret or eventual reversal. There was even some evidence that several of the claims against Zucker were fabricated and possibly political in nature. As one supporter, Deborah Soh, argued in a recent op-ed in the *Wall Street Journal*, "The most current science has been trumped purely because it is at odds with the dominant political view."

But advocates for the practice of childhood social transitioning argue that under the guidance and care of mental health professionals, the practice does not lead to earlier or unnecessary medical or surgical interventions. Those who begin a process of social transitioning, but find that they no longer experience gender dysphoria as they age, can transition back into the gender presentation that is appropriate for them. Claims that transgender activists want to "fast lane" young people into medical or surgical transition are unfounded, and reminiscent of negative "recruitment" stereotypes previously levied at gays and lesbians. Proponents argue that they, along with many medical professionals, simply want young people to have the freedom to explore and navigate a gendered world in ways that are the least harmful to their well-being.

In the following YES and NO selections, Olson and Durwood contend that research findings on the percentage of children with gender dysphoria who eventually identify as cisgender have been misconstrued. They argue that opponents of social transitioning for young people neglect the fact that children's experiences of gender occur within a spectrum, and that professionals cannot simply group all children who express gender variance in one category. Treatment options, they argue, must be individualized to address each unique circumstance, and social transitioning cannot be ruled out. Alice Dreger counters that parents and professionals should be cautious in recommending treatment options to children who may appear gender non-conforming. She argues that encouraging individuals to socially transition in early childhood before they have a full understanding of their gender identity could lead to unnecessary and more permanent treatment options, such as hormonal and surgical treatments.

YES

Kristina Olson and Lily Durwood

Are Parents Rushing to Turn Their Boys into Girls?

Should a boy who grows out his hair, likes to wear pink, and prefers to jump rope at recess rather than play football be raised as a girl instead of a boy? Several recent pieces in prominent media outlets would have us believe that this is a major issue in North America. In the latest such piece, "The Transgender Battle Line: Childhood," an op-ed that appeared in the *Wall Street Journal* on Jan. 4, doctoral student of sexual neuroscience Deborah Soh raises alarm that many feminine boys and masculine girls are being encouraged by their parents and therapists to undergo social transitions, changing their names and pronouns to live full-time in the other gender. Soh characterizes these transitions as premature and in contradiction with established research, citing studies showing that most children who are gender nonconforming do not grow up to be transgender adults.

The central problem with this often-made argument is that it treats all children who violate cultural gender norms as a single category, when in fact there is a wide range of such children in the world. On one end of the spectrum are children who enjoy toys and clothing that are stereotypically associated with the opposite sex (imagine a girl who loves G.I. Joes and rough-and-tumble play or a boy who love Barbies and ballet). In the middle are children who express a lot of unhappiness about being a member of their gender group. For example, a boy who says he wishes he were a girl because then no one would tease him about his preference for nail polish or the fact that he only plays with girls. At the other end of the spectrum are children who consistently, persistently, and insistently assert that they *are* members of the opposite sex and who are beside themselves when they are not allowed to live as such. Such children sometimes resort to self-harm or become anxious and depressed that others will not recognize their gender identity. Importantly, while some children in the last group undergo social transitions, we see no evidence that anyone believes that children elsewhere on the spectrum should do so. We believe these recent articles, whose authors, to our knowledge, do not work with transgender children, overlook key differences within the spectrum of children who do not conform to gender norms, misinterpret past research, and misconstrue interventions to help transgender children.

In describing her own childhood gender dysphoria, Soh praises her parents' approach to her dysphoria. She explains:

> I myself was a gender-dysphoric child who preferred trucks and Meccano sets to Easy-Bake Ovens. I detested being female and all of its trappings. Yet when I was growing up in the 1980s, the concept of helping children transition to another sex was completely unheard of. My parents allowed me to wear boys' clothing and shave my head, to live as a girl who otherwise looked and behaved like a boy. I outgrew my dysphoria by my late teens. Looking back, I am grateful for my parents' support, which helped me work things out.

Soh implies that if only parents weren't so rigid about gender norms, so stuck on the idea that only boys can do boy things and only girls can do girl things, then their children wouldn't feel the need to socially transition. We see the appeal of this argument, and we admit that at least one of us had this view as recently as a few years ago. In the intervening years, we have recruited and studied more than 150 families across the United States and Canada who have supported their children in social transitions. These families are participants in our study, the TransYouth Project, a longitudinal study that aims to track the gender development and mental health of these children, as well as children who would better be described as "gender nonconforming" (children like Soh), through adolescence and young adulthood. After three years of traveling around the country to meet with these families in their homes, in support groups, at camps, and at conferences, our beliefs have changed. Most parents of children who ultimately socially transitioned describe spending months or years doing exactly what Soh praises her parents for doing—explaining to their children that they can play with whatever toys they want and wear whatever clothing they want without having to *become* the other gender. Unlike the young Deborah Soh, these children were decidedly not satisfied with this solution.

In contrast to Soh, a prominent subset of researchers have recommended a more decisive approach, in what they hope will prevent children from ultimately identifying as transgender, than the one Soh describes—to simply limit or even forbid gender nonconforming behaviors in the home and to encourage gender conforming ones instead. At the TransYouth Project, we know many families who employed one *or both* of these strategies at various points in their child's lives—trying to convince their child that that he can play with whatever toys he wants without needing to *be* a girl, or simply forbidding the child from any expression of gender nonconformity. Still other families tried to ignore the gender nonconforming behavior and pleas altogether. These families were ultimately persuaded by the child's persistence—and, oftentimes, by the child's obvious suffering and even self-harm—to try something new, in this case a social transition.

Nearly every piece that raises the issue of social transitions among transgender children cites what we call "the 80 percent statistic," which refers to a 1995 study by Zucker and Bradley that found that, within a group of 45 gender nonconforming children, 80 percent were not transgender at follow-up (usually in the high-school years). Historian Alice Dreger described this finding in a June 2015 article in *Wired*:

> "The data we have indicates that a large percentage of boys who act statistically more "feminine" as children—who dress up in girlish clothing, prefer social role-play games to contact sports, are highly attentive to their mothers and aunts, and feel budding sexual attraction towards male—will end up not as transgender women, but as gay men, at least in our culture. Only a small number will grow up to be straight transgender women.

These findings are used to argue that social transitions should not be encouraged, because according to the logic, around 80 percent of these children who are identified as gender dysphoric will not ultimately be transgender if left alone or given proper therapy. Here, again, the distinction between transgender children and the rest of the spectrum of gender nonconforming children is critical to acknowledge. The studies that found this 80 percent number (or similar numbers) included a broad range of gender nonconforming children. The authors of this particular study, Zucker and Bradley, wrote that it is actually quite rare for children who are brought to gender clinics to believe themselves *to be* the other gender. Much more common were children who showed cross-gender behaviors, who may have wished they were the other gender at times but still saw themselves as members of their original gender group. Thus, most of the children who are argued to have grown out of their gender dysphoria never claimed a transgender identity to begin with.

Perhaps the clearest evidence that most children in these samples were never transgender to begin with is that, when they were directly asked "are you a boy or a girl" as part of a battery of intake questions, an overwhelming percentage (more than 90 percent) of children in these clinics provided the answer that aligned with their natal sex. Is it so surprising that the majority of boys who in childhood believed themselves to be boys in adulthood believed themselves to be men? As one research team based in Amsterdam concluded: "[E]xplicitly asking children with GD [gender dysphoria] with which sex they identify seems to be of great value in predicting future outcomes for both boys and girls with GD." That is, even within samples of gender nonconforming children, the ones who say they *are* the other gender are the ones who are most likely to say the same thing later in life.

This is not to say that a transgender identity in childhood never desists in adulthood. The truth is that we do not know precisely how many transgender children will grow up to be transgender adults, because no long-term studies have recruited a large number of children who believe that they *are* members of the opposite sex nor separated the few they have included in past studies from the broader group of gender nonconforming children. Until the start of our project in 2013, we knew of no studies tracking large numbers of children who specifically identified as transgender in early childhood. Thus, while most popular articles on this topic imply that 80 percent of children with transgender identities will not grow up to be transgender adults, we believe it is more accurate to say that we have no good estimate. What little data do exist suggest that many transgender-identified young children do in fact become transgender-identified teens and adults.

What happens if transgender children socially transition and then change their minds? This is a frequent worry not only in articles on the topic but also of many parents of transgender children. Soh raises this concern:

> Consider a 2011 study of 25 adolescents who had been gender dysphoric as children, published in the academic journal Clinical Child Psychology and Psychiatry. Two girls who had undergone social transitioning to boys—by taking on male-typical appearances—regretted it and struggled to detransition. One wanted to begin wearing earrings, but said she couldn't because she "looked like a boy." The other, hoping for a fresh start with high school, hid childhood photos at home that depicted her time living as a boy. Both feared teasing from their peers.

Importantly, the study that Soh cites here specifically notes that *none* of the children in the study actually socially transitioned. That is, while these two female children appeared such that strangers might have mistaken them for boys because of their haircuts, they did not change their pronouns to live as boys. (Actually, they seem to have had experiences that match Soh's description of her own childhood.) Thus, the degree to which these two children struggled to later assume a more feminine appearance is relevant to the question of whether girls should be allowed to cut their hair short and wear masculine clothing rather than the question of whether girls should be allowed to socially transition to live as boys. From a scientific perspective, we are fortunate that today there are larger numbers of children who *have* socially transitioned, who can be followed to assess rates of regret and the social or psychological costs (or benefits) of "de-transitioning"—some of the many goals of our ongoing study.

Despite the focus of most of the recent articles on prepubescent children, nearly all of these pieces raise alarm about medical intervention. Our experience is that everyone gets nervous when 5-year-olds are mentioned in the same sentence or paragraph as hormones and surgery—and for good reason. Once again, though, care is needed in interpretation. First, and most critically, *the only intervention that is being made with prepubescent transgender children is a social, reversible, non-medical one*—allowing a child to change pronouns, hairstyles, clothes, and a first name in everyday life. No one in mainstream medicine (or elsewhere, to our knowledge) is performing surgery on or providing hormones to prepubescent transgender children. Thus, sentences such as Soh's, "We don't allow children to vote or get tattoos, yet in the name of progressive thinking we are allowing them to choose serious biomedical interventions with permanent and irreversible results" are simply irrelevant to the discussion of social transitions and prepubescent children.

Adolescents and adults—the very people for whom there *is* agreement about the persistence of gender identity—are the ones receiving the "permanent and irreversible" medical treatments. As Soh and Dreger both note in their criticisms of early social transitions, best-treatment practices include the possibility of hormones and surgery for adolescents and adults, and these interventions "can be lifesaving," as Dreger put it.

One final point is relevant here as well: Just because children identify as transgender—and even if they continue to identify that way through adolescence and adulthood—there is no reason to assume that they will necessarily opt for hormones and surgery. Large numbers of transgender adults do not pursue these medical interventions, and we have met adolescents, even ones who have socially transitioned before puberty, who are making that same decision. So even the argument that allowing early social transitions will lead to an inevitable use of hormones and surgery is misleading.

Despite the recent alarmist calls about movements to persuade parents to socially transition their children to another gender and worry that doing so sets them up for a lifetime of hormone and surgical treatment, we know of no evidence suggesting that this is an issue. There are no calls to encourage social transitions among children who merely show preferences for objects, clothing, or hairstyles that are associated in our culture with the other gender, nor for children who sometimes wish they were the other gender. Such children are typically quite content to live in the gender assigned to them at birth, especially if they are allowed to express themselves in a safe environment, with family and peer support.

The consideration of social transitions *for transgender children* is a different discussion entirely. These children, who at first glance might appear similar to other gender nonconforming kids, and who for years were not differentiated within research samples, are actually distinct within the broader group. Transgender children believe themselves *to be* members of the other gender, and researchers, clinicians, and parents can ascertain this information by getting to know these children, and, once trust is gained, asking them. Many transgender adults recall having had this knowledge as children, and many suffered through years of therapy in which they were told they weren't who they knew they were. The causal influence of denial of a deeply held identity and the staggeringly high levels of depression, anxiety, and suicidality observed in unsupported transgender young people—punctuated by the suicides of teens like Leelah Alcorn and Skylar Lee—remains untested, though correlational studies indicate that support is related to better outcomes. This new generation of parents of transgender children—who see statistics on these outcomes and have decided to try social transitions to avoid them—are pioneers.

We do not yet know what the outcomes of social transitions in childhood will be, but this is where people like Soh, the future generation of researchers and clinicians, as well as those who publicly write about these issues, such as Dreger, and those of us studying transgender children can hopefully all agree. By systematically studying the impact of social transitions in *transgender* children, and by studying outcomes in transgender children whose families make a wide array of decisions, we can best discover what is in the best interest of the *transgender* child.

Kristina Olson is an Associate Professor of Psychology and founder of the TransYouth Project at the University of Washington.

Lily Durwood, Project Coordinator at the TransYouth Project.

Alice Dreger

NO

The Big Problem with Outlawing Gender Conversion Therapies

The reception to Caitlyn Jenner's Vanity Fair cover story this week has been mostly laudable. The country, it seems, may finally be ready to approach transgender people with humanity and calm acceptance instead of snark or fear or hate. In fact, even the president continues to put a focus on transgender issues, repeatedly calling for an end to "conversion" therapies for "transgender youth." His intentions are good, but his understanding of gender identity needs to evolve.

Gender is complicated. Gender identity development in children is even more so. Even with our ever-expanding understanding of gender's fluidity and variance, we still err by reducing it to simple labels that do not apply to everyone. When children are developing their gender identities, over-simplifying gender can be especially harmful, as a nudge in one direction or another at this crucial phase might forever change a person's life. Can we respect the expressions of gender-crossing children without being so "affirming" of their declarations that we accidentally steer them to a transgender path they might otherwise not want or need to take?

Let's put a real face on this issue—a thirty-something person I'm going to call Jess. Jess and I know each other through our professional interests in advancing the rights of LGBT people. Although she was born typically female in terms of obvious biology, Jess was always what clinicians call "gender nonconforming." Even as a young child, she gravitated toward "masculine" interests and toys. As she grew, Jess felt sexual attraction to females. Given what our culture says about gender, Jess wondered to herself if all this meant she should have a male body.

"The hardest part for me was puberty," she recalled to me recently. Her body was feminizing even though she continued to feel "masculine" in terms of her self. Jess remembers, "I didn't want my body to have the capacity to reproduce because it didn't fit my concept of my gender." She specifically dreaded having her breasts grow and getting her period.

Jess thinks that if, back then, a clinician had said to her, "you are transgender," that might have made sense to her. She might have chosen to take puberty-delaying hormones that would have kept her from ever developing the anatomy and physiology typical for adult females. She might have followed up with some surgeries. But would that have been the right route for her?

Hard to say. She might have turned out well and happy if she had transitioned. But it's worth reflecting on this: Today Jess identifies as a genderqueer gay person with a female body. And she's fine with that. That means she hasn't needed to get any surgeries and won't need to do hormone replacement therapy, as many people who are trans need to do.

Ontario, Canada, is giving us a glimpse of what President Obama's vision of a legislative end to "transgender conversion therapy" might look like, and why such legislation could actually harm children like the child Jess was. The Legislative Assembly of Ontario is now considering the "Affirming Sexual Orientation and Gender Identity Act," known as Bill 77.

Bill 77 assumes gender identities and sexual orientations are all very simple—as if they are all determined at birth and easily detectable. The bill aims to prohibit any clinical practice that "seeks to change or direct the sexual orientation or gender identity of a patient under 18 years of age, including efforts to change or direct the patient's behavior or gender expression." That is an important goal. Doctors and clinicians should not pressure a child to be any gender or another; that is incredibly harmful. But the problem is that the bill defines "sexual orientation or gender identity of a patient [as] the patient's self-identified sexual orientation or gender identity."

So, under this bill's current form, if a seven-year-old male said he feels he's a girl, then the clinician would have to effectively accept that he's a girl. If the child indicates a belief that s/he's a straight girl, then even if the clinician thinks the patient might be a gay boy—that the child might, with good familial and social support, grow up to be a well-adjusted gay man without the need for sex-altering surgeries or lifelong hormone replacement therapy—the clinician must not "change or direct" the child's understanding.

But by not "changing or directing" the child's understanding—by "affirming" a "transgender" identity as soon as it appears—the clinician might actually be stimulating and cementing a transgender identity. (Consider by analogy how telling a girl who says she hates math that "math is for boys" can stimulate and cement that gendered self-identity.) Maybe the child who is "affirmed" will be just as well off with a transgender identity as she would have been without, but the fact is that being transgender generally comes with non-trivial medical interventions, including hormonal and surgical.

Why would a clinician ever think a feminine male child might grow up to be a gay man rather than a straight woman? The data we have indicates that a large percentage of boys who act statistically more "feminine" as children—who dress up in girlish clothing, prefer social role-play games to contact sports, are highly attentive to their mothers and aunts, and feel budding sexual attraction towards male—will end up not as transgender women, but as gay men, at least in our culture. Only a small number will grow up to be straight transgender women.

Even more concerning is what the Ontario's bill's approach could do to a young adult like Leelah Alcorn, the born-male transgender teenager who killed herself because her parents wouldn't accept her identity. Imagine if Leelah had responded to parental pressure by insisting to a clinician trying to help her that she was not transgender. Under Bill 77, the clinician would have to accept the patient's professed self-identity, even if the clinician believed that gender transition might save this patient's psyche and her life.

Worst of all, if Bill 77 passes, it could very well dissuade many compassionate and progressive clinicians from working with gender-variant youth. That would be a terrible outcome. We need these clinicians, and we need them to follow patients' needs, not cultural trends.

Take Jess's case again. Although she isn't transgender, Jess has no doubt that as a youth she needed clinical help as much as transgender youth do: "I wish someone had worked with me on body image and my relationship to my body, on how my body displays gender and how I can convey gender in a way that makes sense for me." If that had happened, she says, she might have avoided the social withdrawal and eating disorder that ensued from her identity struggles.

Make no mistake—for a child who feels consistently and very strongly the body of the "opposite" sex is what she or he needs to survive and thrive, chemical puberty-blockers followed by gender-affirming surgery and hormone replacement therapy can be lifesaving. But for a lot of children who end up in "gender identity" clinics, the story is more complicated.

Jess says—and I agree—children who may be LGBT and/or gender nonconforming "need to arrive at the identity they will" while adults give them "the space to come to that on their own, providing supportive care along the way." Part of that means not pressing a child to tell us what gender and sexual orientation they "really are," as legislation like Bill 77 would seem to encourage.

Jess tells me, "In retrospect, I'm very happy having the body I have, with just some changes in how I express it. I hold internally an identity that is valuable for me, and knowing I don't necessarily have to pick [from the typical social categories] has been very liberating." The clinical goal, in Jess's words, should not be to solidify labels of L, G, B, and/or T with these children, but to "avoid the harmful impacts of stigma towards this population and promote a healthy sense of self." The outcome that should matter to us clinically is not the label the person might adopt, but the person herself.

Alice Dreger is an author and Professor of Clinical Medical Humanities and Bioethics at Northwestern University.

EXPLORING THE ISSUE

Is "Social Transitioning" a Beneficial Treatment for Transgender Children?

Critical Thinking and Reflection

1. What is social transitioning? What, if any, benefits does it have for transgender children? What, if any, are the risks?
2. Is there any evidence that encouraging social transition in early childhood leads to medical or surgical transition in adolescence or adulthood? Is there evidence that discontinuing social transitioning once it has begun is harmful for children?
3. In what ways might the political climate around advocacy and research impact treatment options for transgender or gender non-conforming children?

Is There Common Ground?

The YES and NO selections within this issue draw attention to the issue of best practices for children expressing gender dysphoria, a relatively new frontier in practice and research. Although treatment protocols for transgender adults are well established, for transgender and gender non-conforming children the path is less certain. The authors most certainly agree that the long-term outcomes of early social transitioning among transgender children are unknown due to the limited research on this topic. However, the focal point of this debate, raised at the end of Olson and Durwood's article, simply asks us to consider what is in the best interest of the *transgender* child?

All authors acknowledge that gender is complicated. However, Dreger argues that due to such complexity, parents and professionals should be wary in steering their child toward one identity or the other. Dreger's discussion focuses less on the use of social transitioning in early childhood and more on the possibility that such early steps could lead to more permanent irreversible changes as the child ages, such as the use of hormones and surgical procedures.

Olson and Durwood call into question the idea that allowing young children to socially transition, via changing their clothing choices, names, and pronouns, will eventually lead to detrimental consequences or the use of medical transitioning. Even if a child ultimately identifies as transgender and continues with social transition, there is no guarantee of hormonal or surgical treatments, as some transgender adults never undergo such procedures. They argue that prohibiting children who express gender dysphoria and identify as transgender from proceeding with social transitioning would cause increased psychological harm. They challenge research statistics that have shown expressions of gender variance in childhood is often temporary. As noted in both selections, there is insufficient evidence to truly know how many children who identify as transgender continue to identify this way as adults. For Olson and Durwood, it is better to accept a transgender child's innate understanding of their own gender rather than assume that it is "just a phase." To them, the benefits of social transitioning for transgender children outweigh the perceived risks. What is your take on the issue? How do the complexities of gender, and our cultural attitudes about the gender and sexuality of children, influence your understanding of this debate?

Additional Resources

Ford, Z. (2016). Transgender kids thrive when their parents embrace their identities. Retrieved from http://thinkprogress.org/lgbt/2016/03/01/3755056/transgender-kids-parents-study/

Green, J. (2012). S/He. *New York Magazine*. Retrieved from: http://nymag.com/news/features/transgender-children-2012-6/

Olson, K. R., Durwood, L., DeMeules, M., & McLaughlin, K. A. (2015). Mental health of transgender children who are supported in their identities. *Pediatrics, 137*(3), 1–9. doi: 10.1542/peds.2015–3223

Soh, D. W. (2015). Why transgender kids should wait to transition. *Pacific Standard*. Retrieved from: https://psmag.com/why-transgender-kids-should-wait-to-transition-c989b21c9179#.9uazgleht

Internet References . . .

Parents, Families, Friends, and Allies United with LGBTQ People to Move Equality Forward (PFLAG)

https://community.pflag.org

The TransYouth Project

https://depts.washington.edu/transyp/

TransKids Purple Rainbow Foundation

www.transkidspurplerainbow.org

World Professional Association for Transgender Health (WPATH), Standards of Care

http://www.wpath.org/site_page.cfm?pk_association_webpage_menu=1351

Unit 3

UNIT

Sexual Identities and Expressions

Few issues have undergone such swift and dramatic change in recent American history than our understanding of, and attitudes toward, the diversity of sexual identities. Gender identities, orientation identities, behavioral identities (e.g., "virgin" or "kinky"), relational identities (e.g., monogamous or polyamorous), and even political identities (i.e., feminist or social conservative) are all ways for a person to both signify their uniqueness and build community. These identifies, however, can also pose a challenge to those who see sexuality through a more traditional lens. As we will discuss issues of understanding, acceptance, and individual rights, we see the effects in our families and in public spaces. In the following unit you are asked to explore five issues concerning sexual identities and expressions.

Selected, Edited, and with Issue Framing Material by:
Ryan W. McKee, *Widener University,* Tracie Q. Gilbert, *Widener University,*
and
Jayleen Galarza, *Shippensburg University of Pennsylvania*

ISSUE

Are Women More "Sexually Fluid" Than Men?

YES: Ann Friedman, from "Why Should Fluid Sexuality Be Women-Only?" *The Cut* (2013)

NO: Joe Kort, from "Going with the Flow: Male and Female Sexual Fluidity," *The Huffington Post* (2015)

Learning Outcomes

After reading this issue, you will be able to:

- Define sexual fluidity.
- Explain and evaluate perceived gender differences in how sexual attraction is experienced.
- Describe the social and political impact of the understanding and acceptance of sexual fluidity.

ISSUE SUMMARY

YES: Ann Friedman, a freelance journalist who writes about gender, media, technology, and culture, notes that while men face more scrutiny for same-sex behaviors, research indicates women experience a greater capacity for same-sex attraction than men.

NO: Joe Kort, a psychotherapist, certified sex therapist, and author, draws on his clinical experience as well as recent studies to argue that men's lack of sexual fluidity is a falsehood.

In 2003, pop megastars Madonna and Britney Spears (and Christina Aguilera, though with somewhat less cultural impact) shook the world with an on-air kiss during the MTV Music Awards. At the time, neither was out as any other sexual orientation than heterosexual; indeed, Justin Timberlake—Britney's boyfriend at the time—was captured shortly thereafter with a look as confused as most others, both in the live audience and at home. In 2008, pop heir-apparent Katy Perry waxed poetic about noncommittal physical affection between women in her smash hit, *I Kissed A Girl*. Today, with an increasing number of Americans having (or admitting to having) same-sex experiences (Twenge, Sherman, & Wells, 2016), one might assume that these two events were mere precursors to an inevitable cultural shift in attitude and experience. That said, a curious question remains: how would those pop culture moments have been received if engaged in by self-identified heterosexual male pop stars? Generally speaking, do we expect women to have a greater capacity for sexual attraction to (or to engage in sexual behavior with) a partner of any gender? If so, does this expectation say something about the inherent sexuality of women and men? Or does it speak to the way that women and men's sexualities are influenced, and policed, by our culture? And what, exactly, does it say about our concept of sexual orientation when increasing numbers of heterosexually identified people report having engaged in same-sex sexual activity?

According to sexologist and researcher Lisa Diamond, the term "sexual fluidity" refers to an individual's capacity for sexual attractions and experiences that run counter to one's sexual orientation. In order to more easily wrap one's head around this notion, it may help to consider differences in sexual behavior versus sexual identity, and both of these versus sexual orientation. Our current popular understanding of sexual orientation refers to the gender a person is romantically and/or sexually inclined to; that said, how one expresses that orientation—through behaviors and identity—may vary based on a mixture of contextual factors (e.g., beliefs about marriage, sexual morality, personal and/or cultural traditions) influencing one's personal development. Having attractions that are inclined toward one gender may not automatically preclude a person from engaging in unexpected sexual behaviors with someone of another gender on a situational basis, such as a heterosexual person kissing someone the same sex at a party (taking Perry's example), or a gay or lesbian college student having sexual intercourse with an ex of another gender while home over summer break. While one may feel that engaging in these behaviors means a person is bisexual, it is important to understand that the behaviors one engages in does not, in each person's case, dictate the way they identify, or label, their own sexual orientation.

Diamond's original research uncovered, perhaps unsurprisingly, significant evidence of sexual fluidity among bisexual and unlabeled women, with increased incidence of identity label ambiguity over time. While Diamond's original research focused solely on women, subsequent studies have reported similar instances of lifetime identity fluidity among bisexual men as well, lending credence to the possibility of fluidity across genders. Does this mean, however, that sexual fluidity is a solely bisexual or queer-identified phenomenon? Not exactly, as those who identify as heterosexual, when surveyed, increasingly report incidences of same-sex sexual behaviors, despite remaining consistent in their sexual identity than sexual minorities over time.

What is the reason for this discrepancy between behavior and identity among self-identified heterosexuals? While it is generally thought to be more acceptable for women to express same-sex attraction and intimate relationships, there are still significant social penalties for those who outwardly identify as lesbian or bisexual (as recent examples of discrimination stemming from proposed "religious freedom" laws have shown). For men, hegemonic notions of masculinity that stigmatize same-sex sexual expression may limit their capacity for exploring sexual fluidity. The risks of outwardly identifying as anything other than heterosexual would be a challenge to these hegemonic norms that could result in discrimination or even violence. However, Diamond and others have found that, when given space to do so, heterosexually identified men are more flexible in their sexual behaviors and identity than originally believed, selecting sexual identities more indicative of a heterosexual-"plus" orientation. Situational examples of men without access to potential female partners reveal that heteronormative pressures do not preempt sexual behavior between heterosexual men (e.g., cases of forced seclusion like prisons, all-male educational facilities, or even some fraternities).

A powerful example of identity versus behavior as it relates to our understanding of sexual orientation comes from a common term used among public health professionals. The term "MSM", short for men-who-have-sex-with-men, was originally employed after finding that when researching same-sex sexual behaviors among men, having had sex with another man did not automatically indicate a person would self-identify as homosexual, or gay. Therefore, asking a person their sexual orientation did not necessarily reveal information about their sexual behaviors. Instead of asking them to identify, asking who they were having sex with revealed the information most relevant to the researchers.

Though much of the discussion centers on the individuals one may choose to become sexually involved with, it is important to recognize that sexual fluidity may, for some, reflect additional aspects of sexual expression. This may and may include a variety of other behaviors such as introducing an additional partner into one's sex life, or even engaging in BDSM play.

The following both YES and NO selections acknowledge sexual fluidity as a real and increasingly acceptable expression of sexuality. However, the authors differ in their beliefs about fluidity in women and men. Ann Friedman argues that, while it is true that men face more scrutiny for same-sex sexual expression, this doesn't account for what she believes to be a more common experience of fluidity among women. Joe Kort argues that, based on his professional experience as a therapist and the most recent research findings, men's orientations can be just as sexually fluid as women.

YES

Ann Friedman

Why Should Fluid Sexuality Be Women-Only?

By now, there's an established celebrity "coming out" narrative. You sit down with a morning talk-show host or write a blog post saying that you're in love with someone who shares your gender. Your true fans profess their continued devotion, LGBT rights groups and opinion writers applaud you, and while you'll get some hate mail, most people are relieved to finally have you "figured out"—especially if your sexuality has been the subject of tabloid speculation.

This doesn't quite apply, however, when you reveal you're dating a man but insist you're still attracted to women. "Of course I still fancy girls," said British diver Tom Daley last week. "But, I mean, right now I'm dating a guy and I couldn't be happier." There were some standard-issue homophobic reactions (which Buzzfeed and HuffPost obligingly collected), but Daley also elicited a more specific sort of disapproval from certain fans—*biphobia*, the Advocate called it. These were the people who assumed Daley was gay but unable to fully admit it, or unwilling to relinquish the privileges of being straight. He was called greedy and accused of trying to have it all. (Which is baffling. It's not as if he's dating six people at once.) By contrast, a few days before Daley's announcement, actress Maria Bello published an op-ed revealing she was in love with a woman after years of dating (and marrying) men. While the headlines were conflicted—some said she'd come out as gay, other said she was bi—her son summed it up best: "Mom, love is love, whatever you are." The idea of a woman being legitimately attracted to both men and other women was heartwarming rather than confusing.

When coming out as not-totally-heterosexual, the rules are different for men and women. Perhaps this is because we've had plenty of cultural cues—like chart-topping hit songs about girls kissing girls—and academic research to acclimate us to the idea of women's fluid sexuality. A new British study found a fourfold increase over the past twenty years in the number of women who've gotten it on with another woman, and 15 percent of American women vs. only 8 percent of men say they've had a same-sex hookups. Research on women's sexual desires (as opposed to their behavior) reveals the female libido to be, in the words of author Daniel Bergner, "omnivorous." When researcher Meredith Chivers showed women clips of erotica—women with women, men with men, men with women, lone men or women masturbating, a pair of fornicating apes—*everything* made their vaginas pulse. There were some variations between straight women and lesbians, and among women of all sexual identities. But while women may not admit it to researchers or even acknowledge it to themselves, we're basically turned on by everything.

"Women have a greater capacity for gender-fluid sexual expression than men do," Chivers told Tracy Clark-Flory at *Salon*. Indeed, men's physical responses track much more closely with what they report their sexual identity to be. Straight men are turned on by women and not men; gay men are turned on by men and not women. While there will always be those who argue that this is because of biological differences, there are strong cultural factors at play. Probably thanks to "lesbian until graduation" stereotypes and "I Kissed a Girl"-style odes to superficial experimentation, we're more comfortable with women whose sexuality is harder to define. "Acceptance of bisexual women hinges in part on straight men's fetishization of it," says a friend of mine who has dated both men and women. "My male friends were endlessly curious about the dirty details of my same-sex relationship." In a Pew Research Center survey of LGBT Americans this summer, 33 percent said there was "a lot of social acceptance" of bisexual women; only 8 percent said the same of bisexual men.

My guess is that as taboos and strict sexual categories begin to fall away, men will be more willing to explore same-sex relationships and hookups—and be more willing to admit as much to researchers—without panicking about which label to claim. For people of all genders, figuring out who we are and what turns us on has always been difficult. But we've failed to accept that many of us continue to question our sexuality well into adulthood. Given that most of us go through dozens of other major changes throughout our lifetime, doesn't it make sense that our sexual desires could shift, too? That we might not be simultaneously attracted to both men and women, but that some of us might go through cycles of being more interested in a particular gender?

There are incredibly important, longstanding cultural and political reasons that people identify with terms like *gay*, *lesbian*, *bisexual*, *transgender*, and *queer*—and, for that matter, *straight*. But such a short list is insufficient to describe many people's complex and varied sexual histories. Online dating, which forces people to choose a label for their sexuality when they create a profile, throws the dilemma into stark relief. OkCupid's now-defunct OkTrends blog reported that 80 percent of users who identified as bisexual only checked out the profiles of one gender. "This suggests that bisexuality is often either a hedge for gay people or a label adopted by straights to appear more sexually adventurous to their (straight) matches," speculated blogger Christian Rudder. The post was insultingly titled "The Biggest Lies in Online Dating."

The problem isn't that self-identified bisexuals who message exclusively men or women are being deceptive; it's that a tiny multiple-choice list of sexual identities doesn't capture the breadth and depth of the human sexual experience. I know women who married men, then divorced them and are now partnered with women. I know women who were in serious relationships with women throughout high school, college, and their twenties, only to meet and marry men in their mid-thirties. I know women who get off on lesbian porn but only sleep with men. I know women who are happily married to men but have an open relationship that allows them to sleep with women occasionally. Some of these women call themselves bisexual, but many don't.

I know far fewer men who transcend traditional sexual categories this way, but I don't think this will be the case forever. Traditional definitions of masculinity—which tend to go hand in hand with homophobia—are going through a real shake-up. More hetero men are tentatively admitting that they're turned on by certain sex acts associated with gay men. And Daley's ambiguous coming-out had some mainstream sports sites sounding like a Gender Studies 101 classroom. "In truth, there should be no need for him to declare his sexuality," wrote a blogger at BleacherReport. This is progress.

Securing broad public approval for concrete rights like gay marriage is one thing, but ending pervasive cultural homophobia is quite a bit trickier. And sometimes those goals can seem at odds. It's hard to fight for the right to be openly gay—to argue that homosexuality is *not* a phase or a choice—while simultaneously acknowledging the people whose experiences defy easy categorization. But as gay rights slowly become mainstream, there's more room for not just women, but men, to proudly claim their undefinable sexual histories. As Frank Ocean replied when *GQ* asked if he was bisexual, "You can move to the next question. I'll respectfully say that life is dynamic and comes along with dynamic experiences."

Ann Friedman is a freelance journalist who writes about gender, media, and technology for *NYmag.com*, the *Los Angeles Times*, and the *New Republic*, among many others.

Joe Kort

NO

Going with the Flow: Male and Female Sexual Fluidity

The assumption that females are more sexually fluid than males is a falsehood. In my 30 years of practicing as an openly gay sex therapist, I have seen and worked with far too many men who exhibit sexual fluidity. What is increasingly happening now is that these men are being discovered and "outed" by their female partners who find their browser histories, and it is causing them distress.

Straight couples often come to me, worried because the man in this couple has looked at gay porn or had bisexual fantasies and may be, in fact, gay or bi—and "what does this mean for our future?" In these situations, I find it crucial to explore the phenomenon of "male sexual fluidity" and how it tends to manifest somewhat differently than the sexual fluidity of women.

Sexual fluidity is the understanding that sexual preferences can change over a lifetime and be dependent on different situations. It is a person's ability to engage in sexual behaviors and interest in members of both genders. Sexual preference and sexual orientation are two different things. One's sexual preference is not always equal to one's sexual orientation, but rather to the things one fantasizes about and enjoys sexually in bed. Sexual orientation is how one self-identifies from gay, lesbian, bisexual, straight, etc., and is separate from, but related to, one's sexual preferences.

In the past few years, evidence has suggested men's sexuality is more fluid than we thought. Lisa Diamond, Professor of Psychology and Gender Studies at the University of Utah, presented a convincing amount of data to this effect in her 2013 lecture at Cornell University. Ritch Savin-Williams is doing his own research on "mostly straight" males at Cornell University, studying men who fall into number one on the Kinsey scale.

But male and female sexual fluidity are expressed in ways that may not yet be showing up on paper. If a guy marks a box on a survey saying, yes, I've been attracted to another man, or, yes, I've had sex with another man in the past year, it may not be at all the same thing as when a woman checks the same box. There's a big difference between sex with an emotional bond and a 5-minute bathroom glory hole adventure.

By culture and biology, men are pushed into limited modes of sexual and tenderness expression. Straight women can touch, hold hands, kiss in greeting, even lie in each other's arms (see recent episodes of The Bachelor) without being vilified or (for the most part) misconstrued as lesbian or bisexual. By contrast, little boys are rigidly de-feminized, discouraged from being affectionate with each other from the time they are about eight years old. While this may be changing, open-minded parenting with regards to gender behavior is far from the current norm. In essence, men, under threat of physical violence and ridicule, learn to compartmentalize tenderness, sex, and love.

Plenty of research exists suggesting that, in general, men are big on objectification and separating sex from feelings. Whereas, a fluid woman (tenderness-entitled) might say, "It's not the gender, it's the person." The fluid man (tenderness-repressed, but sexuality-entitled) might say, "Hey, if my dick likes it, I'm going to go for it."

This corresponds to Diamond's data analysis suggesting that while more women in general tend to report being bisexual, men who consider themselves exclusively-straight, while half as likely to report a same-sex attraction than their exclusively-straight female counterparts, have been shown to be more than four times as likely to get it on with a same-sex partner.

This reminds me of the old Billy Crystal joke: "Women need a reason to have sex, men just need a place!"

There are many various expressions of straight male sexual fluidity. In my clinical experience, the one general commonality is that there is no romantic attachment involved. Authentically straight men who have sex with other men are attracted to the sex itself, not necessarily the guy. It may be just a novelty, or an easy way to get laid, but the question: "Do I need to know this person?" is answered with a resounding, "No."

Because of their ability (or dis-ability) to be impersonal, guys are more often drawn to various kinks and fetishized body parts, able to relate sexually with little personal connection. Research has shown a 20:1 ratio between men and women in terms of fetishes.

Look no further than the ads on the gay app Grindr for affirmation of this tendency. Nothing like a nice direct, unsentimental appeal to raw sexuality between two gay men who understand each other:

> "Come worship my huge 9-inch python . . ."
> "Hairy thick-bearded bear bottom, prepared to take discipline . . ."

Try to imagine a lesbian or straight woman soliciting her partner with this approach:

> "My quadruple D's are lonely for your . . ."

If a straight woman put that in a personal ad, she may wind up being mistaken for an escort. That she should have to even worry about this is a fairly depressing example of the sexual repression of women.

But are women generally interested in creating or responding to many ads like this? Once, I was teaching a sexual orientation course for straight therapists, and talking about gay male ads for dating and sexual hookup partners, and asked how many women would answer an ad like one of the above. Almost immediately, a straight female therapist raised her hand and said, "That would be the reason I would not answer an ad!" Almost every woman in the class agreed. Yes, it's anecdotal, but it does speak to the more relational aspect of women's sexual fluidity.

There are videos online that depict showing gay dating apps to straight men, to which the straight men react with things like, "I am in awe of the directness of these guys around sex." This directness may be one reason a man with an exclusively heterosexual orientation may seek out sex with a person of his own gender (or, for that matter, a female prostitute). He responds to a type of language that is incomprehensible or hurtful to his wife or girlfriend. He seeks to fulfill his fantasies in an arena where they are welcome.

I'm not trying to say men cannot have a personal romantic attachment that is sexual. Just that sexual attraction or activity doesn't necessarily lead to attachment, and that often the language men use in expressing their attraction is different. Nor am I trying to say women can't objectify people or enjoy booty calls. But, I do think it is somewhat less easy for them to navigate casual sex with multiple partners. Is this biological or a matter of culturally shaming women's sexual expression? I don't know. Just like I'm not sure how much of men's sexual expression is culturally- versus testosterone-induced.

No matter what the ratio is between biological vs. cultural, there's no doubt cultural influences play a part. For example, why the recent need to name any sexuality or affectionate relationship between straight men as a special category? If a guy has a new friend, he has a *bromance*. If he has a strong admiration for a male celebrity or sports figure, it's a *mancrush*. If he only digs guys when he's stoned, it's *highsexualism*.

On one hand, the very definition of these terms is that they are non-sexual or non-threatening to their hetero-orientation. On the other, there's something more tender there—and it appears liberating to the guys blurting out the names of their mancrushes on TV. Is this homophobia or biphobia? A chink in the armor of male tenderness expression? Or both?

In contrast, women don't have all these categories for themselves. Why would they? Society doesn't misread affection between women in the same way.

I've found it interesting and rewarding to explore these differences with straight couples in ways that lead to better communication, empathy, and understanding. Maybe it's true that sexual expression is as diverse as human beings themselves.

Joe Kort, a psychotherapist, certified sex therapist, and author of several books on male sexuality and relationships, including *Is My Husband Gay, Straight, or Bi? A Guide for Women Concerned About Their Men.*

EXPLORING THE ISSUE

Are Women More "Sexually Fluid" Than Men?

Critical Thinking and Reflection

1. Are women more innately sexually fluid than men? Or are there simply social forces at play that discourage expressions of male fluidity? Explain.
2. What, according to the YES and NO selections, are some differences between how various genders express sexual fluidity? How might those differences impact how the topic is viewed?
3. Are there other factors to consider when thinking about gender and sexual fluidity, outside of those discussed in this issue?
4. How would you identify your sexual orientation? Do you experience a sense of sexual fluidity in your attractions to, or behaviors to, other people?
5. What, if anything, does the phenomenon of sexual fluidity say about our shared cultural understanding and definition of sexual orientation? Is the term sexual orientation out of step with the realities of current sexual expressions?

Is There Common Ground?

Sexually fluidity is still, for the most part, a largely understudied topic. That said, both the selections presented here suggest at least some general ideas on the best way of thinking about it as it relates to gender. Both authors acknowledge that some gender differences in fluidity exist. Where they differ, however, seems to be in identifying where and how those differences emerge—in how they are both labeled and expressed. In Friedman's assessment, sexual fluidity is less common among men, and suppressed as a function of homophobia in society. From Kort's perspective, sexual fluidity is present in equal rates among the sexes, but it is expressed differently. He believes that fluidity in men is so different that it may not be as identifiable using current research constructs. Is sexual fluidity currently defined in a way that excludes men? Or are current definitions of sexual fluidity and sexual orientation out of step with current expressions of sexuality in general?

In her essay, Friedman lays out clear evidence of a double standard in the social acceptance of sexual fluidity among out nonheterosexual celebrities. That said, many feminists have argued that, while society has seemed more accepting—and even approving—of female same-sex behavior, this social acceptance has only been deemed acceptable to the degree that it serves male-centered fantasies. This acceptance, they argue, is more about male attention and pleasure, than being validated as an expression of sexuality on its own. Do you believe this latter perspective bears out, or does Friedman's point represent a stronger way of understanding society's tolerance of female sexual fluidity?

Finally, despite both perspectives presented, one significant question remains when thinking about sexual fluidity and gender: how is fluidity experienced by those who are transgender, intersex, or gender nonconforming? From Kort's perspective, many of the gender differences existing between cisgender men and women have roots in biology; how, then, is that expectation disrupted if the individual in question is intersex, or is assigned a sex at birth that does not correspond with their gender identity? More research is needed to understand sexual fluidity among people of all genders and sexual orientations. Clearly we have yet to scratch the surface of our understanding this important, yet evolving topic.

Additional Resources

Diamond, L. (2008). *Sexual fluidity: Understanding women's love and desire*. Cambridge, MA: Harvard University Press.

Ward, J. (2015). *Not gay: Sex between straight white men*. New York: New York University Press.

Selterman, D. (n.d.). Debunking myths about sexual fluidity [web log post]. Retrieved from http://www.scienceofrelationships.com/home/2014/10/13/debunking-myths-about-sexual-fluidity.html

Rupp, L. J. (2012). Sexual fluidity "before sex." *Signs: Journal of Women in Culture and Society, 37*(4), 849–856.

Tsjeng, Z. (March 10, 2012). Teens these days are queer AF, new study finds. Retrieved from https://broadly.vice.com/en_us/article/teens-these-days-are-queer-af-new-study-says

Internet References . . .

It's Pronounced Metrosexual

http://www.itspronouncedmetrosexual.org

Queering Sexuality: Fluidity of Women's Sexual Desire

https://prezi.com/j_2r8scgiueu/queering-sexuality-womens-sexual-fluidity/

Sexual Fluidity—After Ellen

http://www.afterellen.com/tag/sexual-fluidity

The Sexual Fluidity Project

http://sexualfluidityproject.tumblr.com/

Selected, Edited, and with Issue Framing Material by:
Ryan W. McKee, *Widener University,* Tracie Q. Gilbert, *Widener University,*
and
Jayleen Galarza, *Shippensburg University of Pennsylvania*

ISSUE

Is "Kink" a Sexual Orientation?

YES: Jillian Keenan, from "Is Kink a Sexual Orientation?" *Slate* (2014)

NO: William Saletan, from "The Trouble with Bondage: Why S&M Will Never Be Fully Accepted," *Slate* (2013)

Learning Outcomes

After reading this issue, you will be able to:

- Describe the concepts of heirloom design, product life extension, and slow consumption.
- Conceptualize a personal definition of sexual orientation.
- Describe the controversy of expanding definitions of sexual identity and orientation to include kink identities.

ISSUE SUMMARY

YES: Jillian Keenan, freelance journalist and author of the book *Sex With Shakespeare,* presents kink as a sexual orientation more complex and nuanced than attraction to a specific set of behaviors.

NO: William Saletan, an author who writes about sexuality, politics, science, and technology, argues against kink as an orientation, noting that BDSM is not about *who* one loves, but *how.*

How do you define sexual orientation? What does it mean to be straight, gay, lesbian, or bisexual? Are you familiar with other ways people identify in relation to sexual orientation, such as queer, pansexual, or asexual? What should we make of phrases often used in humorous ways to describe our attractions or behaviors, such as "heteroflexible" or "try-sexual"? Are they simply witty puns, or do they speak to actual expressions of our sexuality? And what, if anything, does being "kinky" have to do with sexual orientation? Could an interest in kink, a term used to describe sexual behaviors or desires perceived to be nontraditional in nature (such as BSDSM or fetishes), be a sexual orientation in-and-of itself?

Language constantly evolves to meet the needs of an ever-shifting culture, and this is especially true of terminology used to describe sex and sexuality. From euphemisms created to disguise sexually taboo topics, to academic jargon coined to represent a new expression or theory of identity, the ways we talk about, and therefore experience, sexuality is anything but static. Take the concept of "sexual orientation," for example. The idea that someone has, as part of their overall personality or identity, a sexual orientation is a relatively new concept. Despite clear and obvious examples of same-sex attraction, love, and behaviors existing in ancient history, the terms "heterosexual" and "homosexual" have only been around since the mid-nineteenth century. Used then, the terms specifically other- and same-sex sexual behaviors, respectively. Over time, our conceptualization of sexual orientation has shifted thanks to researchers and theorists like Alfred Kinsey, Fritz Klein, and Lisa Diamond. Today, when most people use the term sexual orientation, they reference labels like gay, lesbian, straight, bisexual, or queer. Rather than focusing on specific behaviors, these terms represent identities that signal the sex(es) or gender(s) a person finds themselves attracted to.

But if you dig a little deeper you will find that some describe their sexual orientation as much more than attraction to a specific gender; things like personality and even behaviors can play an important role in their sexual identity. Orientation, for them, is a rich tapestry that describes not only attraction, but also how they experience and identify sexual and romantic desires, fantasies, and behaviors. Some identities like queer, pansexual, omnisexual, or even asexual (and the many identities that fall under the asexual umbrella) provide a more nuanced look at sexual identity. These identities help not only in expressing one's sense of sexual self, but also in connecting with others who identify similarly and in building a sense of community.

This complexity, and the current shared cultural meaning of sexual orientation, may leave many scratching their heads. Is being attracted to people with a good sense of humor, or those with dominant or submissive personalities a sexual orientation? Or are they just traits we are attracted to? Is there a difference? What happens when people start to consider alternate kinds sexual or romantic attraction? This is what is being proposed by many who believe that kink is, in and of itself, a sexual orientation. In making this argument, kink identified individuals are challenging some of the basic conceptualizations of sexual orientation shifting the ways we think about attraction.

How does kink and BDSM fit into this discussion about sexual identity and orientation? With the pop cultural success of books like *Fifty Shades of Grey* there has been an increase in awareness about BDSM, which serves as an umbrella term for a diverse range of sexual acts related to bondage and discipline, dominance and submission, and sadism and masochism. The tight-knit community of people who enjoy these behaviors is often referred to as the BDSM community or kink community. Although popular books, films, and music videos have sparked dialogue and interest about these types of sexual acts among the mainstream and among sexual minority communities.

Many kink-identified individuals support the idea of an expanded understanding of sexuality that includes kink as a sexual orientation. Many report experiencing similar trajectories in the development and expression of their sexuality as those who identify as lesbian, gay, bisexual, or queer (LGBQ). Some kink-identified individuals draw comparisons to shared experiences with those in the LGBQ community, such as being drawn to and recognizing kink early in life, feelings of isolation, and an inability to, or challenges with, "coming out" as interested in kink. These individuals may also describe kink related desires as an inherent part of their sexuality. In addition, supporters of including kink as a sexual orientation often discuss the issue of stigma. Although kink has gained visibility, some members of the community have highlighted incidents of discrimination. Proponents of viewing kink as a sexual orientation propose that the way to de-stigmatize kink and BDSM is to consider it as an integral part of an individual's holistic sense of self, rather than a shameful desire to be hidden. They argue that treating attempts to treat people who enjoy BDSM as disordered, damaged, and in need of treatment is similar to thinking that supports harmful conversion therapies directed at lesbian, gay, bisexual, transgender, and queer (LGBTQ) communities.

Opponents of this view argue that there is a difference between sexual orientation and sexual activities we enjoy; including kink in this category could potentially blur this distinction. To them, kink and BDSM are primarily focused on the behavioral aspects of sexuality, which implies there is a choice or range of options involved. This, opponents fear, could potentially create confusion as to whether the same can be said about same-sex relationships—are they primarily based on behaviors one could choose not to engage in? For those individuals who have fought for the recognition of nonheterosexual identities as an innate or natural part of their being, these implications are problematic. Furthermore, they argue, considering kink as a sexual orientation and drawing parallels to other sexual minorities minimizes the unique history and struggles of LGBTQ communities, especially related to the process of coming out within society and is primarily rooted in LGBTQ history. Making comparisons to coming out as into kink versus coming out as gay or lesbian, for example, also raises concerns among some. Outing or coming out still places LGBTQ individuals in vulnerable positions and sometimes people are physically and/or emotionally harmed as a result.

In the following YES and NO selections, Keenan shows support for the idea of kink as a sexual orientation. She identifies the similar experiences between kink and lesbian, gay, bisexual, and transgender (LGBT) communities, including incidents of marginalization, invisibility, and discrimination. She also highlights how those in the kink community find this expression to be an integral aspect of their sexual identities, and not something that can simply perceived as a choice or hobby. Saletan argues against the notion of BDSM as a sexual orientation as he believes it can never be fully accepted by or integrated into society. He argues that not only is kink more aptly considered a lifestyle, and that acceptance of BDSM in conventional society would "dilute" the ultimate intentions of kink.

YES

Jillian Keenan

Is Kink a Sexual Orientation?

It's summertime, so of course the anti-sex crowd has decided to cool down with a fresh wave of sexual hysteria. The latest panic is that kinky people will lure vanilla children into our sexual hellscape through trendy pop cultural depictions of BDSM, such as *Fifty Shades of Grey*. This nonsense is annoying, but it's also nothing new.

It does, however, raise a question that is often discussed in sexual subcultures but rarely mentioned in the mainstream: Is kink a sexual orientation? I think it is—and if I'm right, the pearl-clutching mobs' concern that fictional depictions of BDSM will lure sexually normative people into our lifestyle are as absurd as the fear that *Brokeback Mountain* would tempt straight people into the subversive fringe lifestyle it portrays. (Shepherding, of course. What did you think I meant?)

Many people, including Dan Savage—who, to be clear, is a vocal and consistent source of advice, support, and advocacy for kinky people—have questioned whether kink qualifies as an orientation. As Savage argued, "While some kinksters identify strongly with their kinks and are open about their sexual interests, being into baby bonnets or bondage isn't about *who* you love, it's about *how* you love."

That's more or less true—I suppose BDSM is *technically* how I love my husband. But, with respect, to reduce the orientation of love to a physical technicality is every bit as reductive (and ultimately inaccurate) as it would be to argue that homosexuality is not an orientation, because penis-in-anus is merely "how" a gay man loves his husband.

Put another way, and with apologies to every relative, teacher, and religious leader who influenced my development: Sexual orientation is far more about *who* is putting his penis in your butt—or *who* is spanking me with a belt—than it is about *how* either activity occurs.

Kink can be such an orienting force that, for many of us, it even overpowers gender. One survey from the National Coalition for Sexual Freedom found that 35 percent of BDSM practitioners identify as bisexual—a rate that is much higher than the 1.8 to 2.8 percent rate reported overall. There are many theories about why bisexuality is so common in the kink community, such as the strong possibility that the kind of people who participate in a BDSM survey are more likely to be open to sexual experimentation. But I have my own theory about this phenomenon.

For years, I identified as bisexual because I'm sexually attracted to both men and women and have acted on that attraction. But in recent years, as I explored my own sexuality more, I've realized that's not quite accurate. I'm not attracted to men *or* women as a group—I'm attracted to "tops," or sexually dominant people, as a group; their gender is irrelevant. Many kinky people describe similar feelings.

This orientation doesn't only, at times, overcome gender; it also overcomes the strong evolutionary human impulse to avoid pain. Perhaps this should go without saying, but kink hurts. It's physically painful. (Sometimes extremely so.) Anything that can swim upstream of such a forceful tide must be rooted in something more fundamental and legitimate than merely what's trendy.

The question of whether kink qualifies as a sexual orientation has been a source of friction between the BDSM and LGBTQ communities for a while. A few months ago, rage erupted when a party promoter scheduled a prison-themed event at a local kinky dungeon during San Francisco's Pride weekend. Although it wasn't an official Pride event, some said it was disrespectful to the trauma experienced by LGBTQ inmates in the U.S. prison system. The subcultural infighting sparked by that event echoed debates that have simmered for years.

"As a lesbian, I would like to say a sincere 'fuck you' to people comparing BDSM to homosexuality," a commenter once wrote on a blog.

"As a queer person myself, I would like to say a sincere 'fuck you' to people who claim I ought to see my BDSM and my queerness differently," replied another.

I have no interest in playing Oppression Olympics with the LGBTQ community. To be clear: LGBTQ people face far more institutionalized oppression than kinky people do. It's always tricky to compare groups. My point is not that our experiences are the same, because they're not. My point is that some shared truths about the experience of sexual and romantic marginalization can be illustrated by acknowledging the places where our paths cross.

Both LGBTQ and kinky people have been irrationally and unfairly accused of preying on children. We've both been told to keep our romantic lives private and to not "shove things in people's faces." We've both been told that our expressions of love, which feel so natural and necessary to us, are damaged, broken, unholy, or less valuable than vanilla, heterosexual, cisgender love. Kinky people, like LGBTQ people (although with less frequency), have also been fired, physically attacked, arrested, or had parenting rights revoked because of our orientations. (One study found that roughly 30 percent of BDSM practitioners reported violence, harassment, or job discrimination because of their sexualities.) Both communities have been told our sexual identities are mental illness.

And both groups have been marginalized or belittled by people who could have been natural allies: Some men and women who marched for interracial marriage rights have mocked the LGBTQ equality movement, just as some people who fought for the LGBTQ community have dismissed kinky people as having, at most, a sexual hobby.

We don't choose kink. Yes, there are vanilla people who, inspired by popular books or movies, choose to experiment with BDSM. (There are also straight people who choose to experiment with same-sex attraction, as anyone who went to college on a coast can attest.) And some people find BDSM later in life, don't feel that it's an orientation they were born with, and yet are full and equal members of the BDSM community (to the extent that such a thing even exists) in every way. But that doesn't minimize the fact that, for a huge portion of kinky people, BDSM is not a choice, a hobby, or a phase. Kink is often so fundamental to our sexual identities that it has to be, at least in some cases, an orientation.

From the outside, "this thing we do" seems like nothing more than weird sex stuff. I understand that. But, from the inside, kink is so much more than merely physical. Our orientation is so deeply rooted that many of us feel we were born with it. For us, kink mixes language, ritual, trust, power, pleasure, pain, and identity in a way that can't be captured by a stereotype.

You know what else mixes language, ritual, trust, power, pleasure, pain, and identity? Love. Every kind of love.

Frankly, I think that to reduce sexual orientation to genitalia does *everyone* a disservice. A gay man whose husband was castrated in an accident would still be "oriented" toward his man. A lesbian whose wife lost her breasts to cancer would still be "oriented" toward her partner. A heterosexual firefighter who was disfiguringly burned would expect his wife to still be "oriented" toward him. Clearly, all sexual orientations are about more than just genitalia. (Chromosomes fail as a simple explanation for sex or sexuality, too.) Perhaps we'd all benefit from an approach to "sexual orientation" that is more nuanced and complex than just which set or sets of genitals one prefers.

So let's imagine that an orientation toward "men" is not an orientation toward genitals or chromosomes but, rather, an orientation toward some kind of intangible, supra-physical "male identities." Let's imagine that the same is true of orientations toward "female identities." If that's the case, is it so strange to imagine that some people might be oriented toward identities that are neither male nor female but, rather, dominant or submissive?

"How" a hetero- or homosexual couple has sex is merely one aspect of their orientation, just as "how" a kinky couple has sex is merely one aspect of our orientation. As its core, orientation is about "who" we love for kinky people, too. We're all oriented toward identities.

To fully argue that kink is a sexual orientation, I'll need a definition of what "sexual orientation" is in the first place. But I'm dissatisfied by the ones I've seen. So I'd like to propose a new definition, stolen from Shakespeare: Perhaps sexual orientation is "an ever fixed mark that looks on tempests and is never shaken." Orientation is any sexual identity that is so fixed and unshakable that it defies choice, reason, and even, at times, simple evolutionary explanation.

Some friends have told me that kink should not be considered an orientation since that could open the door for *any* deeply felt sexual identity to claim that status. Is sexual orientation a slippery slope? Are we two clicks away from a strong preference for nerdy-Jewish-tech-guys-with-dark-hair-and-an-athletic-streak being called an "orientation"? Personally, I don't think it really matters—I doubt that preference could become a legally protected category, so if someone wants to say that's her orientation, what do I care?—but, for the sake of conversation, let's say there needs to be some mechanism to limit what can qualify.

Maybe it's those "tempests" that Shakespeare mentioned. Maybe to qualify as a sexual orientation, an identity must not only be innate, unshakeable, and unchosen, but also stigmatized. Maybe my kink will only remain my "orientation" for as long as people continue to blog that I'm a threat to children, tweet that I'm "damaged and repulsive," and email that I should be forcibly institutionalized. (I could link to examples of all three, but I don't want to feed the trolls.) Maybe "orientation" could be a kind of shelter from the storm only for those sexual groups, or individuals, that need it most.

If you accept this definition, then my kink is my sexual orientation. It's not my choice. It's not my illness. And it's definitely not my hobby.

Jillian Keenan, is a freelance journalist who has written for the *New York Times* and *Slate*, and author of the book *Sex With Shakespeare*.

William Saletan

NO

The Trouble with Bondage: Why S&M Will Never Be Fully Accepted

Is S&M going mainstream?

It looks that way. Twenty to 30 years ago, surveys suggested 10 to 15 percent of Americans had tried it at least once. Five to 10 percent had engaged occasionally in BDSM—an umbrella term for bondage, dominance/submission, and sadomasochism. Fewer embrace it as a lifestyle or identity: Even in big cities, attendance at BDSM conventions is said to be only 1,500 to 2,000. But in the last year, the *Fifty Shades of Grey* trilogy has sold more than 65 million copies. The membership of FetLife, a social networking site for BDSM enthusiasts, has doubled to nearly 2 million. Sales of books and equipment have increased. So has attendance at BDSM events. BDSM-related Internet searches (*domination, master, sex slave, sadism*) went up 70 to 80 percent. College groups devoted to "kink," largely BDSM, gained official recognition at Tufts and Harvard. Pillars of the media establishment—ABC, Fox News, the *New York Times*—are exploring the rise of kink in unflinching detail.

Political advocates for BDSM see themselves as successors to the gay rights movement. They cite *Lawrence v. Texas*. They call themselves "sexual minorities" and depict kink as a "sexual orientation." They seek "legitimacy" by bringing BDSM "into the mainstream eye." They ask to be "accepted," "validated," and "normalized." They wonder, according to the *Times*, whether "they are approaching a time when they, like the LGBT community before them, can come out and begin living more open, integrated lives."

Don't count on it.

I don't mean to be cruel. I know people who have lived this life. I've watched others tell their stories on YouTube. I've read the writings of BDSM teachers, advocates, and organizers. These people are conscientious. Many of them have worked hard to draw boundaries to distinguish domination from abuse. At its best, BDSM is a willing power exchange enveloped in love. But it differs from homosexuality in ways that make it much harder to integrate into normal life.

To start with, BDSM isn't an orientation. It's a lifestyle. In the words of one aficionado, "It's not who you love, it's how you love." That makes it much more reasonable to limit this kind of sexual expression. It's hard to hide the fact that you're in a lesbian relationship. But it's not hard to hide the fact that you like to tie up your girlfriend. You can bring her to the office holiday party. You just can't bring her on a leash.

Second, S&M, by its nature, hurts people. Mild bondage is no big deal. But for sadomasochists, pain is the whole idea. Some stick to spatulas and wooden spoons, but others move on to electric shocks, skewers, knives, and butterfly boards. Women who do S&M porn scenes have described electrical burns, permanent scars from beatings, and penetrations that required vaginal reconstructive surgery. While these injuries were accidental, the BDSM subculture doesn't regard intentional harm as wrong. According to the "Statement on Consent" developed by the National Coalition for Sexual Freedom, injury is wrong only if it "was not anticipated and consented to." The coalition hopes to embed this principle in law, "ensuring that consent will be recognized as a defense to criminal charges brought under assault laws."

I understand the coalition's concern. They don't want nosy neighbors dragging you into court because hot wax burned your nipple. But the BDSM community's position—that "government must stay out of the bedrooms . . . of mutually consenting adults, no matter how violent or shocking the activity"—creates perils of its own.

BDSM can be quite dangerous. Responsible practitioners insist it must be "safe, sane, and consensual." But it attracts people who like to push boundaries. Some submissives are adrenaline junkies: They don't believe in safety. Recently, several men have admitted to or have been charged with or convicted of crimes including sexual abuse, kidnapping, and murder, all under the cover of BDSM. These men don't represent BDSM, but they do represent the far end of sadism. On BDSM sites, you'll find harrowing fetishes such as immersion water bondage and breath play, which some community leaders consider inherently unsafe. Even a standard ball gag can kill the victim by triggering regurgitation.

Every article about BDSM now includes the obligatory professional woman who's secure enough in her feminism to admit she likes to be flogged. It's great that we've come that far, but the message is awkward. While reformers in India battle a culture of rape, Indian BDSM advocates extol the bliss of female masochism. While human rights activists denounce caning and waterboarding, BDSM lecturers teach the joys of caning and waterboarding. Abduction, slavery, humiliation, torture—everything we condemn outside the world of kink is celebrated within it.

The core ethical principle of BDSM is consent. But given the underlying dynamics—one person who wants to dominate, another who wants to be dominated—consent often blurs. BDSM attracts masochists whose boundaries can be pushed. It attracts sadists who like to push those boundaries. According to the *New York Observer*, "In the last year, hundreds of people have come forward to describe the abuse they've suffered within the scene. . . . The stories ranged from more benign assaults (unwanted groping) to tales of being drugged and raped." In a survey by NCSF, more than 30 percent of BDSM participants reported that their pre-negotiated limits on violence or domination had been breached. The coalition's spokeswoman concluded: "There is still confusion between consensual BDSM and assault."

BDSM community leaders stress the importance of "safe words"—distinctive words that the submissive can utter to make the dominant stop. But that doesn't always work. Some dominants refuse to honor safe words. Some say they'll respect them, but then they don't. In the intensity of a scene, a submissive can be beaten into a state of disorientation that puts safe words and the revocation of consent beyond her reach. DomSubFriends, a kink site, warns, "A sub may be in subspace and not have the presence to stop the scene." NCSF agrees: "The physical or emotional intensity of a scene can result in the participants getting carried away, or being unable to revoke or modify consent."

In most BDSM relationships, domination or violence is limited to agreed-upon sessions, known as "scenes." Violence becomes abusive when it occurs "outside the scene." But some couples don't accept this distinction. In a "master/slave" relationship, NCSF guidelines say the slave can "give up contemporaneous consent for the duration of the relationship." "There are people that believe that if you write a contract giving up your freedom, you give it up forever," says one BDSM teacher. In these relationships, "if the slave gives up their freedom, that's it. It's over."

For all these reasons, society can never accept BDSM in its entirety. Nor can BDSM fully accept society. If kinksters ever managed to immerse their leather in what they call the "vanilla" world, the vanilla would ruin the leather. That's what *Fifty Shades* has done: By flooding sex-toy shops with suburban women more interested in bodice rippers than in ripping bodices, it's diluting the netherworld. "They took away my BDSM," sniffed one longtime enthusiast.

Don't persecute kinksters. Most of them just want the freedom to play out their fantasies, within limits and without losing their jobs. But if you can't accept consensual domestic violence as just another lifestyle choice, that doesn't make you a prude. It makes you perfectly normal.

William Saletan writes about sexuality, politics, science, and technology for *Slate*. He is the author of the book *Bearing Right*.

EXPLORING THE ISSUE

Is "Kink" a Sexual Orientation?

Critical Thinking and Reflection

1. How do you define sexual orientation?
2. What influences an individual's sexual orientation? Should we expand current definitions and understandings of sexual orientation? Why or why not?
3. How does the suggestion of kink as a sexual orientation complicate preconceived ideas about sexual attraction and identity?
4. Do you believe describing kink as a sexual orientation minimizes the experiences and struggles of LGBTQ communities? Why or why not?

Is There Common Ground?

Our understanding of human sexuality is constantly evolving. The language used to describe what we now call sexual orientation, and what that term even means, is quite different today than it was just a century ago. Have we, as a culture, finally settled on an accurate definition? Or do you think we must expand our understandings and explore challenges to contemporary thought? Although clearly at odds, both Keenan and Saletan recognize that kink and BDSM are trending, emerging in more mainstream conversations and media images. However, as both authors also confirm, this does not necessarily mean that kink communities are being fully embraced or that they will ever reach the point of acceptance.

One supporter of expanding conceptualizations of sexual orientation to be inclusive of kink identities, Natalie Waschots, stated in an interview with *Feministing:*

> Once we can become comfortable with the idea that BDSM, and all the various permutations and possibilities for identity within that, is a sexual orientation, then we can also begin to appreciate this orientation for the positivity inherent within it. Once we stop regarding BDSM as something dark, something unhealthy practiced only by damaged people, it will be possible to see the joy and pleasure possible within this orientation.

Keenan makes similar arguments in her article, expanding on these ideas to urge individuals to de-pathologize kink identities. In addition, she expresses the idea that sexual orientation cannot be merely reduced to the attraction to genitalia. Keenan argues that sexual attraction is more complex and moves beyond the "it's who you love, not how you love" debate. Could expanding ideas of sexual orientation help decrease the stigmatization of BDSM among mainstream society? Should kink be normalized and accepted or will that diminish some of the unique aspects of the community? Can we deny an individual's ability to understand what is innate to her or his own sexuality?

Saletan contends that BDSM is a lifestyle choice and to fight for acceptance is to undermine the foundations of kink—an alternative lifestyle that prides itself in distinguishing from "vanilla" or non-kink people. However, in framing his arguments, Saletan also raises issues of safety. Should kink be acceptable to mainstream society, or is it too extreme of a sexual expression? He warns of confusion in the understanding of consent and the legal issues that may arise. Is this type of argument helpful or a hindrance to understanding the debate? He further proposes that drawing similarities to the struggles and experiences of LGBTQ communities is invalid and is dismissive of the discrimination faced by LGBTQ individuals on a daily basis. Coming out is a process rooted in LGBTQ history and relates to significant histories of marginalization, oppression, and violence against LGBTQ communities within the United States. Are comparisons between the experiences of kink and LGBTQ communities useful and valid or do they serve to minimize the struggles LGBTQ communities still experience? Often ignored in these discussions are those who identify with kink and as a sexual minority. How might their experiences help shape the debate? Is the concept of sexual orientation too limiting to fully understand the wide range of our sexual and romantic expressions?

Reference

Dusenbery, M. (2013). A conversation about kink with Natalie Zina Walschots. *Feministing*. Retrieved from *http://feministing.com/2012/05/09/a-conversation-about-kink-with-natalie-zina-walschots/#more-48016*

Additional Resources

Thorn, C. (2012). BDSM as a sexual orientation and complications of the orientation model. Retrieved from http://clarissethorn.com/2012/04/09/classic-repost-bdsm-as-a-sexual-orientation-and-complications-of-the-orientation-model/

Wakeman, J. (2014). On making the case for kink as a sexual orientation. *The Frisky*. Retrieved from http://www.thefrisky.com/2014-08-18/on-making-the-case-for-kink-as-a-sexual-orientation/

Yost, M. R. & Hunter, L.E. (2012). BDSM practitioners' understandings of their initial attraction to BDSM sexuality: Essentialist and constructionist narratives. *Psychology & Sexuality, 3*(3), DOI:10.1080/19419899.2012.700028

Internet References . . .

The American Psychological Association, Understanding Sexual Orientation and Gender Identity

http://www.apa.org/helpcenter/sexual-orientation.aspx

The National Coalition for Sexual Freedom

https://www.ncsfreedom.org

Selected, Edited, and with Issue Framing Material by:
Ryan W. McKee, *Widener University,* Tracie Q. Gilbert, *Widener University,*
and
Jayleen Galarza, *Shippensburg University of Pennsylvania*

ISSUE

Is Sexting a Form of Safer Sex?

YES: Brent A. Satterly, "Sexting, Not Infecting: A Sexological Perspective of Sexting as Safer Sex," An original essay written for this volume (2011)

NO: Donald A. Dyson, "Tweet This: Sexting Is NOT Safer Sex," An original essay written for this volume (2011)

Learning Outcomes

After reading this issue, you will be able to:

- Describe potential benefits and risks of sexting.
- Compare and contrast media depictions of sexting with the actual prevalence of sexting, according to contemporary research.
- Describe the harm reduction model as it relates to reducing the risks of sexting.
- Compare the World Health Organization's definition of sexual health to your own personal definition.

ISSUE SUMMARY

YES: Brent A. Satterly, associate professor and bachelor of Social Work Program Director at Widener University's Center for Social Work Education, acknowledges the risks involved in sexting while criticizing fear-based media coverage of the phenomenon. He argues in favor of harm-reduction strategies to reduce the risks associated with sexting rather than continuing the trend of panicked reactions to the expression of youth sexuality.

NO: Donald A. Dyson, director of the Center for Human Sexuality Studies and associate dean of the School of Human Services Professions at Widener University, examines sexting through the lens of the World Health Organization's definition of sexual health and determines that the risks inherent in the digital transmission of sext messages is not a form of safer sex.

The rise in cell phone and social media usage has given rise to a new outlet for sexual expression—sexting. Sexting is the nickname given to the sending of sexual messages or pictures via text or other electronic message. While engaging in steamy conversations is far from a new flirtation method, the ability to send, receive, and forward messages and images in an instant is a relatively new method.

Early media coverage of the phenomenon highlighted the perceived harm done to young victims of the sexting trend. Over the past several years, scandals involving underage teens snapping and sending nude pictures of themselves resulted in child pornography charges being filed against teens in several areas across the United States. In other cases, shared images or messages have been used to bully or embarrass the sender. Scandals involving adults, including professional athletes and entertainers, have caught the public's attention as well. Perhaps the most (in)famous sexting incident involved a politician. In 2011, U.S. Congressman Anthony Weiner was forced to resign after sexually explicit images of him surfaced online. Weiner had been sending the photos, along with explicit messages, to female followers of his various social media accounts. Given the high-profile nature of those involved in the scandals, many felt sexting was a danger that had reached epidemic levels!

Research into sexting, however, tells a different story. A 2009 Pew Research study found that, while some young people text nude and semi-nude images for a variety of reasons, only 4 percent have actually sent an image of themselves to someone they know. Only 15 percent of young people report having received such an image via text (1). A study from 2012, which looked at cell phone and other electronic means of image sharing, found even lower percentages of young people participating. In this study only 2 and 1/2 percent of teens had appeared in nude or nearly nude images, and only 1 percent described the images as sexually explicit (showing breasts, genitals, or their buttocks) (2). These statistics present a different story than the sensational headlines and media coverage of the topic. Even in recent studies of young-adult populations, less than half of respondents report either sending or receiving sexts (3, 4).

If so few young people are actually sexting, why is the phenomenon so controversial? Many sexuality educators have questioned the fear-based response and challenged the assumption that sexting is always unhealthy. At its core, sexting is a form of communication, and communication about sexual thoughts and desires is not, in and of itself, a bad thing. Does the digital mode of communication change this? Does the history of messages stored in phones make sexual communication riskier than sharing feelings in face-to-face conversation? Do images need to be shared in order for a text message to become a sext message?

And what about the images themselves? How much skin needs to be shown for a flirtatious message to become a full-on sext? Does a male sharing a shirtless picture of himself, or female sharing a shot of herself in a bikini count as sexting? Or must there be exposed genitals in the frame? Is it safer for a person to snap and share an image of their genitals if their face (or other identifying features like tattoos) is not visible in the frame (5, 6)?

The controversy has presented sexologists an opportunity to question the "sext-panic" that has clouded the dialogue around sexting and examine what place, if any, the behavior has in sexuality education, and if sexting could be a form of safer sex. In the following YES and NO selections, two professors in Widener University's Center for Education do just that. Brent A. Satterly argues that while sexting does not carry the same risks as exchanging bodily fluids, similar harm-reduction strategies applied to physical behaviors can reduce the risks involved in sexting and translate into dialogue and opportunities that will assist young people in navigating sexual scenarios in the future. Donald A. Dyson applies the definition of "healthy sexuality" developed by the World Health Organization to sexting and finds that qualities inherent in the behavior dictate that it is, in fact, unhealthy and therefore cannot be considered a form of safer sex.

YES

Brent A. Satterly

Sexting, Not Infecting: A Sexological Perspective of Sexting as Safer Sex

According to the Pew Research Center (2009), the use of cell phones to text has become a primary mode of communication among adolescents. Over the course of the last few years, there has been a growing concern over how adolescents are using their texting capabilities around sexual expression. Sexting, the infamous phenomenon where individuals—usually assumed to be adolescents—share naked or partially naked pictures (a.k.a. "pics") or sexually explicit conversations with others, is often touted as a severely dangerous practice that can have far reaching negative outcomes for those who do so. The question of whether or not this practice is "safer sex" simply because it doesn't involve the exchange of bodily fluids is a misnomer. I would posit that it is indeed safe sex [not only] for that reason, but also because parents, educators, and public health officials can teach adolescents about how to reduce the potentially negative risks that sexting may involve.

Incidence

This practice has received wide public "sex-panic" oriented media coverage primarily focusing on adolescents (White, 2009). While this "kids these days" approach conveniently neglects to include the wide numbers of adults who engage in the same behavior, it still remains, however, primarily considered an adolescent phenomenon. The Pew Research Center conducted a 2009 survey citing that:

- 4% of 12–17 year olds who own cell phones have sent nude photos of themselves to someone;
- 15% of 12–17 year olds who own cell phones have received nude photos of someone;
- 8% of 17-year-olds who own cell phones have sent nude photos of themselves;
- 30% of 17-year-olds who own cell phones have received nude photos of someone.

Additionally, a MTV-Associated Press poll found that 1 out of 10 young adults between 14 and 24 have at some point shared nude photos of themselves with others (2009). Whether one considers a 24-year-old as an adolescent is another question entirely.

Is Sexting New?

"There's nothing new about using technology to get sex" (Joannides, 2009, p. 393). Sharing naked pictures or having sexually explicit conversations with others is not a new practice (Joannides, 2009). From naked Polaroids to dirty love letters to phone sex to lustful emails to dirty instant messaging, cell phones have made sexually explicit exchanges more accessible with their prominence (White, 2009).

Potential Negative Outcomes of Sexting?

Regardless of history and the populations who practice this behavior, there are potential negative outcomes for the sender based upon what the recipients of such photos or explicit texts do with it. In the immediate, this may include the public exposure of a nude picture by an angry ex who decides to send the picture to a number of other friends or post it online in an effort to humiliate the original sender. It can also have unintended legal consequences where the sender and/or receiver can be charged with various illegalities, including distribution or possession of child pornography and/or registration as a sex offender depending on state law (Ostrager, 2010).

For example, in the state of Pennsylvania, 17 students were threatened with being charged with child pornography possession or dissemination as a result of sending or receiving nude pictures of two female adolescents (Sexting Girls Facing Porn Charge Sue D.A.). The families of the two female teens countersued the local district attorney stating that since the pictures were distributed with their consent, they could not be charged accordingly. The potential far-reaching effects of this are evident.

While all of this is true, it nevertheless reinforces the quest to control American teen sexuality. Since this "sex-panic" effort to legislate and eliminate teen sexuality is fueled by such frightening incidents as the one previously mentioned, often parents or caregivers recount them as evidence for renewed efforts to squash teenage sexual expression. While this sex-panic bleeds over into how adult sexuality is viewed, ultimately the fear is for children. "Because not only are adults increasingly treated as children—incapable, where sex is concerned, of thinking with anything more elevated than their genitals: but the touchstone for policy in an adult world is increasingly 'what would happen if children got hold of this?'" (Fae, 2011, para. 6). A parental blog from America OnLine exemplifies such fear:

> The intention doesn't matter—even if a photo was taken and sent as a token of love, for example, the technology makes it possible for everyone to see your child's most intimate self. In the hands of teens, when revealing photos are made public, the subject almost always ends up feeling humiliated. Furthermore, sending sexual images to minors is against the law, and some states have begun prosecuting kids for child pornography or felony obscenity. There have been some high profile cases of sexting. (*Parentdish,* 2009, para. 1)

While one may assume that parents' desire here is to protect their adolescent, the result is the same as touting the fear-based abstinence-only message of sexuality education. "Just don't do it because bad things will happen to you" is an insufficient message for teens for behavior change.

Christopher White (2009) addresses such media-based sex-panic of sexting as blaming the victim. He reframes this fear-based reactivity as finger-pointing resulting in further harm:

> Sending photos out to friends and family members or posting them online without the consent of the other person is an assault on that individual in an attempt to cause them great harm and suffering and is where we should be focusing our greatest efforts at stopping a behavior, if that is the action most needed. Instead, certain groups are pointing their finger at the person whose photo was distributed without her permission and putting the blame on the victim. (2009, para. 3)

We cannot control adolescents; rather, we must understand adolescents and help adolescents understand themselves. Hence, the efforts public health officials and sexologists should be centered around is a developmentally appropriate comprehensive sexuality education approach starting from very young. Again, White (2009) poses a poignant solution by encouraging us to redirect our efforts toward working with adolescents around decision-making to safeguard themselves:

> Rather than focusing on how harmful and dangerous sexting is, we should be talking to young people about healthy sexual behaviors including the difference between consensual and nonconsensual acts. We should provide them with the truth about possible unintentional consequences and issues related to trust and dating in relationships. (2009, para. 5)

Is Sexting a Form of Safer Sex?

To frame sexting as a form of safer sex is a misleading question. Sexting, in and of itself, does not necessitate an exchange of bodily fluids. It is a digital exchange of pics and/or texts. The Pew Research Center states that sexting usually occurs within the context of three scenarios: (1) between romantic partners; (2) between partners that share the pics outside of the relationship, and (3) between individuals who aren't in relationship, but would like to be. Each context here carries its own risk of potential exploitation or harm, just as any kind of sexual behavior with another person carries a certain degree of risk, depending upon the variables. Many a sexuality educator has uttered the standard phrase, "What is the only 100% risk-free way to not get pregnant or [to not] get a sexually transmitted infection?" The only acceptable answer is, of course, abstinence.

The same logic holds true for sexting. If an adolescent simply doesn't engage in the behavior, he or she is subsequently abstaining from sexting; therefore, the teen is free of risk of exploitation or harm from someone using a pic, the teen previously sent against them. (This does not account for those individuals who have pictures taken of them without their consent, of course.) If, however, the adolescent is engaging in some kind of sexting behavior, most typically within one of the three aforementioned contexts, she or he needs to consider reducing the risk of potential harm. Teaching healthy decision-making within a comprehensive sexuality education curriculum will aid the teen in considering the risks and benefits of such a behavior.

In the column *Go Ask Alice!,* a reader posed a question about how to become more comfortable with using sexting as a means of bridging the distance between she and her long-distance boyfriend. "Alice" responded with a series of both critical thinking questions and recommendations to reduce risks and increase sensuality. These included consideration of (1) who may view the sext, (2) the potential emotional outcomes should someone else see it, and (3) the level of trust of the recipient of the sext (Go Ask Alice!, para. 3). Alice continues, "If you're comfortable with the potential risks, sexting . . . [is a] great way to explore new and unique ways to sexual satisfaction. If you're not comfortable with the privacy concerns, you may want to let this sexual adaptation of technology slide"(para. 4). She adds some additional points to bear in mind:

- **Character limits.** Sexting a Shakespeare sonnet may callous your fingers and require 30 texts before you even get "there," so you may need to keep it short and sweet.
- **Different sense of time.** If one or both sexters are multitasking, response times may vary from seconds to days. If you're looking for more instant gratification from a distance, phone sex or cyber sex may be quicker. If you're looking for something that fits into a busy schedule, this may be your sexual medium while you're physically away.
- **Beep beep!** If you're expecting a heavy flow of incoming sexts, you may want to switch your mobile device to vibrate or silent to not gather a crowd's attention or disturb bystanders.
- **Keep it discreet.** If you're in a public space, consider stepping aside as your face blushes, heart races, or breaths get deeper. Having a concerned stranger ask if you're hyperventilating may create some awkward moments.
- **Secure the messages.** Consider setting up the security and privacy features of your phone to minimize curious friends . . . and strangers from accessing your sexts. (Go Ask Alice!, para. 5)

Conclusion

Avoiding fear-based and controlling approaches to squashing teen sexuality is an important consideration by which to address the very real risks of sexting. In this rapidly changing world of technology, taking a comprehensive sexuality education-based approach to develop healthy decision-making skills for adolescents around sexting may just allow teens to apply such skills in their lives as a whole.

References

Go Ask Alice! (2010, October 15). *Sexting.* Retrieved from http://www.goaskalice.columbia.edu/11238.html.

Fae, J. (2011, February). *Sex is dangerous. Again.* Sexual Freedom, Retrieved February 24, 2011 from http://www.freedominapuritanage.co.uk/?p=1475.

Joannides, P. (2009). *The guide to getting it on* (6th ed.). Portland, OR: Goofy Foot Press.

MTV-AP Digital Abuse Study, Executive Summary. (September, 2009). AThinLine.org. http://www.athinline.org/MTV-AP Digital Abuse Study Executive Summary.pdf. Retrieved from Pewinternet.org.

Ostrager, B. (2010). SMS. OMG! LOL! TTYL: Translating the law to accommodate today's teens and the evolution from texting to sexting. *Family Court Review, 48*(4), 712.

Parentdish. (February 21). RE: Sexting and your kids [Web log message]. Retrieved from ProQuest Central. (Document ID:2272244681).

Sexting Girls Facing Porn Charge Sue D.A. (2009, March 27). CBS.com. Retrieved from http://www.cbsnews.com/stories/2009/03/27/earlyshow/main4896577.shtml

White, C. (May 2009). Teen sex panic: Media still freaking out about "sexting". Retrieved from Alternet.org.

Brent A. Satterly, is an associate professor and bachelor of Social Work Program Director at Widener University's Center for Social Work Education.

Donald A. Dyson

NO

Tweet This: Sexting Is NOT Safer Sex

In their publication Mobile Access 2010 (Smith, 2010), the Pew Internet and American Life Project identified the current trends in cell phone usage. At the time of the report, 82% of all adults (age 18+) in the United States owned a cell phone. Of those people, 76% used their cell phone to take pictures, 72% used text messaging, and 54% had sent photos or videos using their cell phone.

Leading the charge toward a fully wired populace, the 18–29 year olds in that survey scored higher across the board in their wireless technology utilization. In this age bracket, 90% of the overall population owned cell phones, with 93% of those individuals taking pictures, 95% texting, and 81% sending photos and videos.

Consider as well that the average age for young people to own their first cell phone has decreased dramatically. In the latest data available from Pew on adolescent cell phone use from 2009 (Lenhart, 2009), 58% of 12 year olds owned a cell phone. This number was up dramatically from 18% in 2004.

While ownership has increased, the available technology has moved ahead light years as well. Touch screens with incredible definition join with faster networks to easily facilitate the sharing of pictures and videos from phone to phone. Facetime features allow individuals to live video chat between similarly equipped smartphones. Add to this the increase of smartphone applications (apps) that connect random strangers for live video chat, and the implications are staggering.

For decades, professionals in the technology field have accepted the fact that pornography, in many ways, drives technological innovation (Johnson, 1996). This innovation, often moving faster than the development of ethical guidelines, creates new opportunities for sharing and expressing oneself, including one's sexual self. According to Coopersmith (2009), these technologies offer users the ability to create and share information with both a sense of privacy and with user-friendly interfaces. In essence, it is quick and easy to create and send sexual images in a way that feels, to the user, like it is safe from the judgment and oversight of others.

Out of this technological morass has come the phenomenon popularly referred to as "sexting," or the sending and receiving of sexually explicit text messages (including words, symbols, pictures and videos) using an individual's cell phone.

In the 2009 Pew data of teen cell phone users between 12 and 17, four percent (4%) had sent a sexual image (nude or nearly nude) of themselves to someone via text message and 15% had received such an image. In 17 year olds, those numbers literally doubled, with eight percent (8%) having sent and 30% having received such images (Lenhart, 2009).

Little research has been done on these patterns in adult users, but it is safe to assume that turning 18 years old does not immediately change an individual's behavior, and these trends are likely to continue as technology users get older. As a result, we must begin to acknowledge that sexting is a phenomenon that not only exists, but also exists with little or no oversight and little or no ethical study to guide its use.

Within this experience, some advocates for sexual freedom and expression along with some dedicated to the prevention of sexually transmitted infections, HIV, and unintended pregnancies have begun to consider whether or not sexting can be considered the new "safer sex." Consider the origin of the safer sex terminology. Rising out of the HIV pandemic, first as "safe sex" then as "safer sex," the term has come to be associated with sexual practices that do not risk spreading disease or creating an unintended pregnancy.

With this definition, sexting would certainly seem to be a natural fit. To date, it is not possible to pass human viruses or semen from one mobile device to another through a wireless network.

At issue here, though, is the narrow and reductionist view of sexuality that has too often been embraced as the guiding principle of sex in the current millennium.

Ask most high-school sexuality educators for the core concepts of their curricula, and you are likely to get "safer sex" from almost every one. Lessons about condoms and contraception are surely included if allowed by the administration and school board.

In fact, the abstinence-only education movement succeeded in narrowing the debate about sexuality education to the extent that often, when advocates fight for "comprehensive sexuality education," what they are fighting for is the inclusion of medically accurate information about condoms and contraception (Collins, Alagiri & Summers, 2002).

It is important in this discussion, however, to consider a more holistic approach to sexuality. In response to the global need for a clear construction of what it means to be sexually healthy, the World Health Organization (WHO, 2002) created the following definition:

> A state of physical, emotional, mental and social wellbeing in relation to sexuality; it is not merely the absence of disease, dysfunction or infirmity. Sexual health requires a positive and respectful approach to sexuality and sexual relationships, as well as the possibility of having pleasurable and safe sexual experiences, free of coercion, discrimination and violence. (p. 10)

In this larger context, disease prevention is clearly a part of the physical wellbeing identified. As such, it is certainly an important consideration in sexual decision-making. However, it is far from the only consideration necessary. In fact the definition clearly defines health as beyond mere disease prevention. Using the WHO definition, in order to consider a behavior "safe," one would have to consider the emotional, mental, and social implications associated with the behavior as well.

Briefly consider the act of sexting in the framework provided by the WHO. To do this, one must remember that electronic images sent from one device to another have a few unique qualities. First, they have the potential to remain intact and available for years. Second, because of this longevity, they can be transferred from one device to another and can exist in multiple locations at the same time. Third, this potential for multiplication makes sending or showing them to people who were not the intended recipients remarkably easy.

Now, consider the WHO framework. Is sexting safe physically? Yes, from disease. And while images cannot physically harm an individual, a jealous lover in a fit of rage can certainly cause serious physical harm after seeing a sexual image of another person on a partner's cell phone or computer. Also consider the reality that in some municipalities in the United States, minors who are sending images of themselves, their friends, or their classmates are being charged with both creating and distributing child pornography. This offense can lead to incarceration as well as to inclusion in sex offender registries (Lenhart, 2009). Neither are "safe" locations.

Is sexting safer emotionally? This is a more difficult issue to parse out. Sexting can be flirtatious, fun, and bring an individual a great deal of emotional joy. It is also possible for those images to be kept over time, to be shown to unintended recipients, to be used to blackmail, bully, intimidate, and harass. Imagine the jilted lover who sends your seminude picture to your workplace, or the divorcee who uses stored sexts in a custody battle. The potential for emotional harm certainly needs to be acknowledged.

Is sexting safer mentally? While social networking has changed the nature of privacy in today's online world, sexual images of one's self are still generally considered to be private, and shared with those with whom an individual chooses. The nature of digital communication removes the power of choice from the individual, allowing others the freedom to determine who does and does not have access to these very personal images. That powerlessness, combined with anxiety about the possible unintended recipients of the images, can certainly cause an individual mental anguish.

Finally, consider the "freedom from coercion, discrimination and violence" clause. It is clear that the images captured in sexting can be used for all of those things.

In short, sexting is not and cannot be the new "safer sex." In and of itself, it is NOT safe, and framing it as such teaches individuals to ignore the potential harm that may come from engaging in the behavior. Would you tell your 11-year-old niece that sexting was safe?

In the end, it is far wiser to consider sexting to be like most other sexual behaviors: a mixed bag. It can be fun, flirtatious, exciting, and contribute to some wonderful sexual experiences. It also has risks associated with it, and those risks are beyond mere disease transmission or pregnancy. The key is to educate people about the potential risks, help them to consider how those risks fit into their life, and to make individual choices about their willingness to accept those risks.

References

Collins, C., Alagiri, P., & Summers, T. (2002). Abstinence only vs. comprehensive sex education: What are the arguments? What is the evidence? AIDS Policy Research Center & Center for AIDS Prevention Studies, AIDS Research Institute,

University of California, San Francisco. Retrieved April 1, 2011, from http://ari.ucsf.edu/pdf/abstinence.pdf

Coopersmith J. (2000). *Pornography, Technology and Progress,* ICON 4, 94–125.

Johnson, P (November 1996). *Pornography Drives Technology: Why Not to Censor the Internet.* Federal Communication Law Journal 49(1).

Lenhart, A. (2009). *Teens and Sexting.* Pew Internet & American Life. Retrieved from http://www.pewinternet.org/~/media//Files/Reports/2009/PIP_Teens_and_Sexting.pdf

Smith, A. 2010. *Mobile access 2010.* Washington, DC: Pew Internet & American Life Project.

World Health Organization. (2002). *Defining sexual health: report of a technical consultation on sexual health,* 28–31, January 2002, Geneva. Retrieved April 1, 2011, from www.who.int/reproductivehealth/publications/sexualhealth/defining_sh.pdf.

Donald A. Dyson, is director of the Center for Human Sexuality Studies and associate dean of the School of Human Services Professions at Widener University.

EXPLORING THE ISSUE

Is Sexting a Form of Safer Sex?

Critical Thinking and Reflection

1. What are the risks involved in sexting for teens and adolescents? For young adults?
2. What strategies could be used by young people to reduce the risks of sexting?
3. Are there things that are easier for you to express via nonverbal communication like text messages? Why or why not?
4. In what ways could sexting be seen as a form of safer sex?
5. What other technologies, when first introduced, might have led to a "panic" similar to the controversies surrounding sexting?

Is There Common Ground?

In the YES selection, Satterly presents strategies for reducing the risks involved in sexting. Do you think these steps make sexting a safe practice? Or is it still too risky for teens to engage in the practice? Are there things that are easier to say via text than in person? Can sexting make communication about sexual desires or boundaries easier? Can sexting contribute to healthy sexual dialogue and expression of feelings? Or are the risks still too great? Dyson examines sexting through the World Health Organization's description of "healthy sexuality" and comes to the conclusion that it is not safe. Do you agree with his conclusion? Why or why not? What is your personal definition of sexual health? He states that describing sexting as a form of safer sex "teaches individuals to ignore the potential harm that may come from engaging in the behavior." Do you agree? Finally, Dyson asks "Would you tell your 11-year-old niece that sexting was safe?" What is your answer to this question?

Most of the attention given to sexting has focused on adolescents. But sexting is not limited to the keypad-savvy thumbs of teens. Adults also engage in the practice, and the high-profile sexting mishaps of celebrities and politicians have received media attention as well. Are there different risks for adults who sext as opposed to teens? Why might adults consider sexting a problem for youth while engaging in the practice themselves? What does this say about the risks, benefits, and meaning behind the practice?

Lastly, have you ever sent or received a sext message? What were the reasons behind your actions? How did you feel when you clicked the send button or opened the message? Did you consider both the risks and benefits involved? Did you talk with your partner about what should happen to the images or messages once the conversation (or relationship) has stopped? Do smartphone apps like "SnapChat," which deletes shared images within a few seconds of being viewed, reduce the risks of sexting? In the end, what shaped your final decision? Do you think the conclusions you came to about sexting are the same conclusions everyone should come to? Should sexting be included in conversations of safer sex options?

References

(1) Lenhart, A. (2009). "Teens and Sexting," www.pewinternet.org/~/media//Files/Reports/2009/PIP_Teens_and_Sexting.pdf

(2) Mitchel, K., Finkelhor, D., Jones, L., & Wolak, J. (2012). "Prevalence and Characteristics of Youth Sexting: A National Study," *Pediatrics* (vol. 129, no. 1, pp. 13–20).

(3) Benotsch, E., Snipes, D., Martin, A., & Bull, S. (2013). "Sexting, Substance Abuse, and Sexual Risk Behavior in Young Adults," *Journal of Adolescent Sexual Health* (vol. 52, pp. 307–313).

(4) Gordon-Messer, D. , Bauermeister, J., Grodzinski, A., & Zimmerman, M. (2013). "Sexting Among Young Adults," *Journal of Adolescent Sexual Health* (vol. 52, pp. 301–306).

(5) CBSnews.com "Girl, 15, Faces Porn Charges for Sexting" (February 20, 2009), www.cbsnews.com/stories/2009/02/20/national/main4816266.shtml

(6) Quaid, L. (December 3, 2009). "Think Your Kid Isn't Sexting? Think Again," www.msnbc.msn.com/id/34257556/ns/technology_and_science-tech_and_gadgets/

Additional Resources

Benotsch, E., Snipes, D., Martin, A, & Bull, S. (2013). "Sexting, Substance Abuse, and Sexual Risk Behavior in Young Adults," *Journal of Adolescent Sexual Health* (vol. 52 pp. 307–313).

Gordon–Messer, D., Bauermeister, J., Grodzinski, A., & Zimmerman, M. (2013). "Sexting Among Young Adults," *Journal of Adolescent Sexual Health* (vol. 52, 301–306).

Jaishankar, K. (2009). "Sexting: A New Form of Victimless Crime?" *International Journal of Cyber Criminology* (vol. 3, no. 1).

Lenhart, A. "Teens and Sexting" (2009), www.pewinternet.org/~/media//Files/Reports/2009/PIP_Teens_and_Sexting.pdf

Levine, D. "Sexting: A Terrifying Health Risk . . . or the New Normal for Young Adults?" *Journal of Adolescent Health* (vol. 52, no. 3, pp. 257–258).

Shafron-Perez, S. "Average Teenager or Sex Offender? Solutions to the Legal Dilemma Caused by Sexting," *The John Marshall Journal of Computer and Information Law* (February 2009).

Internet References . . .

MTV—A Thin Line Campaign

This page, from MTV's Thin Line Campaign, reports on research and lays out the risks of teen sexting.

www.athinline.org/facts/

Older Adults and Sexting

This article, from the American Association of Retired Persons (AARP) discusses trends in sexting among older adults.

www.aarp.org/relationships/love-sex/info-11-2009/sexting_not_just_for_kids.html

Sexting: Risky Actions and Overreactions

This is the FBI's infosheet on youth sexting. It addresses legal and other issues.

www.fbi.gov/stats-services/publications/law-enforcement-bulletin/july-2010/sexting

Youth+Tech+Health (YTH)

YTH, formerly known as ISIS, is an organization dedicated to advancing the health and wellness of youth through technology.

www.yth.org

Selected, Edited, and with Issue Framing Material by:
Ryan W. McKee, *Widener University,* Tracie Q. Gilbert, *Widener University,*
and
Jayleen Galarza, *Shippensburg University of Pennsylvania*

ISSUE

Is the Addiction Model Appropriate for Treating Compulsive Sexual Behaviors?

YES: Isaac Abel, from "Was I Actually 'Addicted' to Internet Pornography?" *The Atlantic* (2013)

NO: Marty Klein, from "Why 'Sexual Addiction' Is Not a Useful Diagnosis—And Why It Matters," *martyklein.com* (2016)

Learning Outcomes

After reading this issue, you will be able to:

- Describe several sexual behaviors/scenarios that could be classified as problematic ("compulsive" or "addictive").
- Compare the addiction treatment model for behaviors like drinking or gambling and contrast it with the addiction model for sexual behaviors.
- Describe the importance of medical and academic sources like the diagnostic and statistical manual (DSM) on the legitimacy of the "sex addiction" model.
- Explain the influence personal values have in determining whether sexual behaviors/scenarios are seen as problematic.

ISSUE SUMMARY

YES: Isaac Abel, a journalist who writes (under a pen name) about sexuality and gender, shares his story of compulsive sexual behaviors while arguing that the sex addiction model, while not perfect, gave support to his struggle.

NO: Marty Klein, an author and Certified Sex Therapist, argues that the sex addiction model is harmful to clients, treating normal sexual behaviors as pathologies and gives undue authority to moralizing, sex-negative "experts."

The name Tiger Woods was once conjured images of competition, championships, and multimillion-dollar endorsements. The champion golfer was on pace to win more major tournaments than anyone in history. But after his multiple extra-marital affairs were revealed, his name became synonymous with one term—"sex addict." Woods sought to keep much about his situation private, but soon apologized to family and fans at a press conference. Questions and diagnoses were tossed about from television studios to dining rooms world-wide. *"Why would he risk his family and fortune?" "He MUST be addicted to sex!" "Sex wasn't his problem, hubris was!"*

While Woods' behavior was blamed on addiction by many in the general public, the concept of sex-addiction is a controversial subject among experts in the fields of sexology and sex therapy. At the heart of the controversy is a seemingly simple question that has no easy answer: *how much sex is too much?*

Consider this exchange from the movie, *Annie Hall*. Two characters, Alvy and Annie, have just been asked by their therapists if they have sex "often".

> Alvy: Hardly ever. Maybe three times a week.
> Annie: Constantly. I'd say three times a week.

Whether or not one can (or is) having too much sex might be a matter of perspective, as it seems to be for Alvie (wanting more) and Annie (wanting less). On the other hand, some members of the sexological community will clearly tell you that there is a point at which sex can become too much.

Another important consideration is how a person defines sex. Does it include masturbation? Does it include oral or anal intercourse, in addition to vaginal intercourse? Are nongenital touching behaviors, like kissing or massage, sexual in nature? And how about the viewing of online pornography, or the reading of an erotic novel like *Fifty Shades of Grey*? Is sex outside of a committed relationship or marriage necessarily a sign of addiction? The answers will depend on who you ask.

Much of modern understanding of sexual addiction comes from the work of Patrick J. Carnes, who authored *Don't Call It Love: Recovery from Sexual Addiction.* Carnes cofounded the Society for the Advancement of Sexual Health in 1987, an organization dedicated to "helping those who suffer from out of control sexual behavior." Today, Carnes is considered a leading authority on sexual addiction, in a field that includes prevention services, treatment services (including a 12-step recovery model), professional conferences, an academic journal *(Sexual Addiction and Compulsivity),* and more.

The website for Sex Addicts Anonymous (saa-recovery.org), which points visitors to links for resources and meeting information, details the frustration of sex addicts who feel they are "powerless over our sexual thoughts and behaviors and that our preoccupation with sex was causing progressively severe adverse consequences for us, our families, and our friends. Despite many failed promises to ourselves and attempts to change, we discovered that we were unable to stop acting out sexually by ourselves."

The framing of sex, masturbation, or even viewing explicit materials as a compulsive and addictive behavior is nothing new. The idea that masturbation and frequent intercourse could send a person into a downward spiral of unhealthiness was presented in advice columns, "health" journals, and other periodicals during the Victorian Era and the early 1900s. Consider the following excerpt about masturbation from John Harvey Kellogg's *Plain Facts for Old and Young,* written in 1891:

> As a sin against nature, it has no parallel except in sodomy. It is known by the terms self-pollution, self-abuse, masturbation, onanism, voluntary pollution, and solitary or secret vice. The habit is by no means confined to boys; girls also indulge in it, though it is to be hoped, to a less fearful extent than boys, at least in this country. Of all the vices to which human beings are addicted, no other so rapidly undermines the constitution, and so certainly makes a complete wreck of an individual as this, especially when the habit is begun at an early age. It wastes the most precious part of the blood, uses up the vital forces, and finally leaves the poor victim a most utterly ruined and loathsome object.

Nineteenth-century preacher Sylvester Graham also described a litany of ailments that would affect the masturbator, or anyone who had "frequent" intercourse before age 30. If the names Kellogg and Graham ring a bell, it may be because the food products they created, cornflakes and graham crackers, were developed in order to (supposedly) help suppress the sexual urges of some of the earliest "sex addicts" (which, by their definitions, could have been just about anyone)!

More recently, attempts at measuring sexual addiction have taken on more a more scientific tone. Critics, however, argue that it is simply the same old Victorian idea, repackaged for a new century. Many modern-day sexologists call the idea of sexual addiction nonsense, stating that the very term "sexual addiction" invites comparison to other addictions in which the object of dependence (heroin, nicotine, alcohol, gambling, etc.) is inherently harmful. They explain that sex, as a normal biological drive, should not be placed in the same category. Efforts to create an addiction out of sex do nothing more than feed a hungry new addiction treatment industry that is erotophobic, at its core.

This subject was at the forefront of the mental health community's debate over revisions to the fifth edition of the *Diagnostic and Statistical Manual of Mental Disorders (DSM),* published by the American Psychiatric Association in 2013. The workgroups charged with updating what is considered by many to be the "holy scripture" of psychology poured over research on sex addiction and letters from advocates and organizations on all sides of the debate. They considered the scientific evidence for and against the phenomenon, the impact and validity of terms like "out-of-control," "compulsion," and diagnoses such as "sex addiction" and "hypersexual disorder". Ultimately, both sex addiction and hypersexual disorder were omitted from inclusion in the updated DSM.

This lack of inclusion, however, has not stopped the debate. From the pages of scientific journals to Hollywood films, from academic list-servs to advice columns in the back of weekly independent newspapers, everyone seems to have an opinion. So much ink (and online video) has been spilled discussing sex addiction, that social and behavioral scientists who actually research the phenomenon have a hard time breaking through the cultural noise.

In the following YES and NO selections, Issac Abel (a pen name) explores the nature of his own sexual compulsions in order to find out the truth about sexual addiction. He argues that, while the term "addiction" may not be the best descriptor, it gives those who feel their behaviors are problematic a foothold in addressing their problems. Sex therapist Marty Klein rejects the notion of "sex addiction" as unscientific and moralistic. He argues that much of what is labeled problematic behavior is quite typical, and that applying the addiction treatment model to these behaviors preys on people's sex-negative insecurities.

YES

Isaac Abel

Was I Actually 'Addicted' to Internet Pornography?

I was staring at an inbox overflowing with emails about porn. Not spam, but hundreds of personal emails from people I'd never met, detailing their relationships with Internet pornography.

The emails were in response to a piece I wrote for *Salon,* in which I described the history of my Internet porn use. It began in pre-pubescence and continues to infect my intimacies today, despite an ongoing four-year boycott. Through the honesty of my digital pen pals, I found out I wasn't alone in having problems with porn or being disoriented about what that said about me. I mean, I'm not really a porn "addict" or anything, right? But if I'm not, then what am I?

Fortunately, some of my readers felt like they had discovered resources to understand, if not resolve, their porn-related tensions. This cadre of anonymous porn veterans pointed me toward a cache of research, which launched me on a rather academic investigation with some of the world's leading experts on "porn addiction," to find out what's been going on inside my head and what it says about who I am.

What Happened to My Brain?

There's not a consensus on the science of how porn affects the brain, but there is a lot of information on the topic. So much that it can be difficult to sift through.

Marnia Robinson and Gary Wilson, a science writer and science teacher who are married and the founders of YourBrainOnPorn, are leading voices in the space. They admit that they don't have the academic credentials, but think they've compiled some reliable information from years of following the research.

I sat down to watch Wilson's TED talk—now viewed over 900,000 times—with the proud skepticism of a recent university graduate. Wilson laid out his hypothesis: "natural addictions" arising from needs like food and sex have essentially the same neurochemical effect on the brain as drug-related addictions by hijacking evolutionarily useful mechanisms.

Wilson cites one such evolutionary mechanism called the "Coolidge Effect." This describes how male sheep typically take longer to ejaculate when having sex with the *same* ewe, but can ejaculate with a *new* partner in about two minutes every time. Wilson says that mammals developed tools designed for binging on natural rewards in case they needed to pack away food after a hefty kill or got their moment as Alpha male.

According to Wilson's theory, Internet porn perverted this evolutionary mechanism. It tricked my brain into thinking that I had the opportunity to procreate with limitless new mates, prompting repeated "hits" of dopamine, a neurotransmitter associated with reward and motivation. These persistent spikes of dopamine triggered the release of another chemical—ΔFosB—that's necessary for binging on rewards like sex and food.

With a reward like food I would eventually get full and my brain would cease its excitement for new bites. But the continuous stream of new sexual mates in Internet porn overrode my normal satiation mechanisms for sex, causing ΔFosB to *accumulate* in my brain. The accumulated ΔFosB ultimately led to physiological changes—a numbed pleasure response, hyper-reactivity to porn, and an erosion of willpower—that resulted in my cravings and addiction-like symptoms.

According to Wilson, Internet porn's power to sustain arousal with mass numbers of novel mates at-a-click has sensitized many people's brains to porn sex rather than real sex, leading to a wave of porn-induced brain-based sexual dysfunction. This is distinct from past pornography, because even fiends flipping through magazines could only fool their brain into thinking that there were a dozen or so different partners at a time with whom they could copulate.

Wilson contends that these new Internet porn "addicts" tend to exhibit specific symptoms related to these new conditions of porn, like compulsive novelty seeking and mutable (shifting) sexual tastes. This can further exacerbate stress if users' porn-based sexual fantasies morph to the point where they clash with their self-identified sexual desires or orientation.

Wilson's theory resonated with me, as did the trove of candid narratives of porn addiction and recovery hosted on YourBrainOnPorn.com that color the portrait of a user I can understand—who can't get it up or can never cum, who watches gay porn or fetishes like "scat" despite having no real-world interest in those scenarios, and who spends hours a day masturbating with a tight-squeeze "death grip" that just can't be matched by vaginal sex.

While I was tempted to run with these corroborating accounts, I recognized that anecdotes were just that, and I wanted to see more rigorous investigations before drawing any conclusions.

The critics of YourBrainOnPorn.com feel the same way. They point out that there has never been a study that specifically examines the brain changes of Internet porn users with the scientific robustness of a randomized control trial, so the brain changes that Wilson and Robinson speculate are occurring in heavy porn-users have not actually been observed.

It's true, but that standard might not be feasible here. In 2009, University of Montreal professor Simon Lajeuness tried to set up such a study, but was thwarted because he "could not find any adult men who had never viewed sexually explicit material."

In lieu of such a study, Wilson and Robinson link to a slew of studies that show how the underlying brain changes observed in *all* addicts have already been seen in the brains of overeaters, compulsive gamblers, video gamers, and more recently in "Internet addicts" (including porn-watchers).

These changes include desensitization (reduced responsiveness to pleasure), sensitization (hyper-reactivity to addiction-related cues), abnormal white matter (a weakening of the communication between reward circuits and the frontal cortex), and hypofrontality (a decrease in frontal-lobe gray matter that is involved in impulse control and decision-making).

Still, the lack of scientifically rigorous research that isolates Internet porn users from other "Internet addicts" has forced Wilson and Robinson to cite testimonials—and is why the couple's detractors cry "anecdotal pseudoscience!" and "mass hypochondria!" Sometimes, Wilson and Robinson do seem to get carried away, like by claiming that ex-Internet porn addicts are a valid, albeit "informal," control group to study this phenomenon (but, of course, they're not randomly selected, so there may be a common trait among these folks that made them use and stop using that could affect their results).

If the duo comes off as overzealous in their defense of the legitimacy of porn addiction, it may be because their counterparts are so dogmatically dismissive. Well-known sex therapist Dr. Marty Klein argues in *The Humanist* that these "addictions" are likely secondary to other root causes like bipolar disorder, OCD, borderline personality disorder, or just masturbating too much, and that focusing on porn masks the problem—and the individual's responsibility to deal with his own immature decision-making. Dr. Klein categorically refutes the addiction model, stressing that most people who watch porn have no problem with it. He declares, "[U]sing porn does NOT cause brain damage, erectile dysfunction, or loss of sexual interest in one's mate."

Klein elaborated on his perspective on a January episode of *the Savage Love Podcast* with the celebrated sex advice columnist Dan Savage (who backs him up):

> "When a lot of people who label themselves as sex addicts or porn addicts say, "I'm out of control," what they really mean is "You know, it would be really uncomfortable to make different decisions about sex than the ones that I'm making. When I'm lonely it would be really uncomfortable to not look at porn."

On air, Dr. Klein constructed a straw man of a porn addict who is too undisciplined "to stop looking at porn for five minutes," too unwilling to address the emotional roots of his behavior, and too socially inhibited to have a "decent" relationship alternative. I was feeling exhausted at the thought of contorting myself to fit this description, but gave up even trying when Dr. Klein informed me by email that I was more alone than I thought: "[I] do NOT see the epidemic of young men with porn-created erection problems that Robinson wants to help . . . she's probably making a sampling error."

However, Dr. Klein's critics note that he has been defending pornography against censorship since the 1980s (apparently to the adoration of the industry; he is listed as a "porn star" on Adult Video News' website) and assert that he has not adequately taken into account just how different Internet porn is from its antecedents.

In academic circles too, the debate on the primacy of porn's role in problematic sexual behavior (as opposed to a secondary symptom or coping mechanism) is paramount.

Dr. Jim Pfaus of Concordia University, a leading researcher in the science of porn, claims that Internet porn can lead to chronic masturbation, but that the masturbation itself is the primary issue. Author Naomi Wolf quotes Dr. Pfaus in her book *Vagina: A New Biography*:

> "With each ejaculation, as with orgasm, you are turning on refractoriness. With each successive ejaculation, for chronic masturbators, the inhibition gets stronger—because of the increased serotonin—making it less likely for these men to achieve another erection, much less another ejaculation . . . It's not the porn, per se, but its use in chronic and obsessive masturbation. The addiction is not actually to the porn but to the orgasm and the predictability of reward."

But this only makes sense if "porn addicts" are all chronic masturbators, using Internet porn to jerk off twice in a half hour or however long their post-ejaculatory refractory period is, which would override their natural sedation. I did not do this. And most testimonials I've read do not include this feature. I got in touch with Dr. Pfaus to get a more detailed explanation, but found that his theory rests completely on refractoriness.

Once again, the seeming disconnect between "experts" and the qualitative experience of my readers (and me) was leading me back to Wilson and Robinson. So were they right—was I suffering from a physiologically based addiction? I wanted to hear it from the physicians and diagnosticians themselves.

In 2011, after a four-year process, the American Society of Addiction Medicine (ASAM) released a sweeping new definition of addiction as a *primary* illness, not just a coping mechanism for something like depression. The definition also states that all addictions imply the same fundamental brain changes, sexual behavior addictions included.

Since then, the American Psychiatric Association has at least partially followed suit, determining that addiction no longer applies only to substances like alcohol, but also to behaviors like pathological gambling—adding the newly-codified "behavioral addiction" category to the fifth edition of *The Diagnostic and Statistical Manual of Mental Disorders* (DSM).

While the DSM committee is still far more conservative in its approach to behavioral addictions than the ASAM, this new category does create room for a variety of behavioral addictions to eventually be recognized by psychiatrists. Some argue that this is precisely the intention of creating the new category, especially since sex addiction and Internet addiction were placed in the appendix of the DSM-IV, pending further research.

Furthermore, labeling behavioral addiction as a disease in the DSM-IV is significant in and of itself because it implies that conscious choice plays little or no role in the state of such compulsive behavior, which gets at one of the ASAM's primary goals—extinguishing the moral stigma around addiction.

And the more I read, the more I felt myself letting go of my own self-stigma. Maybe this wasn't really all my fault. Maybe I deserved treatment. Maybe I shouldn't be so scared to tell people about it for fear of moral retribution. But the copious criticism refilled me with doubts.

I worried: was this new definition really just a slippery slope towards diagnosing anything we like to do a lot as a mental disorder, as some critics were saying? Could pathologizing sexual behavior lead to legitimizing "conversion therapy" for sexual deviants, as people like Dr. David Ley, the author of *The Myth of Sex Addiction*, feared?

But as I did more research, these fears seemed increasingly unfounded. In fact, the long history of politics around definitions of sex addiction made it seem, if anything, sex addiction (and perhaps porn addiction) would have been recognized much earlier if various vested interests hadn't dragged the debate.

Also, I wondered, if people are so afraid of calling my condition an "addiction," then what do they call it? And how are they defining it?

Well, one of the main alternatives that critics have used to describe my porn habits is "compulsion." But Gary Wilson of YourBrainOnPorn.com argues that compulsion implies the same fundamental constellation of brain events that promotes persistent overconsumption initiated by ΔFosB—just to a lesser degree. He cites several studies that demonstrate how the level of ΔFosB in the brain correlate with the profundity of addiction-related brain changes. So, true compulsive behavior *is* addictive behavior.

Still, many continue to believe that this is a bottomless debate. That just like every other politicized question, there are two entrenched sides with endless arguments and counter arguments, definitions and redefinitions, shifting proofs and truths, and so we throw our hands up and say: I guess we just can't know.

But defaulting to agnosticism in the face of complicated evidence isn't neutral; it reaffirms of the status quo. And those troubled by their relationship with porn will continue to suffer without support, unsure of how to feel about themselves or how best to seek treatment.

Neurosurgeon Dr. Donald Hilton, the author of *Understanding Pornography and Sexual Addiction*, gets this. He makes an incisive comparison in a paper for the Society for the Advancement of Sexual Health to illustrate how the absence of randomized trials should not stop us from having a declarative opinion on porn addiction:

> "Where is the comparative prospective study with tobacco in children? The one that divides the kids, gives half cigarettes, protects the others, and follows them? It doesn't exist, of course, and never will, and therefore those so biased will still say that smoking is not addictive, even now."

Hilton argues that even though tobacco executives still tell Congress that smoking is not addictive, a "tapestry of research over the decades" has convinced virtually everyone that it is.

Personally, I do see a "tapestry" of evidence that porn addiction exists. Others may not. But I think that in a few decades, it's likely that most people will think of it as similar to eating disorders or gambling addictions—yes, I have "chosen" to do destructive things, but it's because I have a condition, an illness, and it should be treated as such.

Rich qualitative data and physiological evidence may never be enough to "prove" the existence or non-existence of porn addiction as was true with tobacco, so it's worth asking: would the consequences of formally recognizing "porn addiction" be good or bad?

In the aforementioned episode of *Savage Love,* Klein is upfront about his consequentialist bias, which is quite sympathetic:

> "I think a lot of the whole sex addiction movement is simply an attempt to pathologize sexual expression that somebody else doesn't like. It's pretty easy nowadays to use that expression, "sex addiction," to say this person has a disease and with the addiction industry being so popular in this country, the infrastructure of handling that "disease" of sex addiction is all set up."

This is not a porn addiction model I would stand behind. We should stand guard against a hegemonic addiction industry and the over-pathologizing of sexual expression. But the prominent pro-porn addiction model folk don't advocate for this. Just about everyone in that camp prescribes therapy *and* a regimen of behavior change, targeting the emotional-psychological roots of the user's decision making while simultaneously curbing problematic behaviors.

Furthermore, addictions are often intertwined with other emotional and behavioral issues (which perhaps renders the "primary illness" debate a bit inane). But by denying the possibility that porn could be a primary factor in such troublesome behavior, we fail to support people who would benefit from targeting porn directly with cognitive behavior therapy or twelve step treatment programs to complement psychotherapy.

Tellingly, Marnia Robinson and Gary Wilson also take a consequentialist perspective, and it's exactly why they push so hard for the addiction model:

> "We don't necessarily think everyone having symptoms from overconsumption of porn is 'an addict,' but we think the addiction model is still the best one for helping guys understand how they could have conditioned their sexuality in unwanted ways."

What Robinson and Wilson understand that Klein doesn't is that there are profound psychological effects of being unrecognized—suffering, and being told it's either your fault, you're making excuses for yourself, or you're making it up altogether.

If we codify the category of "porn addiction," everyone will more accurately appreciate the potential power of porn to condition sexuality (brains are most plastic as teens, so be careful) and perhaps most importantly, porn users will be more precisely differentiated under the porn addiction umbrella.

If we know how different types of Internet porn use interact with various emotional conditions and stages of development, we can provide a rigorous conception of who fits this category and who might be better suited by another model.

Like Violet.

Violet is a reader I really connected with who wrote that although she is *not* addicted to watching porn, "I've been brainwashed so that anytime I experience erotic feelings they channel through mainstream hetero porn images" (she identifies as lesbian). She didn't experience "the involuntary impulse to watch or read porn," which is how she conceived of addiction, but instead she experienced "the involuntary internal hijacking of erotic expression, which I don't have a short term for at the moment."

Addictive behaviors are often classified as recreational use, abuse, and dependence. The earlier the use, the more profound the effects and the more difficult to treat. Maybe if this is officially recognized, I'll know if I'm a recovered porn addict, a porn abuser, or an early-stage recreational user experiencing an internalization of porn-based eroticism that has profoundly impacted what sexual stimuli I find salient (still searching for that shorter term). But for now, I'm allying myself with addiction.

I am not advocating for victimhood or pathologizing sexuality, I just want to have my struggle recognized. I've been battling this for a long time alone. To get past it, I need to find affinity and support. To find that, I need this to have a name.

Isaac Abel is the pen name of a Brooklyn-based journalist. He writes about sexuality and gender for sites like *theatlantic.com* and *salon.com*.

Marty Klein

NO

Why 'Sexual Addiction' Is Not a Useful Diagnosis—And Why It Matters

If convicted mass murderer Ted Bundy had said that watching Bill Cosby reruns motivated his awful crimes, he would have been dismissed as a deranged sociopath. Instead, Bundy has said his pornography addiction made him do it–which many people treated as the conclusion of a thoughtful social scientist. Why?

There's a phenomenon emerging in America today that affects everyone, particularly those in the helping professions. Not caring about it, or having no opinion about it, is no longer an option.

I am not interested in trashing 12-step programs. AA performs a great service every year in helping people handle their addiction to alcohol and other drugs. The question that has been put to us is, is the addiction model a good one for diagnosing sexual problems, and is the 12-step model a good one for treating sexual problems?

And if it is, is it as appropriate for treating rapists as it is for people who masturbate more than they think they should?

How the Sexual Addiction Movement Affects Professionals

People are now self-diagnosing as "sex addicts."

They're also diagnosing their partners. Non-sexologist professionals such as ministers and doctors are diagnosing some of their clientele as sex addicts, too. As a result of these trends, many people who should be seeing therapists or sexologists are not. And many who don't need "treatment" are getting it.

The sexual addiction movement is aggressively training non-sexologists, such as marriage counselors, in the treatment of sexual problems.

Many professionals are now taking these programs instead of those offered by sexologists. Also, some professionals now feel incompetent to treat certain systemic problems without this sexual addiction "training." It is important to note that the content of this sexual addiction training is sexologically inadequate: there is little or no discussion of systems, physiology, diagnoses, cultural aspects, etc.

The concept of sexual addiction affects the sexual climate of the society in which we work—negatively.

This negativity is reflected in anti-sex education legislation, anti-pornography ordinances, homophobic industry regulations, etc.

Sex addicts now have cachet as sex experts.

Mass murderer Ted Bundy, widely quoted as an expert on the effects of pornography, is only one example. Right-wing crusaders now routinely quote "sex addicts" to justify repressive beliefs and public policy suggestions.

Defining Sexual Addiction

In the literature, the sex addict is typically described as:

> Someone who frequently does or fantasizes sexual things s/he doesn't like; Someone whose sexual behavior has become unstoppable despite serious consequences (including, according to Dr. Patrick Carnes, unwanted pregnancy) Someone whose sexual behavior and thoughts have become vastly more important than their relationships, family, work, finances, and health; Someone whose sexual behavior doesn't reflect her/his highest self, the grandest part of her/his humanness.

According to the National Association of Sexual Addiction Problems, "6% or 1 out of 17 Americans are sexual addicts." That's about 14 million people.

From this literature and from meetings of groups like Sexaholics Anonymous (SA), the beliefs of people committed to the sexual addiction model appear to include:

Sex is most healthy in committed, monogamous, loving, heterosexual relationships The "goal" of sex should always be intimacy and the expression of our highest self. There are limits to healthy sexual expression, which are obvious (e.g., masturbation more than once a day) Choosing to use sex to feel better about yourself or to escape from problems is unhealthy.

Clinical Implications of the Concept

It sees powerlessness as a virtue.

Step 1 of the traditional "12 steps" of all AA-type groups is "we admitted we were powerless over X (alcohol, our sexual impulses, etc.) . . ."

Controlling our sexuality can be painful, not because we lack self-control or will power, but because sexual energy is powerful and demands expression. The primitive, infantile forces behind those demands often make sexuality feel like a matter of life and death—which, in the unconscious, it is.

"Sex addicts" say they are "out of control," but this is just a metaphor—i.e., they feel out of control; controlling their impulses is very painful. We've all had that experience, with sex and with other things. Virtually everyone has the ability to choose how to control and express their sexual impulses (we'll discuss the small group who can't later). The concept of sexual addiction colludes with peoples' desire to shirk responsibility for their sexuality. But powerlessness is far too high a price to pay.

It prevents helpful analysis by patients and therapists.

The concept of sexual addiction prevents any examination of the personality dynamics underlying sexual behavior. It prevents the assessment and treatment of sexual or personality problems, because identifying and dealing with the "addiction" is the goal.

By encouraging people to "admit" that they are powerless, the concept of sexual addiction prevents people from examine how they come to feel powerless–and what they can do about that feeling. This careful examination, ultimately, is the source of personality growth and behavior change. The expression "That's my addiction talking" is creeping into the popular vocabulary. This translates into "don't confront or puncture my defenses."

It trivializes sexuality.

The concept of sexual addiction ignores the childhood passions at the source of sexual guilt. Aggression, lust for power, and greedy demands to be pleasured are all part of normal sexuality, which every adult needs to broker in some complex fashion.

People learn to feel guilty about their sexual impulses as infants. "Sex addicts" are told they have nothing to feel guilty about, that they can learn to feel better one day at a time. But people know all the "good" reasons they have for feeling sexual guilt. By denying the dark side of normal, healthy sexuality that most people know they have, the concept of sexual addiction increases guilt.

Self-identified "sex addicts" want us to remove the darkness from their sexuality, leaving only the wholesome, non-threatening part–which would, of course, also leave them as non-adults. Rather than collude with this understandable desire, competent therapists are willing to confront this darkness. Instead of snatching it away from patients, we can help them approach, understand, and ultimately feel less afraid of it.

Another way to describe this is that:

It lets people split—i.e., externalize their "bad" sexuality.

Once a person describes her/himself as a "sex addict," s/he can say, "I don't want that sexual feeling or behavior over there; the disease wants it." Good therapists know how to recognize splitting, how it blocks adult functioning, and how to move patients away from it.

It makes a disease out of what is often within reasonable limits of sexual behavior.

High levels of masturbating and any patronage of prostitutes, for example, are typically condemned as "abnormal" and reflecting a "disease," according to SA-type groups. Which experts get to make judgments about acceptable sexual behavior? Exactly where do their criteria come from?

It doesn't teach sexual decision-making skills or how to evaluate sexual situations.

Rather, the concept uses a "just say no" approach. As experience with family planning shows, "just say no" helps people abstain from self-destructive sex about as well as "have a nice day" helps people deal with depression.

SA-type groups say that ultimately, sexual abstinence is more like abstinence from compulsive eating—that is moderation—than it is like abstinence from compulsive drinking—that is, zero participation. On what theoretical basis has this critical judgment been made? Simple expediency.

Where is the healthy model of sexuality?

The sexual addiction model of human sexuality is moralistic, arbitrary, misinformed, and narrow. Excluded from this model are using sex to feel good; having "bad" fantasies; and enjoying sex without being in love. Where is the theoretical justification for this moralistic position?

We've seen this before: the concept of sin as sickness. It has led to sincere attempts to "cure" homosexuality, nymphomania, and masturbation—by the world's leading social scientists, within our own lifetime. It is outrageous to treat sexual problems without a model of healthy sexuality that relates to most people's experience.

The sexual addiction concept shows a dramatic ignorance of the range of typical human sexuality.

At the end of competent sex therapy or psychotherapy treatment, the patient is a grown-up, able to make conscious sexual choices. Sex addiction treatment offers a patient the chance to be a recovering sex addict. Which would you rather be?

Professional Implications of the Concept

It reduces the credibility of sexologists.

Prospective patients are now asking therapists a new set of questions: "Are you in recovery yourself?" "Have you treated sex addicts before?" What if a therapist is emotionally/sexually healthy and therefore not "in recovery?" Is s/he then disqualified as a professional?

The public, I'm afraid, is now getting a picture of us as being ivory tower types out of the touch with the real—i.e., destructive—sexuality out on the street. They're feeling, "You want to waste time discussing systems, regression, defenses, and meanwhile there are kids buying Playboy out there!"

It replaces professional sexologists as relevant sex experts.

There are two groups of people behind this:

a) Addictionologists, often in recovery themselves (i.e., they have unresolved sexual and impulse control issues). They typically have little or no training in sexuality; and
b) 12-steppers themselves, lay people who love being in recovery. Their missionary zeal has nothing to do with science or clinical expertise. They freely generalize their own experience with sexual problems and "recovery" to all people and to human sexuality.

Both groups of people are now being quoted–and are actively portraying themselves—as sex experts.

By offering training from people with little or no sexological background, the concept suggests that all sex therapists offer is just another "theory" about sexual functioning. Just as creationists now want (and frequently get) "equal time" when scientists teach or discuss evolution, addictionologists now want—and are beginning to get—" equal time" regarding sexual functioning.

Graduates of such training programs believe that they have learned something about sexuality, when they haven't. They have learned something about addiction. And they are taught that they are competent to treat addiction in any form, whether its vehicle is alcohol, food, gambling, love, or sex.

Most addictionologists admit they lack skills in differential diagnosis. They and their 12-step programs let anyone define him/herself as a "sex addict". How many personality disorders, how much depression, how many adjustment reactions are being treated as "sex addiction?"

Political Implications of the Concept

It strengthens society's anti-sex forces.

"Sexual addiction" is the Right's newest justification for eliminating sex education, adult bookstores, and birth control clinics. They are using the same arguments to eliminate books like The Color Purple from school libraries, even in supposedly liberal California. Businessman Richard Enrico, whose group Citizens Against Pornography takes credit for eliminating the sale of Playboy magazine from all 1,800 7-11 stores, did so, he says, "because smut causes sex addiction." And he was able to convince one of America's largest corporations of this complete fiction. We should not be colluding with this destructive force.

It emphasizes negative aspects of sex.

Sex addiction treatment is essentially creating a special interest group of people who feel victimized by their own sexuality. Not others' sexuality, like rape victims—their own sexuality. This lobby/interest group is growing as increasing numbers of people are recruited into identifying themselves as sex addicts. With the agenda of protecting people from their own sexuality, they are a dangerous group, easily exploited by the Right and other sex-negative points of view.

It frightens people about the role of sexuality in social problems.

Increasingly, "sex addicts" and trainers are talking in public about how sexual impulses took over their lives and made them do things like steal money, take drugs, and see prostitutes. This frightens people about their ability to control their own sexuality—as if they're vulnerable to being taken over. It supports public ignorance about sexuality.

"Sex addicts" and trainers spread stories about how childhood masturbating to Playboy leads to porn addiction, and about how prostitutes become so alluring that people destroy their marriages. The public, of course, takes the additional step that this could happen to anyone—even though there is no data to support this idea.

The movement continues to spread dangerous lies about sex, even though, for example, the ultraconservative Meese Commission was unable to find any evidence that pornography leads to child molestation, and even though no medical society in the world has ever proven that masturbate of any kind is harmful.

It focusses on the "dignified" "purpose" of sex.

These words always seem to mean a rigid sex role system, with sex needing love to give it meaning. Sweating and moaning never seem dignified to people concerned with the dignity of sex. Ultimately, the "purpose of sex" can only be a political, rather than a scientific, concept.

It obscures the role of society in distorting our sexuality.

Sexologists understand that our moralistic American society constricts healthy sexual expression. We all know the sexual and intimacy problems this creates; in fact, we are now beginning to understand how such distortion even helps create sex offenders. But the sexual addiction movement only sees society as encouraging "promiscuity," instead of discouraging pleasure and healthy sexuality. This simplistic analysis cannot see how the media and other institutions make guilt-free sex almost impossible.

The sexual addiction concept attempts to heal society's sexual pain while keeping its economic, political, and social foundations intact. This is not only naive and ineffective, it is dangerous.

Why Is the Sexual Addiction Concept So Popular?

It distances personal responsibility for sexual choices.

As Loyola University's Dr. Domeena Renshaw says, "my illness makes me have affairs" is a very popular concept. The concept seems to allow sexual expression without the punishment our infantile side fears. This is a great childhood fantasy. But the price is too high.

It provides fellowship.

SA-type meetings provide structure and relaxed human contact for people who have trouble finding these in other ways. The program also allows alcoholics in AA to work the steps again. This is one of the single biggest sources of self-described "sex addicts." In fact, Patrick Carnes claims that 83% of all sex addicts have some other kind of addiction.

It provides pseudoscientific support for the intuitive belief that sex is dangerous.

In doing so it legitimizes sex-negative attitudes and supports sexual guilt.

It lets people self-diagnose.

This is very American, very democratic. People like to feel they are taking charge of their lives, and self-diagnosing gives them the illusion that they are.

It encourage people to split.

When people are troubled by their sexuality, it is comforting to imagine the problem "out there" rather than "in here." A striking example is Jimmy Swaggart, who railed against immorality out in the world, while behaving in the very ways he was condemning.

It also encourages a kind of splitting among non-"sex addicts." In answering the defensive question "how can people be sexual like that?" It makes people who behave in certain ways essentially different from us "normal" folk. Basically, people use the concept of sexual addiction as a projection of their fear about their own sexuality. Its very existence is sort of an exorcism of sexuality on a societal level.

It helps people get distance from their sexual shame.

Most of us have deep shame about our sexuality—either our overt behavior, or the more primitive urges and images left over from childhood that we've never accepted. This profound sense of shame is what people would really like to get rid of; the behavioral symptoms they're supposedly addicted to are just a symbol of that shame.

SA-type groups reframe this same into a positive thing. It is a badge for membership; it lets "addicts" know they're heading toward a solution; it affirms that a sex-crazed society is victimizing them; and it suggests they're being too hard on themselves. Good therapy does the opposite: it helps people feel their shame, relate it to an even deeper pain, and temporarily feel worse—before helping them resolve it.

Why Do So Many People Claim to Get Relief from Sexual Addiction Programs?

First, we should keep in mind that simply because people claim that something gives them emotional relief doesn't mean it works in the way they claim. Astrology apparently helped reduce Nancy Reagan's anxiety about husband Ron's career, but that doesn't mean it actually helped either of them make better decisions.

The recovery process can be emotionally reassuring for many people.

It offers structure, goals, fellowship, and an accepting social environment. In fact, since most of the talk at SA-type groups is about sex and relationships, it's a relatively easy place to meet people for dating. And that does go on.

Conversation at SA-type meetings is exclusively about material that each individual is already focusing on. Thus, all conversation feels like it's about the individual "addict," and so participants can feel connected with others without having to abandon their own narcissistic focus. This feels intimate, and gives the illusion that an individual is making progress. And, of course, virtually everyone gets to hear stories of people who are worse off than they are, and so they feel better.

People enjoy feeling like they're heading somewhere.

While "addicts" learn to enjoy the process of recovery, they also learn they're never going to fully get there. So they set their sights lower–and do accomplish never being cured.

Because the sexual addiction movement is not interested in personality change, it can offer symptom relief without any ethical conflicts. In many cases people do get that relief–although it's at the expense of the rest of their character structure. Finally, as "addicts" continue learning how to distance themselves from their "bad" sexuality, they feel an increasing sense of direction and relief.

Addicts transfer some of their compulsivity to the SA-type group meeting itself.

For many "sex addicts," meetings (sometimes many times per week) are the most important part of the week. In a predictable setting and way, with comforting regularity, they get to listen to and talk about sexual feelings and behavior they dislike.

This feeling is perfectly conveyed by a "sex addict" quoted in a recent Contemporary Sexuality. He notes that, "Every Thursday night for the past year and a half I have repeated that statement [about his so-called addiction] to my 12-step support group." By itself this is a trivial point; in the context of a program supposed to heal compulsive behavior, it is troubling.

What About Sexual Compulsivity?

Most self-described sex addicts aren't out of control; they are relatively "normal" neurotics for whom being in control is painful. In fact, as the National Association of Sexual Addiction Problems says, "most addicts do not break the law, nor do they satisfy their need by forcing themselves upon others."

Those who are really sexually compulsive are typically psychotic, sociopathic, character-disordered, etc. Some of these people have impaired reality testing. Others have absolutely no concern about the consequences of their behavior. Dr. Renshaw states that "undifferentiated sexual urgency is a symptom of manic-depression." These people don't need help laying off one day at a time. They need deep therapy, medication, structured behavioral interventions, or other intensive modalities. The University of Minnesota's Dr. Eli Coleman, for example, reports treatment success with lithium, comparable to the clinical results lithium produces with other compulsives. It is absolutely indefensible to suggest that the same mechanism is operating in the rapist and in the guy who masturbates "too often." The concept of sexual addiction does nothing to diagnose serious problems, assess danger, discuss beliefs about sex, take a history, or change personality. There are no treatment statistics on true obsessive-compulsives using the sexual addiction model. We must also, and this is much harder, continue to resist and interpret society's demand for simple answers and easy solutions about true sex offenders.

Sexual energy scares people; distorted expressions of that energy terrify people. We need to continually educate policy-makers and the public as to why the treatment of sex offenders is so complex and difficult, and why quick-fix solutions are worse than partial solutions. We must find a way to say "I don't know" or "We're still working on it" without apologizing. Cancer researchers, for example, have done a good job of making partial answers—like early detection and quitting smoking—acceptable.

Summary

The concept of "sex addiction" really rests on the assumption that sex is dangerous. There's the sense that we frail humans are vulnerable to the Devil's temptations of pornography, masturbation, and extramarital affairs, and that if we yield, we become "addicted." Without question, being a sexual person is complex, and we are vulnerable—to our sex-negative heritage, shame about our bodies, and conflict about the exciting sexual feelings we can't express without risking rejection. Sexuality per se, however, is not dangerous—no matter how angry or frightened people are.

Professional sexologists should reject any model suggesting that people must spend their lives (1) in fear of sexuality's destructive power; (2) being powerless about sexuality; (3) lacking the tools to relax and let sex take over when it's appropriate.

Addictionologists have cynically misled the public into thinking that "sexual addiction" is a concept respected and used by sex therapists and educators. Even a brief look at our literature, conferences, and popular writing shows how rarely this is true. But addictionologists don't care about sexual truth or expertise—only about addiction. The sexual addiction movement is not harmless. These people are missionaries who want to put everyone in the missionary position.

In these terrible anti-sex times, one of our most important jobs is to reaffirm that sexuality—though complicated—is precious, not dangerous. Now more than ever, our job is to help people just say yes.

Marty Klein is a Licensed Marriage & Family Therapist and Certified Sex Therapist. He is the author of six book, including *American's War on Sex: The Attack on Law, Lust, & Liberty,* and *Sexual Intelligence: What We Really Want from Sex, and How to Get It.*

EXPLORING THE ISSUE

Is the Addiction Model Appropriate for Treating Compulsive Sexual Behaviors?

Critical Thinking and Reflection

1. What is the difference between addiction and compulsion?
2. At what point would a person's sexual behaviors, or frequency of sexual activity, lead you to become concerned for their health or well-being?
3. What are the benefits of the addiction model of treatment for sexual addiction or compulsivity? What are the limitations?
4. Who should be leading the conversation about sex addiction or compulsive sexual behaviors, and why? Consider the roles that doctors, researchers, therapists, addiction specialists, media, as well as those who feel their sexual behaviors are problematic, have in shaping this conversation.

Is There Common Ground?

Thanks in-part to celebrity sex scandals, sex addiction is presented as a very real and problematic issue in the popular media. Among sexologists, however, the legitimacy of the sex addiction model is far from settled. At the heart of this debate is the true meaning of a word many have trouble defining—addiction.

Think of the many things that might be considered addictive—alcohol, caffeine, tobacco, other drugs—and assess whether or not they are part of your life, or the lives of your family or friends. What makes something addictive? Is it how often a person indulges in it? Is it the degree to which it seems recreational or compulsive? Is it how much control a person has in deciding whether or not to engage in it? Or, is addiction more about what might be considered a social vice?

How about nonchemical behaviors that some might consider compulsive? Are people who surf the Internet for hours "addicted"? How about a political "junkie" who constantly scours newspapers and blogs for new information? The person who never misses an episode of their favorite TV crime drama? Teens (and adults) who play video games for hours at a time? What about the person who spends every Sunday glued to the TV watching football, or the one who builds their life around their favorite reality TV shows? The person who constantly checks and updates their social media accounts? Can a person be addicted to their artistic or musical pursuits? Fitness and exercise? Are these problematic addictions or harmless habits that allow one to relax and blow off steam? Which behaviors escape the realm of "addiction" because they are more socially functional (or accepted)?

While arguments over the issue are common at academic conferences and professional list-servs, one thing everyone can agree on is that many, many people feel insecure or worried about their sexual behaviors. The Ted Talk mentioned by Abel (which had around 900,000 views when the essay was originally published in 2013) now has, at the time of this writing, nearly 6.5 million views. Abel notes that the description of sex addiction as a disease, like alcoholism, isn't one that he is comfortable with. Here, he and Klein see eye-to-eye. Despite this, Abel feels the addiction model gives his struggle a structure or from which he can begin to transition into a more comfortable place. Klein, on the other hand, would see the labeling of certain sexual behaviors as an addiction as playing into the hands of a predatory industry, ready to sell a cure for a disease that doesn't exist.

Additional Resources

Ley, D. (2014). *The myth of sex addiction.* Lanham, MD: Rowan and Littlefield.

Klein, M. (2015) *America's war on sex. Praeger.*

Maltz, W., & Maltz, L. (2008). *The Porn trap.* New York: Harper.

Wilson, G. (2015). *Your brain on porn. Commonwealth Publishing.*

Internet References . . .

The Great Porn Experiment

https://www.youtube.com/watch?v=wSF82AwSDiU

Why I Am No Longer a Sex-Addiction Therapist

https://www.psychologytoday.com/blog/understanding-the-erotic-code/201511/why-i-am-no-longer-sex-addiction-therapist

Your Brain on Porn

yourbrainonporn.com

Your Brain on Porn—It's Not Addictive

https://www.psychologytoday.com/blog/women-who-stray/201307/your-brain-porn-its-not-addictive

Selected, Edited, and with Issue Framing Material by:
Ryan W. McKee, *Widener University,* Tracie Q. Gilbert, *Widener University,*
and
Jayleen Galarza, *Shippensburg University of Pennsylvania*

ISSUE

Should Group Marriage Be Legal?

YES: Fredrik deBoer, from "It's Time to Legalize Polygamy," *Politico Magazine* (2015)

NO: Jonathan Rauch, from "No, Polygamy Isn't the Next Gay Marriage," *Politico Magazine* (2015)

Learning Outcomes

After reading this issue, you will be able to:

- Define group marriage, polygamy, and polyamory.
- Describe the "slippery slope" argument, as it relates to same-sex and group marriages.
- Describe at least two arguments in favor of group marriage.
- Describe at least two arguments against group marriage.

ISSUE SUMMARY

YES: Fredrik deBoer, a writer, researcher, and Continuing Lecturer at Purdue University, believes that despite opposition from both conservatives and progressives, the next logical step in marriage equality is the legalization of polygamy.

NO: Jonathan Rauch, an author and Senior Fellow at the Brookings Institution, asserts that there are many reasons, supported by extensive research, to oppose polygamy.

Throughout the debate over marriage equality, the phrase "one man and one woman" was a common refrain. To opponents of same-sex marriage, this succinctly described what they believed to be the makeup of the ideal, traditional marriage. Anything else, they claimed, would be redefining an institution that had been universally accepted for thousands of years and, for many, tied to deeply-held religious beliefs. If same-sex marriage were to be legalized, it would most certainly lead to other officially recognized styles of marriage, including group marriage. Some critics went further, questioning what would stop people from marrying family members, or even their pets! This argument, that one event would eventually lead to an undesirable series of other events, is referred to as a "slippery slope" argument.

Advocates for marriage equality argued that the slippery slope assertion was simply a scare tactic to take the focus off of a very real injustice that resulted in social and economic harm to same-sex couples. They simply wanted the opportunity to share in the rights and responsibilities of marriage, described as an agreement or covenant between two people, regardless of sex or gender, and no more. In June of 2015 the U.S. Supreme Court, in a 5–4 decision, ruled that same-sex couples have a fundamental right to marry. Still, many who opposed the ruling (including a dissenting Chief Justice John Roberts) expressed concern over the idea that the ruling could lead to even more styles of formally recognized marriages.

Slippery slope arguments aside, the idea that marriages between one man and one woman are, and have been, a universal norm ignores many cultures in which group marriage occurs. While monogamy, or having only one spouse or partner, is typically expected, relationships—including, in some cultures, marriages—can be organized in many different ways and be made up of more than two partners. Before going forward, it is important to clarify a few terms related to group marriage and group relationships. The following definitions are from the website of Franklin Veaux, coauthor of *More Than Two: A Practical Guide to Polyamory.*

> Group Marriage—A relationship in which three or more people consider themselves married to one another; in the polyamory community, most often a relationship involving more than one man and more than one woman, who may live together, share finances, raise children together, and otherwise share those responsibilities normally associated with marriage.
>
> Open Relationship—Any relationship that is not sexually monogamous. . . . that permits "outside" sexual entanglements, but not loving or romantic relationships.
>
> Polyamory—The state or practice of maintaining multiple sexual and/or romantic relationships simultaneously, with the full knowledge and consent of all the people involved.
>
> Polygamy—The state of practice of having multiple wedded spouses at the same time, regardless of the sex of those spouses.

Over the last several years, polyamorous and nonmonogamous relationships have become increasingly visible, if not increasingly common, as an alternative to traditional relationships. For some more accustomed to monogamy, the reality of high divorce rates or personal experience with infidelity may spur a desire to think differently about their sexual and romantic lives. For others, polyamory may remove pressure to be all things to one partner, or to conform to a relationship ideal that never felt attainable. In response to the growing interest in nonmonogamy, a number of dating websites and apps have added options for those in who identify as polyamorous or are in, or seeking, open relationships. Despite this, the cultural expectation of monogamy remains strong and nonmonogamous relationships remain somewhat stigmatized.

Historically, many polygamous cultures have supported polyandry (women having multiple husbands) but not polygyny (men having multiple wives). As polyandrous cultures are relatively rare, criticism levied at polygamous relationships is largely based on the assumption that most are of a polygynous nature. Many women's' rights advocates have asserted that such relationships are inherently inegalitarian; multiple wives are desirable only to service the husband and produce children. In some areas, more than one wife is seen as a symbol of status for a man. In addition, spousal abuse is not an uncommon experience in polygynous cultures.

Supporters of polyamory and group marriage argue that their relationships should not be judged by the cultural proscriptions of societies a world away. Modern monogamous relationships are not immune from spousal abuse or forcing women into traditional roles. In the West, men and women enjoy (at least theoretically) a more equitable status within society. Women are highly educated and heavily integrated into the workforce, and there are legal protections in place to prevent, and respond to, abusive situations. Furthermore, group marriage need not follow a traditional heterocentric model. Partners of all genders and sexual orientations can come together in loving, supportive relationships. And if marriage is about love, as same-sex marriage advocates argued, why do limits have to be placed on the number of people who can enter into a loving, legally sanctioned, relationship?

In the following YES selection, Frederik deBoer argues that after the legalization of same-sex marriage, the next logical step is the legal recognition of group marriage. Polyamorous people and relationships exist, and to deny them the right to marry replicates the same injustices same-sex couples fought to overcome. In the NO selection, Jonathan Rouch counters by noting substantial research on the detrimental impact of state-sanctioned polygamy. Comparing monogamous same-sex marriages to group marriage, he asserts, is a tired and fallacious argument.

YES

Fredrik deBoer

It's Time to Legalize Polygamy

Welcome to the exciting new world of the slippery slope. With the Supreme Court's landmark ruling this Friday legalizing same sex marriage in all 50 states, social liberalism has achieved one of its central goals. A right seemingly unthinkable two decades ago has now been broadly applied to a whole new class of citizens. Following on the rejection of interracial marriage bans in the 20th Century, the Supreme Court decision clearly shows that marriage should be a broadly applicable right—one that forces the government to recognize, as Friday's decision said, a private couple's "love, fidelity, devotion, sacrifice and family."

The question presents itself: Where does the next advance come? The answer is going to make nearly everyone uncomfortable: Now that we've defined that love and devotion and family isn't driven by gender alone, why should it be limited to just two individuals? The most natural advance next for marriage lies in legalized polygamy—yet many of the same people who pressed for marriage equality for gay couples oppose it.

This is not an abstract issue. In Chief Justice John Roberts' dissenting opinion, he remarks, "It is striking how much of the majority's reasoning would apply with equal force to the claim of a fundamental right to plural marriage." As is often the case with critics of polygamy, he neglects to mention why this is a fate to be feared. Polygamy today stands as a taboo just as strong as same-sex marriage was several decades ago—it's effectively only discussed as outdated jokes about Utah and Mormons, who banned the practice over 120 years ago.

Yet the moral reasoning behind society's rejection of polygamy remains just as uncomfortable and legally weak as same-sex marriage opposition was until recently.

That's one reason why progressives who reject the case for legal polygamy often don't really appear to have their hearts in it. They seem uncomfortable voicing their objections, clearly unused to being in the position of rejecting the appeals of those who would codify non-traditional relationships in law. They are, without exception, accepting of the right of consenting adults to engage in whatever sexual and romantic relationships they choose, but oppose the formal, legal recognition of those relationships. They're trapped, I suspect, in prior opposition that they voiced from a standpoint of political pragmatism in order to advance the cause of gay marriage.

In doing so, they do real harm to real people. Marriage is not just a formal codification of informal relationships. It's also a defensive system designed to protect the interests of people whose material, economic, and emotional security depends on the marriage in question. If my liberal friends recognize the legitimacy of free people who choose to form romantic partnerships with multiple partners, how can they deny them the right to the legal protections marriage affords?

Polyamory is a fact. People are living in group relationships today. The question is not whether they will continue on in those relationships. The question is whether we will grant to them the same basic recognition we grant to other adults: that love makes marriage, and that the right to marry is exactly that, a right.

Why the opposition, from those who have no interest in preserving "traditional marriage" or forbidding polyamorous relationships? I think the answer has to do with political momentum, with a kind of ad hoc-rejection of polygamy as necessary political concession. And in time, I think it will change.

The marriage equality movement has been both the best and worst thing that could happen for legally sanctioned polygamy. The best, because that movement has required a sustained and effective assault on "traditional marriage" arguments that reflected no particular point of view other than that marriage should stay the same because it's always been the same. In particular, the notion that procreation and child-rearing are the natural justification for marriage has been dealt a terminal injury. We don't, after all, ban marriage for those who can't conceive, or annul marriages that don't result in children, or make couples pinkie swear that they'll have kids not too long after they get married. We have insisted instead that the institution exists to enshrine in law a special kind of long-term commitment, and to extend certain essential logistical and legal benefits to those who make that commitment. And rightly so.

But the marriage equality movement has been curiously hostile to polygamy, and for a particularly unsatisfying reason: short-term political need. Many conservative opponents of marriage equality have made the slippery slope argument, insisting that same-sex marriages would lead inevitably to further redefinition of what marriage is and means. See, for example, Rick Santorum's infamous "man on dog" comments, in which he equated the desire of two adult men or women to be married with bestiality. Polygamy has frequently been a part of these slippery slope arguments. Typical of such arguments, the reasons why marriage between more than two partners would be destructive were taken as a given. Many proponents of marriage equality, I'm sorry to say, went along with this evidence-free indictment of polygamous matrimony. They choose to side-step the issue by insisting that gay marriage wouldn't lead to polygamy. That legally sanctioned polygamy was a fate worth fearing went without saying.

To be clear: our lack of legal recognition of group marriages is not the fault of the marriage equality movement. Rather, it's that the tactics of that movement have made getting to serious discussions of legalized polygamy harder. I say that while recognizing the unprecedented and necessary success of those tactics. I understand the political pragmatism in wanting to hold the line—to not be perceived to be slipping down the slope. To advocate for polygamy during the marriage equality fight may have seemed to confirm the socially conservative narrative, that gay marriage augured a wholesale collapse in traditional values. But times have changed; while work remains to be done, the immediate danger to marriage equality has passed. In 2005, a denial of the right to group marriage stemming from political pragmatism made at least some sense. In 2015, after this ruling, it no longer does.

While important legal and practical questions remain unresolved, with the Supreme Court's ruling and broad public support, marriage equality is here to stay. Soon, it will be time to turn the attention of social liberalism to the next horizon. Given that many of us have argued, to great effect, that deference to tradition is not a legitimate reason to restrict marriage rights to groups that want them, the next step seems clear. We should turn our efforts toward the legal recognition of marriages between more than two partners. It's time to legalize polygamy.

Conventional arguments against polygamy fall apart with even a little examination. Appeals to traditional marriage, and the notion that child rearing is the only legitimate justification of legal marriage, have now, I hope, been exposed and discarded by all progressive people. What's left is a series of jerry-rigged arguments that reflect no coherent moral vision of what marriage is for, and which frequently function as criticisms of traditional marriage as well.

Fredrik deBoer is a writer, researcher, and Continuing Lecturer at Purdue University.

Jonathan Rauch NO

No, Polygamy Isn't the Next Gay Marriage

I am a gay marriage advocate. So why do I spend so much of my time arguing about polygamy? Opposing the legalization of plural marriage should not be my burden, because gay marriage and polygamy are opposites, not equivalents. By allowing high-status men to hoard wives at the expense of lower-status men, polygamy withdraws the opportunity to marry from people who now have it; same-sex marriage, by contrast, extends the opportunity to marry to people who now lack it. One of these things, as they say on Sesame Street, is not like the other.

Yet this non sequitur just won't go away: "Once we stop limiting marriage to male-plus-female, we'll have to stop limiting it at all! Why only two? Why not three or four? Why not marriage to your brother? Or your dog? Or a toaster?" If there's a bloody shirt to wave in the gay-marriage debate, this is it.

The shortest answer is in some ways the best: Please stop changing the subject! When you straights give yourselves the right to marry two people or your brother or your dog or a toaster, we gay people should get that right, too. Until then, kindly be serious.

If I sound exasperated, it's because the polygamy argument doesn't stand up to scrutiny. That doesn't stop it from popping up everywhere. A good example of the species can be found in this publication, where Fredrik deBoer welcomed Politico Magazine's readers "to the exciting new world of the slippery slope."

"Now that we've defined that love and devotion and family isn't [sic] driven by gender alone, why should it be limited to just two individuals?" he asked. "The moral reasoning behind society's rejection of polygamy remains just as uncomfortable and legally weak as same-sex marriage opposition was until recently."

The assumptions here seem to be two. Point 1: If there's no good reason to oppose same-sex marriage, then there's no good reason to oppose polygamy. Point 2: The Supreme Court ruled in Obergefell v. Hodges that gay marriage is a fundamental right, so polygamy must also be a fundamental right.

In his dissent in Obergefell, the ordinarily astute Chief Justice John Roberts goes in for this logic. Point 1: The majority, he says, "offers no reason at all why the two-person element of the core definition of marriage may be preserved while the man-woman element may not"—implying that, because the majority offered no rationale against polygamy (in a case that was not about polygamy), none exists. Point 2: "It is striking how much of the majority's reasoning would apply with equal force to the claim of a fundamental right to plural marriage." And so, says Roberts: "There may well be relevant differences that compel different legal analysis. But if there are, petitioners have not pointed to any."

No relevant differences? Let's help him with that.

Unlike gay marriage, polygamy is not a new idea. It's a standard form of marriage, dating back, of course, to Biblical times and before, and anthropologists say that 85 percent of human societies have permitted it. This means we know a thing or two about it.

Here's the problem with it: when a high-status man takes two wives (and one man taking many wives, or polygyny, is almost invariably the real-world pattern), a lower-status man gets no wife. If the high-status man takes three wives, two lower-status men get no wives. And so on.

This competitive, zero-sum dynamic sets off a competition among high-status men to hoard marriage opportunities, which leaves lower-status men out in the cold. Those men, denied access to life's most stabilizing and civilizing institution, are unfairly disadvantaged and often turn to behaviors like crime and violence. The situation is not good for women, either, because it places them in competition with other wives and can reduce them all to satellites of the man.

I'm not just making this up. There's an extensive literature on polygamy.

Here's a 2012 study, for example, that discovered "significantly higher levels of rape, kidnapping, murder, assault robbery and fraud in polygynous cultures." According to the research, "monogamy's main cultural evolutionary advantage over polygyny is the more egalitarian distribution of women, which reduces male competition and social problems."

The study found that monogamous marriage "results in significant improvements in child welfare, including lower rates of child neglect, abuse, accidental death, homicide, and intra-household conflict." And: "by shifting male efforts from seeking wives to paternal investment, institutionalized monogamy increases long-term planning, economic productivity, savings, and child investment."

There's more, but you get the idea.

In this article, I noted other research suggesting that societies become inherently unstable when effective sex ratios reach something like 120 males to 100 females, such that a sixth of men are surplus commodities in the marriage market. That's not a big number: "The United States as a whole would reach that ratio if, for example, 5 percent of men took two wives, 3 percent took three wives, and 2 percent took four wives—numbers that are quite imaginable, if polygamy were legal for a while."

By abolishing polygamy as a legal form of marriage, western societies took a step without which modern liberal democracy and egalitarian social structures might have been impossible: they democratized the opportunity to marry. It's no coincidence that almost no liberal democracy allows polygamy.

With all due respect to the Chief Justice, if reducing rather than expanding marriage opportunity and destabilizing rather than stabilizing society aren't "relevant differences" between polygamy and same-sex marriage, I don't know what would be.

Now, people who want to take issue with the theoretical and empirical literature on polygamy should feel free to do so. What they should not do is what Chief Justice Roberts and Fredrik deBoer do, which is to ignore the literature altogether. Blandly asserting that there's no good reason to oppose polygamy once gay couples can marry makes no more sense than saying there's no reason to oppose date rape or securities fraud once gay couples can marry. It doesn't follow, and it isn't true, and the intellectual laziness implicit in asserting it is epic.

Next, a point of law: In order to stand up in court, a challenged law normally needs only to survive what's called a rational-basis test. That's a low bar: the government merely needs to be able to claim that its law is rationally related to a legitimate government purpose.

The trouble that gay-marriage opponents kept running into was that they could not surmount this very low bar, because they couldn't explain how preventing gay couples from marrying served any of the state's claimed goals. Nor could they show any plausible harm from gay marriage. Justice Anthony Kennedy's opinion for the majority in Obergefell makes this point explicitly: "With respect to this asserted basis for excluding same-sex couples from the right to marry, it is appropriate to observe these cases involve only the rights of two consenting adults whose marriages would pose no risk of harm to themselves or third parties."

Jonathan Rauch is an author and Senior Fellow at the Brookings Institution.

EXPLORING THE ISSUE

Should Group Marriage Be Legal?

Critical Thinking and Reflection

1. How do you define marriage?
2. Can polyamorous relationships be as secure, or as successful, as monogamous relationships? Why or why not?
3. What is the value in having one's relationship legally recognized and validated by the state? Consider personal, cultural, legal, and economic factors in your answer.
4. Do you agree with the "slippery slope" argument put forth by critics of same-sex and group marriage? Why or why not?

Is There Common Ground?

While offering very different perspectives on group marriage, both deBoer and Rauch see value in the institution of marriage. In his argument, deBoer argues that critics of same-sex marriage who warned of a slippery slope were correct in their logic, to a certain extent. If marriage is about love, and not traditional norms, then why are only two people allowed to be legally wed? Rather than truly challenging the definition of marriage, same-sex marriage advocates drew a distinction between monogamous relationships and polyamorous relationships. Is there potential for great harm to society if polyamorous relationships become polygamous marriages?

Rauch, on the other hand, notes that he is tired of hearing comparisons between same-sex marriage and polygamy. As a talking point of marriage equality opponents, the argument was meant to disparage of the validity of same-sex relationships. Same-sex marriage, like so-called traditional marriage, is simply about equality and love. Research on polygamy, Rauch notes, indicates that such relationships are often linked to a host of social problems and foster gender inequality.

What do you think about nonmonogamous or other polyamorous relationships? Can they be as successful as monogamous relationships? And just how successful are humans at monogamy? With infidelity and divorce commonplace, many have made the argument that polyamory may hold the key to true relationship happiness. What is the purpose of legal marriage? Should the state have any say over the way we structure our relationships? How would you feel if group marriage were a legitimate, legal possibility for yourself and others?

Additional Resources

Veaux, F., & Rickets, E. (2014). *More than two: A practical guide to polyamory*. Thorntree Press.

Taormino, T. (2008). *Opening up: A guide to creating and sustaining open relationships*. Cleis Press.

Witte, Jr., J. (2015). *The western case for monogamy over polygamy*. Cambridge University Press.

Internet References . . .

Opening Up

openingup.net

More Than Two

morethantwo.com

The Secret to Desire in a Long Term Relationship: Esther Perel TedTalk

https://www.youtube.com/watch?v=sa0RUmGTCYY

Why We Love, Why We Cheat: Helen Fisher TedTalk

https://www.youtube.com/watch?v=x-ewvCNguug

Unit 4

UNIT

Sex and Society

Competing philosophical forces drive concerns about human sexuality on a societal level. Some are primarily focused on the well-being of individuals (or groups of individuals) and their rights to individual expression; others are mainly concerned with either maintaining or questioning established social norms. Still others are engaged by the extent to which the law should impose on a citizen's privacy. In this unit we invite you to explore five such issues that affect our social understanding of sexuality.

Selected, Edited, and with Issue Framing Material by:
Ryan W. McKee, *Widener University,* Tracie Q. Gilbert, *Widener University,*
and
Jayleen Galarza, *Shippensburg University of Pennsylvania*

ISSUE

Is Having a Sex-Positive Framework Problematic?

YES: Melissa Fabello, from "3 Reasons Why Sex Positivity Without Critical Analysis Is Harmful," *Everyday Feminism* (2014)

NO: Eric Barry, from "I'm Sex-Positive, and Most People in Chicago Have No Idea What That Means," *The Huffington Post* (2014)

Learning Outcomes

After reading this issue, you will be able to:

- Define sex-positivity.
- Explain the connection between sex-positivity and feminism.
- Assess the usefulness of applying a critical lens to discussions on sex-positivity.

ISSUE SUMMARY

YES: Melissa Fabello, a body acceptance activist and a Managing Editor of the *Everyday Feminism* media site, argues that without critical analysis, the mainstream sex-positivity movement can ultimately be harmful.

NO: Eric Barry, writer, comedian, and creator of the *Full Disclosure* sex-positive podcast, believes that sex-positivity allows people to embrace sex and without feeling shame or applying other inextricable meanings to behaviors.

Imagine the following scenario: Maria, an unmarried woman in her early 20s, has never been sexually active. She's not very religious, but remembers hearing lots of messages growing up about sex being risky and "dirty." Women who pursue sex for pleasure, she has been told repeatedly, lack control and have no class—an image she has always tried to avoid. Recently, Maria started seeing Derek, another 20-something she met on a popular dating app. Maria finds Derek very attractive, and he seems to feel the same way about her. One weekend, Derek invites Maria to dinner at his house; afterwards, they begin to watch a movie and begin to make out. Maria is nervous, but excited, and enjoys the feelings she is experiencing. As the kissing becomes more intense, Derek asks Maria if she wants to have sex. She says yes, but her body immediately becomes tense. When Derek steps away to find a condom she takes deep breaths, but still struggles to relax. While she strongly wants to have sex with Derek, she begins to wonder if having sex will make her like the type of people she has judged this whole time. Her desire is there, but it is accompanied by anxiety, shame, and guilt. She tells Derek that tonight may not be the best night to go all the way. Derek, sensing her discomfort, says that it's ok, and that they can just enjoy the movie together. Imagine this scenario . . . then imagine if Maria hadn't grown up receiving those types of messages. Instead, imagine conversations with parents and educators about sex and sexuality as a positive expression of one's health, wellness, or even spirituality. Imagine media messages that described those who enjoy sex as healthy and focused on what they want. Imagine discussions about safer sex as a pleasurable way to enjoy sex, rather than a way to simply mitigate risk. Could having fewer negative ideas about sex have changed Maria's experience with Derek? Would this change her attitudes about others who engage in sexual activities outside of marriage? Proponents of sex-positivity would respond with a resounding "YES!"

In 1931, psychoanalyst Wilhelm Reich asserted that neuroses was a function of unresolved sexual repression, the only cure for which being the establishment of regular, healthy sex—a "genital love life," as he called it. His ideas were unconventional for the field to say the least; that said, he is often cited as the original stimulus for the sex-positivity movement, which would gain traction during the Sexual Revolution of the 1960s and 1970s. Since that time, scholars, activists, artists, and laypersons alike have offered varying perspectives on what, exactly, sex-positivity is, as well as how it should be expressed. At its core, the sex-positive approach focuses on three basic principles: (a) that sex is good, (b) that individuals should feel comfortable expressing the sexuality that is most affirming for them, so long as (c) all partners involved are of legal age and engaging consensually in the behaviors expressed. While sex-positivity originally emerged in response to problematizing clinical diagnoses of sexual phenomena (homosexuality, masturbation, and women's sexual urges, specifically), many proponents of sex-positivity also cite religion—and Christianity in particular—as a common source for spreading erotophobia and sexual repression at large. It follows, then, that diversity is an additional core aspect of sex-positivity. As sexologist Carol Queen notes, "'Sex-positive' respects each of our unique sexual profiles, even as we acknowledge that some of us have been damaged by a culture that tries to eradicate sexual difference and possibility" (Queen, 1997). Sex-positivity, as an approach to sexual behaviors and sexuality in general, has been expressed and supported in a variety of areas, from pop culture to comprehensive sexuality education for young people.

Sex-positivity became a growing discussion in the 1980s among second-wave feminists, centered predominantly on how to navigate the struggle between sexual autonomy and resisting sexual ideals deemed misogynistic and/or patriarchal. The height of this debate is most commonly known as the "Feminist Sex Wars." Pornography was the biggest target of criticism during this time, as many feminists believed it to be directly responsible for inciting violence against women. Anti-pornography feminists of the time were clear in their assessment that pornography, as well as sex work of all kinds, and even consensual BDSM, could never be empowering because they were inherently antiwomen and historically constructed to benefit men. Many sex-positive feminists, on the other hand, took a stand against these notions, asserting that much of concern over pornography was sex-negative, paternalistic, and hetero-centric. Such a stance, they argued, erased or invalidated some erotic expressions of lesbian and bisexual women. They also believed that women could consent to participate in, and be consumers of, porn or sex work, and that such choices could be an empowered expression of one's sexuality. Furthermore, they argued that BDSM allowed for expressions of both dominance and submission on the part of women, and that sex acts involving power exchange could be simply for pleasure—not a political statement. Still, critics of sex-positivity have seen this acceptance of perceived transgressive sexual acts as an "anything goes" attitude.

Over time, the concept of sex-positivity found a home in the feminist and queer blogosphere, as a critique of sex-negative media, education, and research. While it may seem unusual, sex-negativity can be found in much sexual health research and policy. Consider research that focuses on the risks consequences of sexual behavior rather than the benefits, or policies that aim to dissuade people from certain communities (often marginalized communities) from becoming pregnant or even being sexual. On a more individual level, sex-negative attitudes can, like the story of Maria above, lead to physiological consequences. Erotophobia, or the general fear of sex, for example, is often cited as a cause of vulvodynia, or extreme pain and/or irritation of the vulvar area. Adverse thoughts about sex, sexual partners, and even anxiety over sexual orientation may work together with the body's parasympathetic nervous system to produce this condition. When left untreated, vulvodynia can produce additional anxiety and guilt, leading to later cases of dyspareunia (pain from penetrative vaginal intercourse), vaginismus (uncontrollable spasms of the vaginal cavity), lowered self-esteem and poor general self-concept. Adverse responses from sexual partners and/or doctors may add to the problem, causing additional feelings of anxiety or guilt. Could adopting a sex-positive attitude alleviate some of the symptoms noted above? Perhaps, but the dismantling of years of sex-negative messages is not an easy task. Even the most progressive advocates of sex-positivity have been shaped by their cultural environments. It is also important, again, to consider the intersections of sex-positivity and marginalization. Are there some communities or sexual identities that are under more scrutiny for their sexual attitudes and behaviors than others? If so, how might expressing a sex-positive attitude look different for them than for members of privileged groups?

At its core, sex-positivity may seem like a basic idea to which the average person should subscribe. After all, who wouldn't want their sex life to be more pleasurable?

That said, not everyone sees sex-positivity as a universal ideal. For them, there are factors that complicate both one's understanding of sex-positivity and their willingness to espouse it as a worldview. As such, the question is raised: can having a sex-positive framework be problematic? In the following YES selection, Melissa Fabello argues that an unexamined approach to sex-positivity can have negative consequences. In the NO selection, Eric Barry counters with a discussion of the positive aspects of a sex-positive approach to sex and sexuality.

YES

Melissa Fabello

3 Reasons Why Sex Positivity Without Critical Analysis Is Harmful

I'm a feminist, and I'm also a sex educator.

As such, I get a lot of people asking me to explain sex-positivity, usually under the assumption that I identify as sex-positive.

Which I don't (quite)—at least, I don't feel 100% committed to it yet.

And I want to talk about it.

According to everyone's favorite oh-so-academic source, Wikipedia, the sex-positive movement is "a social movement which promotes and embraces sexuality with few limits beyond an emphasis on safer sex and the importance of informed consent."

It's, in the words of Allena Gabosch's "A Sex Positive Renaissance," "an attitude towards human sexuality that regards all consensual sexual activities as fundamentally healthy and pleasurable and encourages sexual pleasure and experimentation."

Basically what it boils down to is (1) not making moral judgments, (2) respecting everyone's personal preferences, and (3) encouraging people to be active agents in discovering what does *(and doesn't)* make them tick.

And I'm not against this notion.

In fact, I'm all about it—both in theory and in praxis.

The problem for me comes in the way that many people *practice* sex-positivity—namely, without a critical analysis component.

I like what sex-positivity *sets out to do*, but there are *factions of the movement* that I think need a little work.

Sex-positivity isn't about exclaiming "YEAH!" to every conversation around sex any more than feminism is about exclaiming "YEAH!" to any conversation about women.

There's more to it than that.

The argument in sex-positivity, especially using a feminist framework, is that any decision that *we make* around our sexuality is inherently empowering because we exercised choice in the face of a society that tries to deny us that.

It's the idea that if a person—*particularly a woman*—freely, openly, honestly, and enthusiastically engages in a sex act, then she is operating against the status quo, and isn't that feminist?

And I'm not here to say whether or not any individual act or situation is feminist.

Rather, I want us to talk about some ways to think through the question instead of carelessly labeling *everything* an example of liberation in the name of sex-positivity.

So here are three points that I consider when I think through this stuff. And I'm hoping that you'll also adopt them into your sex-positive attitudes in order to include more critical analysis in your thinking and in the movement as a whole.

1. We Don't Make Decisions in a Vacuum

I wish we did. But we don't.

It is entirely impossible for us to untangle ourselves from our socialization. It plays a part in every single thing that we do—including sex.

And while I (*obviously*) absolutely believe in and advocate for trying to unlearn the dangerous and oppressive messages that we've been handed down, I think it's uninformed to assume that we are above them.

For example, I wear make-up. I like it. I think it's fun. I think it's pretty. I use it because for me, it's an important part of my gender expression, and I actively make the personal choice to use it.

However, I'm also bombarded daily—*and have been for my entire life*—with the message that I'm ugly (and therefore, especially as a woman, worthless) without it.

Do I make my own choice every day about whether or not I want to put on make-up? Yeah. And can it be empowering for me to make a choice for myself? Sure.

But do I come to the conclusion to buy mascara in a vacuum? No.

So can I ever know for sure whether or not I'd still make the same decision under different circumstances? No. I can't.

The same goes for sex.

A friend of mine who is also in the not-quite-but-almost-sex-positive camp recently brought up to me at a party the concept of bimbofication, which is a fetish involving women playing up the bimbo stereotype—from her looks (long, blonde hair; large breasts) to her personality (ditzy, man-pleasing, sexually available).

The question that my friend presented was: *"What do you think of this?"*

And at its core, that's awesome. If you want to do that, cool. You're an adult. Do what makes you happy. I want people to lead healthy, satisfying sex lives. If extensions, high heels, and an air of vapidness do that for you, rock on.

But on the other hand, I think it's fair to go a step beyond that. Because I *am* curious about understanding why certain preferences exist: What messages are we receiving from society at large that are telling us that this is sexy? *Is it* coming from somewhere?

And I think that *matters* if we want to understand sexuality as a field.

At the end of the day, I'm always going to be all for people doing what makes them happy, so long as it's consensual.

But my problem with sex-positivity without critical analysis is that it always ends there without engaging people in a conversation around how socialization affects the choices that we make.

And asking why doesn't have to be judgmental. It can be curious. And I think that curiosity is *(largely)* missing from the mainstream movement.

2. Empowerment for One, But Oppression for All?

Let's just jump right into talking about facials, since it's been a popular topic in feminist discourse lately.

Again: Consenting adults? Awesome. Stay safe, folks.

But there has been a lot of conversation in the feminist community over the past few years about sex acts that are quote-unquote *"degrading"* in that they position women as submissive to men by playing out male-pleasure-centric tropes in pornography.

On the one hand, one argument is the sex-positive side: If I want a dude to ejaculate on my face—*if I really, honestly want and like that*—then isn't it empowering to let him do it?

Sure. Maybe.

But the other side of the argument is: Maybe *you* think it's awesome, but because we live in a society where women's submissiveness to men is the status quo and in which penises are often weaponized *(as in common phrases like "Suck my [bleep]")*, then does this perpetuate rape culture? And if so, how can it ever, ever be feminist?

The same arguments can be (and is, tirelessly) applied to sex work: If a woman decides of her own accord that she wants to perform in pornography, feminism says that [it] should be sanctioned. But is pornography—particularly of the mainstream variety—empowering to women on a larger scale?

The argument is that just because it's empowering for *you personally* doesn't mean that it does *women on the whole* any good. So then the question becomes *what* is feminist, then? *Your* personal empowerment? Or the lifting up of a community? And how can one ever control the latter?

The truth is: There isn't actually an answer here. There are a million other details to take into account, and there's always the argument that any woman who is personally empowered is empowering women on the whole.

My issue here is that all of these arguments attempt to be black-and-white. You're either a sex-positive feminist—believing that your personal empowerment is paramount—or a sex-negative feminist—believing that if an act doesn't directly oppose oppression, it isn't empowering.

But these issues *aren't* black-and-white. They're *not* easy. They're not one-size-fits-all. They deserve a conversation.

That's what "sex-positivity with critical analysis" means for me.

3. A Redefined Status Quo

I've talked about this before—in my "Party Girl Pop" video and my "Conflating 'Objectification' with 'Liberation'" article—and it isn't anything that I came up with myself.

Both Susan J. Douglas and Ariel Levy, among others, have written on this topic extensively, and I recommend their work if you want to delve deeper into this.

But at the core of this issue is a question about whether or not the sexual availability and flexibility of women is really liberation or if it's "new sexism."

I teach kids. That's what I do. That's my life's work. And when I ask my high school students to describe their ideal partner to me, the straight men will almost always—*like, nine out of ten times*—put "freak" on their list.

And when I ask them to elaborate, they always tell me that they want a partner who's down for whatever and wants it all the time. Okay.

Similarly, in both my personal and professional lives, I have encountered people—mostly men—who (I'm assuming mostly through the pornification of our psychosexual development) have normalized sex acts that to some are still taboo.

From the seemingly innocent desire for anal sex to pushing boundaries around pain play to demanding participation in one-way-street fetishes, there is suddenly a lot of pressure on women to perform more and more daring sex acts.

What we've created is an expectation. And as soon as we create an expectation, we're in dangerous territory.

Most feminists, I imagine, would agree that the pressure for women to get married and have children is an unfair gender expectation that should not be pushed onto all of us and that acquiescing to this standard may or may not be feminist, depending on your level of choice in the matter.

But if the "new normal"—*or the "new ideal"*—of womanhood is to be "sexually liberated" (most often seen as being appealing and pleasing to men, just *openly*), then how is that any different?

Where do we draw the line between what is authentically liberating and what is just sexism presented in a shiny new package?

Again: There is no easy answer here. There is no litmus test to determine whether your decision is yours or the product of surrounding pressures.

But when sex-positivity means assuming that all choices are automatically liberating, that we've moved so far beyond "real" sexism that women are now completely independent from patriarchal idealism, I can't get on board.

Sex-positivity is a movement that arose from a need for us to accept and value sexuality without guilt, shame, and hurt.

I'm about that.

But when we stop asking hard questions in favor of assuming that everything is revolutionarily enlightened and therefore devoid of the intricacies of oppressive structures, I have to step back and question whether or not that's a movement I want to be a part of.

And unless that critical analysis is present, I don't.

Melissa Fabello is a body acceptance activist and a Managing Editor for the website *Everyday Feminism.*

Eric Barry

NO

I'm Sex-Positive, and Most People in Chicago Have No Idea What That Means

I recently moved from San Francisco to Chicago. One of the great fears I had about moving halfway across the country was how the cultural norms I was raised with might differ from that of more traditional, midwestern values.

I had lived in the Bay Area my whole life and attended UC Berkeley, a notorious bastion for liberal views and activism. While back home not everyone agrees with each other's views, there is a prevailing sense of "looking forward"—that marijuana will be legalized, that healthcare is a right, that marriage should be accessible to all. How and when all that may happen is up for debate—but generally we all agree that the status quo is never something upon which our ethics should be rooted.

In my short time here, I've learned how to make friends fast—frequently going out to bars and approaching groups of strangers. I favor an earnest introduction, which always carries with it a necessary amount of awkwardness, but that typically subsides, particularly when people find out I'm "not from around here."

Recently, I approached two women and we began talking. I was lamenting the fact that a friend of mine, who I was casually dating, had gone home with another friend of mine earlier in the night.

"Wow, she sounds like a total slut," the women replied.

"Not at all. We've just been hooking up. We haven't set any terms. It just kinda bummed me out," I responded. "I don't own her. I definitely embrace sex-positivity."

As it turned out, sex-positivity was a term these women had never heard. I was a bit taken aback; sex-positivity was one of those words that it seemed everyone in San Francisco knew. One of those words we learned in our first gender studies course at Berkeley. But as I've discovered, it's a term *most* Chicagoans have never heard.

You can read all sorts of books on sex-positivity, but generally speaking, it's the idea that one's sexual preferences are a matter of personal choice, and that within the confines of informed consent, those preferences should not be subject to the moral imposition of others.

So if sleeping with 10 different people 10 days in a row (or hell, at the exact same time) is your thing—more power to you! As long as all those involved have consented and you're not knowingly spreading some gnarly STIs, no one should be *tisking* at you in judgment.

Similarly, if you're the type of person that's embracing a period of celibacy, or perhaps you like to wait longer periods of time before engaging sexually with someone, that's fantastic too! The point is that your lifestyle is your choice, and what you do in your bedroom has no impact on what I do in mine.

All too often I hear the term "slut" used as a pejorative. In fact, it's the only way many of us have heard it used. So it might come as a surprise that many people in the sex-positive community, myself included, don't regard the term as inherently negative. In fact, I openly describe myself as a slut. Yes, I am promiscuous, as are many of my friends. But that doesn't mean that we're of low moral standards, or incapable of forming meaningful, lasting relationships with others, including those we sleep with. For us, we're just not hung-up on the idea that penis-in-vagina (or any place of your choosing) carries with it some inextricable meaning, or at the very least, we're aware that that meaning varies greatly from individual to individual.

We are completely transparent with our partners. We respect our partners. We are not "players." We are ethical sluts.

Frequently there's a misconception that those who are sex workers (meaning anyone involved in the sex industry from escorts to porn performers, sex therapists to strippers) are somehow damaged. That they're either uneducated or their career path is the result of a poor childhood. Sex-positivity looks to challenge that notion.

As the host of *Full Disclosure*, a podcast which looks to humanize those in the sex industry and generally destigmatize the cultural taboos surrounding sex, I've interviewed a number of adult performers, sex workers, sexologists and the like. The overwhelming majority of those I've interviewed are exceptionally intelligent and well-rounded individuals, those who do not come from a background of child abuse or neglect—certainly no more than anyone else working in any other industry. I'd feel pretty silly chalking up Jim in finance's decision to become an accountant to his father leaving him when he was five, and I'd feel just as silly saying that's why Lexi is now a webcam model.

Being sex-positive doesn't just inform our own personal relationships. It's an attitude that sexuality, in its many forms, is an innate part of who we are as humans. And with that belief, sex education needs to be an integral part of our schools' curriculum. Children should know that not everyone, perhaps themselves, need [to] be defined by a male/female sexual binary. Students don't just need to hear "it gets better," we need our schools to lead the charge in being able to tell them "it **is** better." Young women should not be told that their pleasure and shame go hand-in-hand. All too often sex is presented to our youth as something abnormal, immoral and "other," and consequently when sex does rear its head, it's often in unhealthy, irresponsible and uninformed fashions.

Unfortunately, most of this was lost on the women back at the bar. They had never heard of sex-positivity, and it was a lot for them to soak in. It directly challenged everything they'd ever been told about the lens through which we view sexuality. When they first heard the term sex-positive, they thought I was talking about something related to HIV status, or inviting them to a sex club. I'm exceptionally grateful for how hospitable Chicagoans have been to me, inviting me into their home. I think we both have a lot we can learn from each other.

Sex isn't something we're going to get rid of. It's why we're all here after all. And that's not something any of us should feel shame over, but instead we should be celebrating and educating ourselves about, and embracing with an attitude of positivity.

Eric Barry is a writer, comedian, and the creator of the *Full Disclosure* sex-positive podcast.

EXPLORING THE ISSUE

Is Having a Sex-Positive Framework Problematic?

Critical Thinking and Reflection

1. Is critical analysis a necessary addendum to a sex-positive ideology? Why or why not?
2. Is sexism the only lens through which a sex-positive lens may be usefully examined?
3. What impact does sex-positive feminism have for those of other genders?
4. What are two to three ways an individual could incorporate a sex-positive framework in their own life?

Is There Common Ground?

While an awareness of sex-positivity is increasing, there is still much debate over the concept. The two perspectives presented here do their respective parts to work through what is a complex, multilayered discussion.

Melissa Fabello strikes a potential middle ground by encouraging critical "curiosity" in one's sex-positive embodiment, even while refusing to write off any sexual expression automatically. Her perspective offers a keen, yet often overlooked distinction between sex-positivity and feminism, owning the idea that even consensual behaviors enacted by adults may miss the mark in forging equitable, empowered relations between sexes. Ultimately, Fabello's article begs an important question: Can sex-positivity be fully accepted without placing limitations on how it is expressed? Could sexual acts that threaten the social position of women count as sex-positive, even if it they are fully consensual? Extending from this discussion, Fabello uses examples and discourse to shape her argument that are specific to feminist analysis. But are there other critical lenses through which similar analyses could occur? If one's critique could unpack gender, could it not also unpack race, skin tone, size, and/or physical ability?

While Fabello appears to engage a community that is already well versed in the language and ideology of sex-positivity, Eric Barry acknowledges that these conversations are not yet universal, and may even remain among a privileged few. What responsibility do proponents of the sex-positivity movement have to those in the mainstream, for whom this discourse is presently inaccessible? Is sex-positivity a realistic perspective for everyone to take? What does sex-positivity look like for marginalized individuals and groups such as sex workers, asexuals, racial and ethnic minorities, and transgender or gender nonconforming individuals? What might sex-positivity look like for adolescents, who are, in most cases, legally unable to consent to sexual activity?

Reference

Queen, C. (1997). *Real live nude girl: Chronicles of sex-positive culture.* Pittsburgh: Cleis Press.

Additional Resources

Jones, F. (2016). The case for sex positivity. *Ebony, 71*(5), 98–101.

Farajaje-Jones, E. (2000). Holy fuck. In K. Kay, J. Nagle, & B. Gould (Eds.), *Male lust: pleasure, power, and transformation* (pp. 327–335). New York: Harrington Park Press.

White, R. (May 9, 2012). 8 ways to be positive you're sex positive. *The Frisky.com.* Retrieved from http://www.thefrisky.com/2012-05-09/8-ways-to-be-positive-youre-sex-positive/

Pflug-Back, K. R. (Oct. 1, 2013). Sites of violence: Why our notions of "sex-positive feminism" are in need of an overhaul. *TheFeministWire.com.* Retrieved from http://www.thefeministwire.com/2013/10/sites-of-violence-why-our-notions-of-sex-positive-feminism-are-in-need-of-an-overhaul/

Internet References . . .

Center for Positive Sexuality

http://positivesexuality.org/

Center for Sex Positive Culture

http://www.cspc.org

Foundation for Sex Positive Culture

https://thefspc.org/

"Sex-Positive" Feminism Archives—Feminist Current

http://www.feministcurrent.com/tag/sex-positive-feminism/

Selected, Edited, and with Issue Framing Material by:
Ryan W. McKee, *Widener University,* Tracie Q. Gilbert, *Widener University,*
and
Jayleen Galarza, *Shippensburg University of Pennsylvania*

ISSUE

Is Pornography Harmful?

YES: Pamela Paul, from "The Cost of Growing Up on Porn," *The Washington Post* (2010)

NO: Megan Andelloux, from "Porn: Ensuring Domestic Tranquility of the American People," An original essay written for this volume (2011)

Learning Outcomes

After reading this issue, you will be able to:

- Explain the limitations and difficulties in defining "pornography."
- Describe some of the recent research that has been done on pornography.
- Critique research methods on the effects of pornography.
- Discuss specific reasons why pornography might be considered harmful, or beneficial.

ISSUE SUMMARY

YES: Pamela Paul, author of *Pornified: How Pornography Is Transforming our Lives, Our Relationships, and Our Families,* argues that studies declaring the harmlessness of pornography on men are faulty, and that consequences of porn consumption can be seen in the relationships men have with women and sex.

NO: Megan Andelloux, sexuality educator and founder of the Center for Sexual Pleasure and Health, argues that the benefits of porn on American society outweigh the questionable consequences.

"The Internet is for porn!" Or, so sings a muppet from the hit Broadway show *Avenue Q.* As in-home access to the Internet has risen, so has access to a seemingly unlimited supply of pornography. But is pornography harmful? And whom, if anyone, does it harm? While the debate over erotic and explicit material is nothing new, the widespread availability of online pornography has raised new concerns about an old issue.

Debates over pornography in the United States have largely focused on the perceived negative impact of porn versus free-speech arguments that oppose censorship of any kind. While many see this conflict as a feminist issue, even feminists can find themselves on opposing sides of the argument. In the 1970s and 1980s, an often intense academic debate (referred to as the feminist sex wars) raged between "radical feminists" and a new school of feminist thinkers who labeled themselves "sex-positive." Radical feminists, such as Andrea Dworkin and Catharine MacKinnon, opposed pornography. Sex-positive feminists were weary of calls for censorship and alarmed by anti-porn feminists who were now allied with the conservative movement they saw as in opposition to women's liberation.

A key part of the debate hinges on the effects of the consumption of pornography. Opponents point to researchers who have found connections between porn and a decrease in compassion toward rape victims and the support of violence against women. Recently several popular authors (including Pamela Paul, whose essay is featured in this issue) have warned against the negative impact easily accessible porn can have on relationships, masculinity, and femininity.

On the other hand, supporters of porn point to other studies that show no significant correlation between sexually explicit material and attitudes that are supportive of violence against women. Anti-censorship advocates like Nadine Strossen and sex-positive feminists like Susie Bright and Violet Blue have written about the ways pornography can empower both performers and viewers. The growing market for feminist and queer erotica, featuring films produced and directed by women such as Candida Royalle, Tristan Taormino, and Jayme Waxman, suggests women are supporting porn in increasing numbers.

While the feminist sex wars cooled over time, the debate was never settled—thanks in large part to the ambiguous definition of porn. What, exactly, is pornography? Is there a line between art and pornography? Between pornography and obscenity? In 1964, Supreme Court Justice Potter Stewart, in an opinion stating the scope of obscenity laws should be limited, famously said of hard-core porn, "I know it when I see it." Nearly 50 years later, controversial porn producer Max Hardcore was sentenced to 46 months in prison (though the sentence was later reduced) for violating federal obscenity laws by distributing his films and promotional material via mail and over the Internet.

The issue of pornography and its potential harms, particularly in reinforcing the subjugation and humiliation of females, is a perplexing one. Efforts to censor speech, writing, and pictorial material (including classical art) have been continuous throughout American history. The success of censorship efforts depends mainly on the dominating views in the particular era in which the efforts are being made, and on whether conservative or liberal views dominate during that period. In the conservative Victorian era, morals crusader Anthony Comstock persuaded Congress to adopt a broadly worded law banning "any book, painting, photograph, or other material design, adapted, or intended to explain human sexual functions, prevent conception, or produce abortion." That 1873 law was in effect for almost a hundred years, until the U.S. Supreme Court declared its last remnants unconstitutional by allowing the sale of contraceptives to married women in 1963 and to single women in 1972.

In 1986, a pornography commission headed by then-Attorney General Edwin Meese maintained that the "totality of evidence" clearly documented the social dangers of pornography and justified severe penalties and efforts to restrict and eliminate it. At the same time, then-Surgeon General C. Everett Koop arrived at conclusions that opposed those of the Meese commission. Koop stated that "Much research is still needed in order to demonstrate that the present knowledge [of laboratory studies] has significant real world implications for predicting [sexual] behavior.

It is doubtful that Justice Stewart, the feminists of the 1970s, or the Meese commission could have foreseen the impact of the Internet and "smart phones" (such as iPhones, Androids, and Blackberries) on the availability or distribution of porn. The seemingly unlimited availability of free hard-core porn at our fingertips has been cited by many as a need for further restrictions. The implications of porn consumption, however, are still hotly debated. While accurate statistics are difficult to come by, there is no debating porn's popularity or billion dollar revenues.

As you read the selections, think about how *you* define pornography. Does it need to be explicit to be considered pornographic? How should feminist, gay, lesbian, or queer-produced porn that portrays people of various genders and body types enjoying sex be viewed in the conversation? What about erotic novels, like *Fifty Shades of Gray*, or paintings, illustrations, and sculptures depicting nudity or sex? Should soft-core porn be treated the same way as hard-core? What about animated scenes of nudity or sexual intercourse that are often depicted in video games? Consider your own porn-viewing habits, or the habits of people you know. Do you think it has had an impact on your (or your friends') attitudes toward women, men, or sex in general? If you believe pornography to be harmful, do you feel it is more damaging to women or men? Do you believe society would benefit from restricting or banning some types of sexually explicit material? Where would you draw the line (or lines) in deciding something was illegal?

In the YES selection, Pamela Paul, author of *Pornified: How Pornography Is Transforming Our Lives, Our Relationships, and Our Families*, calls into question the findings of a Canadian researcher who found that viewing pornography had no negative effects on men in his sample. In the NO selection, Megan Andelloux, sexuality educator and founder of the Center for Sexual Pleasure and Health, argues that pornography is not only healthy, but it is a valuable part of the fabric of American society.

YES

Pamela Paul

The Cost of Growing Up on Porn

Guess what, guys? Turns out pornography—the much-maligned bugaboo of feminists, prigs and holy rollers—is nothing more than good, not-so-dirty fun.

The proof comes from the University of Montreal, where recent research showed that connoisseurs easily parse fantasy from reality, shudder at the idea of dating a porn star (what would Maman think?) and wholeheartedly support gender equality. "Research contradicts anti-pornography zealots," gloated a column's headline in the *Calgary Sun*.

So, I've been contradicted. Presumably, I'm one of the zealots in question. My anti-porn fanaticism took the form of a 2005 book, "Pornified," in which I dared to offer evidence that all is not well in the era of Internet porn. Today, 20-somethings, teenagers and even—sorry to break it to you, parents—tweens are exposed to the full monty of hard-core pornography.

Wasn't it time someone asked some obvious questions? What will happen now that the first generation of men raised on Internet porn is making its way onto the marriage market? What influence does the constant background blare of insta-porn have on their ideas about women and monogamous relationships?

The answers I found to those questions were less than cheering. In dozens of interviews with casual and habitual porn users, I heard things such as: "Real sex has lost some of its magic." "If I'm looking like eight or 10 times a day, I realize I need to do something to build my confidence back up." "My wife would probably think I was perverted and oversexed if she knew how much I looked at it every day."

In the years since I wrote the book, I have heard from dozens of readers who described the negative effects of porn. One was a student at Berkeley, who observed that "ever more deplorable acts needed to be satiated" and noted: "As a child, we are exposed to things that we may not realize have formative effects. As adults, many times we simply continue without questioning." (Women, it seems, also turn to iVillage.com, where a board devoted to "relationships damaged by pornography" contains more than 32,280 messages to date.)

Yet there's still so much we don't know. Perhaps we can learn from the scintillating news out of Montreal. Let's have a closer look at that—oops!—turns out there is no study. Simon Louis Lajeunesse, a postdoctoral student and associate professor at the university's School of Social Work, has yet to publish a report. His findings, such as they exist, were based on interviews with 20 undergraduate males who detailed their views on sex, gender and pornography in one to two lickety-split hours.

Granted, it's qualitative, not quantitative, research, but the brevity of the interviews is concerning. While reporting "Pornified," I felt the need for more than four hours with many of my 100 interviewees. Of course, my guys could talk anonymously to a disembodied voice on the phone; the poor fellows in Montreal had to sit down and look a male social worker in the eye before confessing a penchant for three-ways. Lajeunesse asked 2,000 men before he found 20 willing subjects. Most of them, he said, were referred by women in their lives. Hmm.

And just how did Lajeunesse learn that pornography hadn't affected their views of said women? Why, he asked and they said so! "My guys want to have equal relationships, equal income, equal responsibility domestically," Lajeunesse told me. Color me dubious, but I hardly think most men would own up to discriminating against women, spurred on by porn or not.

To be fair, researching the relationship between men and pornography isn't easy. My methods had flaws, too. The most methodologically sound study would involve gathering a sample of men, scheduling regular sessions to view online porn, and comparing their subsequent sexual attitudes and behaviors with those of a control group that did not use pornography. Through a series of measures—interviews, questionnaires, observations—the data would be collected and analyzed by a team of objective academics.

That's not going to happen now, though it once did. Back in 1979, Jennings Bryant, a professor of communications at the University of Alabama, conducted one of the most powerful peer-reviewed lab studies of the effects of porn viewing on men. Summary of results: not good. Men who consumed large amounts of pornography were less likely to want daughters, less likely to support women's equality and more forgiving of criminal rape. They also grossly overestimated Americans' likelihood to engage in group sex and bestiality.

Yet Bryant's research (conducted with colleague Dolf Zillmann) was carried out long before the Internet brought on-demand porn to a computer screen near you. So why no update? Other than a spate of research in the '80s and '90s that attempted to link pornography with violence (results: inconclusive), nobody has looked at the everyday impact of hard-core porn. "That's a catch-22 with most studies about media effects," Bryant told me. "If you can't demonstrate that what you're doing to research participants is ultimately beneficial and not detrimental, and you can't eradicate any harm, you're required not to do that thing again."

Every university has a review board for the protection of human subjects that determines whether a study is ethically up to snuff. "It is commonly the case that when you get studies as clear as ours, human subjects committees make it difficult to continue to do research in that area," Bryant explained. "Several graduate students at the time wanted to follow up, but couldn't get permission." In other words, the deleterious effects were so convincing, ethics boards wouldn't let researchers dip human subjects back into the muck.

No matter—people will take care of that on their own. As one young man explained, after mentioning that "porn may have destroyed my relationship with my girlfriend" in an e-mail: "I always feel that I'm over porn, but I find myself keep coming back to it. There seems to be an infinite number of porn sites with limitless variations, one never becomes bored with it. . . . It's a very difficult habit to break."

Or as one 27-year-old female lawyer noted recently: "All of my girlfriends and I expect to find histories of pornographic Web sites on our computers after our boyfriends use it. They don't bother erasing the history if you don't give them a lot of hell." The implications troubled her. "I fear we are losing something very important—a healthy sexual worldview. I think, however, that we are using old ideas of pornography to understand its function in a much more complex modern world."

Of the many stories I've heard revealing the ways in which young men struggle with porn, I offer here just one, distilled, from a self-described "25 year old recovering porn-addict" who wrote to me in October. "Marc" began looking at his father's magazines at age 11, but soon, he wrote, he "turned to the Internet to see what else I could find." This "started off as simply looking at pictures of naked women. From there, it turned into pictures of couples having sex and lesbian couples. When I got into watching videos on the Internet, my use of porn skyrocketed." At 23, he began dating a woman he called "Ashley." "However, since Ashley's last boyfriend had been a sex/porn addict, I was quick to lie about my use of porn. I told her that I never looked at it. But after 5–6 months, Ashley discovered a hidden folder on my computer containing almost a hundred porn clips. She was devastated."

Marc and Ashley broke up, got back together and spent several months traveling in India. He continued to look at porn behind her back, and on a trip to Las Vegas, he got lap dances despite promising not to. Ashley broke up with him again. "I had never thought about the adverse effects of my use of porn. . . . I want to change. I want to be a respectful human being towards all human beings, male and female. I want to be a committed and loving boyfriend to Ashley."

This is hardly solid lab research. But it is one of many signs of pornography's hidden impact. And flimsy "if only it were true!" research isn't an acceptable substitute for thorough study. An entire generation is being kept in the dark about pornography's effects because previous generations can't grapple with the new reality. Whether by approaching me (at the risk of peer scorn) after I've spoken at a university or via anonymous e-mails, young people continue to pass along an unpopular message: Growing up on porn is terrible. One 17-year-old who had given up his habit told me that reading about porn addicts "was like reading a horrifying old diary, symptoms, downward spirals, guilt, hypocrisy, lack of control, and the constant question of to what degree fantasy is really so different from reality. I felt like a criminal, or at the very least, a person who would objectively disgust me."

Let's not ignore people like him, even if it's tempting to say, as one headline did, "All men watch porn, and it is not bad for them: study."

That's just one more fantasy warping how we live our real lives.

Pamela Paul is a journalist and author. Her books include *Parents, Inc.*, and *Pornified: How Pornography Is Damaging Our Lives, Our Relationships, and Our Families.*

Megan Andelloux

NO

Porn: Ensuring Domestic Tranquility of the American People

Pornography. Images of happy people rolling over one another, flashes of arched backs, moans that cannot be ignored, and giggles pouring from the mouths of stars. Out of the corner of the eye a flash of skin on the monitor catches our attention and draws us in. Porn has become ubiquitous on the Internet in the modern day, but its existence has graced the surface of the Earth since humans first began tracing stick figures on cave walls. One of its earliest forms comes to us from the town of Santillana del Mar, in the Cantabria region of northern Spain during the Upper Paleolithic Period.[1] Coital scenes were drawn out on cave walls 40,000 years ago depicting oral sex, voyeurism, and sex for the sake of fun! Records of these "graphic" images coming from France, Portugal, and Egypt beg the question: did rulers like the great Pharaoh Ramses have to hide his papyrus porn from the royal court? Were our ancestors riddled with angst and shame about the potential damage of gazing at naked bodies drawn on scrolls? Probably not. The danger of depicting human nudity wasn't a social concern until the middle of the 18th century, when the written word made erotica available to the common man.[2] Suddenly, politicians, clergy members, and authority figures of all types decried the erotic word and spread fear of its supposed dangerous and corrupting influence. Today, alas, we still face the same argument: Is pornography harmful?

Not all porn is created equal, but it is a form of speech that has been and must continue to be protected in our society. What may be found offensive by one citizen or group of citizens should not dictate whether or not the rest of society is to be allowed free access to it, lest tyranny of minority opinion rule the day. It's clear the American court systems agree.[3] If the US Supreme found that the Westboro Baptist Church's hate speech is to be afforded protection, how could one ever think to outlaw pornography's message of pleasure? Porn virtually embodies everything the founders envisioned when they penned "the right to life, liberty, and the pursuit of happiness!"

It's been reported that over 372 million websites are devoted to displaying images of people having sex of one sort or another.[4] There are untold thousands of magazines, flash drives, comic strips, and pornographic images that circulate around us every day. Porn is a major part of our American culture, and it could be argued that watching porn is America's real pastime. Now before I start getting hate mail for an inflammatory statement like that, let me point out that regardless of a person's religious preference or political affiliation, about 36% of the American population uses porn at least once a month.[5] One would never know it because very few people publicly claim to enjoy pornography. It's understandable why. Acknowledging that you watch pornography is tantamount to identifying yourself as a "pervert" in our society.

It is astonishing that 40 years after a conservative administration spent years and millions of dollars trying to find a correlation between violence and porn (which they were unable to do), and show that porn has damaging effects on individuals and their personal relationships (which they have not), Americans are still shamed when they enjoy such a basic, ancient part of our humanity.

So, when we have hard, reputable data that tens of millions of Americans have watched porn in the past month, that our crime rates are lower when we have access to it,[6] that the most prevalent images *by far* are of adults having sex,[7] and that the performers in the field like the work they do,[8] why then is porn still vilified? It's because a group of highly motivated, yet select few people yell hard, long, and loud. They shame both people who watch and the actors who perform in porn. They portray those who stand up for porn as being misguided, or as duped by the industry itself, and browbeat people with their opinion that looking at images of people having sex is somehow immoral. We rarely hear that using porn is beneficial, empowering and a healthy choice in sexual development, exploration and expression.

Let's look at why pornography is indeed, good for society and individuals.

Pornography Shows Human Beings as Being Sexual Creatures

Pornography exposes sexual desire, and it is unashamed of what it produces. It shows the lust, the yearning, and the appreciation of other human bodies and their sexual energy. Pornography rejoices in the very things society works so hard to suppress.

Whether stumbled upon or sought out intentionally, porn is a part of society because we enjoy it. People derive pleasure seeing other people be sexual. Porn helps individuals explore behaviors they may feel alone in experiencing, such as fetishes, non-heterosexuality, or even simple masturbation. The anti-porn folks are right in at least one thing: We do learn from the images. Although, the moral crusaders will then go on to argue that we in the audience are without free will and are forced to mimic the most degrading images we see in pornographic films. But just as I will continue to come to a full stop at the next red light I see despite having enjoyed *The French Connection* last night, free will gives us the option to imitate movie scenes or not at will. Nearly everyone is sexual. Porn helps us to share in our sexuality without overriding or sublimating it.

> "Old, young, black, white, male, female, trans, pretty, ugly, tall, short, big, little, all types are represented on screen. A wider variety of body types are welcome on the porn screen as opposed to mainstream media representations of love, sex and romance. We may not look like Angelina Jolie, but we can find someone on a porn screen who looks a lot like we do, having a fun time and living to tell the tale. That's no small thing."
>
> —*Nina Hartley*
> *Porn Performer, Sex Educator*

Pornography Shows the Wide Variety of Human Sexual Desires and Actions

Porn gives hope to those who feel alone and/or sexually isolated. Queers, women, the elderly, or any marginalized group can see, with full representation, that there may be others out there, sexual like they are.

> "I started performing in pornography so that I could participate in what I felt is much needed visibility of queer sexuality, gender expressions, and sex-positive behaviors and culture. My work reflects the minority/marginalized communities that I am a part of, while allowing me to connect with a universal audience who can all appreciate great sex."
>
> —*Jiz Lee, Feminist Porn Award's Boundary Breaker and AVN Nominated Best New Web Star*

And now with amateur porn being the highest accessed sexually explicit material,[9] we have more evidence of the sex-lives of average Americans! We have proof that it's not just the "evil" porn industry that wants ejaculation scenes or spankings. We see normal bodies on film, flaws and all, having the best most creative sex.

And rather than a for-profit corporation behind the production, amateur porn has become the sexual art of folk. It's Bob and Jane playing here, or Jane and Jane, or Bob and Bob—beer belly, thick legs, short hair and . . . all frolicking around in sexual bliss.

> "Porn has afforded me the ability to feel out my sexuality without the fear of rejection or humiliation."
>
> —*Mark Farlow*

Ethically made pornography is a sub-genre of porn comprised of actors who are paid living wages for depiction of realistic sex. Ethically made pornography allows a performer to participate as more than just an actor in the sexual act being depicted. Ethical porn is an emerging powerful field within the adult market. The individuals and companies behind this movement seek out participants who DON'T look like the typical porn-stars. The ultimate goal seems to be to bring real sex to the masses. Some notable companies in this field include:

- Comstock Films
- Pink and White Productions
- Good Releasing
- Fatale Media
- Reel Queer Productions
- Sir Video
- Tristan Taormino's Expert Guide Series
- Nina Hartley's Guide Series

> "Independent and feminist porn especially can be an incredible validation for those who don't see their own desires reflected in mainstream media."
>
> —*Alison Lee, Good For Her Feminist Porn Awards*

Pornography Is a Risk Reduction Method It Is the Safest of Safe Sex

Watching porn is one of the safest ways to explore sexuality. There is no risk of STI transmissions, no risk of an unwanted pregnancy, no risk of feeling disappointed by the way our body performed, no risk of cheating, and no risk of violence. Human beings fantasize about forbidden fruit. We often wonder what it would be like to be with someone of the same gender, experience a threesome, engage in anal play, explore power dynamics, or talk dirty to our lover. Porn lets us find out, risk-free.

> "Pornography can be a great way for people to explore their sexuality and fantasies without affecting others in society. Through pornography, they are able to jump their pizza delivery person or proposition their car dealer without actually disturbing others."
>
> —*Shanna Katz, Sexologist*

Pornography Gives Access to Sex Information to All

While pornography isn't the best way to educate individuals on how to have sex, it does grant access to sexual information. It allows a great number of people to see what it means to have oral sex, pull-my-hair-play, or cis-gendered experiences. They say a picture is worth a thousand words. There is a clear difference between reading about it in a book and seeing it live in front of you, where you can watch the emotions, see the actual behaviors that take place, and process that information in a different way.

A person may feel titillated or disgusted, intrigued or off put, but all of these feelings are important parts of the learning process. What better starting point could one have when making decisions about the type of sexual behavior one wants to engage in?

I'm not arguing that pornography pretends to be educational. But it does purport to be experiential. Not everyone goes to college, nor do they have access to a sex educator, nor sex education programs, nor even a well stocked sex-ed self-help bookshelf. Accessing pornography can often be the first guidepost pointing the way to what one may want to do (or not do) in bed. The experience that porn brings, surrogate to real life as it may be, helps create a more informed decision making process.

> "We know that many people turn to porn for sex information because there is a dearth of sex ed media. So even if we're making a movie that is in no way intended to be primarily educational, (that is, porn) we want to show sex as people actually have it."
>
> —*Carol Queen, Good Releasing Films*

Pornography Encourages Conversations to Take Place about Sex

Hate it or love it, pornography is part of America.

Whether you call the risqué PETA commercial banned from prime-time porn, or find Charlie Sheen's latest sexual adventures pornographic, porn can start a conversation. We can turn to our neighbor or friend and ask, with all good intentions and proper decorum, "What do you think about Sasha Grey going into mainstream movies? Do you think she's going to make it? Why?" These probing questions serve a vital public service of allowing us to learn the sexual attitudes of our neighbors and friends.

American culture doesn't speak openly about sexuality yet harbors a judgmental attitude. Knowing the sexual mores of our peers can be vital for our social well-being. With the pornography industry putting "sexy time" out there for everyone to see and critique, seize the opportunity and talk about it!

> "Viewing porn was helpful to convey what turned me on (and off) to my partner, ultimately making the sex and relationship stronger."
>
> —*Kim Chanza*

Myth-Busting

In cultures that have access to pornography, violent crimes rates decreased. Yes, decreased. The US Government shows there is no correlation between violence and having access to and watching pornography.

The media routinely blares headlines bearing shocking titles such as "Porn made him sodomize his child!" Therefore, one would think that porn contributes to all manner of bad outcomes. The facts show, however, that pornography has been established not to increase rates of sexual violence. In 1970, the President's Commission on Obscenity and Pornography (also known as The Lockhart Report) found no link between pornography and delinquent or criminal behavior among youth and adults.[10] William B. Lockhart, Dean of the University of Minnesota Law School and chairman of the commission, famously said that before his work with the commission he had favored control of obscenity for both children and adults, but had changed his mind as a result of scientific studies done by commission researchers.

Similarly, in 1984 the Metro Toronto Task Force on Public Violence against Women and Children failed to demonstrate a link between pornography and sex crimes,[11] as did the 1994 US National Research Council Panel on Understanding and Preventing Violence.[12] Even the Meese Report, a famously biased hand-picked group of anti-pornography advocates hired by Ronald Reagan to prove the damaging effects of pornography failed to show any hard evidence. In fact, they got more than they bargained for when they hired Canadian sociologist Edna F. Einsiedel to summarize the current scientific studies linking pornography and violence. Her conclusion was that "No evidence currently exists that actually links fantasies with specific sexual offenses; the relationship at this point remains an inference.[13]"

Those talking heads who cling to the canard that porn leads to violence, rape, sexual assault, or child molestation are preaching from emotion, not facts. They fear what horrors "might" come to pass, and their fear is contagious. Terrifying tales without background or prelude are woven in the media to provoke a base response in their audience. Unfortunately, American history is littered with examples of just such emotional arguments being more powerful than well-reasoned counterparts. Witness the Salem witch trials, Japanese internment camps during WWII, or the sordid history of the House Un-American Activities Committee.

The anti-porn community (be it conservative religious or liberal feminist) stuffs the news media with anecdotal evidence of the danger posed by porn. Anecdotal evidence is of course the least reliable type of scientific data; one person, with a pretty face and a sob-story, can be more convincing than stacks of peer-reviewed journal articles. Though it can be moving to hear stories such as "Porn made me masturbate all day," or, "Porn made me see people as if they were naked," porn has not been actually shown to cause any such behavior.

Porn is an easy target for attack, but here is the thing: Humans have free will. We can choose to act one way or another, but pornography does not force us to do evil.

In all seriousness, rape and sexual assault are caused by violent antisocial tendencies, complete disregard for another's rights, and pure self-interest. To pin it on porn relieves the rapist of the guilt and blame.

One may not like certain aspects of pornography, but that discomfort should not restrict other's access to it. A society that produces legal pornography, a people that have access to pornography, is a sexually healthy nation. Pornography, a blessing of liberty, creates for us a more perfect union.

Resources

- Feminists for Free Expression
- ACLU
- Woodhull Freedom Foundation
- National Coalition for Sexual Freedom
- Free Speech Network
- Society for the Scientific Study of Sexuality
- America's War on Sex, Marty Klein
- Planned Parenthood of Western Washington, Pornography: Discussing Sexually Explicit Images, Irene Peters, Ph.D.

References

1. Cave paintings show aspects of sex beyond the reproductive. (2006, May 2). *Dominican Today,* Retrieved from http://www.dominicantoday.com/dr/people/2006/5/2/12982/Cave-paintings-show-aspects-of-sex-beyond-the-reproductive.
2. Carroll, J.L. (2007). *Sexuality now.* Belmont, CA: Wadsworth.
3. Corry v. Stanford University, Case No. 740309 (Cal. Super. Ct. 1995); Dambrot v. Central Michigan University, 839 F. Supp. 477 (E.D. Mich. 1993); Doe v. University of Michigan, 721 F. Supp. 852 (E.D. Mich. 1989).
4. Joseph, M. (Producer). (2007). *Internet porn* [Web]. Available from http://www.good.is/post/internet-Porn.
5. Media Metrix Demographic Profile—Adult. (2008, June). comScore
6. Kendall, T.D. (2006). Pornography, rape, and the internet. *Proceedings of the law and economics seminar* Stanford, CA: http://www.law.stanford.edu/display/images/dynamic/events_media/Kendall%20cover%20+%20paper.pdf.
7. Diamond, M. (2009). Pornography, public acceptance, and sex related crime: a review. *International Journal of Law and Psychiatry* 32 (2009) 304–314;

corrected with Corrigendum IJLP 33 (2010) 197–199.

8. Paulie & Pauline. (2010). *Off the set: porn stars and their partners*. Glen Rock, NJ: Aural Pink Press.
9. Klein, M. (2006). *America's war on sex: the attack on law, lust, and liberty*. Santa Barbara, CA: Praeger.
10. The Commission on Obscenity and Pornography, (1970). *President's commission on obscenity and pornography*. Washington, DC: U.S. Government Printing Office.
11. Task Force on Public Violence against Women and Children, Final Report (1984). *Metro Toronto*. Toronto, Canada.
12. Reiss, A.J., & Roth, A.J. National Research Council, (1993). *Understanding and preventing violence*. Washington, DC: National Academy Press.
13. United States Attorney General, Commission on Pornography. (1986). *Attorney general's commission on pornography*. Washington, DC.

Megan Andelloux, a certified sexologist and sexuality educator, is the director of the Center for Sexual Pleasure and Health, a sexuality resource center for adults in Pawtucket, Rhode Island. Ms. Andelloux lectures at major universities, medical schools, and conferences on issues surrounding sexual freedom and the politics of pleasure.

EXPLORING THE ISSUE

Is Pornography Harmful?

Critical Thinking and Reflection

1. What types of harm or benefits could result from consuming pornography?
2. Do you think that the ways men and women consume pornography are different? Explain.
3. How has technology changed the way porn is consumed?

Is There Common Ground?

Is there the potential for middle ground between vehemently anti-porn and resoundingly pro-porn camps? Is all porn bad and inherently harmful? How does the age of the viewer impact the potential for harm? There does appear to be general consensus that child pornography is harmful. However, defining child pornography may prove just as challenging as defining all porn. And should the viewer's age be taken into account? At what age should the line be drawn? 12? 16? 18? 21? Is there a difference between a 14-year-old watching online porn versus a 24-year-old? Should two high school students "sexting" each other be viewed the same way as a much older adult looking at nude images or video of a high school student?

In his book, *America's War on Sex*, Marty Klein reports that 50 million Americans use legal adult pornography. A 2013 *Huffiington Post* article reported that 30 percent of all data transmitted on the Internet is porn, and that porn websites are visited more frequently than Amazon, Netflix, and Twitter combined. Most people do not publicly acknowledge their use of pornography, and many even adopt shameful attitudes about it. So, in this way, the arguments presented by Paul and Andelloux may reflect American attitudes and experiences, in general. The common ground may be that people will continue to consume pornography, while many—even the same consumers of pornography—will be silent about it, or condemn it.

Additional Resources

Blue, V. (2006). *The Smart Girl's Guide to Porn.* San Fransisco, CA: Cleis Press.

Klein, M. (2012). *America's War on Sex.* Santa Barbara, CA: Praeger.

Levy, A. (2006). *Female Chauvinist Pigs: Women and the Rise of Raunch Culture.* New York, NY: Free Press.

Nathan, D. (2007). *Pornography.* Toronto, ON: Groundwood Press.

Paul, P. (2006). *Pornified: How Pornography Is Transforming Our Lives, Our Relationships, and Our Families.* New York, NY: Holt.

Sarracino, C. & Scott, K.M. (2009). *The Porning of America: The Rise of Porn Culture, What It Means, and Where We Go from Here.* Boston, MA: Beacon Press.

Internet References . . .

Academia Does Porn

This article describes a brand new peer-reviewed academic journal devoted to pornography.

www.salon.com/2013/05/03/academia_does_porn/

Cindy Gallop Wants to Change the Future of Porn

Cindy Gallop, creator of www.makelovenotporn.com, shares some of her thoughts on intimacy, pornography, social media, and how these things will come together in the future.

www.businessinsider.com/make-love-not-porn-cindy-gallop-2013-4

Porn Study: Does Viewing Explain Doing—Or Not?

This is a discussion of a new study investigating the relationship between porn use, risky behavior, and erectile dysfunction.

www.psychologytoday.com/blog/cupids-poisoned-arrow/201304/porn-study-does-viewing-explain-doing-or-not

The History of Pornography No More Prudish than the Present

A history of pornography from the ancient to the current.

www.livescience.com/8748-history-pornography-prudish-present.html

Selected, Edited, and with Issue Framing Material by:
Ryan W. McKee, *Widener University,* Tracie Q. Gilbert, *Widener University,*
and
Jayleen Galarza, *Shippensburg University of Pennsylvania*

ISSUE

Should Condoms Be Required in Pornographic Films?

YES: Sadhbh Walshe, from "Condoms and Porn Don't Mix Is a Stupid and Unhealthy Belief," *The Guardian* (2013)

NO: Shay Tiziano, from "Keep Concern Trolling Laws Out of Our Porn: A 'Workplace Safety' Based Argument Against Mandatory Condoms in Adult Films," *Stefanos & Shay* (2016)

Learning Outcomes

After reading this issue, you will be able to:

- Explain the existing policy on testing for sexually transmitted infections (STIs) in the adult film industry.
- Discuss the public health arguments for mandatory condom usage in adult films.
- Discuss both the business and free-speech arguments against mandatory condom usage in adult films

ISSUE SUMMARY

YES: Sadhbh Walshe, a filmmaker and television writer who also writes about social justice issues for publications around the world, believes arguments against condom use in porn are more about studio profits than performers' rights.

NO: Shay Tiziano, an emergency room nurse who is also an educator, host, performer, and advocate within the BDSM community, argues that concerns over workplace safety on pornographic film sets are overblown, and an example of sex-negative moralizing in disguise.

For years, the production and economic center of the adult film industry, which generates billions of dollars annually was Los Angeles, California. In a typical year, there were about 500 applications for adult film permits. But between January 1 and April 14, 2013, only two were requested. Why the sudden drop? In November 2012, Los Angeles County voters passed a controversial law, the *County of Los Angeles Safer Sex in the Adult Film Industry Act*, also known as "Measure B." The new law required adult film performers to use condoms during all scenes involving anal and vaginal intercourse filmed in Los Angeles.

Like all industries that operate within the United States, the adult film industry is subject to health and safety regulations developed and enforced by government agencies. The California Occupational Safety and Health Act (Cal/OSHA), passed in 1973, mandated

> ". . . safe and healthful working conditions for all California working men and women by authorizing the enforcement of effective standards, assisting and encouraging employers to maintain safe and healthful working conditions, and by providing for research, information, education, training, and enforcement in the field of occupational safety and health . . . . Employers must protect employees from blood-borne pathogens and not discriminate against employees that complain about safety and health conditions. Companies are required to prevent workers from coming into contact with blood or other potentially infectious material, including semen and vaginal fluid, and to provide post-exposure prophylaxis."
>
> (Grudzen & Kerndt, 2007)

While this law was not written specifically for adult performers, the occupational risks are similar to health

care workers or researchers who may come into contact with such "infectious material." In 2006, Cal/OSHA recommended, but did not require, several policies to increase safety on porn sets, including the use of condoms and latex dams during filmed sexual activity.

Though Cal/OSHA regulations were on the books, enforcement of the law was minimal. Porn producers had traditionally required mandatory monthly testing of each performer to stay in compliance, but did not require that condoms be used. The adult industry occasionally experienced outbreaks of various STIs, including HIV, during which production would stop and all performers who had been put at risk were immediately retested. Many industry insiders felt that this policy was the best way to protect the safety of performers.

But in 2012, a performer altered his paperwork, hiding a positive syphilis test result and infecting several of his fellow performers. This event was the impetus for the AIDS Healthcare Foundation, an HIV advocacy group, to successfully push for legislative change in the industry. Measure B which, again, requires the use of condoms for all on-camera acts of vaginal and anal sex on adult film sets, passed with nearly 57 percent of the vote. Those in favor of the law, including some performers, said that it would help to ensure the safety on the set and help promote condom usage among viewers. They likened the law to those requiring the use of hard-hats and safety goggles on construction sites. Opponents, including other performers, argued that, thanks to rigorous testing, the mandatory use of condoms was not needed. They feared film productions would go "underground," shooting without permits or workplace safety norms. They also predicted that the change would lead adult film companies to take their highly profitable businesses outside of Los Angeles, to other counties in California, states like Nevada, or even countries like Brazil, with fewer regulations.

Since 2012, legal challenges and red tape have made the law difficult to enforce. However, as of late 2015, requests for production permits in Los Angeles had fallen 90 percent. Despite the legal wrangling, legislators in other parts of the country have attempted to enact similar laws. The AIDS Healthcare Foundation, emboldened by their success in Los Angeles, has pushed for the same regulations to be enacted on a larger scale throughout California. In November of 2016, *The California Safer Sex in Adult Film Act* will appear on ballots statewide, giving voters the opportunity to decide if adult films throughout the state should be held to the same regulations as Los Angeles County.

In the following YES selection, filmmaker and social justice advocate Sadhbh Walshe argues that those opposed to condom laws in the adult film industry care more about profits than safety. She argues that the standard practice of regular testing does little to prevent outbreaks of HIV and other STIs, and that mandated condom usage is much more effective. In the NO selection, Shay Tiziano, an emergency room nurse as well as a BDSM community advocate, educator, and performer, identifies concern over workplace safety as nothing more than sex-negative moralizing. Her experience in both the health care and adult industries reinforces her belief that being an adult film performer is an incredibly safe profession.

References

Grudzen, C., and Kerndt, P. (2007). The Adult Film Industry: Time to Regulate? *PLOS Medicine, 4*(6). doi: 10.1371/journal.pmed.0040126

YES

Sadhbh Walshe

Condoms and Porn Don't Mix Is a Stupid and Unhealthy Belief

One might think that when a person makes their living having sex with strangers, as porn industry performers do, using condoms would be a no-brainer. Yet despite the prevalence of STDs in the industry, the ill-conceived notion that condoms and porn don't mix seems to have trumped common sense.

Apparently, the sight of a condom clad penis is a buzz kill for end users, and performers don't want to wear them anyway. Or, at least, that's what the Free Speech Coalition (FSC), the trade association for the adult entertainment industry, would like us to believe as it continues its fight against mandatory condom use. With another performer testing positive for HIV and the Los Angeles—based industry facing another moratorium in production, the time may have come for both the profiteers of porn and those who get their kicks from watching it to get over their condom phobia.

Recently, the FSC announced that one of their LA-based performers had tested positive for HIV, and that all filming would be suspended while they try to determine if anyone else in their talent pool had been exposed to the virus. This is the third time in the past four months that the industry has had to shut down production after performers tested positive. Despite these repeated blows to the industry's bottom line, never mind the pain and suffering of the infected performers who have been hit with the double whammy of contracting a life-long disease and losing their livelihood, the opposition to mandatory condom use persists. At the same time, the industry's justification for its opposition—that performers just don't like condoms and that they prefer to rely on testing systems—is getting harder to swallow.

The arguments put forth by the industry against mandatory condom use are as creative as they are varied, ranging from violation of performers' first amendment rights (the industry's trade association is not called the "Free Speech" Coalition for nothing) to the risk of condom-induced vaginal irritation known as "floor burn." Porn sex, as aficionados will attest, is not the same as civilian sex—put simply, performers go at it for hours on end, while for most of us mere mortals the penetrative part of the act can be over in a matter of minutes. Some female performers say that in shoots that last several hours, condoms can be irritating and can lead to internal abrasions. The industry claims that these abrasions could make it easier to transmit infection, and that this is the reason that many performers prefer to not use condoms at all.

While floor burn is a legitimate concern recognized by doctors, the second part of this argument (that using condoms ultimately makes it easier to transmit infection) makes little sense. If performers consistently use condoms, which have been proven to provide protection against disease, then the risk of transmitting infections can only be reduced. Yet this rather lame argument against condom use, that has been embraced by an industry that claims to care so deeply about its performers' wellbeing, kind of leaves a lot of them (the female ones in particular) stuck between a rock and a hard place. Basically female performers are left with a rather dismal choice—use condoms and risk being afflicted with the painful but treatable condition of floor burn, or don't use condoms and risk contracting chlamydia, gonorrhoea, syphilis, and even HIV.

For now the only recourse most performers have to protect themselves against HIV and other STDs is to be constantly tested and hope that their fellow performers do the same. To the industry's credit, it has a fairly rigorous testing system in place. Prior to the three cases of HIV being detected in September, performers were being tested monthly. Now the industry requires performers to be tested every 14 days (at their own expense) before they can be cleared for participation in a shoot. While testing has its place, it doesn't quite hold up as a preventative measure, however. As Ged Kenslea, spokesperson for the Aids Healthcare Foundation put it:

> *"Relying on testing to prevent the transmission of HIV is a bit like using a pregnancy test as a form of birth control."*

As the industry continues to push testing as the best form of prevention, it seems to have forgotten that using condoms is a legal requirement not an option, at least in Los Angeles where the majority of all porn films produced in the US are made. Last year voters in Los Angeles County passed Measure B, which mandates the use of condoms in the adult entertainment industry. Even before this measure passed, condom use was already technically required under the state's Occupational Safety and Health Administration [OSHA] laws but was difficult to enforce.

Measure B was supposed to change that, but according to Kenslea, who has reviewed a representative sample of straight porn films, over 90% are still condom free. (This is in stark contrast to the gay porn industry which has voluntarily complied with condom laws and is still managing to thrive.) So despite laws being in place to protect all performers, the industry continues to mostly defy them, all the time claiming to be acting according to the performers' wishes and in their best interest.

Could it be that the industry has a more self-serving reason to favor testing over mandatory condom use that has little to do with the wellbeing or otherwise of performers and a lot to do with profits? According to CNN, when the industry experimented with condom use over a decade ago after another HIV outbreak, revenues declined by 30%. It may well be that the concern that "Debbie does Condoms" will not be a big seller among porn users is what's driving the industry to move out of Los Angeles to cities like Las Vegas where condoms are not (yet) required, rather than any real concerns that condoms are injurious to performers' health.

I hope before any more performers learn through the industry's mandatory testing that they have contracted HIV, which could have been easily prevented by observing mandatory condom laws, they will at least question their employer's motives.

Sadhbh Walshe, a filmmaker and television writer who also writes about social justice issues for publications around the world, including *The Guardian* and *The New York Times*.

Shay Tiziano

NO

Keep Concern Trolling Laws Out of Our Porn: A "Workplace Safety" Based Argument Against Mandatory Condoms in Adult Films

There are many excellent reasons to oppose government mandated condoms in porn—as an example of "sex work savior" legislation crafted while explicitly ignoring input from actual sex workers, a freedom of speech issue, another example of government trying to tell us what the "approved" forms of sex between consenting adults are, a safety risk to performers when these laws push the industry underground, and more. When politicians and special interest groups (*cough*Aids Healthcare Foundation*cough*) "sell" this legislation to the public, though, the angle they use doesn't have much to do with any of those arguments- they come at this type of legislation pleading for workplace safety. "We just want to give adult film performers the same OSHA workplace protections as people in other occupations!"

This is a difficult argument because on its face, it sounds totally reasonable, even to allies of sex workers. Who's against safety? I mean, shouldn't porn performers have the same on-the-job protections as, for example, nurses?

I'm an ER nurse with experience in porn and a partner who works full time in the adult industry, and I'd answer that particular question with a resounding "NOPE." The "workplace safety" argument falls apart in two basic ways—first, in terms of actual job-related risk, and second, in terms of the approach and implementation of "safety" regulations offered in bills like the (fortunately now dead) AB 1576 and the (unfortunately still quite alive) Measure B in LA.

Starting with risk being an adult film performer is an incredibly safe job. Since the current testing standards were implemented in 2004, there have been ZERO transmissions of HIV on industry-regulated adult film sets. The adult industry has shown over the last decade of successful self-regulation (read about the current guidelines here http://www.stefanosandshay.com/articles/mandatory-condoms-in-porn/) that sex on an adult film set is the safest sex you can have, and being an adult film performer is extraordinarily safe! Of course every job (and really everything we do) involves some amount of risk, but let's contrast the risk of contracting HIV on a porn set to the risk I face when I work in the ER. Every day I have many patients with a variety of contagious diseases or of unknown status. In 2005 (the most recent year for which I could find numbers), there were 1,350 health care worker (HCW) exposures (needlestick or mucocutaneous) to HIV positive sources recorded by the CDC, and 8,859 exposures to sources of unknown HIV status. Those are just the ones reported, and we know that HCWs wildly under-report their exposures. The International Healthcare Worker Safety Center has estimated that as many as 35 new cases of HIV are transmitted annually to health care workers in the US (1). Globally, there are estimated to be around 1000 cases per year (2). And HIV is just the start of the serious risks I face as an ER nurse- I'm exposed to patients with TB, MRSA, hepatitis, meningitis, C. diff, and many more. Several years ago, one ER I worked in had such a severe outbreak of workplace-acquired C. diff among the staff that about a third were out on sick leave and they almost had to shut down the ER. I've also been assaulted on the job. So where am I safer—having sex without a condom on an industry-regulated adult film set, or working as an ER nurse? I know my answer to that question. Yet organizations like the Aids Healthcare Foundation (AHF) try to sell the idea that there's some sort of epidemic or wildly unsafe working conditions in the adult industry. As has been pointed out by others, adult performers are not a risk to the general population—the general population is a risk to adult performers!

So that's the risk angle—the risks on an adult film set are fundamentally not anywhere near the same as the risks I face in the ER, so it doesn't make sense to apply the same "workplace safety" standards.

The second way that these claims about "workplace safety" fall apart is that legislation to mandate condom use in porn likes to call upon OSHA standards, yet handle these issues ENTIRELY DIFFERENTLY than the OSHA regulations that apply to hospital workers. Occupational Safety and Health Administration (OSHA) regulations as they apply to jobs like nursing are focused on making sure the employer provides protective equipment like gloves, masks, and isolation gowns. They're focused on making sure the employer takes on the burden of paying for my bi-annual TB tests and n-95 mask fit tests and hepatitis B vaccinations and all that (3).

There's actually quite a bit of space for worker choice in the OSHA regulations that apply to HCWs. There are exceptions for me not taking the time to put on personal protective equipment if I make a professional judgment that in a specific instance its use would prevent the delivery of healthcare or public safety services or would pose an increased hazard to the safety of myself or co-worker. There's even exemptions for worker choice—some nurses and phlebotomists don't like to wear gloves because they can "feel the veins better" without them. Does that rationale sound familiar to anyone, with regards to people not liking to use condoms? Well, there's actually an entire section of OSHA regulations specifically outlining exemptions for employees to choose not to routinely glove for blood draws (3). That's after an interesting section stating that "mouth pipetting/suctioning of blood is prohibited"—which was kinda an odd subject to read about on the US Department of Labor web site. In any case, this is in stark contrast to laws like AB1576 & Measure B, which make no exceptions at all, and focus on punitive, criminal consequences for failure to comply with these "protections"—to quote from AB1576: "Because a violation of the act would be a crime under certain circumstances, the bill would impose a state-mandated local program by creating a new crime." (4) Measure B also imposes penalties, including fines of up to $1,000 and jail time (5). These penalties explicitly apply not only to producers and directors, but to anyone involved in production, including and up to the performers supposedly being protected! This is an entirely different approach than lawmakers take towards job safety for occupations like nursing and it is very telling as to the real intentions behind this type of legislation.

So at their base these are concern-trolling laws that address a non-problem "problem." Organizations like the Aids Healthcare Foundation *know* that there's no crisis in the adult industry. What are they hoping to accomplish—taking the number of on-set HIV transmissions down from zero to . . . what? If they actually gave a shit about preventing HIV infections on the job they could come to hospitals and implement programs to move to IV cannulas with one-way valves or needleless IV tubing or spend their time and resources on some of the 49,000 people who are diagnosed with HIV per year (NONE of them infected on a regulated adult film set). It's an outrage to see a non-profit like AHF wasting money to publicity-monger with crap like AB 1576 and Measure B.

Mandatory condom in porn legislation uses "workplace safety" as a Trojan Horse. Inside the Trojan Horse you'll find the real reasons behind this type of legislation—moralizing, controlling sexuality and especially the female body (similarly to legislation about birth control and abortion), garnering publicity, etc. Whenever you see legislation that proposes to "help" a group of people who vehemently oppose said "help," you should be very wary. Sex workers don't need legislative "saviors."

References

1. Preventing Needlestick Injuries among Healthcare Workers: A WHO–ICN Collaboration. http://www.who.int/occupational_health/activities/5prevent.pdf
2. Center for Disease Control http://wwwnc.cdc.gov/travel/yellowbook/2014/chapter-2-the-pre-travel-consultation/occupational-exposure-to-hiv
3. United States Department of Labor https://www.osha.gov/pls/oshaweb/owadisp.show_document?p_id=10051&p_table=STANDARDS
4. AB 1576 Bill Text http://www.leginfo.ca.gov/pub/13-14/bill/asm/ab_1551-1600/ab_1576_bill_20140130_introduced.html
5. Measure B Text as linked from http://www.smartvoter.org/2012/11/06/ca/la/meas/B/

Shay Tiziano is an emergency room nurse and a host, performer, and advocate in the BDSM community. She is also the Education Director for the well-known BDSM event *Dark Odyssey: Surrender* and for the BDSM club the San Francisco Citadel.

EXPLORING THE ISSUE

Should Condoms Be Required in Pornographic Films?

Critical Thinking and Reflection

1. What safety precautions were taken to protect performers before the passage of Measure B? What new practices did Measure B mandate?
2. What are the arguments in favor of mandated condom usage in pornography? What are the arguments against the mandate?
3. How might mandatory use of condoms in porn impact the performers? The producers? The viewers?
4. Do you think adult films become more or less erotic with on-screen condom use? Or does it make no difference to the viewer?

Is There Common Ground?

Some may wonder why condoms aren't already mandatory in porn production, or why performers aren't more interested in using them. Economics, producers argue, is the driving factor. The lack of condoms in porn is simply a response to viewer demand. Consumers, producers say, don't want to watch porn with condoms. Additionally, some filmmakers and performers feel that requiring performers to use condoms would infringe on their artistic freedom. Supporters of the law note that condom use has been the norm in the majority of gay male-oriented porn films, and that consumers have raised few concerns. Additionally, they argue that condom requirements for porn produced in other parts of the world have not hindered the sale of those films.

Public health advocates, adult film performers and producers do agree that safe work environments for those involved in the porn industry are important. What they disagree on is the role of government in regulating safety practices. Opponents of laws like Measure B argue that increased regulation could actually decrease safety, as productions move "underground" or to areas with even fewer safety regulations. Those in favor fear more, or more dangerous, outbreaks like the one in 2012.

What is your take on the controversy? Do you agree with Walshe, who believes that producers' concern over safety regulations is more about the companies' bottom line than the safety of the performers? Or, do you trust Tiziano, whose expertise as both a nurse and adult performer, has convinced her that mandatory condom use is porn unnecessary and paternalistic? Are analogies between condoms and hard-hats appropriate? Is a porn set just another work environment? Why might condoms only be required for vaginal and anal sex and not oral sex? Should condoms and dams be required for oral sex as well? Would the use of condoms make you more or less likely to watch adult films? Why? Does the porn industry have a responsibility to lead by example and promote safer sex practices? Or are adult films, simply a form of artistic expression like any other film? Do the creators of other types of media, like action films or music, for example, have a responsibility to promote healthy behaviors?

Additional Resources

Abram, S. (April 14, 2013). Porn film permits have dropped dramatically in L.A. County. *Los Angeles Daily News*. Retrieved from http://www.dailynews.com/article/ZZ/20130414/NEWS/130419731

Brown. E. B. (January 22, 2016). Stalemate over porn condom law in Los Angeles. Retrieved from https://reason.com/blog/2016/01/22/las-condoms-in-porn-law

Hess, A. (October 25, 2012). Porn stars may soon have to wear condoms. Will you still watch? *Slate*. Retrieved from www.slate.com/blogs/xx_factor/2012/10/25/california_s_measure_b_what_s_so_bad_about_condoms_in_porn.html

Los Angeles Times (October 18, 2012). No on Measure B. Retrieved from http://articles.latimes.com/2012/oct/18/opinion/la-ed-end-measure-b-20121018

McGreevy, P. (November 4, 2015). California will Vote in 2016 on condoms for porn actors. *The*

Los Angeles Times. Retrieved from http://www.latimes.com/local/political/la-me-pc-california-initiative-requiring-condoms-for-porn-actors-makes-2016-ballot-20151104-story.html

Snow. A. (October 18, 2012). Condoms in porn: One adult performer says yes to Measure B. *The Daily Beast*. Retrieved from http://www.thedailybeast.com/articles/2012/10/18/condoms-in-porn-one-adult-star-says-yes-to-measure-b.html

Internet References . . .

AIDS Healthcare Foundation

http://www.aidshealth.org/

Free Speech Coalition

https://www.freespeechcoalition.com/

Selected, Edited, and with Issue Framing Material by:
Ryan W. McKee, *Widener University,* Tracie Q. Gilbert, *Widener University,*
and
Jayleen Galarza, *Shippensburg University of Pennsylvania*

ISSUE

Should Sex Work Be Decriminalized?

YES: Matt Hershberger, from "Legalized Prostitution Is a Mess. Here's Why It Has to Happen Anyway," *Matador Network* (2015)

NO: Demand Abolition, from "The Evidence Against Legalizing Prostitution," *Demand Abolition* (2016)

Learning Outcomes

After reading this issue, you will be able to:

- Distinguish between the terms sex work and prostitution.
- Distinguish between the terms legalization, criminalization, decriminalization, and regulation as they related to prostitution.
- Examine and assess potential connections between the stigmatization of sex work and adverse side effects of current decriminalization efforts.
- Consider the significance of prioritizing prostitution when thinking about sex work as a whole.

ISSUE SUMMARY

YES: Matt Hershberger, writer and blogger, uses the "lesser of evils" argument to suggest that decriminalization may be the best chance society has at present to ensure a safe working environment for today's sex work population.

NO: Demand Abolition argues there is insufficient evidence from efforts to legalize and/or decriminalize prostitution in the past to suggest either as a useful option in any sense.

Whether it's pornography, prostitution, web-camming, or exotic dancing, sex work is a large part of the global economy. Loosely defined, sex work refers to the exchange of sexual services for money and/or other goods (clothing, housing, transportation, education, etc.). People who engage in sex work are diverse, ranging in age, gender, sexual orientation, ethnicity, socioeconomic status, and participant motivation. The variety and intensity of activities sex workers engage in is also, including many behaviors, not thought of as inherently sexual. Prostitution is the most commonly discussed type of sex work, and while many—if not most—sex work is illegal in most places, prostitution has been the subjects of much conversation on legalization and decriminalization.

Prostitution is well-known colloquially as the "oldest profession in the world." While it legally refers to the exchange of money or goods for sexual services, the specific expectation held by most people is that prostitutes engage in direct sexual activity with their clients. Despite the fact that prostitution is legal in only a handful of countries (and regulated in still fewer), it is estimated that nearly 42 million individuals engage in some type of formal prostitution service, worldwide. Prostitution ranges from solicitation in outdoor settings (e.g., parks, streets), to setting up residence in brothels, to high-end escort services. Though individuals from various walks of life engage in prostitution, nearly 80 percent of them all are women, including sizeable numbers of transgender women of color. Additionally, 75 percent of all prostitutes are under the age of 25; coercion is a significant part many of these younger workers' experiences.

It may be helpful when examining the debate on sex work to clarify distinctions between *criminalization*, *decriminalization*, and *legalization*. Those who seek to end the practice through the criminalization of prostitution would take an abolitionist perspective, meaning that all aspects of prostitution would be illegal and punishable by law. On the other hand, the decriminalization of prostitution would remove any criminal penalties associated with the trade, and allow prostitutes to operate in a similar manner to independent contractors or other independently licensed businesses. As a third option, legalization of prostitution would call for state licensing and regulations, including the possibility of mandated testing for sexually transmitted infections and, in the United States, official registration of the occupation with the Internal Revenue Service. According to the US Department of State Bureau of Democracy, Human Rights, and Labor, the legality of prostitution varies across the world with it being illegal in many countries, legalized and regulated in others. Additionally in some parts of the world, the act of prostitution itself is legal, though other activities related to it are illegal, such as soliciting sex in a public place.

In the United States, Nevada has consistently been the only state in which prostitution is legal. (In recent history, prostitution was also allowed de facto in Rhode Island, though a 2009 law made it a misdemeanor in that state.) Nevada legalized prostitution in 1971; at present, the state is home to 28 legal brothels and nearly 300 registered female prostitutes. Brothels in Nevada are only allowed in counties that have fewer than 400,000 residents, which excludes major metropolitan areas, including the county where Las Vegas is located. That said, researchers have found that 90 percent of prostitution in Nevada takes place (illegally) in Las Vegas and Reno. Legalized brothels in Nevada are highly regulated; state law requires that brothel prostitutes receive weekly tests for Chlamydia and Gonorrhea, as well as monthly tests for HIV and Syphilis. Condom use is also required, though its enforcement can, obviously, be tricky. Among prostitutes affiliated with Nevada brothels in recent years, there have been no cases of HIV, and rates for gonorrhea have remained around 1 percent. As a whole, prostitutes at brothels are found to fare significantly better than those who work independently on the streets. Indeed, one such case study in Australia found that prostitutes (and those who solicit on the streets, specifically) working outside of the legalized and regulated system experienced drastically higher rates of bacterial STIs (80 times greater) than those who worked in brothels.

In the last few years, prostitution and sex work have found a firm home on the Internet, through such online advertising websites as Craigslist and Backpage. In these cases, advertisements may be created on a permanent or temporary basis, with workers arranging and performing fly-by-night sexual experiences at an offline location, as brokered through third parties (i.e., pimps). While these can involve consensual participants, it is reported that many women and children are forced into these avenues against their will, with many of them having no knowledge of how and to whom these advertisements are promoted. In addition to using the Internet to promote offline work, websites have also cropped up offering other Internet-only sexual experiences, including web camera video chat hosting. "Chat hosts" or, in some circles, "Cam Girls", as they are called, use their cameras to broadcast erotic acts live to viewers in public for-pay chat rooms. Many also offer private pay options, where viewers may engage in greater interactivity, depending on client preferences and website capabilities.

Different views about prostitution may depend on the specific way in which it is conceptualized. Organizations such as the Coalition Against Trafficking in Women (CATW), for example, consider prostitution to be sexual exploitation. A common concern affirming this logic centers on the mental, emotional, and socioeconomic circumstances informing many women's decisions to become sex workers—all of these having been routinely cited as significant participant motivation for those lowest in the earning stream, and those considered most at risk for experiencing violence and other mistreatment. On the other hand, sex worker activist organizations like Call Off Your Old Tired Ethics (COYOTE), and the North American Task Force on Prostitution, focus on the labor of sex work, likening the energy exerted as a prostitute with that one might expend through any other profession, including construction or clerical work. With this in mind, proponents of decriminalization prefer to focus on organizing/educating sex workers, and securing worker rights around safety, harm reduction, and economic empowerment.

In the following YES selection, writer and blogger Matt Hershberger presents a rationale for decriminalizing prostitution, outlining the potentially inevitable challenges of maintaining the current system. In the NO selection, Demand Abolition cites a collection of research evidence iterating that prostitution is a violation of human rights, leading to the dehumanization of women and children, and should, thusly, remain criminalized.

YES

Matt Hershberger

Legalized Prostitution Is a Mess. Here's Why It Has to Happen Anyway

On August 11, Amnesty International, the world's largest and most prominent human rights organization, voted to support the worldwide decriminalization of prostitution. It has been a tremendously controversial decision, with celebrities like Lena Dunham, Nick Kristof, and Kate Winslet speaking out against it, and with many (including another writer on Matador) arguing that decriminalization actually serves to make life easier for pimps and sex traffickers rather than the women they exploit.

But sex workers and sex worker advocacy groups tend to support decriminalization as a way to better protect their health and well-being while refocusing law enforcement's attention not on the worker's themselves, but on those who are trafficking or harming the women instead.

The one thing that everyone seems to agree on is that decriminalized prostitution is not even *remotely* close to perfect. No one—aside from truly terrible people—wants women to be abused, sold, killed, or exploited, and the world's many experiments with decriminalizing prostitution have never totally eliminated these risks. It needs to happen anyway.

There are three basic options, all of which can be implemented in a billion different ways. They are total criminalization, partial decriminalization, and full legalization. Total criminalization (which much of the world subscribes to) is by far the worst approach. It leads to the targeting and arrest of the sex workers, who may have been forced into the industry, meaning they're getting arrested for *something they desperately do not want to be doing*. It also means that, with the entire industry pushed underground, abused women are less likely to seek help from law enforcement, as they are technically complicit in a criminal act. Many sex workers in countries with total criminalization say that police will often demand they perform sex acts on them in order to avoid being arrested.

Full legalization is a lot trickier. The standard, go-to argument for the legalization of prostitution is that it's the world's oldest profession and it isn't going anywhere, so we should try and bring it out of the shadows and reduce the potential harm as much as humanly possible. Legalization—which, we should note, is technically different from decriminalization, as legalization refers to the imposition of regulation while decriminalization refers to the removal of criminal punishments—would, ideally, bring prostitution into a place where it could be practiced safely and regulated so that the government could focus their energy instead on targeting traffickers. Legalization would also ideally make it easier to provide prostitutes with health services, thus preventing the spread of STDs.

Opponents of legalization (aside from the people who simply oppose it for moral reasons) typically say that increased legalized prostitution leads to increased sex trafficking. The evidence for this is a bit shaky, though: often, as German Lopez points out in his excellent article on Vox it conflates sex trafficking with human trafficking, which are not one and the same, and human trafficking is notoriously difficult to reliably study, as it is illegal and is thus underground. It may simply be that, when prostitution is legalized, it becomes easier to track sex trafficking, and as a result, we may see a spike in it. If this is the case, our response shouldn't be "let's make prostitution illegal again to get these numbers down," it should be, "let's use this new information to make trafficking more difficult."

The approach that people like Lena Dunham and Gloria Steinem support, partial decriminalization, is the approach Sweden and Norway have adopted. In 1999, Sweden decriminalized the *selling* of sex, while simultaneously criminalizing the *buying* of sex. So rather than targeting the sex workers, it targets the johns. Proponents claim this legislation has had a number of effects: first, it has drastically reduced the number of prostitutes working in Sweden, and second, it has drastically reduced the number of women being trafficked in Sweden.

The problem with the Sweden approach is that the evidence of actual improvements are pretty shaky, and

Hershberger, Matt. "Legalized Prostitution Is a Mess. Here's Why It Has to Happen Anyway," *Matador Network*, August 2015.

pro-Sweden claims that full legalization in countries like Germany have led to an increase in sex trafficking have been proven to be totally wrong. Sex worker advocates oppose the Sweden model because it still stigmatizes sex workers, and because police will often target sex workers as a way of getting to the johns, making it a kind of indirect criminalization.

Legalized Sex Work in the U.S. Is a Mess

So what has legalization looked like in the U.S.? I actually have some first hand experience of this: Last summer, as part of a press trip, I went to Sheri's Ranch, one of Nevada's 19 legal brothels. Sheri's Ranch is typically acknowledged as one of the "nicer," and certainly one of the more expensive brothels in the state, in part due to the fact that it sits just across the border from California, and in part because at an hour and a half away, it is the closest a legal brothel can get to Las Vegas (most of the more populated counties in Nevada do *not* have legalized prostitution). An hour at Sheri's Ranch can cost you as little as $1,000, and as much as $20,000.

The setup in Nevada is not what most advocates for legalization of prostitution are looking for. The women at Sheri's Ranch are not employees but rather are contractors in the complex, which is owned by a madam. They pay for the right to stay there, they pay for weekly STD tests, they pay taxes, and they pay for a "sheriff's card," a kind of county permit which struck me as being remarkably close to a legalized bribe.

Nevada's system works more in the favor of the brothel owners (who could be reasonably equated to pimps) and the customers, rather than the workers themselves, and there's still no shortage of reports of abuse. 90% of prostitution in Nevada is still illegal, and while the brothels do provide a safe space for the women there, they often don't do much to prevent illegal prostitution.

The vision I saw of legalized prostitution in Pahrump, to be honest, kind of grossed me out. There was an actual "Sex Menu" that included items like "Hot and Cold Blowjob" ("you will not know whether you are going or cumming!"), and a "Tongue Body Licking Massage" ("Erotic Sex Tongue Pleasure!"). Grossest of all, one of the rooms had an *actual corporate sponsor:* Landshark Beer. The room was covered in Landshark wallpaper and had its trademark sign—that surfboard with a bite taken out of it—hanging on the wall.

. . . But It's Still the Best Option

This "ick" factor is in part what makes this debate so damn hard to have. I don't have to live as a woman or as a prostitute, so it's easy for me to feel grossed out about Sheri's Ranch. I have the luxury of being judgmental and condescending. And it's hard to divorce this instinctive "ick" from any compassionate opinions I could have about prostitution and how it should be handled.

It's also extremely difficult, in a world as shady as prostitution, to be sure what works and what doesn't work. Legalization policies in one place may be horribly put together and horribly implemented, making the problem the worse, while legalization policies in another place may be really well done and may help protect prostitutes from trafficking and abuse. There's so much nuance to this issue that categorizing policies as simply "good" or "bad" is a totally useless practice.

At the end of the day, the people who can best speak for sex workers are the sex workers themselves. And while sex workers as a whole are not united in their opinions about the sex trade—there are an estimated 42 million of them worldwide, after all—they and their advocates don't support the Sweden model, calling it "indirect criminalization." Because they are the people these policies are supposed to protect, they are the ones whose testimony we should give the greatest weight to, especially when the data the other sides are using is so unreliable.

Full legalization will still have its problems. It will not solve violence against women, and it will not end trafficking. It may, especially to us outsiders, still appear to be gross or morally reprehensible. But Amnesty is right: the only way to fix the problems with the world's oldest profession is to finally bring it out of the shadows.

Matt Hershberger is a writer, blogger, and human rights activist who writes about ethical travel. His work has been published on sites such as matadornetwork.com, foxnews.com, thoughtcatalogue.com, and businessinsider.com.

Demand Abolition **NO**

The Evidence Against Legalizing Prostitution

The idea that legalizing or decriminalizing commercial sex would reduce its harms is a persistent myth. Many claim if the sex trade were legal, regulated, and treated like any other profession, it would be safer. But the research says otherwise. Countries that have legalized or decriminalized commercial sex often experience a surge in human trafficking, pimping, and other related crimes. The following research affirms that legalization or decriminalization is not the answer to reducing the harms inherent to commercial sex.

Prostitution, regardless of whether it's legal or not, involves so much harm and trauma it cannot be seen as a conventional business.

- Interviews with prostituted individuals in New Zealand reveal that a majority of prostituted people in the country did not feel as if decriminalization had curbed the violence they experience, demonstrating that prostitution is inherently violent and abusive. (*Report of the Prostitution Law Review Committee*: p. 14)
- One study of prostituted women in San Francisco massage parlors found that 62% had been beaten by customers. (*HIV Risk among Asian Women Working at Massage Parlors in San Francisco*: p. 248)
- An investigation of the commercial sex industry in eight American cities found that 36% of prostituted people reported that their buyers were abusive or violent. (*Estimating the Size and Structure of the Underground Commercial Sex Economy in Eight Major US Cities*: p. 242)
- The "workplace" homicide rate among prostituted women in Colorado is seven times higher than what it was in the most dangerous occupation for men in the 1980s (taxi driver). (*Mortality in a Long-term Open Cohort of Prostitute Women*: p. 783)

Prostitution and human trafficking are forms of gender-based violence.

- Most persons in prostitution are either female or transgender (male-to-female). (*Estimating the Size and Structure of the Underground Commercial Sex Economy in Eight Major US Cities*: p. 219 and *The Impact of the Prostitution Reform Act on the Health and Safety practices of Sex Workers*: p. 61)
- In contrast, the vast majority of sex buyers are male. (*Executive Summary of the Preliminary Findings for Team Grant Project 4—Sex, Safety and Security: A Study of Experiences of People Who Pay for Sex in Canada*: p. 3)
- Prostituted persons are mostly women and face exceptional risks of murder (p. 784) and violence at the hands of male sex buyers (p. 248), signifying that the practice is on the continuum of gender-based violence. This remains true even in areas where prostitution is legal or decriminalized. (p. 14)
- In many countries, human trafficking tends to be a result of women's "disadvantageous position in the society that is often reflected in increasing preference for sons and neglect for daughters." (*Girls for Sale? Child Sex Ratio and Girls Trafficking in India*: p. 1)

Legalizing or decriminalizing prostitution has not decreased the prevalence of illegal prostitution.

- An investigation commissioned by the European Parliament found that in countries with legal prostitution, such as Austria, "the effect of regulation can be a massive increase in migrant prostitution and an indirect support to the spreading of the illegal market in the sex industry." (*National Legislation on Prostitution and the Trafficking in Women and Children*: p. 132)
- Denmark decriminalized prostitution in 1999, and the government's own estimates show that

the prevalence increased substantially over the decade that followed. (*Prostitutionens omfang og former 2012/2013*: p. 7)

- Interviews with prostituted persons in the Netherlands reported that "legalization entices foreign women to come to the Netherlands, causing an increase [in prostitution]." (*Prostitution in the Netherlands since the lifting on the brothel ban*: p. 38)

Legalization or decriminalization has not reduced the stigma faced by prostituted people.

- After New Zealand decriminalized prostitution in 2003, there were still reports among prostituted persons of "continuing stigma" and "harassment by the general public." In addition, there was little difference in disclosure of occupation to healthcare professionals before and after decriminalization. (*The Impact of the Prostitution Reform Act on the Health and Safety practices of Sex Workers*: p. 11 and 12)

Legalization or decriminalization increases human and sex trafficking.

- One study with data from 150 countries found that those with "legalized prostitution experience a larger reported incidence of trafficking inflows." (*Does Legalized Prostitution Increase Human Trafficking?*: p. 76)
- Another quantitative analysis similarly reported that sex trafficking is "most prevalent in countries where prostitution is legalized." (*The Law and Economics of International Sex Slavery: Prostitution Laws and Trafficking for Sexual Exploitation*: p. 87)
- Regulated prostitution increases the size of the overall market for commercial sex, which benefits criminal enterprises that profit from sex trafficking. (*Does Legalized Prostitution Increase Human Trafficking?*: p. 67 and *National Legislation on Prostitution and the Trafficking in Women and Children*: p. 132)

Attempts to regulate prostitution have failed and adherence is low.

- A large-scale evaluation of the legalization of prostitution in the Netherlands, coordinated by the Ministry of Justice, found that licensed brothels did not welcome frequent regulatory inspections. This undermines their willingness "to adhere to the rules and complicates the combat against trafficking in human beings." (*Prostitution in the Netherlands since the lifting on the brothel ban*: p. 11)
- A review of the empirical evidence on the Dutch legalization of prostitution found that many prostituted persons still rely on anonymity, secrecy, and cash transfers, demonstrating that a legalized prostitution market operates much like a criminal market. (*Legale sector, informele praktijken. De informele economie van de legale raamprostitutie in Nederland*: p. 115–130)
- New Zealand's Prostitution Law Review Committee found that a majority of prostituted persons felt that the decriminalization act "could do little about violence that occurred." (p: 14) The Committee further reported that abusive brothels did not improve conditions for prostituted individuals; the brothels that "had unfair management practices continued with them" even after the decriminalization. (p. 17)

Attempts to provide prostituted individuals with rights through legalization or decriminalization have failed.

- New Zealand's Prostitution Law Review Committee found that after decriminalizing prostitution, there still is a problem with lack of respect for employment arrangements among brothel operators. (*Report of the Prostitution Law Review Committee*: p. 159)
- The German government's own evaluation of the 2001 law that legalized prostitution suggested that fewer than 8% of prostituted individuals are "officially insured as a prostitute." (*Report by the Federal Government on the Impact of the Act Regulating the Legal Situation of Prostitutes (Prostitution Act)*: p. 26)
- It's estimated that only 1% of prostituted persons in Germany have a contract of employment. (*Report by the Federal Government on the Impact of the Act Regulating the Legal Situation of Prostitutes (Prostitution Act)*: p. 17)

Legalization and decriminalization promotes organized crime.

- Evaluations have found that regulation of prostitution creates a façade of legitimacy that hides sexual exploitation, and that brothels can "function as legalized outlets for victims of sex trafficking." (*The challenges of fighting sex trafficking in the legalized prostitution market of the Netherlands*: p. 227)
- An example of how sex trafficking can operate behind a veil of legalized prostitution is the so-called "Sneep case." German pimps traveled across the border to the Netherlands and took over large parts of the Red Light District in Amsterdam, using intimate relationships and brutal violence to coerce women to sell sex and hand over their profits. (*Relationships Between Suspects and Victims of Sex Trafficking. Exploitation of Prostitutes*

and Domestic Violence Parallels in Dutch Trafficking Cases: pp. 49–64, and *The challenges of fighting sex trafficking in the legalized prostitution market of the Netherlands*: p. 218)

The Nordic Model (criminalizing the act of buying sex, but legalizing the act of selling sex) has lowered the prevalence of street prostitution.

- An evaluation of the impact in Sweden found that street prostitution had been cut in half. (*Förbud mot köp av sexuell tjänst: En utvärdering 1999–2008*: pp. 34–35)
- Similarly, an evaluation of Norway's implementation of the Model in 2009 found that it "has reduced demand for sex and thus contribute to reduce the extent of prostitution" (p. 11), a result that has been confirmed in additional analyses. (*Kriminalisering av sexkjøp*: p. 13)

The Nordic Model has prevented an increase in prostitution overall.

- While Sweden's neighbors, such as Denmark and Finland, experienced increases in prostitution, data suggest that it remained flat in Sweden for the decade that followed the implementation of the Nordic Model. (*Förbud mot köp av sexuell tjänst: En utvärdering 1999–2008*: p. 36)

Countries that have implemented the Nordic Model have seen lower prevalence of human trafficking than countries that have legalized prostitution.

- Since legalizing prostitution results in an increase in trafficking (p. 76), it should not be surprising to learn that the Nordic Model has been effective at combating trafficking. According to the European Union's harmonized data on human trafficking, Sweden and Norway, for instance, have much lower trafficking rates than the Netherlands. (*Trafficking in Human Beings: 2015 Edition*: p. 23)

Prostituted individuals often come from vulnerable populations and lack choice, while most sex buyers have abundant resources.

- Individuals who are prostituted are often poorly educated (p. 248) and they are forced into prostitution by the lack of opportunities. (*Estimating the Size and Structure of the Underground Commercial Sex Economy in Eight Major US Cities*: p. 220)
- An evaluation of New Zealand's decriminalization revealed that 73% of prostituted individuals needed money to pay for household expenses, and about half of those who were street-based or transgender had no other sources of income. (*The Impact of the Prostitution Reform Act on the Health and Safety practices of Sex Workers*: p. 9)
- In sharp contrast, sex buyers are more likely to be employed full-time, more likely to have graduated from college, and have higher-than-average incomes. (*Ordinary or Peculiar Men? Comparing the Customers of Prostitutes With a Nationally Representative Sample of Men*: p. 812 and *Executive Summary of the Preliminary Findings for Team Grant Project 4—Sex, Safety and Security: A Study of Experiences of People Who Pay for Sex in Canada*: p. 2)

Demand Abolition is an organization dedicated to eradicating the illegal commercial sex industry in the United States and beyond by combatting the demand for sex work.

EXPLORING THE ISSUE

Should Sex Work Be Decriminalized?

Critical Thinking and Reflection

1. What are the benefits and challenges of legalizing, decriminalizing, or regulating prostitution and sex work in general?
2. How, if at all, might decriminalization of sex work prevent sex trafficking and/or violence against sex workers?
3. How do social perceptions and stigmatization of sex work adversely affect the experiences of individual sex workers?
4. Do you feel that people who become involved in prostitution or other sex work really have a choice in the matter? Explain.

Is There Common Ground?

Addressing the negative side of sex work is an ongoing debate—the end of which, at times, appears out of sight. That said, both perspectives here do their part to add to the discussion. A point of consensus between Hershberger and Demand Abolition rests in acknowledging both the desire to do away with sex trafficking and sex worker abuse, and the impossible sustainability of the current system. Where their stances diverge, however, is in exactly how to address the issue.

Hershberger affirms the idea that legalizing prostitution comes with its own set of problems, particularly in cases where it is not implemented in an organized way. He also acknowledges that much of the perspective against prostitution itself may represent one's own biases against the nature of sex work itself. How much of a role might biases against sex work have in harming those who involved in the trade? Are there biases among even those who aim to affirm sex workers' voices?

Demand Abolition presents solid evidence detailing the harm and trauma experienced by both consensual sex workers and those who become victims of sex trafficking, as well as the lack of choice many sex workers have in securing alternative employment. In countries that are significantly under-resourced, what options, if any, present viable alternatives for sex workers who are believed to lack other options? What impact might client prosecution, rather than sex worker prosecution have on the industry? Is it enough to shift prosecution focus, or are additional efforts necessary?

Additional Resources

Grant, M.G. (February 2, 2013). When prostitution wasn't a crime: The fascinating history of prostitution in America. *Alternet.org*. Retrieved from http://www.alternet.org/news-amp-politics/when-prostitution-wasnt-crime-fascinating-history-sex-work-america

Dank, M. et al. (2014). Estimating the size and structure of the underground commercial sex economy in six major US cities. Washington, D.C.: Urban Institute. Retrieved from http://www.urban.org/research/publication/estimating-size-and-structure-underground-commercial-sex-economy-eight-major-us-cities/view/full_report

Heineman, J., MacFarlane, R., and Brents, B. G. (2012). Sex industry and sex workers in Nevada. In Shalin, D. N. (Ed.) *The social health of Nevada: Leading indicators and quality of life in the Silver State.* Las Vegas, NV: UNLV Center for Democratic Culture. Retrieved from http://cdclv.unlv.edu/mission/index.html

MacInnes, T. (Director), & Nason, K. (Director). (2013). *Buying Sex* [DVD]. Canada: National Film Board of Canada.

Bauer, J. (Director) et al. (2015). *Hot Girls Wanted* [DVD]. Bloomington, IN: Two to Tangle Productions, LLC.

Internet References . . .

Children of the Night

www.childrenofthenight.org

Stella

www.chezstella.org

The Coalition Against Trafficking in Women—International

www.chezstella.org

COYOTE: Call Off Your Tired Old Ethics

http://coyoteri.org/wp/

Selected, Edited, and with Issue Framing Material by:
Ryan W. McKee, *Widener University,* Tracie Q. Gilbert, *Widener University,*
Jayleen Galarza, *Shippensburg University of Pennsylvania,* and
Tanya M. Bass, *North Carolina Central University*

ISSUE

Do State Laws on Abortion Clinic Safety Make Women Safer?

YES: Mary Kate Cary, from "Safety First for Abortion Clinics," *U.S. News and World Report* (2013)

NO: The American Civil Liberties Union, from "What TRAP Laws Mean for Women," American Civil Liberties Union (2014)

Learning Outcomes

After reading this issue, you will be able to:

- Discuss three regulations and requirements made of abortion providers in states that have enacted Targeted Regulation of Abortion Providers (TRAP) laws.
- Compare and contrast the requirements these regulations place on abortion providers with requirements made of other medical providers.
- Describe the logistical impact these laws have had on those seeking abortion services.

ISSUE SUMMARY

YES: Mary Kate Cary, a former White House speechwriter for President George H.W. Bush and contributing editor for U.S. News and World Report, argues that states have the right to regulate abortion clinics as they see fit, and that increased regulations are in the best interest of patients.

NO: The American Civil Liberties Union, a nonprofit organization working to defend and preserve individual rights and liberties, argues that states are increasingly regulating abortion providers in an attempt to restrict and ultimately eliminate women's access to abortion services.

In the political sphere, abortion is often referred to as a "wedge issue"—one that divides people (more specifically, voters) along deeply held moral and ethical lines. On one side are those who oppose abortion, and identify as pro-life. Those who are against abortion believe that it is morally wrong to terminate a pregnancy. They find the legality of abortion to be problematic, and have argued for government restrictions that reduce the availability of the procedure. On the other side of the spectrum are those who consider themselves to be pro-choice. Broadly speaking, they believe that the decision to terminate a pregnancy should be made by the woman faced with that choice. Women obtain abortions for a variety of reasons and pro-choice advocates believe that the procedure should, like other health care options, be available to those who need it without undue burden.

Binary frames like pro-choice and pro-life present an "if you're not for us, you're against us" image of the abortion debate. While pundits on talk shows polarized the issue as black-and-white, there are many evident shades of grey. In reality, many folks who are pro-choice see no problem with *some* regulations, such as a ban on late-term abortions. And many who are pro-life are ok with *some* exceptions, as in the case of pregnancy from rape or incest, or when a pregnant woman's life is at risk. In the United States, these regulations and exceptions are negotiated and enacted mostly in the court system, thanks to the Supreme Court's landmark ruling in *Roe v. Wade*.

The Court's ruling in *Roe v. Wade* essentially made abortion legal, but with limitations. States, the Court ruled, could not prohibit abortion during the first and second trimester of pregnancy; they were free, however, to enact restrictions during the third trimester. Challenges to the law seeking an expansion of state power to regulate abortion have been commonplace ever since. In 1977, the Hyde Amendment restricted the use of federal Medicaid funds to pay for abortions. In 1992, the Court moved away from the trimester as the unit of measurement in the *Planned Parenthood v. Casey* ruling. This decision stated that states could impose limited regulations during the second trimester, and, if they desired, completely restrict abortion after "fetal viability." This imprecision in language has been the cause of much debate over when, exactly, viability occurs (especially as medical technology has advanced over time). The ambiguity has led to more court challenges over the years, and states have also moved to restrict abortion access through other legal means.

Many of the state regulations on abortion, anti-abortion advocates argue, seek to protect women's health and safety. Those who support the regulations claim that they protect women from jeopardizing future pregnancies or being subjected to physical or emotional harm. The regulations may change over time, becoming more or less restrictive, due to court challenges and the passage of new laws. As of March 2016, 38 states require counseling prior to obtaining an abortion, and 28 of these require an additional extended waiting period before the procedure can be performed. Others have enacted laws that require those providing abortions to disclose certain information to patients such as any risks involved (25 states), descriptions of the specific procedure sought (25 states) or all abortion procedures (23 states), the gestational age of the fetus (33 states) as well as descriptions of the fetus at its current gestational age (27 states). Additionally, some states mandate that patients be told information about the ability of a fetus to feel pain (12 states) or that "personhood" begins at conception (6 states) (Guttmacher, 2016b). Twenty-five states have policies that mandate or regulate the use of ultrasounds before an abortion, and three states require that the image be shown and described to the patient.

Those who oppose these regulations argue that the laws are thinly veiled attempts to completely eliminate access to abortion at the state level by making them harder to obtain. Requiring a waiting period, for example, means having to make two separate trips on two different days to the provider's office. Requiring an ultrasound prior to abortion can significantly increase the cost. Describing the potential health risks associated with abortion ignores its relative safety in comparison to childbirth. The American College of Obstetricians and Gynecologists (ACOG) asserts that when legally provided, abortions are an extremely safe procedure. Almost 90 percent of all abortions occur within the first trimester, the period of gestation when abortion is safest. Even when performed later, there are few serious complications from abortions at all gestational ages. Such regulations, which have been in place for decades in some states, significantly impede (and potentially eliminate) women's access to abortion according to supporters of abortion rights.

More recently states have attempted, in some cases successfully, to place requirements on abortion providers that are not required of other health care providers. In some cases, the regulations are based on factors unrelated to the abortion procedure itself. These regulations, labeled Targeted Regulation of Abortion Providers (TRAP) laws, by pro-choice advocates, may require the costly remodeling and renovation of office space in order to meet hospital-style building codes (e.g., elevators large enough for two gurneys, specifying corridor width and office size). These building requirements may even be made in sites where medication abortion, rather than surgical abortion, takes place. Other regulations include requiring a site where abortions are performed, to be within a certain distance from a hospital, and that abortion providers have admitting privileges at said hospital (Guttmacher, 2016a). Again, anti-abortion advocates argue that the laws are designed to protect women's health, while pro-choice advocates believe the requirements to be part of the systematic restriction of women's rights.

In the following YES selection, Mary Kate Cary argues that additional regulations are common sense actions that ensure women are provided the best care possible. In the NO selection, the American Civil Liberties Union asserts that these additional conditions are simply unnecessary and also impede access to reproductive health services that were made legal in 1973.

Editor's note regarding the NO selection from The American Civil Liberties Union:

> Since submitting this manuscript for publication, the United States Supreme Court ruled that the Texas laws described in this issue were, indeed, unconstitutional. The decision in *Whole Women's Health v. Hellerstedt* (2016) made clear that when evaluating the constitutionality of an abortion

restriction the court must weigh the benefit of the law against the burden it imposes on women's access to abortion services. In the case of the Texas TRAP laws, there was no evidence that the laws protected women's health and substantial evidence that they posed real problems for a woman seeking an abortion. While this ruling was seen as a victory for supporters of reproductive rights, those who support TRAP laws expressed dismay over the ruling and vowed to continue efforts to restrict abortion access.

References

Guttmacher Institute. (2016a). Targeted regulation of abortion providers. *State Policies in Brief.* Retrieved from https://www.guttmacher.org/sites/default/files/pdfs/spibs/spib_TRAP.pdf

Guttmacher Institute. (2016b). Counseling and waiting periods for abortion. *State Policies in Brief.* Retrieved from https://www.guttmacher.org/sites/default/files/pdfs/spibs/spib_MWPA.pdf

YES

Mary Kate Cary

Safety First for Abortion Clinics

What does having a doorway 32 inches wide have to do with having a safe abortion? Not a thing, say abortion rights advocates. In fact, they argue that state restrictions on abortion clinics are arbitrary, cosmetic and aimed at ending women's access to reproductive health care services. But that 32-inch rule isn't from out of the blue: it is in the Life Safety Code (LSC), which is now part of the U.S. Code and was originally written by the National Fire Protection Association. The LSC regulates everything from exit signs to sprinklers to revolving doors to elevators—you name it—in day care centers, health clinics, hotels, schools, prisons, businesses and homes across America. Alabama's latest abortion law, for example, doesn't mention 32-inch doors anywhere; it simply says abortion clinics must abide by the LSC.

And so when I read that several states have required abortion clinics to meet the same standards as ambulatory surgical centers—with doorways wide enough for ambulance gurneys, in case things go wrong—that didn't strike me as "extremist" or a "war on women." It struck me as common sense. I've been in a situation where a gurney couldn't fit through a door to help save someone who was dying, and it was horrendous. It's also common sense to have nurses on duty, a safe blood supply, and a hospital within 30 miles. Having a doctor with hospital admitting privileges, so there won't be an hours long wait in the emergency room, seems like a good idea too.

So does limiting abortions to no later than 20 weeks, as Republican Sen. Marco Rubio of Florida is considering, with exceptions for rape, incest and when the life of the mother is threatened. Most abortions take place prior to 12 weeks; fewer than 0.2 percent take place after 24 weeks. Contrary to what you'd think from reading about Wendy Davis' filibuster, Texas would have been the 9th state to enact a 20-week limit for abortions, not the first.

When you look overseas, you see where the rest of the world stands on this issue. France, Spain and Germany all limit abortions to 14 weeks, according to the Center for Reproductive Rights. Sweden restricts them after 18 weeks. Italy bans them after 90 days. South Africa imposes increasingly tough restrictions from 12 to 20 weeks, and allows abortions after 20 weeks only if the life of the mother is in danger or there is a severe malformation or injury to the fetus. In a twist on Bill Clinton's mantra that abortion be "safe, legal and rare," the preamble to the South African law calls for abortion to be "early, safe and legal."

Where is this evolution coming from? I suspect sonograms have a lot to do with it. And it makes a difference to people if the baby is viable and able to survive outside the womb, which takes place somewhere between 20 and 24 weeks, right in the middle of the second trimester. Over the last few decades, as the technology has changed—both in terms of technological advances that allow better sonograms of the babies and medical advances that allow premature infants to survive—public opinion has been shifting as well.

In January of this year, Gallup found that 64 percent of Americans support outlawing abortion in the second trimester, and a whopping 80 percent in the third. A National Journal poll last month reported that more women (50 percent) than men (46 percent) support banning abortions after 20 weeks, except in cases of rape and incest. Nearly two-thirds want Roe v. Wade to stand. Most think abortion should be legal, but safe.

The Supreme Court agrees. In the 1992 case of Planned Parenthood v. Casey, the court upheld Roe, but also upheld the right of states to regulate abortion providers. So, it's no surprise that 17 states have enacted restrictions this year, according to the Guttmacher Institute. Despite what you may hear on cable TV, it's perfectly legal for states to regulate abortion clinics.

Mary Kate Cary is a former White House speechwriter for President George H.W. Bush. She currently writes speeches for political and business leaders, and is a contributing editor for U.S. News & World Report.

The American Civil Liberties Union

NO

What TRAP Laws Mean for Women

What TRAP Laws Mean for Women

Abortion restrictions known as TRAP laws can have a devastating impact on women and force clinics to close completely, with the end goal of making abortion access not just difficult, but impossible.

What you need to know:

What Are TRAP Laws?

TRAP stands for Targeted Regulation of Abortion Providers. TRAP bills single out abortion providers for medically unnecessary, politically motivated state regulations. They can be divided into three general categories:

- a measure that singles out abortion providers for medically unnecessary regulations, standards, personnel qualifications, building and/or structural requirements;
- a politically motivated provision that needlessly addresses the licensing of abortion clinics and/or charges an exorbitant fee to register a clinic in the state; or
- a measure that unnecessarily regulates where abortions may be provided or designates abortion clinics as ambulatory surgical centers, outpatient care centers or hospitals without medical justification.

What Is the Impact of These Regulations?

These laws take a variety of forms, but one of the most detrimental requires that abortion providers obtain admitting privileges at a nearby hospital. This is the type of law at the crux of federal court cases concerning Alabama, Wisconsin and Mississippi. Other types of TRAP laws force clinics to make medically unnecessary—and incredibly costly—renovations by setting requirements about the width of hallways, the size of closets and even the color of paint on the walls. The end result of these regulations is the same: Clinics are forced to close down and women are denied access to safe and legal abortion.

Why Can't Abortion Providers Comply with These New Requirements?

Admitting privileges are extremely difficult, if not impossible, for doctors who provide abortions to obtain for reasons that have nothing to do with the doctor's medical qualifications. Privileges can be granted—or denied—for variety of reasons that have nothing to do with medical quality or credentials. Some hospitals, for example, require that physicians with admitting privileges admit a certain number of patients per year. Because of abortion's high safety rate, providers will never meet this requirement.

Also, many hospitals are hostile to doctors who provide abortions. For example, two doctors in Texas recently had their admitting privileges revoked specifically because they provide abortion on their own time, off site. Do these laws make women safer? No, the leading medical groups uniformly oppose these restrictions. We all want women to be safe, but the doctors and medical groups oppose these laws because they aren't necessary for patients' safety. In 1 From the National Abortion Federation fact, far from making women safer, they put women's health in jeopardy by shutting down clinics and making it more difficult for women to access safe and legal abortion care. In fact, the American Medical Association and the American College of Obstetricians and Gynecologists have said "there is simply no medical basis" for the TRAP law and that it "does not serve the health of women . . ., but instead jeopardizes women's health by restricting access to abortion providers."

These Laws Address a Phantom Problem—Abortion Is Already Extremely Safe.

Abortion is already very safe—safer in fact that childbirth. Colonoscopies, for example, have a much higher rate of complication, and are commonly performed in similar outpatient clinics. Yet those clinics and doctors are not submitted to these types of regulations, and the politicians pushing for TRAP laws are not calling for them to be. Rather, they have singled out only doctors who provide abortions. It's clear that the real motivation behind these laws has nothing do to with women's health and everything to do with shutting down clinics and preventing women from getting safe and legal abortions. As the federal district court in Wisconsin explained when blocking that state's law, the "complete absence of an admitting privileges requirement for [other outpatient surgical] procedures including those with greater risk is certainly evidence that the . . . Legislature's only purpose in its enactment was to restrict the availability of safe, legal abortion."

Does This Issue Spread Beyond Texas?

Yes.

Because the courts allowed the Texas law to take effect it provides a dramatic example of how harmful these laws are. Already clinics in that state have stopped providing abortions, and when the second half of the law takes effect in September, only be a handful of clinics could remain in the whole state. The effect of this law has already been devastating for Texas women, particularly those who live outside major metropolitan areas. There are no abortion providers in huge swaths of the state, which means women either have to travel hundreds of miles to get care, carry a pregnancy to term against their will, or resort to attempting to induce abortion on their own. This situation is only going to get worse if the courts don't block the other part of the law that is scheduled to take effect on Sept. 1. If that part of the law takes effect, the state will have gone from more than 35 abortion providers to 8 in less than one year.

And, unfortunately, the problem spreads far beyond Texas. In fact, laws like the ones passed in Texas, are spreading throughout the South. Mississippi has a law that is currently blocked in the courts that would shut down the only clinic left in the state. Alabama has a law that if the courts allow it to take effect would leave only 2 clinics in the entire state. The legislatures in Oklahoma and Louisiana are close to passing similar laws that would have devastating effects on women's access. And, this issue has spread beyond the South as well. Wisconsin has a similar law that has been blocked by the courts that would drastically reduce a woman's access to abortion in that state as well.

The American Civil Liberties Union (ACLU) is a nonprofit organization working to defend and preserve individual rights and liberties. The ACLU is a champion of segments of the population who have traditionally been denied their rights, with much of our work today focused on equality for people of color, women, gay and transgender people, prisoners, immigrants, and people with disabilities.

EXPLORING THE ISSUE

Do State Laws on Abortion Clinic Safety Make Women Safer?

Critical Thinking and Reflection

1. Should each state have the flexibility to create individual policies regarding abortion or other health services?
2. Which, if any, of the TARP laws do you think have an impact on women's health and safety?
3. Which, if any, of the TARP laws do you think pose an undue burden on women attempting to access abortion services?

Is There Common Ground?

The two essays selected for this issue present a compelling contrast between worldviews. The American Civil Liberties Union believes that TRAP laws reduce access to a medical procedure that has been legal for decades. They highlight examples of the hardships many women, particularly in rural areas, may have in accessing abortion services. In addition to the ACLU, there are numerous professional organizations from the medical field that have spoken out against requirements they deem unnecessary for patient safety. In fact, they argue, such laws do the opposite of what their supporters claim. By restricting access to health services, the laws actually jeopardize women's health.

Supporters like Mary Kate Cary believe precautionary requirements like expanded corridor width and hospital admitting privileges should be a commonsense norm. Taking additional steps to ensure patient safety should be required for any medical facility, including abortion clinics. In addition to supporting TRAP laws, she feels that abortions should take place no later than 20 weeks into a pregnancy. Many states have enacted this 20-week ban but, as with most laws related to abortion, the courts may ultimately decide the legality of such a measure. While there are exceptions for rape and incest in some of the state laws, they are omitted from others.

While many people strongly identify as pro-life or pro-choice, this do not mean that people are incapable of compromise. Is there an opportunity for compromise on such a hotly contested issue? Do you believe having a facility meet hospital standards will increase the safety of an abortion procedure? What about the size of hallway corridors or admitting privileges to hospitals? Do you feel that these requirements, or those changing the date at which late-term abortion can be accessed from 24 to 20 gestational weeks, present an undue burden for women? Based on your understanding of TRAP laws, are there compromises that can be made that would satisfy those on both sides of the debate?

Additional Resources

Buchbinder, M. et al. (2016). Reframing conscientious care: Providing abortion care when law and conscience collide. *Hastings Center Report 46*(2), 22–30.

Leinwand, T. R. (2015). Strange bedfellows: The destigmatization of anti-abortion reform. *Columbia Journal of Gender and Law, 30*(2), 529–548.

Mercier, R. J. et al. (2015). The experiences of abortion providers practicing under a new TRAP law: A qualitative study. *Contraception, 91*(6), 507–512.

Internet References . . .

American Civil Liberties Union

www.aclu.org

American College of Obstetricians and Gynecologists

www.acog.org

Guttmacher Institute

guttmacher.org

Secular Pro-Life

secularprolife.org

Selected, Edited, and with Issue Framing Material by:
Ryan W. McKee, *Widener University,* Tracie Q. Gilbert, *Widener University,*
and
Jayleen Galarza, *Shippensburg University of Pennsylvania*

ISSUE

Has Marriage Equality Set the Gay Rights Movement Back?

YES: Karma Chavez, from "Intersectional Equality," *Against Equality* (2015)

NO: Keegan O'Brien, from "In Defense of Gay Marriage," *Jacobin Magazine* (2015)

Learning Outcomes

After reading this issue, you will be able to:

- Define marriage equality.
- Name two benefits the Supreme Court ruling on marriage equality has given same-sex married couples that they did not have access to previously.
- Name two issues of inequity between LGBT citizens and straight-identified citizens that the ruling on same-sex marriage did nothing to address.

ISSUE SUMMARY

YES: Karmen Chavez, an activist, author, and Associate Professor of Rhetoric, Politics, and Culture at the University of Wisconsin-Madison, argues that the singular focus on marriage equality resulted in inaction on a number of other issues important to the LGBT community, and that continued progress and support for LGBT issues and organizations is now at risk.

NO: Keegan O' Brien, a queer social activist and writer, argues that marriage equality is but one step on the path toward LGBT liberation, and that it should be celebrated as a major victory.

In June, 2015, the Supreme Court issued their ruling in the case of *Obergefell v. Hodges*, which officially affirmed that same-sex marriage was a constitutional right within the United States. Specifically, the Court held that same-sex couples were protected under the Fourteenth Amendment and states were required to issue marriage licenses to same-sex couples as well as recognize same-sex marriages performed out of state. Although many individuals can recall where they were when this ruling was reached, some may have minimal understanding of the road toward such a landmark victory in equality. For several decades, lesbian and gay rights organizations pushed toward the legalization of same-sex marriage, facing numerous cultural and legal challenges at the state and federal level along the way. Between 2004 and 2015, nearly 40 states had achieved marriage equality though hard-fought legal challenges. In 2013, the ruling in another Supreme Court case, *U.S. v. Windsor*, effectively dismantled the federal Defense of Marriage Act, signed into law in 1996 by President Bill Clinton. This law had, for federal purposes outlined and defined marriage as being between one man and one woman. It also held that a state was not required to recognize a same-sex marriage performed in another state as valid. Same-sex marriage licenses issued in New York, for example, were not legally valid in Texas. The victory struck down section 3 of the Defense of Marriage Act, deeming it unconstitutional and paving the way for the *Obergefell v. Hodges*, which made marriage equality the law of the land.

For many, these rulings were a sign of significant social and political changes within the United States.

As soon as the decision in the case of *Obergefell v. Hodges* was made public, media outlets took to the streets to hear public opinion. Same-sex couples flooded local county offices to apply for marriage licenses, while others held impromptu wedding ceremonies. Many couples shared personal testimony regarding the impact of marriage equality on their lives and relationships, including obtaining access to marital benefits like covering a spouse under health insurance plans or gaining protections when making necessary financial or medical decisions. Beyond the economic benefits that a legally binding marriage could now afford couples, many supporters felt that this was a step toward personal and political validation. For some, it was the culmination of a decades-long struggle to be seen as more than as second-class citizens.

The Supreme Court rulings were not, however, without controversy or opposition. There were immediate challenges posed by some religious fundamentalist groups and individuals. In some states, journalists highlighted the refusal of several county clerks to issue licenses to same-sex couples, claiming infringement on their religious liberty. Shortly after the verdict, Alabama State Supreme Court Chief Justice Roy Moore instructed his state's probate judges to refuse marriage licenses to same-sex couples. In order to circumvent this federal legislation, lawmakers in several states pushed legislation known as religious freedom laws, offering protection to religious institutions and officials from having to perform same-sex marriage ceremonies. According to some of the proposed laws, private business owners or employees could even refuse service to same-sex couples or anyone perceived to be a sexual minority. Currently several states have proposed and even passed such laws, drawing fierce criticism and, in some cases, boycotts from people and businesses opposed to what they feel is state-sanctioned discrimination. Thus, the marriage equality ruling has created another pressing legal issue for the LGBT community.

Despite their frustration with the proposed religious freedom laws, marriage equality advocates were not surprised by backlash from fundamentalist circles. What did surprise many throughout the fight for same-sex marriage was that the movement had been a source of contention for several groups within the larger LGBT community for years. Several LGBT activists, including members of the group *Against Equality,* have criticized mainstream LGBT organizations for dedicating so many resources to marriage equality, what they believe is a single-issue political agenda, and neglecting other intersectional issues that continue to affect many LGBT communities (e.g., incidents of violence, access to health care regardless of marital status, discrimination in employment and housing, and the lack of clear and effective immigration policies). Some are asking critical questions about who is guiding the goals of the larger LGBT movement. Specifically, LGBT activists opposed to marriage equality criticize mainstream social justice organizations for representing the interests of affluent, White, gay men by promoting marriage equality, and not reflecting the interests of individuals at the margins of the movement. Some question how marriage equality addresses more immediate issues impacting the lives of LGBT people of color? Further, opponents argue that many mainstream LGBT activists fail to challenge the systematic flaws that perpetuate oppression, violence, and discrimination against LGBT populations.

In the following YES selection, Karma Chavez emphasizes the negative effects of the fight for marriage equality on LGBT organizations, including the impact on funding for many gay rights groups not focused on marriage. Chavez argues that the singular focus of same-sex marriage has limited LGBT organizations' ability to advocate for change regarding other important social issues and that mainstream LGBT organizations lack an intersectional lens, often excluding people of color from their agendas. In the NO selection, Keegan O'Brien recognizes that marriage equality is a small victory in a larger struggle for full equality. However, he argues, people should not neglect the impact of the achievement on community morale, as well as the potential to open new opportunities and avenues toward progress.

YES

Karma Chavez

Intersectional Equality

Equality Maryland announced on June 30, 2015 that it was considering cutting significantly or stopping its daily operations. The reason? Despite all the work that the organization says it has accomplished, it reports that "funding from individuals and major donor sources dropped significantly after securing marriage equality," which Maryland has had since 2012. While this fact may surprise some readers, many queer and trans people of color and poor and disabled queers and allies are anything but shocked.

The gay and lesbian movement's limiting of "equality" to the issue of marriage (and before that open military service and hate crime protections) has had devastating impacts on many members of the LGBTQ community for a long time. In 2010, journalist Lisa Dettmer talked to several leaders of LGBTQ organizations who served the community on issues ranging from health to low-income housing for people with AIDS to youth homelessness. They all reported difficulty securing funding from foundations and individuals who only wanted to support the issue of gay marriage, at the same time that states were cutting their funding. Many closed their doors. The lesson? Single-issue politics informed by the agendas and needs of the most privileged are not just narrow; they actually have negative material consequences for the most oppressed among us.

Many radical queer activists like the collective Against Equality have tried to draw attention to problems with the mainstream gay and lesbian movement's definition of equality. That definition centers the experiences and needs of those who suffer oppression primarily based on their sexual orientation, ignores the needs of those marginalized in multiple ways (race, class, gender identity, ability, education and citizenship status), and sidelines how capitalism oppresses all people regardless of sexual orientation.

In short, the mainstream gay and lesbian rights movement has fed us an anti-intersectional definition of equality. Intersectionality has become a buzzword, but it means more than just saying facets of identity like race, class, gender and sexuality are important. Intersectionality, as introduced by women-of-color feminists in the '60s and '70s, is the idea that the interlocking nature of oppression (but also privilege) impacts how we view the world and how the world lets us exist. When we craft a political agenda based only on one form of oppression (sexual orientation) while minimizing other forms of oppression and privilege, we bolster our own privilege, and reinforce the structural disadvantage others suffer.

Several statements released by queer and trans people around the country after the Supreme Court decision on marriage made this point. The local groups, Young Gifted and Black and Freedom Inc., issued a statement to clarify their position after supporters of marriage equality attacked some of YGB's leaders in heated exchanges on social media for refusing to celebrate the decision. YGB's and FI's position does not go as far as some others, but they offer insight into what it means to lead an intersectional movement through the lens of queer and trans Black people. One way they offer is to broaden definitions of family.

They write, "Based on our experiences in Black communities we know that grandparents, neighbors, even whole communities are often doing the work of family, including getting food on the table, taking care of elders as they age, caring for ill loved ones, putting kids to bed at night, helping with their homework, and just generally keeping things together. We also know as queer folk that people in a variety of relationships, whether romantic or not, including those who are single, in polyamorous relationships, in families with nonresidential stepparents, or in families with loved ones who are incarcerated, in communally raised families, in communities of friendship, and those in the foster system, continue to experience discrimination . . ."

An intersectional approach to equality considers these factors in creating a political agenda, recognizing that state-sanctioned marriage disregards people who exist in alternative families, and may reinforce their marginalization. In fact, already there is talk in Wisconsin about ending domestic partner benefits now that marriage is legal, a move that has happened elsewhere. Ending domestic partnerships could be devastating for disabled people who cannot marry because they would lose their government benefits, but who may currently enjoy rights like hospital visitation as registered domestic partners. Moreover, state and federal governments have often passed policies that punish women of color on welfare and promote heterosexual marriage as an antidote to declining state support. Strengthening the institution of marriage may further marginalize those also disadvantaged based on gender and sexuality, rendering their families less legitimate and more open to scrutiny.

These are the kinds of insight that taking an intersectional approach to gender and sexual liberation provide. Local groups like YGB, FI, and Alianza Latina are doing it on the ground. One key takeaway is this: We cannot simply reduce struggles to one aspect of identity and imagine that we are in the service of values like justice or equality.

Karma Chavez is an Associate Professor of Rhetoric, Politics, and Culture at the University of Wisconsin-Madison. Her work is influenced by queer people of color theory and women of color theory. She is the author of *Queer Migration Politics*.

Keegan O'Brien **NO**

In Defense of Gay Marriage

While millions celebrated the Supreme Court's historic ruling on June 26, 2015 making gay marriage the law of the land in all fifty states, it wasn't just right-wingers who were raining on the big rainbow parade. A number of activists on the queer left, plenty of whom I respect and agree with on other issues, were less than enthusiastic.

Prominent South Asian trans spoken word duo Darkmatter, who recently did a tour called "Gay Rights Are Wrong," and the collective Against Equality were among those making the case that the Court's ruling was at best insignificant, and at worst a step backwards. Darkmatter's posts in particular struck a cord, generating several thousand likes and shares on Facebook.

Here's why they're wrong.

For starters, critics argue that marriage equality only affects rich, white, cisgender gays and lesbians. But this is simply not true. Marriage equality is a class issue that provides real, material benefits to working-class same-sex couples—cisgender and trans, and black, white, and brown.

One would have to be out of touch with the day-to-day reality of working-class people's lives to argue it's insignificant that same-sex couples can now visit one another in the hospital, secure access to crucial tax benefits, share custody over their children, and gain citizenship for their partner. What's more, trans people who didn't have the means to legally or medically transition can now be covered under their partner's health insurance.

But marriage equality is about more than just material benefits—it's about dignity. In a society that has told LGBTQ people they are less than equal for decades, it matters that queer people will be able to hold their head up a little higher, that coming out and living openly will be somewhat easier, and that future generations will have access to rights and social freedoms that would have been unimaginable to queers just a couple decades ago.

And given the scarcity of left victories over the last few decades, winning gay marriage is substantial. Aside from small wins here and there, until last month there was nothing this generation could point to in our lifetime as a major victory, as a confirmation that when ordinary people organize and fight back they can force the people in power to cave. For those of us whose political horizons extend well beyond marriage, this is good news.

Ironically, leftist arguments against marriage equality have something in common with Gay Inc.—they both attribute this victory to politicians. However, far from being a gift delivered from on high, gay marriage was opposed by almost the entire Democratic Party establishment until just a few years ago. It is pressure from below that has decisively pushed this struggle forward.

The legalization of gay marriage also shows just how flexible and dynamic capitalism can be. As long as profitability isn't threatened, the economic system will allow all sorts of adjustments, including to the gender make-up of the nuclear family.

But that doesn't mean progress was automatic. Every gain has required relentless struggle from below. This win doesn't belong to gay-friendly corporate America, the Democratic Party, or the Supreme Court—it belongs to the thousands who protested, sat in, spoke out, and organized even when they were told their demands were unrealistic. It belongs to us.

In 2008 California passed Proposition 8, which banned gay marriage and stripped same-sex couples of their civil rights. Prop 8's passage sparked an eruption of protests organized largely over social media by young activists independent of established LGBTQ organizations and led to the formation of new grassroots activist groups such as Join the Impact, One Struggle, One Fight, and Queer Rising. A year later, this momentum culminated in the National Equality March in Washington, DC.

The march was organized by a ragtag, multiracial band of working-class LGBTQ activists from all across the country and had one simple demand: full LGBTQ equality now. March organizers included veteran fighters like AIDS activist and union militant Cleve Jones and socialist activist and writer Sherry Wolf; well-known artists like spoken word poet Stayceann Chin; and new activists, young and old, like high school organizer Jose Richard Alvis and union militant and trans activist Tara Le. Broadway performers organized dozens of buses from New York City alone.

Despite opposition until very late in the organizing process by the Human Rights Campaign and other established LGBTQ organizations, the march drew over 250,000 people, wildly exceeding organizers expectations of 5,000 to 10,000, and making it the first and largest demonstration for LGBTQ rights since 1993.

The explosion of protests nationwide after Prop 8 and the National Equality March marked a turning point in the fight for marriage equality. The demonstrations took the gay marriage debate national, helped push public support into the majority, and invigorated local activism, paving the way for future successful campaigns.

A common argument made by critics is that fighting for issues such as marriage equality or ending discrimination in the military assimilates LGBTQ people into oppressive systems that radicals should have no business in. Instead, they insist, the focus should be on struggling for liberation. This strategy leaves activists with radical slogans and little else.

Small adjustments to such a fundamentally rotten system are of course insufficient. We need a revolution, a world where working class and oppressed people run society collectively and democratically, and harness the immense wealth they've created to build a system based on human need and solidarity, not war, poverty, and oppression. But I also know that revolution won't happen in one spontaneous swoop, and rarely do radicals—especially at a time when the Left is weak—get to determine when and where mass movements break out.

Marriage equality is of course a partial victory that provides limited improvements to people's lives while still leaving the system intact.

But socialists support raising the minimum wage to $15 and the right of workers to unionize, even though it doesn't change the fundamental relationship of exploitation between labor and capital. We fight to abolish the death penalty, even though the system of mass incarceration persists. We struggle for a more democratic political system, even if capitalism constantly threatens political equality.

We do so not only because these advances improve the lives and conditions of the people they affect, but because history proves time and time again that reform movements, rather than being a barrier to future struggles, have the potential to build a higher level of confidence, organization, and consciousness that sets the stage for future victories.

Whether reforms have a radicalizing effect or are co-opted and defanged by those in power is significantly dependent on the size, rootedness, and influence of the organized left and its ability to contend politically against the influence of more conservative, status quo forces in the movement—such as the Human Rights Campaign.

That's why the decision by many good radical activists to stand on the sidelines over the last decade as hundreds of thousands of people were drawn into struggles for marriage equality was wrongheaded. It weakened the left wing of the movement and made it easier for Gay Inc.'s conservative, myopic politics to dominate.

Another claim of skeptics is that winning gay marriage will put an end to the LGBTQ movement altogether. Some activists have cautioned that since rich gays and lesbians have gotten what they want, the funding for political organizations will suddenly dry up and the issues affecting the most vulnerable and marginalized LGBTQ people will go unaddressed.

But this argument only reflects how much political activism has become steeped in the nonprofit world, where a movement's ability to win is determined by how big of a grant it can get from some foundation. While movements need to be independently funded and self-sustaining, it's bottom-up pressure that drives social change—not cash.

Outside of maybe a few gay millionaires, no one's proclaiming the struggle is over. Even the *New York Times*, hardly a mouthpiece for the radical left, ran a front-page article the day after the Supreme Court's ruling titled "Next Fight for Gay Rights: Bias in Jobs and Housing."

Far from cutting the movement short, the public opinion see change over the past decade, the increasingly awful economic situation that huge numbers of people are experiencing, and the emergence of the Black Lives Matter movement have created fertile ground for activists to agitate around issues that Gay Inc. de-prioritized, including LGBTQ youth homelessness, violence against trans women (disproportionally trans women of color), and the racist, anti-queer criminal justice system.

Considering the Left's string of losses over the past forty years, it's not surprising that many good activists have lowered their expectations and embraced the idea that there's a limit to what our movements can achieve—that we can only pick between winning gay marriage and combating anti-trans violence.

But this is a ruling-class zero-sum game that leaves our side picking for scraps, lowers our movement's horizons, and narrows our conceptions of what's possible. The job of the Left is to challenge the ruling class's definition of what's realistic and raise people's expectations of what we can achieve.

Leftists such as Solidarity member Mehlab Jameel are right to criticize efforts by Gay Inc. and the Democratic Party to use LGBT rights to give a progressive veneer to settler colonialism and imperialism, but that doesn't mean the fight for civil rights is hopeless. The ruling class has always appropriated progressives' language for its own ends. George W. Bush used the mantle of feminism and women's rights to carry out a "war on terror" that left thousands of Afghans and Iraqis dead. That didn't prompt the Left to dismiss the struggle for women's rights and reproductive justice as a project of imperialism.

Radicals can—and must—fight to advance civil rights for LGBT people while also organizing to challenge pink-washing and oppose racism and empire.

Above all, these left criticisms are a manifestation of a tendency among radical activists to view movements and reform victories only in terms of what they haven't accomplished. But while it's good to resist being placated by small reforms, what this approach misses is that mass movements open up new possibilities for large numbers of people to become radicalized.

When calls for radical change take the place of figuring out how to dynamically relate to people other than committed leftists, activists have created an echo chamber that only inhibits movement building. Demands to abolish marriage or smash the state may generate support from other radicals, but they remain empty slogans without the popular forces required to bring about social transformation.

What is threatening to the system, however, is a radical politics that prizes figuring out how we can relate to the world as it actually exists today, meeting people where they are at, and trying to move things forward from there. Those of us who want to effect social change have an opportunity right now to insert ourselves into a process in which wider layers of people are getting a taste of their own power, increasing their confidence, and expanding their vision of what's possible.

This requires being able to assess the dynamics of each moment and figure out what makes sense tactically; knowing when to advance, and when to retreat; and most importantly, being willing to patiently argue and debate with others as we continue to struggle alongside them.

Long-term, patient organizing may not be the revolution. But it's the only way to get us there.

Keegan O'Brien is a Boston-based writer whose work has written for *The Nation* and *Jacobin Magazine*. He is a queer-identified socialist and activist.

EXPLORING THE ISSUE

Has Marriage Equality Set the Gay Rights Movement Back?

Critical Thinking and Reflection

1. Why is marriage equality a point of controversy within the LGBT rights movement? Is marriage equality a setback, or a point of progress for the movement?
2. Who should influence the political agenda of the LGBT rights movement?
3. How can LGBT rights movements and organizations be more inclusive of diverse needs within the communities they serve and represent?

Is There Common Ground?

Justice Kennedy authored the ruling in *Obergefell v. Hodges* and wrote,

> No union is more profound than marriage, for it embodies the highest ideals of love, fidelity, devotion, sacrifice, and family. . . . It would misunderstand these men and women to say they disrespect the idea of marriage. Their plea is that they do respect it, respect it so deeply that they seek to find its fulfillment for themselves. Their hope is not to be condemned to live in loneliness, excluded from one of civilization's oldest institutions. They ask for equal dignity in the eyes of the law.

In reading his concluding statement and reflecting on the articles on this topic, can you identify potential benefits and limitations of marriage equality within LGBT communities? Does the right to marry translate to full societal equality for sexual minorities?

As O'Brien emphasized in his article, strides toward equality are being made. We must, however, reflect on some difficult questions sparked by Chavez's arguments in order to fully understand the implications of the long fight for marriage equality. Did the focus on same-sex marriage reduce the LGBT rights movement to a single-issue cause representing the most privileged members of the community? Can we celebrate political achievements such as this even though some individuals may not benefit? While both sides present frustrations in navigating opposing views, these conversations do help us move beyond the idea of marriage equality as the central issue to LGBT equality. Both authors offer alternate perspectives for discussing what it means to achieve equal rights within the United States and which gaps need to be addressed. In either case, there is evidence that this goal has not been completely realized.

Additional Resources

Angelo, G. (2015). A conservative case for marriage equality, *Washington Examiner*. Retrieved from http://www.washingtonexaminer.com/a-conservative-case-for-marriage-equality/article/2567744

Chemerinsky, E. (2015). Symposium: A landmark victory for civil rights, *The SCOTUS Blog*. Retrieved from http://www.scotusblog.com/2015/06/symposium-a-landmark-victory-for-civil-rights/

Dark Matter (2015). The other side of pride: In the fight for LGBT rights, visibility for some doesn't mean justice for all, *Creative Time Reports*. Retrieved from: http://creativetimereports.org/2015/06/26/dark-matter-the-other-side-of-pride-lgbt-rights/

Phillips, A. (April 2016). Why religious freedom bills could be just the beginning of the gay marriage debate, *The Washington Post*. Retrieved from https://www.washingtonpost.com/news/the-fix/wp/2016/04/13/why-religious-freedom-bills-could-be-just-the-beginning-of-the-gay-marriage-debate/

Internet References . . .

Against Equality

againstequality.org

Human Rights Campaign Marriage Center

hrc.org/campaigns/marriage-center

Pew Research Center, Gay Marriage and Homosexuality

pewforum.org/topics/gay-marriage-and-homosexuality/

CPSIA information can be obtained
at www.ICGtesting.com
Printed in the USA
FFOW01n0418271116
29744FF